WHAT INVESTORS ARE SAYING ABOUT
The Millionaire Real Estate Investor

"The Millionaire Real Estate Investor *finally brings a book to the real estate investing market that's been missing . . . A real model for success that works in the real world and not just in the bookstore."*

Tony E. Holloway
Winston-Salem, NC

"Gary Keller has captured the essence of the successful real estate investor. If you have the desire and you apply the lessons of The Millionaire Real Estate Investor, *wealth and success are sure to follow."*

Dyches Boddiford
Marietta, GA

"Fear keeps so many aspiring investors from taking that first step. This book turns that fear into the confidence they need to begin building their financial future."

Pat Puckridge
Asheville, NC

"I was honored to be asked to participate and to share my ideas on how to build wealth through real estate investing but was skeptical that the experience of 120 diverse investors from all parts of the country could be consolidated and put into text. Gary and Dave have done an exceptional job of pulling it all together. The Millionaire Real Estate Investor *is a concise, easily understandable, very engaging, condensed version of the combined experience of us all. I read it cover to cover at the first sitting!*

It's a must for real estate investors, at any level. Great for the novice investor and required reading for everyone thinking about building a real estate portfolio. The systems in the book will work for anyone. I only wish I had had it 25 years ago. It could have saved me 10 years of trial and error and gotten me off to a head start in building my portfolio."

George Castleberry
Austin, TX

"*The Millionaire Real Estate Investor gives investors a road map to greater success based on their personal financial goals. It's a must-read for the attentive investor.*"

Mike Brodie
Plano, TX

"*The Millionaire Real Estate Investor will awaken the sleeping giant in us all, with purpose, systems, and proven models led by confidence. The possibilities are endless. This truly is 'The Blueprint' for the future of residential investors.*"

Bobby and Janet Faulk
Lake Norman, NC

"*What a realistic way to identify, analyze and purchase investment property to become independently wealthy. The sky's the limit with these proven models and systems.*"

Gene Arant
Austin, TX

"*The Millionaire Real Estate Investor is absolutely ideal for investors. I've been helping people build and manage their wealth through buying real estate for years and this book will help me serve my network of investors even better! Thanks, Gary.*"

Chris D. Hake
Madison, WI

"*This book provides the most direct and easy-to-understand platform from which to take my investment portfolio to its next level.*"

W. Darrow Fiedler
Los Angeles, CA

"*Thanks, Gary, Dave, and Jay, for the opportunity to participate in the research for* The Millionaire Real Estate Investor. *I look forward to sharing it with like-minded people!*"

Pat LaMonica
Charlotte, NC

"*An excellent, comprehensive, common sense primer on real estate investing.*"

Joe Arlt
Virginia Beach, VA

THE
MILLIONAIRE
Real Estate Investor

Anyone can do it—
not everyone will

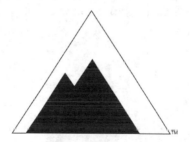

Gary Keller

with Dave Jenks and Jay Papasan

New York   Chicago   San Francisco   Athens   London   Madrid
Mexico City   Milan   New Delhi   Singapore   Sydney   Toronto

28   LCR   21 20

ISBN 0-07-144637-0

Printed and bound by LSC Communications.

The illustration titled "Standard Deviation of Various Portfolio Mixes" appears courtesy of Ibbotson Associates, Inc. It is used with their permission, and they reserve all rights. Copyright © 2005.

McGraw-Hill Education products are available at special quantity discounts to use as premiums and sales promotions or for use in corporate training programs. To contact a representative, please visit the Contact Us pages at www.mhprofessional.com.

Financial Wealth (fĭ-năn'shəl, wĕlth) n. The unearned income
to finance your life mission without having to work.

The Millionaire Real Estate Investor *is dedicated to the
men and women who have a passion for their work and yet dream
of someday achieving financial independence, of someday being
able to finance their mission in life without having to work.
It's dedicated to all those who want the biggest life possible,
who are actively seeking ways to finance that vision,
who want to go as far as possible with as few roadblocks as possible,
and who want to say at the end of the day,
"I'm glad I did" instead of "I wish I had."*

ACKNOWLEDGMENTS

While the research for this book began in the spring of 2002, the idea was born nearly two years earlier when we interviewed Cristina Martinez for our first book, *The Millionaire Real Estate Agent*. Cristina had built an amazing real estate sales business that generated over $4 million in gross income each year by catering to residential real estate investors. The stories she told inspired us and pointed us down the winding path that ends with these pages. Thanks, Cristina.

I'd be remiss not to mention Michael Allen, who was my original wealth-building mentor. Many of the ideas in this book about money and wealth building came to me long ago during our breakfast discussions. Although Michael is no longer with us, he has been ever-present in my thoughts, especially during the writing of this book. He has my deepest gratitude.

We began the search for investor interviewees by focusing on the wonderfully talented and successful real estate agents and investors we've known for years and kept asking for referrals until we expanded our list past those initial contacts. While everyone who agreed to be interviewed was helpful and insightful, several people really stand out because they went above and beyond to introduce us to more investors or supply more information. The first name that springs to mind is Dyches Boddiford, who, even though he didn't really know us, extended himself again and again by putting us in touch with numerous investors, sending us his material on entity planning, and participating in teleconferences to discuss the early systems and models we had developed. Don Zeleznak,

George Castleberry, Tamara Fuller, Renata Circeo, Don Beck, and Elmer Diaz also participated in those teleconferences and wowed each of us with their incredible knowledge about the finer details of market analysis, property acquisition, and property management. Not only are they all incredible investors, they are all teachers at heart. Jimmy and Linda McKissack shared their insights into how they parlayed their real estate sales business into a phenomenal investing business. Jimmy's knowledge of the Texas foreclosure process lit our way through that thicket of information. Early on, Chris Hake took it upon himself to devise a spreadsheet that laid out how many properties one would have to own and how much cash flow those properties would have to generate to net a million dollars in annual income. George Meidhof and Michael Huang guided us through the early stages of how to set up legal entities for investments and how to structure every kind of partnership. George also visited us in Austin and walked us through the aisles of a home improvement store to show us how he shops for bargains when fixing up properties. Both Rick Villani and Rob Harrington, Jr., spent many hours with us, on the phone and in person, detailing how they built their uniquely different but highly successful investment businesses. Rick has made fixing and flipping houses into a science, and Rob's done the same with evaluating and acquiring commercial properties. They were huge allies in the writing of this book, and their wisdom and insights touch more sections than we can name here. We'd also like to extend a special thank you to bestselling investment authors Robert T. Kiyosaki and Robert Shemin, who generously took time off to talk with us at length about their investment philosophies.

What follows is a complete list of all the Millionaire Real Estate Investors who we interviewed for this book: Al Abramson, Gene Arant, Joe Arlt, Stanley Armstrong, Susan Barbour, Ray Barr, Leanne Barschdorf, Don Beck, Armand Bedirian, Rische Beeson, Dwan Bent-Twyford, Mike Bergida, Chris Bird, Dyches Boddiford, Dottie Bowe, Mike

Brodie, Charles Brown, Jim Castagnari, George Castleberry, Steve Chader, Renata Circeo, Jerry Clevenger, Bill Cook, Judy Cook, Kim Daugherty, Alex Delgado, Don DeRosa, Elmer Diaz, Linda Dolese, Greg Dorriety, Barbara Drake, Ron Duguid, Brannon Fain, Dave Fairweather, Janet and Bobby Faulk, Darrow Fiedler, Charlie France, Tamara Fuller, Ron Garber, Jane Garvey, Leo Gee, Rick Geha, Bill Goacher, John Grossmann, Bob Guest, Chris Hake, Nancy Halberg, Brian Hammermeister, Robert Harrington, Jr., Carlos Herbon, Dave Herries, Pat Hiban, Tony Holloway, Michael Huang, Chris Jessey, Vena Jones-Cox, Ken Jordan, Donnis King, Robert T. Kiyosaki, Leona Kline, Robert Kohorst, Jon and Amy Kubas, Nikki and David Kupfer, Pat LaMonica, Don Leiby, Allen D. Leone, Cathy Manchester, Barbara Mattson, Arnold May, Mary McDonald, Patricia McDonald, Bobbi McKenna, Jimmy and Linda McKissack, George Meidhof, Jack Miller, Anna Mills, Tim Minnix, Paul Morris, Jimmy Napier, Mike Netzel, Dennis Nevius, Erv Norgren, Bill O'Kane, Rocco Pangallo, Glenn Papineau, Wendy Patton, Craig Power, Pat Puckridge, Marshall Redder, Sharon Restrepo, Sally Richards, Carlos Rivero, Peggy Rollins, Joe Rozanski, Steve Scheffe, Robert Shemin, Rick Smith, Will Stewart, Patrick Swint, Mike Tavener, Geidre Trahan, Robert Trahan, Todd Tresidder, Robert P. Tucker, Rick Villani, Lyle Wall, Pat Wells, Danny Williams, Bob Witcher, Jean Yevic, Jen and Jay Yilmaz, Charles Young, Don Zeleznak, and Ryan Zeleznak.

Many of these investors joined us for a Millionaire Real Estate Investor Mastermind session in Austin in summer 2003, and for two days we just talked and brainstormed about every aspect of investing. The results were amazing, and many of the ideas, "ahas," and insights reflected in this book originated at that inspirational gathering. A special thanks to all of them for making an investment in us. Although Charles Sullivan was unable to attend, he provided detailed feedback on the manuscript. Thanks, Charles.

We'd be negligent not to mention several people who, while not full-time real estate investors themselves, were invaluable resources because of their industry expertise: noted economist Harry S. Dent, Jr.; real estate editor of CBS.MarketWatch.com Steve Kerch; Ron Kubek, a prominent real estate agent and broker in Canada; and the foreclosure experts at Wells Fargo. We relied on their vast knowledge more than they know. To each and every person on this list we offer heartfelt thanks, and we hope that what we've captured on paper accurately reflects the sum of all your knowledge.

Perhaps the best testimony to the power of the systems and models we lay out in this book are two that are very close to home. Heather M. Iarusso, our researcher, and Rachel Proctor May, our transcriber and profile writer, transformed their lives and their mindsets while working on this project. When Heather interviewed her first Millionaire Real Estate Investor for this book, she was helping her landlord pay his mortgage. Eight months and 114 interviews later, a friend rents two rooms in her four-bedroom, two-bathroom house. More important than the logistics of this move, however, is the mental "move" she made going from renter to homeowner to investor. She's now on the path to building wealth and passive income. After spending hours upon hours transcribing Heather's interviews with Millionaire Real Estate Investors, Rachel and her husband, who were both graduate students at the time, bought their first house. Armed with all the knowledge from these investors, Heather and Rachel have teamed up to buy their first investment property. Way to go!

Special thanks to the team at McGraw-Hill, particularly Mary Glenn, our exceptional editor, and her talented assistant, Ed Chupak. This book was a marathon, not a sprint, but their patience never flagged. Thanks for the help and the encouragement. Our managing editor, Peter McCurdy, also deserves our gratitude for guiding this book through the production process in a remarkably efficient way. We were tardy, but Peter got us back on track.

The staff here at Keller Williams® Realty International has been incredibly supportive while we have focused on this book. A special thanks

Acknowledgments

Figure 1: Millionaire Real Estate Investor Mastermind Group 1

Back Row: Gary Keller, Dave Jenks, Bobby Faulk, Ryan Zeleznak, Rische Beeson, Jody McAnally, Ed Berry, and Sean Seaton.
Middle Row: Chris Hake, David Osborn, Jane Maslowski, Pat LaMonica, Steve Scheffe, Jimmy McKissack, Mary Taylor, and Rick Smith.
Front Row: Chris Jessey, Leona Kline, Janet Faulk, Cathy Manchester, Heather Iarusso, and Linda Dolese.

Figure 2: Millionaire Real Estate Investor Mastermind Group 2

Back Row: Bill O'Kane, Gary Keller, Pete Reeser, George Castleberry, George Meidhof, Dennis Nevius, Bob Guest, Mike Colohan, and Jay Papasan.
Middle Row: Terry Dyroff, Todd Orrill, Rocco Erker, Adam Robinson , Darrow Fiedler, Gene Arant, Sandy Murphy, Mike Brodie, and Mike Netzel.
Front Row: Bonita Joy Yoder, Michael Huang, Joe Jackson, Leith Seegers-McKahan, Dottie Bowe, and Leanne Barschdorf (Steve Chader was present but is not pictured).

to Mo Anderson, Mark Willis, Todd Butzer, and Sharon Gibbons for their leadership and encouragement. My and Dave's executive assistants, Valerie Vogler-Stipe and Mindy Hager (truly "assistant executives" in our minds), gave us phenomenal leverage while we were writing this book. We thank them dearly, as well as Allison Odom and Jeannine Abbott, who in turn gave them leverage to do all that had to be done while we were locked away writing toward our deadline. Thanks to Toni Tolerico, our PowerPoint wizard, and designer Justine Smith who helped design some of the graphics. This book is much more polished thanks to the efforts of Casey Blaine, a freelance editor, who gave us excellent feedback on the final drafts of the manuscript.

Over the past two years we've given close to 50 presentations of this material in the form of "sneak preview" training sessions. Thanks to the thousands of enthusiastic attendees who stayed afterward to share their investing wisdom and comment on our evolving models. Speaking of these events, the MillionaireSystems team deserves our gratitude for tirelessly scheduling and organizing these events as well as overseeing product sales and development. So big thanks to Molly Brown and Dawn Sroka. Laura Morgan and her events team also played a huge role in making these learning events happen.

My coauthors, Dave Jenks and Jay Papasan, have earned my sincere gratitude for their stamina and skill in pursuing this project from start to finish. We worked through lunches week after week (subsisting on Marye's Red Turkey and Turkey #1 sandwiches) and often took our writing home on weekends and nights. Thanks for their dedication to excellence through draft after draft and to their families and loved ones for lending them to this process for so long.

Professor Walstein Smith, former head of the real estate department at Baylor University, is also due thanks for letting a struggling student work for his real estate company part-time and get an inside look at what would become his profession of choice. And thanks to my lifelong friend Kim

Brightwell, who through our childhood games of chess and Monopoly taught me to think strategically.

Thanks to my wife, Mary, and my son, John, the true loves of my life, for their willingness to constantly be my guides and teachers even when I didn't want guidance or teaching. Thanks to my parents, Lew and Minnie Keller, for their loving parenting and sound advice throughout my life. And special thanks to my father, who, before he passed away, shared his investing stories with me and gave me permission to share them with you. Always the teacher—thanks, Dad.

A special thanks to you, the reader. It has been my experience that the best ideas are those shaped by many, which is why so many people were involved in the writing of this book. But the process doesn't have to end here with this printed edition. I encourage you to share your thoughts and suggestions for improvement and your experiences working with these models. Just visit www.KellerINK.com and drop us a line.

Finally, thanks to God, from whom all things come.

Gary Keller
January 14, 2005

CONTENTS

PART ONE: CHARTING THE COURSE

Part One:

CHARTING THE COURSE

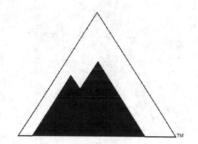

PREFACE

I am haunted. I'm haunted by the fear that our children may lose their way in a world that values money for what it can buy and not for the good it can do. I am haunted by the idea that our children are growing up in a society that places too much emphasis on the job you have, the salary you make, and the title you wear. An impatient world measured in days, not years, and populated by instant winners, lottery lovers, and a battery of million-dollar game shows. A time when investing has become a romantic notion of high-flying day traders and IPO millionaires or, worse, has become synonymous with a crapshoot plagued by corporate scandal, worthless stock options, and bankrupt pension funds. Most of all I'm haunted that we're teaching a generation that riches come quickly or not at all. My preoccupation with this fear began after I had a conversation with my son in the car.

Big Money—Little Money

"Dad, I need to talk to you."

I met his eyes in the rearview mirror as if to say, "Fire away."

"I'm serious, Dad."

I turned off the radio and gave him my immediate, undivided attention. John stared out the window and for a moment seemed to grapple with the right way to express what was troubling him. Parents know this brief pause before the big question. You experience a mix of curiosity and worry over what could be on your 12-year-old's mind. But it's important, so you wait and you listen.

"Dad, I need money, serious money, and I need it fast."

I relaxed. As a businessperson and an investor I knew a few things about money. This probably was a problem I could address and, hopefully, teach John a thing or two in the process.

"What do you mean? Why do you need that kind of money?"

"I want money. I want my own money so I can buy things, so I can buy the things I want."

This was my opening, and I shared with him my belief that a big part of making money is about work ethic and patience and having a good plan. I tried to express the satisfaction that comes from rolling up your sleeves and making your own way. I finished with some suggestions for ways he might make some money on his own.

"How about mowing yards? We could make some flyers when we get home, and I'll help you canvass the neighborhood."

"But I don't want to do that."

"That's how I made money when I was your age."

"No, no. It's not fast enough, Dad."

We kept going. I made suggestions, and he shot them down. My plans, it seems, either took too long or didn't create the serious big money he had in mind. After a few minutes I was frustrated and upset—parentally angry. So I collected myself and offered one last constructive suggestion. But as I shared it, I could see in the mirror that he was already struggling to find a polite way to tell me he had no interest.

Honestly, at that point I wanted to quit in frustration, to just let it go. But I made a critical decision to stay engaged and continue to search for a plan that would work for both of us. The great thing is that we did just that. Later that afternoon, back at home, we looked at his resources, went over his options, and created a broad plan for him to earn extra cash on his own—something he could build on and grow over time. As the plan came together, his confidence grew and the mood that had gripped him earlier was dispelled.

I really don't blame John for wishing that money came easily. There have been many times when I wanted to believe that too. But here is a truth you can count on: Little money comes easy—big money doesn't. This is a foundational truth I hope you will learn and come to understand as I have, and as I hope my son will too.

This book is about the plans that create big money. If I've learned anything in my entrepreneurial career, it's this: Small plans at best yield small results, and big plans at worst beat small plans. So, when I want big results, I need a big plan. The best outcomes—in any of life's endeavors—are almost always the result of a big plan powered by persistent effort over time. That approach will not only give you the best possible chance to win, it will also put you in the best possible position to win big.

In terms of creating financial wealth—big money—one of the best ways I've seen, one that is truly accessible to anyone, is to invest in real estate. Real estate investing can be an awesome avenue to wealth. It can absolutely change your life and your family's future. In fact, it can provide you with not only the minimums you need but also the maximums you deserve. This book is not about your minimums; it's about your maximums—your maximum potential as an investor.

Whether you are a beginner or a seasoned real estate investor, this book was written for you. It was written to help you succeed and succeed big. All you need is a plan, a good plan—a proven big plan that can guide you from the beginning to the highest levels of investing. *The Millionaire Real Estate Investor* will share that plan with you. We want you to become a successful real estate investor, to achieve your goals, to prosper and flourish over time, and even—should you so choose—to become a Millionaire Real Estate Investor.

Of course, I'd wish the same thing for my son, and maybe that's the course he'll choose. Not long after our afternoon together, John came up to me and unexpectedly asked, "Dad, will you ever teach me to make big money?"

"John," I told him, "when you're ready, it would be one of the greatest pleasures of my life to teach you."

INTRODUCTION

Ideas are the beginning points of all fortunes.

Napoleon Hill

ARE YOU READY?

Are you ready? Are you ready to become a Millionaire Real Estate Investor?

I am a lifelong teacher, and there is one thing I believe to be absolutely true: Real learning begins only when the student is open to the message. I've heard many people say, "When the student is ready, the teacher will appear," as if this were some strange or mysterious coincidence. The truth is, a teacher is almost always there and learning is simply a matter of the student being ready and willing to learn. For me this holds true whether I'm teaching an entrepreneur how to create a business plan or showing my son how to make money. If they're not ready, they don't learn! Becoming a successful real estate investor is no exception. The journey begins when you're ready to take it.

I'd like to share a few real-life stories from people who discovered one day that they were ready to start their investment journey and did:

- As a registered nurse, Barbara Mattson struggled to support her disabled husband and two children. Barbara transformed their lives when instead of paying off an avalanche of accumulated medical bills she used a long-overdue disability settlement to buy an investment property. In five years she accumulated $9 million in real estate, and now she runs her own real estate company.

- Donis King left her secretarial job of 16 years to pursue real estate investing and never looked back. She supported herself solely on rental income and now owns 27 houses free and clear. Donis was able to retire at an early age.

- Ken Jordan, a career biologist, left the security of his government job after buying his first multifamily investment property. He now works for himself, living off rental income and his property management company.

- As the mother of three, Barbara Drake was determined to get a college education to set an example for her children. Not only did her first two investment properties pay for her degree, they put her children through school as well. Barbara quit her job to pursue real estate investing full time. Now in her sixties, she owns 36 single-family homes and lives off the cash flow.

- When Wendy Patton bought her first investment property, she was living in a hotel, made $20,000 a year, and owed that much in student loans. Today Wendy has bought and sold more than 600 houses. She lectures around the country and lives off her investment income.

- When Danny Williams accepted an early retirement package from Delta, he owned 11 rental properties and had two children in college. Danny says he's now "totally unemployable" by choice and in complete control of his destiny.

- Jimmy and Linda McKissack struggled for years to turn a restaurant and nightclub into a sustainable business. They began supplementing their income through investment properties, and before long they "got it." Within five years they went from a handful of investment homes to 83 residential properties worth over $10 million.

■ Carlos Herbon and his wife immigrated to the United States from Argentina with $150 in their pockets. The couple and their sons now own several million dollars worth of real estate and run a property management company. For them the American dream has become a reality.

What did these investors have in common? On the surface, not much. They came from all over and began their investment journeys with vastly different resources. Some had stable jobs and equity in their homes, while others began with massive debt, no credit, and not much more than the change in their pockets. What they *did* share was a burning desire and a readiness to change their lives, to succeed on their own, without a job or a boss, without a pension plan or a safety net, in the entrepreneurial world of real estate investing.

Their drive and will to succeed were strong enough to lead them to do the right things day in and day out for months and years as their net worth steadily grew. None were "instant millionaires," won the proverbial lottery, or tapped into some "secret formula" for overnight financial success. They were ready and they were willing. They got a plan, and they implemented it with persistence and patience.

The Millionaire Real Estate Investor is about building great financial wealth, and although there are ways to make money fast even in real estate investing, this book is not about "get-rich-quick" schemes and techniques. Frankly, there are no express elevators to the top in financial wealth building—just a long flight of steps. But it is a worthy journey, and reaching the top takes both patience and perseverance. This book is about a tried and true financial wealth-building vehicle that rewards those who have patience and perseverance—that vehicle is real estate.

I'm a Millionaire Real Estate Investor too, but perhaps more important, I've also had the privilege, as the founder of one of the largest and fastest-growing real estate franchise companies in history, to oversee and consult on thousands of real estate transactions. In my career I've seen a lot of financial wealth built through real estate. I've also seen money lost. As an agent and broker, a business owner and investor, and an advisor and consultant, I've explored almost every angle of real estate. And I've been taking notes.

In the end, though, this book isn't about me, and even though we interviewed over 100 of them, it's not about the other Millionaire Real Estate Investors you'll meet in these pages. *The Millionaire Real Estate Investor* is about you, your choices, and your possibilities. It's about the millionaire in you. The millionaire in you who dreams of fulfilling all the thoughts and visions in your head and heart. It's about the unrealized you, the you that wants to focus on how big your life can be and act accordingly. I believe *The Millionaire Real Estate Investor* is about the real you, not some idealized you or some new person you need to become. It's about the actual, factual, bona fide you, the naked-before-the-mirror, indisputable, unquestionable, honest-to-God (you know what I mean) authentic you. I firmly believe that the opportunity to build financial wealth—even big financial wealth—is open to you. In fact, it is open to all people who are ready and willing to accept the challenge, no matter what their shortcomings, no matter what their current station in life.

Please don't let any doubts or fears you might have turn into excuses such as "I don't have any credit; I've got too much debt; I don't know what to do; and besides, I'm no good with money." I'm here to tell you that in the end none of that really matters. It didn't matter to the Millionaire Real Estate Investors we interviewed, and it won't matter to you. It's time to set aside those doubts that whisper things like "It's not possible" or, worse, "I can't do it" and those fears that stealthily subvert your best ambitions. I want to encourage you to sidestep this kind of self-sabotage and begin the journey with confidence. With confidence it's possible for anyone, and if you're ready—possible for you.

The Millionaire Real Estate Investor

MONEY LIVES ON THE OTHER SIDE OF FEAR

Money lives on the other side of fear. I didn't always know this, but I now know it is true. Fear keeps us from getting what we want, especially in matters of money. It is true for me, and it is true for you. All of us can look at our lives and count the times when fear stepped in, prevented us from taking action, and cost us a precious financial opportunity. In this way fear becomes a building block of future regret. It blinds us to possibilities. It keeps us where we are, stuck in a financial box—a box built by fear, a box built by our own hands.

But just as fear can stop us in our tracks, it can make us move faster than we ever imagined. Just as it can give us a negative focus, it can give us a positive focus that can galvanize us to take positive action. What is interesting is that in this moment, when we're afraid that something won't happen or even that it will, fear points out what is most important to us. It shows us what matters most in our lives. In truth, fear isn't all bad. Don't be afraid of fear. Respect it, keep going, and move past it.

Just like a river of water, fear can be bridged. Fear is only as big or as wide as you allow it to be. And as is often the case, once you've crossed that river of fear and experienced the wonders on the other side, you look back and question why you were ever afraid. But here's the catch: The only people who actually know this are those who have crossed that river and are standing on the other side. It is my hope that just like the millionaires we interviewed, you will be among those who choose to cross that river of investment fear and stand financially tall on the other side.

One of the things my coauthors and I will do in this book is dispel the kinds of unproductive fears that prevent good real estate investors from becoming great investors and, even worse, prevent many people from investing in real estate at all. At the same time we'll highlight areas where fear is a good thing and caution should be exercised. The truth is that when you have the confidence that comes from understanding what to do, why you should do it, and how to do it right, most of your uncertainty will be left behind. Knowledge and insight can wash away more fear than anything else can. It's our sincere hope that *The Millionaire Real Estate Investor* will be a great source of knowledge, insight, and confidence for you.

Money does live on the other side of fear. But in a bigger sense opportunity lives on the other side of fear as well. Money just represents one tangible form of opportunity. It gives you options and allows you to choose. That's one reason we called this book *The Millionaire Real Estate Investor*. To us the word *millionaire* represents big opportunity, unlimited options, a large life. That's what this book is ultimately about—living a large and limitless life. The first step on that journey is to acknowledge any fears that might be holding you back and then cross that bridge. Your financial opportunity lies on the other side of your investment fears.

ANYONE CAN DO IT— NOT EVERYONE WILL

While *The Millionaire Real Estate Investor* is a handbook for investing in real estate, it is also—at its core—a manual for creating financial wealth. Creating financial wealth begins with an understanding of the best time-tested principles for making and managing money. Creating wealth is about recognizing that *wealth* and *riches* are not the same, that the gap between a *good* deal and a *great* deal is a vast chasm created by a lack of wisdom. Learning the difference can change the way you look at the world, and eventually it can change the shape of your life.

How you think matters. In fact, it matters a lot. So, before we can share with you these fundamental truths about money, investing, and real estate, we need to make sure you agree with us on two important points:

1. Building financial wealth through real estate is possible.

2. Building financial wealth through real estate is possible for you.

We think history has proved the first point, and chances are, you already know that investing in real estate has made others wealthy. Our primary concern is that you agree with the second point—that you really believe it's possible for you. In our experience many people can't get their minds around the idea that they too can attain real financial wealth through investing. There's a whole laundry list of excuses, but they all boil down to one thing: self-doubt. This book will encourage you to confront that doubt and step past it to the opportunities that lie unrealized before you. Remember, as Shakespeare pointed out, "Our doubts are traitors, and make us lose the good we oft might win by fearing to attempt."

As you'll discover, *The Millionaire Real Estate Investor* is really two books in one. The first part is devoted to your thinking. In that part you'll confront some of your myths about money, real estate, and yourself. You'll also learn some timeless truths about the way money works. If you can learn to think like a millionaire, you'll have a much better chance to become one. The second part of the book is about taking action. It's the "how-to" part and will outline a proven path to follow as well as tested models to employ.

Remember, anyone can do it—not everyone will. The only question is: Will you?

OVERVIEW

> *A casual player of Monopoly might think that it's a game of chance and that the winner is determined by rolls of the dice. Watching the best players in the world has shown me it's not. The winners are actually masters of strategy and negotiation. They know how to minimize the impact of bad luck—and to put themselves in the way of an undue share of lucky breaks.*
>
> Philip Orbanes, Game Designer
> *Harvard Business Review*

CHAMPIONS TAKE THE LUCK OUT OF THE GAME

Luck. Blind luck, dumb luck, Lady Luck. No matter what you call it, many people believe that luck is one of the essential ingredients in real estate investing. Finding a great investment property, the perfect tenant, or the right buyer at times can feel beyond your control or anyone else's. These key elements often seem to be a matter of fortuitous timing or simple coincidence, but here's the truth: Success in real estate investing is no more about luck than is success in anything else in life. This is not to say that Lady Luck doesn't play her hand from time to time, but you can't plan on it, rely on it, or predict it. It is by definition beyond your control. That's what luck is, and the best investors, the tried and true champs, don't count on good luck showing up. Through the use of proven strategies and time-tested models, they make luck unnecessary—they take it out of the game.

One afternoon, over a game of Monopoly with my wife and son, I got the opportunity to illustrate to my son how champions use models to circumvent luck and maximize their likelihood of winning.

"John, don't trade with your dad," Mary, my wife, said. "That's how he always wins."

I gave my wife a mock frown, which she answered with a playful smile.

John hesitated. He wasn't sure of the right move. But in the end he made the trade and gave me the final piece of a key monopoly. He justified the move, saying, "Well, it's all luck anyway."

"Really?" I asked. "I don't think so."

Quickly, I mortgaged other properties and put hotels on my new monopoly. Within a handful of turns John landed on one of my hotels and had the misfortune of going to jail and the double misfortune of rolling out only to land on my monopoly again. Just like that, he was knocked out of the game.

Afterward John asked me what I meant when I said Monopoly is not just about luck. I replied, "In almost every game there are usually tried and true ways to win. And if you follow them, you may not win *every* time, but you will significantly increase your odds of winning *most* of the time."

"So you know how to do that with Monopoly?"

"Sure. Do you want to learn?"

Of course he did, and so I went to my office and dug out an article written by a game designer that outlined a simple strategy for winning at Monopoly. We read it together, and I could see that for him a realization was sinking in. There was a way to win—a model to follow—and when you understood what to do, it seemed that it would be harder to lose than to win.

John looked me in the eye and asked, "Dad, have you been letting me win?"

"Sometimes," I admitted. "But I wanted you to have fun while you were learning how to play. If it makes you feel any better, I don't think you'll be needing any more help from me after this."

Sure enough, we played again and John won without any help from me. He now knew the difference in the game between the good real estate deals and the great ones. He knew what to do and what to avoid. One resounding victory wasn't enough. John later talked his uncle into playing and whipped him soundly too.

Almost everyone has played Monopoly at one time or another, but very few people understand that there is a clear way to maximize their chances of winning the game. The best players know which spots on the board get the most traffic and which ones have the highest return on investment. They also know how to acquire the most advantageous monopolies without having to land on those spaces. They network, they trade, they barter and find ways to make deals work. It may be an over-simplification, but to me this all sounds a lot like the real-world game of real estate investing.

The question is: How do you take luck out of the *real* real estate investing game? First, you learn to play the game. Second, you learn to win the game. Playing well and winning consistently both start with learning proven, time-tested models.

BIG MODELS—BIG GOALS— BIG SUCCESS

Early in life I started making the connection between how I approached something and the outcome I achieved. Do it one way and get one result; do it another way and get a better result. I began to understand that for me there was clearly a good way of doing things. Along the way I also learned there was an even better way of doing things.

However, my biggest epiphany came when I discovered that if I wanted the best, most predictable results possible, I couldn't just put forth a good or even a great effort: I had to do things the best possible way. In school, when I studied one way, I'd get a C. If I studied another way, I'd get a B. And if I studied the best way, I'd get an A. When I was learning to play the guitar, if I rehearsed one way, the music sounded good. If I rehearsed another way, the music sounded great. But if I rehearsed the best way over time, it sounded awesome. In retrospect it seems obvious, but it took time for me to notice the pattern: The way I did things mattered. It mattered a lot.

By paying close attention to my outcomes, I started to uncover the best ways to do the things that mattered to me. By being intentional and purposeful, I started to find success in the things I pursued. Let's be honest: I don't think you can or should be this purposeful in every area of your life. The danger in bringing that kind of intensity to every task is that you risk wasting lots of time and energy perfecting things that really don't matter. That's being a "jack of all trades but a master of none," or what I sometimes refer to as misplaced focus. But when the outcome really does matter, this kind of careful approach makes all the difference.

In my effort to achieve more and more success, I discovered that my own learning and experience weren't always enough. Naturally, I started looking elsewhere and turned to books, teachers, mentors, and even consultants for advice; that became my path. And they all seemed to point in one direction—You could learn from history. Books recounted success stories. Teachers alluded to research. Mentors taught from experience, and consultants often cited the specific best practices in an industry. I didn't have to start at the beginning and learn from my own mistakes. I could start in where someone else had left off. I could give up my need to do in order to learn. In fact, in this way I could learn even faster. This was a breakthrough in my life and, quite truthfully, one of my biggest "ahas" ever. Some of the biggest successes I've had in business and investing are due to this simple concept. In fact, I like to say that some of my best thinking was done by other people.

One book in particular, *Unlimited Power*, by Anthony Robbins, helped me both put a name to what I was looking for—modeling—and devise a process for finding those proven models. Simply put, if you look to the very best people in a field and study what they do, you often can repeat their success. The key is to learn how they achieved their goals and then understand why they did it that way. When you grasp these two things, you can start where they left off.

Thus, I became a collector of success stories and models, and over time I discovered that every success story worth exploring had three fundamental parts: what a person thought he or she could do, how that person did it, and what that person accomplished. That process—think, plan, produce—soon became the basis for my personal success formula: Big Goals powered by Big Models lead to Big Success. Big Goals—Big Models—Big Success.

The Big Goals push you to think big and see new possibilities for your life. And Big Models make those possibilities more probable by giving your actions the foundation of proven, time-tested methods. That's a formula for Big Success.

We all have personal ceilings of achievement that are based on our current thoughts and habits. Implementing the lessons learned from your own trial and error can raise that ceiling, but only so far and so fast. Proven models, in contrast, can help you raise your level of achievement dramatically in a relatively short period of time.

It's a little like the difference between running on your own and being part of a relay team. With models you get to skip whole legs of the race and get the momentum and speed of those who ran before you. The baton they hand you is the gift of learning from their experience, the gift of benefiting from how far they've advanced the race. Models help us

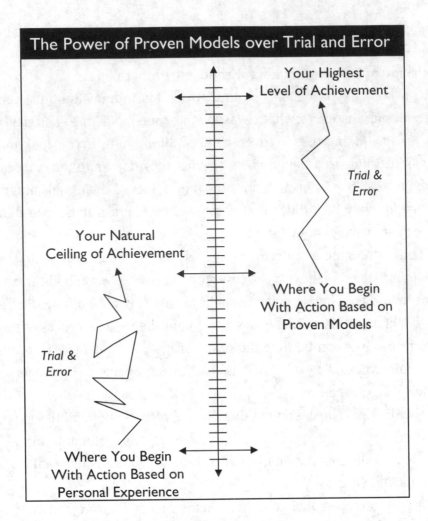

The Power of Proven Models over Trial and Error

Your Highest
Level of Achievement

Trial &
Error

Your Natural
Ceiling of Achievement

Where You Begin
With Action Based on
Proven Models

Trial &
Error

Where You Begin
With Action Based on
Personal Experience

Figure 1

avoid known stumbling blocks and reach our objectives faster than we could alone. It is a huge leap of faith to assume that those starting at the bottom, with only their own knowledge and experience, will ever reach the place where a proven model begins.

To move forward in life, everyone has to learn from mistakes. The only question is whose: yours or those of the great achievers who lived before you?

That's why, when we set out to research *The Millionaire Real Estate Investor*, we went on a quest for the very best real estate investing models we could find, the ones used by the best players in the investment game. Through many months of intensive research, interviews, and mastermind group meetings, we did just that. The models we'll share with you represent the "best practices" of some of the most successful real estate investors today. In fact, all the real estate investors we interviewed to build the models presented in this book owned at least $1 million worth of real estate not including their personal residences, and over 60 percent had achieved in excess of $1 million in equity in their investment portfolios. They averaged almost 50 rental units and over $100,000 in net annual cash flow from their investments. These were career investors who had purchased an average of around 150 properties and even a few who had bought and sold over 1,500 properties in their investment careers.[1] Our research was thorough, and the results were compelling: Successful investors clearly follow proven models, and those proven models for selecting, buying, and owning real estate can generate the kinds of remarkable results those investors have achieved. They are the models presented in these pages.

Let's be very clear. A proven model is simply a method or system used to produce desirable, repeatable results. Although no model can guarantee success, a proven model built on the best practices of high achievers almost always will maximize your chances for big success over time. In other words, big models lead to big success. They also give you confidence in your actions, an understanding of whether you are doing the right things.

Models aren't really new. They are everywhere. I follow them. You follow them. Everyone follows them. Most people just aren't aware of the specific repeatable processes they've developed, such as the best way to

---

[1] Profiles of some of our Millionaire Real Estate Investors appear toward the end of this book.

brush their teeth, lace up their shoes, bake a cake, balance a checkbook, iron a shirt . . . even the best way to drive to work. You use these models to maximize the effectiveness and efficiency of your actions. That is how you get what you want more predictably, more of the time.

Just as these models help take the stress out of your daily life, you can use models to reduce stress, improve efficiency, and maximize results in your investment life. The models featured in *The Millionaire Real Estate Investor* are the ones master real estate investors use to minimize risk and maximize profit when buying, holding, and selling properties. Their knowledge didn't come for free. They paid for it with their own time, effort, and money. My initial education in real estate investing didn't come for free either. It cost me $100,000, and it forever changed the way I look at the world.

THE $100,000 THAT GOT AWAY

One summer weekend while vacationing at a popular beach resort, Mary and I ran into a real estate agent in the elevator. My wife asked, "So, how's the real estate market? Heard of any good deals?"

"Actually, I know of a great one right here in the building. It's a condo that just came on the market. Would you like to see it?"

At first we weren't sure. Buying wasn't really on our minds. But it seemed like a fun thing to do, and so we agreed to take a look.

It turns out the agent lived in the building, and even though it wasn't her listing, she knew a lot about the property. She related that the owners lived out of town, as did their agent. Although it was on a corner with beach views and was in great shape, the condo was listed for only about $160,000. Mary and I had been coming to that beach for years and, being real estate agents, always picked up the real estate magazines and perused the market. We had a decent understanding of values and immediately recognized that the condo apparently was listed well under its market value. The agent agreed. I remember her words to this day. She said, "Honestly, this is a steal."

Like any good agent she asked us if we wanted to put in an offer. Even though I knew that we could afford it and that it was obviously a good deal, I hadn't yet become a true investor, the kind who won't allow a good deal to pass him or her by. I thanked the agent for her time and told her we'd think about it.

Normally, "we'll think about it" is just a polite euphemism for "no thanks." But sometime the next week the condo came up again in a conversation between my wife and me. After a short discussion at the dinner table I got up, found the agent's card, and called her with our offer. To give you a sense of how this memory has stuck with me, I remember every aspect of that moment. I was sitting in the den in my favorite armchair and calling from my black cordless phone. When the agent picked up and I told her we wanted to buy the condo, she just laughed and laughed.

"I told you that condo was a steal," she said. "It sold the next day!"

I hung up the phone, turned to Mary, and said, "Honey, we just lost $100,000."

I'll never forget that feeling. Truthfully, I feel sorry for my wife, who had to spend the rest of that evening with me. I was embarrassed, preoccupied, and a little grumpy. Here I was with every advantage. I had been working in real estate for over a decade. I knew the business. I knew how much money could be made through investing in real estate, and still I had let this opportunity pass me by in a moment of indecision.

Anyone could have bought that condo! It was priced at $160,000 at the time and would have resold immediately for $260,000—an instant $100,000 windfall before expenses. Even people who might not have qualified for financing personally probably could have bought a short-term option for a few hundred dollars and had investors lining up outside their doors to partner on the deal. What I learned was that I wasn't thinking like a real investor. Plus, I was asking the wrong questions. I was asking, "Should I make an investment?" when I should have been asking, "Is this the deal?" A *true* real estate investor would not have walked away from a great opportunity like that. A *true* real estate investor would have had the confidence to act when the opportunity presented itself. What I've come to know as a fundamental truth is that all of us, as real investors, should wake up every morning and say to ourselves, "I'm an investor. I'm building financial wealth. Is this the day I find an opportunity and make a deal?"

It wasn't until I lost such a great opportunity that I finally got it: I needed to learn how to become an investor. That meant I would have to learn to think like an investor and then act like one.

$100,000 lesson learned. I vowed never to make that mistake again. I knew that I had to learn. I had to learn how to recognize an opportunity when I saw one and understand the appropriate action to take. I needed to know how to build financial wealth through smart investing. I needed to learn how to become an investor—a great one. And I knew that somewhere there had to be the best models for doing that. Within weeks I began having regular breakfasts with Michael, an old college pal who was then a financial advisor with his own television show. It was with Michael that I started to awaken the investor inside me and discover some of the fundamental financial wealth-building models that are the foundation of what we'll share in this book.

MORNINGS WITH MICHAEL

It was Michael's television show that got the ball rolling. One day he called me up and said, "Hey, Gary, I want to interview you for my show." He wanted to talk about how I had made the leap from building a great small business to building a great big business. After the show we met for breakfast and continued visiting. We had so much fun and learned so much talking about business that I suggested that we do it on a regular basis. Before long we were meeting every other Tuesday morning for breakfast.

At the very first meeting Michael quickly discovered that I was a businessperson, not an investor, and so the topic of discussion each breakfast was investing or, to put it another way, how to grow financial wealth. This was my personal investment group, a club with only two members. Michael was committed to turning me into an investor, and it worked. We read every important financial author from Buffett to Rohn and shared our observations. Michael encouraged me to keep a personal balance sheet, a one-page document that summarized my net worth. Each meeting he'd ask me one simple question: "Gary, how can you make your net worth grow?"

One of the things I learned was the simple difference between financial riches and financial wealth. Being rich is about having money. You can have a job and be very rich. The problem with this is that the money stops coming to you when you stop working for it. Financial wealth, by contrast, is about owning assets, such as businesses or real estate, that generate money for you. Those assets can have aspects of a "job" in that they demand some of your time, but the dollars they generate are generally disproportionate to the time you invest. Quickly, Michael taught me that I wanted to be financially wealthy instead of just rich.

For over 10 years I met with my friend and learned. After a time I began acting on that new knowledge. One of the first things I did was to recognize a good real estate opportunity and act on it. Coincidentally, my first investment as a *true* real estate investor also happened to be a condo deal.

While I was interviewing someone for a sales position in one of my real estate offices, the conversation turned to commercial real estate. I asked, as the investor I had become, what I now always ask: "Do you know of any good deals?" It turned out that he knew of a building of business condos that were about to go on the market at a terrific price. This time there was no hesitation. I immediately set up a showing for the next morning. I looked at the property, understood that it was priced below market value, and quickly made an offer.

I'm so glad I didn't hesitate. It turned out that the price was a steal, and other buyers quickly lined up to buy it, only to find out it was already sold. The good news is that I bought it the way an investor would. I recognized the opportunity, acted on it, and many years later sold the property for just under half a million in net profits. Although I paid dearly for my first lesson in real estate investing, after a little time spent learning to think and act like a real investor I was able to replace a $100,000 lost opportunity with a success story worth almost five times as much.

Although consistent results didn't show up overnight, during the last decade, by constantly searching for great opportunities, recognizing them when I found them, and acting on the best ones quickly, I've made millions through traditional investing, investing in businesses, and investing in real estate. I now know that I'm out to build financial wealth. I'm an investor all the time. And I'm always looking for an opportunity to make a deal!

What's astounding is that the simple lessons I learned with Michael aren't anything new. They have been around for ages. Most timeless truths are like that: incredibly simple and obvious yet overlooked by those not ready to see. When you understand the timeless truths about financial wealth building—how money really works—when you can recognize a great opportunity and are ready to act on it, your world changes. That's what this book is about. And there is no better place to begin learning these financial wealth-building lessons than the arena of real estate investing.

THE THREE AREAS OF FOCUS FOR THE MILLIONAIRE REAL ESTATE INVESTOR

In the late 1940s, quality control manager Dr. Joseph M. Juran documented a life-changing universal principle that he called the "vital few and trivial many." The idea was that a relatively small percentage of your efforts lead to the vast majority of your results. He attributed some of his findings to the statistical work of the Italian economist Vilfredo Pareto, who had observed that 80 percent of the wealth in his country was owned by 20 percent of the population. As fate would have it, that broadly embraced principle came to be known not as Juran's Law but as Pareto's Principle. These days we simply call it the 80:20 Rule.

The idea that 20 percent of your actions lead to 80 percent of your results may be one of the most powerful principles you can apply to your life. It's about getting the most from your time and effort. It's about maximizing your results. It's about having focus.

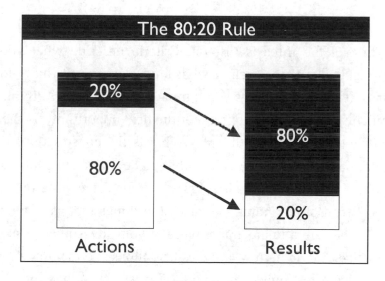

Figure 2

Focus is the key to great success, more than effort, experience, or even natural ability. Look at the highest achievers in any field and you'll discover that they have powerful focus; just as important, you'll learn that they focus on the right things: the handful of truly important issues that make the biggest difference. They know what matters and when it matters most. As you move toward becoming a successful real estate investor, you too will gain that level of focus. Although the results that come from that focus may start slowly, over time they will grow substantially.

When we conducted our interviews with high achievers in the real estate investment world, our goal was to discover the fundamental concepts they focused on day in and day out without distraction. In which areas did they strive to achieve mastery? What we discovered is that these investors focus on three simple but incredibly dynamic forces at the heart of real estate investing. In fact, these three forces are at the core of all investing: Criteria, Terms, and Network. We've come to refer to them simply as CTN. They are for us the "Dynamic Trio of Investing."

CRITERIA: WHAT YOU BUY

The first of the three is Criteria. Criteria describe what you buy. They're the standards that define what kind of property you're looking for. Your Criteria are the things you ultimately list on your APB (all properties bulletin) when you're hunting for the next opportunity. Is the property a single-family or a multifamily? What is the construction? Does it have the right features and amenities that make it attractive for resale or rental? Most important, where is it located? Your Criteria are the aspects of the property that are immutable facts, the things that can't be negotiated away. They are a foundational piece of your investment strategy.

In practice Criteria narrow an investor's choices to the properties that represent the greatest opportunity and the least risk. When the property

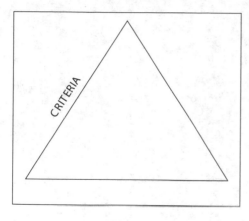

Figure 3

you find matches your Criteria, what you get in return is something with predictable value. Think of your Criteria as an "opportunity filter" that keeps out the bad and lets in the good. And just as good Criteria are the backbone of successful real estate investing, bad Criteria (or no Criteria at all) have been the downfall of many a would-be investor. In the "Buy a Million" section of this book, we'll discuss the specific Criteria successful investors use to select their investment properties. Criteria are ultimately about identifying predictable value, and that is why they are the first area of focus for the Millionaire Real Estate Investor.

TERMS: HOW YOU BUY IT

If Criteria define an opportunity, Terms define how you turn it into a deal. Once a property meets your Criteria, Terms determine its value to you both now and for the future. Terms are the negotiable aspects of a purchase, and they include everything from the offer price, down payment, and interest rate to conveyances, occupancy, and closing costs. Every investor we asked told us that Terms are where a great deal can be created from even the most modest Criteria. A skillful negotiation of Terms can lead to a better equity position, improved cash flow, and sometimes both. It's about how much money you need to acquire a property and close a transaction and how much the property will yield over time. Terms are about maximizing financial value and represent the second area of focus for the Millionaire Real Estate Investor.

Later, in "Buy a Million," we'll home in on the key Terms of any transaction that can make the biggest difference in the relative success of an investment. You don't have to be a gifted negotiator like Roger Dawson or Donald Trump to capitalize on Terms. It is about understanding the financial fundamentals of a transaction, knowing which elements are flexible, and being systematic about getting all you can from every deal. It's also about knowing when to walk away. Remember, you make your money going in, not going out. You buy right and let the market go to work for you as opposed to buying less than right and hoping the market will save you. Buying right means getting the right Terms.

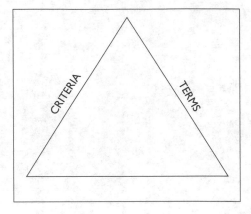

Figure 4

NETWORK: WHO HELPS YOU

The last member of the Dynamic Trio is Network. Your Network is who helps you in your investing. When we were attempting to pin down the critical areas that make the biggest difference in real estate investing, Network was a surprise contender. We just didn't see it coming. The idea of the individual entrepreneurial investor beating the streets for deals is what comes to mind for most people. But again and again, throughout our research, investors referred to all the people who helped them succeed. They had relationships with people who sent them opportunities, mentored them, helped them buy and maintain their properties, and in many cases provided services that enabled them to do more while spending less time and effort. As a businessperson, I call this leverage: the fact that you can accomplish more with qualified help than you can accomplish alone.

The Dynamic Trio of Real Estate Investing

CRITERIA

TERMS

NETWORK

Figure 5

When we review Network in detail in "Buy a Million," we'll help you understand how to establish a "dream team" for your investment career. From real estate agents to contractors and property managers, you will need help. In fact, although it was the last of the three items we identified, Network will come first in your investing career, as you'll rely on those people to help get your investment career launched safely, reliably, and profitably. The advice we provide in these pages will help you both select the best and work successfully with them over time.

The three areas of focus for the Millionaire Real Estate Investor—Criteria, Terms, and Network—answer the questions of what you'll buy, how you'll buy it, and who will help you. Remember, Criteria identify, Terms determine, and your Network supports all the investing you do. Mastering these three areas will give you the greatest chance for long-term success and place you solidly on the path to becoming a Millionaire Real Estate Investor.

Criteria, Terms & Network

Your CRITERIA identify potential deals

Your TERMS determine the real deals

Your NETWORK supports all your deals

Figure 6

THE FOUR STAGES OF GROWTH ON THE PATH TO A MILLION

The path of the Millionaire Real Estate Investor is a progression through four stages. First, you must learn to Think a Million (think like a Millionaire Real Estate Investor) before you make your first move. How you think matters. Whether this strikes you as a cliché or as a timeless truth, my experience has taught me that the bigger I think, the more I can accomplish. I've learned that what I hold in my mind is what shows up in my life. Learning to think like a Millionaire Real Estate Investor will give you the greatest chance of becoming one.

The next step is to Buy a Million, in which you'll get a thorough understanding of the best models for investing in real estate and, more fundamentally, an understanding of money: the ways it is made and the ways it can be lost. The goal is to equip you with the working models you need to purchase investment properties with a market value of a million dollars or more. Believe it or not, this is not the huge leap you might imagine, and many investors reach that mark long before they ever expected they would. Buy a Million is about the fundamentals of acquiring properties, holding them, and in some cases selling them. Buy a Million applies the power of Criteria, Terms, and Network to launch your career in investing.

After you Buy a Million, you'll set your sights on having an equity position of a million dollars or more in your properties. We call this stage Own a Million. This is when you will realize that the investing you have done has blossomed into a bona fide business. With that transformation come a set of issues specific to that level of ownership. Acquiring properties through credit potentially becomes more difficult, cash becomes a commodity, and managing your investments could require help from several quarters. This stage involves dealing with and often balancing cash flow with asset or equity buildup. It may involve selling, trading up, or exchanging. It certainly involves understanding the surprisingly simple realities of tax and owner entity issues. The good news is that by understanding these issues from the beginning you can plan for them. That is what the models in this book are intended to help you do. By beginning with the right models, proven ones that can handle the big issues, you'll never have to stop and scratch your head or, worse, start over and reinvent what you do.

The last stage of growth for a Millionaire Real Estate Investor is Receive a Million. Think of it as the summit, a place where only the best have gone. Receive a Million is when you are in a position to receive an annual income of a million dollars from your investments. Pivotal to this stage is that your investment business be designed so that you can choose to get out of the day-to-day work and enjoy the benefits of what you've created. Although you can step out at any point along the way, it is my hope that you will set your sights on a big goal.

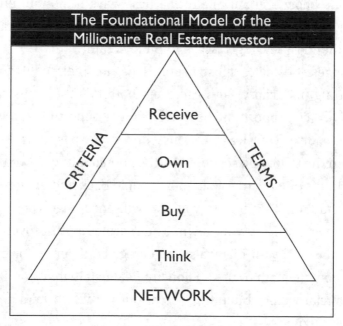

Figure 7

Exactly when you decide to move into the "receive mode" is up to you. Obviously, you don't have to wait until you're receiving a million dollars a year. Like some of the investors we met in our research, you can accept the cash flow you've built and step out of the business sooner. Or you can wait and receive more down the line. The point is that if you've followed the models of *The Millionaire Real Estate Investor*, you will have more choices, and that is a very good thing to have in your financial wealth-building life.

MOVING FORWARD

I believe that everyone has a chance to be financially wealthy. It begins with a state of mind, a way of looking at the world, and ultimately evolves into a way of life. Financially wealthy people think differently from the rest and as a result make different choices and enjoy more freedom in their lives. It's about living a large life. It's about having greater choices. This book is about one of the best ways I know to build financial wealth: real estate investing. Real estate is accessible to all and is easily one of the most leveraged ways to build wealth.

The biggest obstacles most people face are their own doubts and fears. Building financial wealth can seem both daunting and dangerous. But as we've said, opportunity, especially great opportunity, always lives on the other side of your fears. Learning how to get past those fears is our next task. In the following section, "MythUnderstandings," we're going to reveal the kinds of fears that hold most people back and explore with you why they should not do that to you. We will encourage you to shed any baggage that might slow you down. Then, armed with proven big models and powered by your big goals, you can go confidently for big results. You can follow the path of the Millionaire Real Estate Investor. It is a journey of financial wealth building. It is a journey worth taking. It can be your journey too.

POINTS TO REMEMBER

■ Each of us should wake up every day and say to ourselves, "I'm an investor. I'm building financial wealth. Is today the day I find an opportunity and make a deal?"

■ A proven model is a process or method used to produce desirable, repeatable results. A proven model built on the best practices of high achievers in a given area will produce the most desirable and predictable results as well as maximize your chances for continued success over time.

■ High achievers use models to take the luck out of the game. They implement big models to minimize risk and maximize profit when buying, holding and selling real estate.

■ The three areas of focus for the Millionaire Real Estate Investor—Criteria, Terms and Network—determine what you'll buy, how you'll buy it and who will help you.

■ CTN—The Dynamic Trio of Investing:
  • Criteria identify potential deals.
  • Terms determine the real deals.
  • Your Network supports all your deals.

■ The path of the Millionaire Real Estate Investor progresses through four stages—Think a Million, Buy a Million, Own a Million, and Receive a Million—and they are best pursued in that order.

MYTHUNDERSTANDINGS

Fears are educated into us, and can,
if we wish, be educated out.

Dr. Karl A. Menninger

THE DEVIL'S WEDGE

In the old fable "The Devil's Best Tool" the Devil is going out of business and selling all the tools of his trade. For sale are implements such as the hammer of hatred, the scythe of spite, the maul of malice, and the dagger of deceit. As one would expect, the Devil's tools are all ominous, but oddly, the highest-priced item in his arsenal is an extremely worn and harmless-looking wedge. When asked why it is so expensive, the Devil slowly smiles and replies, "To be totally candid, this may be my most powerful weapon of all. I call it the wedge of doubt. When all my other tools fail me, I know I can always rely on doubt and discouragement to break the heart and shatter the will of man."

How upsetting that something so small and often dismissed can be so devastating. As surprising as this is, the moral of this fable is quite clear: Don't underestimate the power of doubt to keep you from becoming your best. Yet that's exactly what often happens in the world of investing. People doubt either their abilities or the possibilities. They simply don't believe they can really be investors or that investing can help them reach financial freedom.

When I talk with people about investing, what often becomes clear is that they don't initially recognize that fear or doubt is playing a significant role in their financial lives. They feel that investing is simply an intellectual option they have or haven't taken advantage of. While they can acknowledge the value of investing, they can't quite justify why they aren't doing it more often or at all. Only when I press, asking questions such as "Then why don't you do that?" do they finally realize that their doubts and fears are at least part of the reason they've been unable to give investing a serious and sustained try. That's when they finally have the "aha" that the opportunities of investing live on the other side of their fears and doubts, that the best financial rewards more than likely will be found outside their comfort zones. That's when they finally understand that fears and doubts undermine their confidence and their actions and ultimately can drive a powerful wedge between them and their dreams.

EIGHT MYTHUNDERSTANDINGS BETWEEN YOU AND FINANCIAL WEALTH

In the process of interviewing Millionaire Real Estate Investors for this book, a clear pattern emerged. Almost without fail, at one time or another, these high-achieving investors had to confront a persistent fear or a nagging doubt about investing that later proved to be unfounded. In fact, we were able to identify eight of those limiting beliefs that would-be investors commonly hold about becoming an investor and about investing itself. While these doubts and fears seldom are addressed in other invest-

> *"There's never a perfect time to start, so people should just start. Because there are always deals. You just learn your market and always buy below value, and you can't go wrong."*
> Jimmy and Linda McKissack
> Millionaire Real Estate Investors
> Highland Village, TX

ment books and seminars, the Millionaire Real Estate Investors we talked to impressed on us how important it is to address these subtle yet powerful misgivings early in the game. "Rest assured," they told us. "Everyone who intends to become financially wealthy will deal with them sooner or later." It suddenly became obvious to me that these doubts don't go away on their own; left unexamined or not dealt with, they can keep you from becoming a great investor.

We came to understand that these are the "MythUnderstandings" (part myth and part misunderstanding) that people have about investing. And after some consideration, two distinct categories of MythUnderstandings emerged from the research:

1. Your MythUnderstandings about the way you look at yourself as an investor

2. Your MythUnderstandings about the way you look at investing

This surprised us. We thought the MythUnderstandings would be about money and investing, but the more we thought about it, the more it made

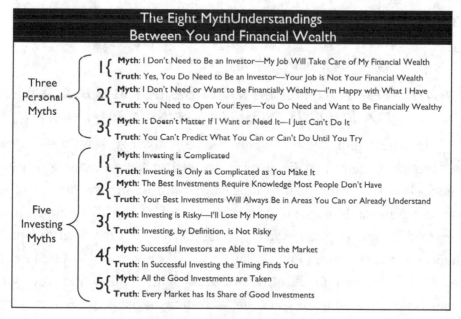

Figure 1

sense. People generally have two ways of looking at anything: the way they see themselves in the world and the way they see the world and how it works. You might think it would be reversed—that your perceptions of how the world works would inform your sense of how successful you could be—but for some strange reason it isn't. The image you have of yourself as an investor becomes the lens through which you see the world of investing, and that self-image will either guide or misguide you. Interestingly, any myths you have about yourself as an investor tend to magnify your misunderstandings about investing. That's why we call the MythUnderstandings about the way you view yourself as an investor the "Big Three."

THE BIG THREE: MYTHUNDERSTANDINGS ABOUT THE WAY YOU LOOK AT YOURSELF AS AN INVESTOR

PERSONAL MYTH 1: I DON'T NEED TO BE AN INVESTOR— MY JOB WILL TAKE CARE OF MY FINANCIAL WEALTH

TRUTH: YES, YOU DO NEED TO BE AN INVESTOR— YOUR JOB IS NOT YOUR FINANCIAL WEALTH

It is almost epidemic how many people think they don't need to be an investor. Usually that happens because they believe consciously or unconsciously that the path to financial wealth is through one's job. If you're like me and believe that financial wealth is about having enough unearned income to finance your life mission without the need to work, chances are your current job income and savings plan will not be nearly enough to build true financial wealth. It is highly unlikely that your job creates enough income for you to set aside a manageable percentage of it and, at an average rate of interest, still achieve true financial wealth.

Many years ago this was a common and encouraged practice that I call the "myth of the modest saver." Thrifty individuals would stash small sums of money in coffee cans, under mattresses, and in personal savings accounts, believing they eventually would achieve financial freedom. In more modern times this "modest saver" has evolved into the "modest investor." This is the person who takes a small percentage of his or her annual income and invests it in his or her company pension plan, a 401(k), or a mutual fund. In this time when many people don't save or invest at all, these modest savers and investors are actually ahead of the game, but their investments almost never amount to true financial wealth. All the modest saver of old and the modest investor of today actually build is a small financial nest egg to provide for their most basic needs. When most people stop to do the math, they are shocked at how little income their current investment plan will provide when they quit working.

The truth is that only a tiny percentage of people, probably less than 1 percent, make enough income from their jobs to become financially wealthy. I'm talking about people such as highly paid athletes, actors, musicians, and executives. The extraordinary compensation these people receive is so large that they easily could live off a fraction of their income, invest the rest, and even with modest rates of return achieve financial wealth. The operative word here is *could*. I'm continually amazed at how many of these high income producers think they do not need to be investors.

Here's the problem: They cling to a far-fetched assumption that their jobs will continue to provide these extraordinary streams of income. In fact, the more money people make, the more overconfident they tend to be about their financial future. Prosperity can provide a false sense of security. They may overspend and underinvest to the point that one day they wake up and realize they are on the downslope of their primary income-earning years and their lifestyle is about to come to an end. Others understand they should be investing but then delegate all responsibility for their financial wealth building to other people.

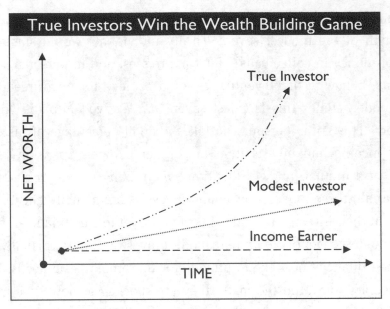

Figure 2

As presumptuous as it is to count on your income to be there always, I find it even more presumptuous to trust others to tend to your financial future. How many times have you read about athletes, actors, musicians, and businesspeople filing for bankruptcy? The fact is that people tend to spend money in direct proportion to the amount they earn, and any extra money that comes along (gifts or bonuses) is earmarked for consumption before it ever arrives in their bank accounts. It seems strange, but a high income doesn't necessarily translate to financial wealth.

One of the most startling examples I can think of is the story of former heavyweight boxing champion Mike Tyson. Over a period of 20 years, Tyson reportedly earned over $400 million.[1] Despite that, records reveal that he filed for bankruptcy in 2003 after falling $23 million into debt through extravagant spending habits and by allowing others to watch over his money. Not only did he not manage his money well, it appears

---

[1] As reported in the August 5, 2003, edition of *The New York Times*.

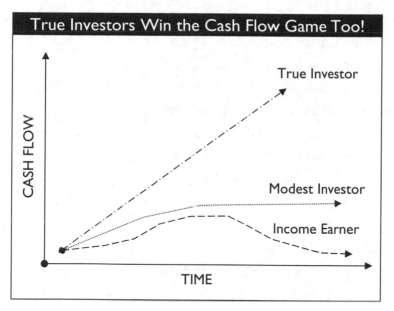

Figure 3

that neither did those he put in charge of it. I'm certain he never felt he was capable or even that he should play an active role in his financial well-being. Like so many others, he might have said, "I don't need to be an investor. My work is my financial wealth, and others will manage my money." As we all know, Tyson eventually lost his job and his financial wealth. It is a sad tale but one that, from a financial standpoint, is all too common among high income earners. It is, as they say, easy come, easy go. And in a consuming society, that's exactly how it does go.

I don't want to diminish the value of financial advisors. To the contrary: I engage them, have great faith in them, and believe everyone should have them. What I am saying is that wherever your money is, you need to be there too. No matter how you make your money or how much you make, if you don't take an active role in your financial planning and money management, you're at grave risk of seeing your investments underperform or, worse, be lost. As the old saying goes, a fool and his money are soon parted. While we're not calling anyone a fool, not acting like an investor or not being active in your investments is one of the most financially foolish positions you can take.

I encourage you to look at your job differently. Your job is the venue where you can earn your initial investment capital, and a percentage of your wages must be dedicated to building up your investment stake. I don't want to shock you, but the legendary investor Sir John Templeton tells the story of how he and his wife lived off as little as 50 percent of their income at the beginning of his investment career. They made a game of seeing how well they could live on only a fraction of their household income.

While you may not be like Templeton, choosing the path to financial wealth will require that you live off less than you make and consume less than the world tells you to. You can't let the media and advertisers set your values for you. Just as kids sometimes decide what to eat based on television commercials, adults tend to let the media convince them what they should spend their money on if their financial decisions aren't guided by a stronger compass. Don't get caught keeping up with the Joneses. The faster you reach a position where you can begin your investment career, the faster you'll be able to achieve financial independence.

I love the story of James Sorenson. In the 1940s Sorenson had a job selling medical supplies in the Salt Lake City area and got in trouble for not spending enough money on his sales visits with physicians. When he turned in his first expense report for less than $5, his supervisor told him he needed to spend, or at least report, $30 or more for his client entertainment expenses each week or he'd "spoil the business for everyone." But instead of taking doctors out for drinks or fancy meals, Sorenson would buy them a coffee or a soda. Then he'd take the difference and invest it in real estate. In those days he would buy plots of land in Utah for as little as $25 an acre. About a decade later the uranium boom hit, and those plots sold for thousands. Rather than just enjoy the perks, Sorenson didn't count on his job for his financial wealth. He started early and started small. He spent a lifetime thinking like an investor—working at a job he had a passion for and investing for his future. As a result, by 2004 he was reportedly worth approximately $4 billion.

Ideally, you should look at your work this way: It can be a passion that pays you money for doing what you love to do. Some passions pay more than others, but as history indicates, they rarely pay enough to create financial independence. Your job is your job; financial wealth building is something else. That is how I think Sorenson looked at it, and I encourage you to do the same thing.

Most people think that earning money in a job and saving some of it or sticking it in the company retirement plan makes them investors. It doesn't—but they think it does or think it is close enough that they don't need to be an investor. It is this MythUnderstanding that causes many people not to become true investors. Don't let that be you. Realize that whatever your job or work is, you also need to be an investor. You must wake up in the morning telling yourself, "I'm an investor. I'm building financial wealth. Today's the day I could find an opportunity and make a deal!"

PERSONAL MYTH 2: I DON'T NEED OR WANT TO BE FINANCIALLY WEALTHY—I'M HAPPY WITH WHAT I HAVE

TRUTH: YOU NEED TO OPEN YOUR EYES—YOU DO NEED AND WANT TO BE FINANCIALLY WEALTHY

You have no idea what you will need or want beyond today. You cannot predict what life will offer down the road for good or for bad. As hard as you may try, you can't predict with any confidence the resources you'll need to deal with life's uncertainties. Complicating everything is the fact that it takes time to grow money. Financial wealth building is not something that can be accomplished in reaction mode. It is really difficult to find more money just because you all of a sudden want or need it. As I've said all along, small money comes easily—big money does not.

Becoming an investor—someone who pursues financial wealth building every day—is all about preparing for the minimums and maximums in your life: the unpredictable financial minimums you may need and the unforeseen financial maximums you may want. If you choose not to pursue financial wealth, your future more than likely will be defined by extremely limiting financial choices. You may have to scramble to meet your changing needs or do without the things you eventually wish for. At a point in your life when settling for less might devastate you, you might have to do just that.

Let me share with you a revealing conversation I had with one of my students on the pursuit of big financial wealth.

> **STUDENT:** You know, Gary, I hear you talk about building financial wealth, and I understand the logic of what you're saying. The problem with that is I'm not motivated by money. I'm happy with what I have. I really don't need or want anything else. Life is going great just the way it is.
>
> **GARY:** Fair enough. I truly appreciate your honesty and respect your answer. Now, I'd like to ask you a question. Do you have insurance? Do you have any car, homeowner, disability, or medical insurance?
>
> **STUDENT:** Sure. It's the prudent thing to do. Insurance takes care of the unplanned or unexpected, right?
>
> **GARY:** Right. That's exactly the way I feel too. Things can happen that are beyond your control, and it's good to be prepared. My question for you, though, is this: How can you be sure that the unexpected won't happen in areas of your life that insurance won't cover?
>
> **STUDENT:** I'm not sure what you mean.

GARY: Well, what happens if you suddenly lost your job or, worse, your ability to earn a living?

STUDENT: Honestly, I haven't ever really thought about it. I guess you just don't expect things like that to happen. I have no idea what I'd do in that situation.

GARY: I understand. But it is a real possibility, and you really should think about it. And by the way, we're just talking about you. What if that sort of thing were to happen to someone you loved and that person wasn't financially prepared?

STUDENT: You know, that scares me a little bit. The thought that a friend or family member might someday need my help and that I wouldn't be able to provide it saddens me. If they had health issues or experienced a financial disaster, I think I might feel very bad if I were not in a position to help in a meaningful way.

GARY: That's actually what I'm talking about. If something like that happened and you weren't prepared, at the very least you might have to make incredible sacrifices in order to be of any help. You're a giving, caring person, and I'd hate to see you in that position. But you're not alone in this. No one can know beyond today what he or she might or might not need in the future. And because that's true, doesn't it make sense to pursue more financial wealth than you currently need it for no other reason so that financial wealth can serve as an umbrella insurance policy for your life?

I gave my student a moment to let the truth of our conversation sink in, and I honestly think it did. Sometimes it's hard to think in terms of future possibilities, especially unpleasant ones. As we talked more, I also let her know that all unanticipated needs aren't bad. What if she had a gifted child who needed special educational opportunities? What if an unforeseen opportunity arose that required more money to take advantage of than she currently had? I wanted to go in this direction because we hadn't yet discussed the other side of the issue: the idea that some needs are also about seizing valuable opportunities to move forward in life and that sometimes you may want money beyond your current needs and necessities. Here's how the rest of the conversation went:

GARY: Just for argument's sake, let's imagine that you have all the money you'll ever need. You also have enough to take care of the critical unforeseen needs that might arise for your friends and loved ones. Now, if you still had an abundance of financial wealth after all those needs had been taken care of, are there other things you might do with your money?

STUDENT: Sure. I guess everyone daydreams about what they'd do if they had a lot of money. My first thought is that I'd love to take my parents on a long trip around the world. They've always wanted to travel, but they've never quite been able to. That would make me feel great.

GARY: That's awesome. I love the idea of your traveling the globe with your folks. Is there anything else you'd do if money were no object?

STUDENT: Oh, gosh, that's so hard to imagine. I guess maybe I'd help out a friend of mine. She's a single mom, and I know that helping her out a little would be a huge lift for her.

GARY: That's great, but now I want you to think even beyond your family and friends. Are there things you'd like to see happen in your community?

STUDENT: Well, of course. I'd go crazy with this. I'd fix up the homeless shelter downtown. I'd donate money to provide meals for the needy; I'd set up an after-school recreation program for kids. And actually, we need an emergency blood bank, and I'd fund that too. Honestly, Gary, there is so much that is needed right here in town.

GARY: Absolutely. I got it. But let's go even bigger than that for a second. What if you had financial wealth such that even after you did all those things, your reach could extend even beyond this town? What could you do?

STUDENT: Wow, that's even tougher. Who thinks about that? I mean, I guess I'd do something huge like support cancer research. Or maybe I'd want to create an organization to help fund the fight against heart disease. I might even be able to help put a dent in world hunger.

GARY: Now listen to yourself. Earlier you said it felt bad to think about pursuing more money. Now it sounds a lot like you're imagining a very exciting life where you're able to make a big difference in the world and in the lives of people.

STUDENT: I've never really thought about it the way we're talking today. I guess I've always been afraid that money might own me.

GARY: That's perfectly normal. I think a lot of people feel that way. There's this idea that having more money or pursuing it will change them or, even worse, corrupt them in some way and make them bad people. However, it's been my personal experience that having more money won't change you at all. What it will do is *amplify* who you already are. I believe that in the end people are exposed to new possibilities by financial wealth and empowered by it. Instead of being changed by money, it simply allows them to be more of who they really are.

STUDENT: That makes sense to me. More money just makes you more of what you already are.

GARY: Exactly. Your hypothetical responses just prove the point. You're one of the most generous souls I know. Having more wealth would just amplify your generosity. So tell me, how does this new view of your financial potential make you feel?

STUDENT: Honestly, it makes me feel inspired.

GARY: Inspired?

STUDENT: Yes, inspired. Inspired that my life could be so much bigger than I ever thought was possible.

GARY: You know what? You're inspiring me too. See, this is the kind of thing that happens when you pursue maximums for your financial life instead of minimums. Suddenly money can become good for the good it can do. And the more you have, the more good you can do.

I appreciated the candidness of my student and her willingness to allow me to talk to her in this manner. What's fascinating is that she really did get it. She realized that there are two types of people in the world: First, there are those who (because they chose not to build financial wealth) have limited opportunities to care for themselves and their loved ones. Second, there are those who (because they chose to pursue financial wealth as an investor) have much larger opportunities to care not only for themselves and their loved ones but also for so much more. It's the difference between a focus on the minimums life can require and a focus on the maximums life can offer. It comes down to what kind of person you want to be and the life you want to lead.

Later, as you might expect, she and I began to talk about how to make more money. This curiosity is the natural result of

> *"My biggest mistake was not investing more."*
>
> Mike Netzel
> Millionaire Real Estate Investor
> Pittsburgh, PA

imagining how big your wants and needs might become. You progress from seeing that it might be possible to believing that it should be, and then you realize that you are now motivated to seek financial wealth to your highest potential.

Most people are taught to live within their means, but I was taught differently and encourage you to think differently as well. Instead of forgetting your dreams and living within your means, try pursuing the means to live your dreams.

PERSONAL MYTH 3: IT DOESN'T MATTER IF I WANT OR NEED IT—I JUST CAN'T DO IT

TRUTH: YOU CAN'T PREDICT WHAT YOU CAN OR CAN'T DO UNTIL YOU TRY

I really struggle with this way of thinking. I just don't understand why people seem to want to place judgment ahead of effort and unproven opinions before a willingness to try. There's no way for you, or anyone else for that matter, to know your true financial potential. And because your true financial potential is unknown, it makes no sense to place limits on it. "I can't do it" becomes another rationale for not trying, for not stretching, for not exploring your potential. Some people have told me they don't want to set themselves up for disappointment. The unfortunate irony is that the people who would rather not set themselves up for disappointment by going for it are the very ones destined for disappointment. The moment you buy into the idea that you can't achieve financial wealth, you put yourself on the path to complacency, compromise, and, ultimately, regret.

Years ago the online job search company Monster.com ran a provocative Super Bowl ad showing a series of children describing their "financial dreams and aspirations." The award-winning commercial combined humor with poignancy to make a powerful point about settling for what you thought you could do instead of pursuing what might be possible. The litany in the commercial went something like this:

CHILD ONE: When I grow up, I want to file—all day.

CHILD TWO: When I grow up, I want to claw my way up to middle management.

CHILD THREE: I want to be replaced on a whim.

CHILD FOUR: I want to be a yes man. Yes woman. Yes, sir; coming, sir; anything for a raise, sir.

Three or four other children continued this refrain until the commercial closed with a surprisingly touching question: *What did you want to be?*

With that question, the contrast between the modest aspirations and resigned attitudes of the children in the commercial and the shoot-for-the-stars hopes real children have went from humorous to sobering. That was when you realized that you may have made more compromises along the way than you would have imagined, that somewhere along the journey of your life you stopped wondering what was possible for you and started thinking in terms of what was probable.

In my experience there are basically two ways people view their financial potential. There are those who think in terms of what's financially probable and those who think in terms of what's financially possible. Probability thinkers base their view of their future financial selves on their past history and current capabilities. They say to themselves, "Based on who I've been and who I am, this is probably what I can financially accomplish in the future." They use words such as *realistic* and *likely* when they discuss their financial potential. As a result, when they are presented with a new opportunity that doesn't fit their preconceived notions of their financial potential, they often conclude that they simply "can't do it." For them, their financial future is determined, predictable, and ultimately static.

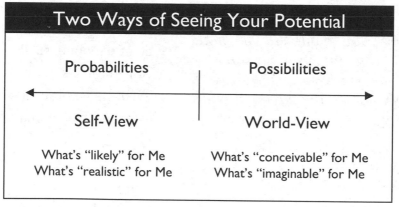

Figure 4

Possibilities thinkers, in contrast, rarely utter the words "I can't do it." They set aside any limiting notions they might have about their financial potential and base their view of their future financial selves on what they imagine themselves to be capable of accomplishing. And they use an altogether different vocabulary. Their potential is described in terms of what's "conceivable," what's "imaginable," and what's "possible." They say to themselves: "I have dreams for a reason. Based on who I can become, this is what I can financially accomplish." They take into account that they might have to learn new things, acquire new skills, or change their habits to reach their full financial potential. For them, their financial future is flexible, active, and, ultimately, alive.

A great example of this is Trammell Crow, who rose from humble beginnings to amass one of the largest real estate empires of all time. A child of the Depression, Crow and his seven brothers and sisters grew up in a Dallas home with no bath or hot water. But Trammell didn't let his modest beginnings dictate the size of his future. In 1948 he went into real estate and saw a world of unlimited possibilities. He quickly realized that through loans and private investors he could achieve his goals long before he could on his own. Crow's big idea was the commercial shopping mall. We take them for granted now, but in 1955 Crow's idea was

> *"I bought one house for $5,000, sold it for $36,000, and made $10,000 on it. I was 25 at the time, so that was pretty good money when you're just going to school and waiting tables, and just having fun."*
>
> Carlos Rivero
> Millionaire Real Estate Investor
> Austin, TX

revolutionary. By the 1960s he was the leading developer of shopping malls in the United States, and by the 1980s he was the largest real estate developer and property manager in the country. Today, because he saw no limits to his potential, the Trammell Crow Company is one of the largest diversified commercial real estate services companies in the world.

Many of the real estate investors we interviewed told similar stories about how before becoming investors they would have been voted least likely to become financially wealthy by the world. A good example is Barbara Mattson, whom I mentioned briefly in the Introduction.

Barbara worked as a home health nurse, and her husband, Tom, was in construction. They were a typical family living in a modest home with two cars and a pair of young daughters. Then, in 1997, Tom came home not feeling well. The next morning he couldn't move. Suddenly Barbara was left to care for her children and an ailing husband while also having to earn enough income to cover two car notes, a mortgage, and a mountain of medical bills.

Month after month the Mattsons battled unsuccessfully to get worker's compensation. "I'm living on macaroni and cheese here," she complained to her labor attorney. "I can't do this. You have to help me." But his only response was, "Ms. Mattson, this is a long process." In her efforts to keep the bills paid and the creditors at bay, Barbara was often just circulating her debt, "robbing Peter to pay Paul." In the end she was encouraged to declare bankruptcy and start over, but she was determined not to give up.

In one of those positive coincidences, Barbara bought some tapes on investing in real estate. They originally were intended for Tom, to fill his time and possibly eventually provide a way for him to earn income for the family. After all, he worked in construction and understood real estate. But he didn't show much interest, so Barbara listened to the tapes at night while caring for her youngest daughter. She also listened to them on the way to her home-care appointments.

Then, in July 1998, almost nine months after he became ill, a simple sneeze caused Tom's legs to go numb. He emerged from surgery cocooned in a body cast. Coincidentally, just when things were darkest, his worker's compensation was approved, and they received a $20,000 check covering nine months of back payments.

Here is one of those defining moments when the difference between probability thinking and possibility thinking is revealed. Barbara had very little knowledge of investing; in fact, she'd just listened to that single set of tapes. Between work and looking after her husband and family, she had almost no time. Even though she had temporary possession of a large sum of money, her bills and debts added up to a lot more; in essence, she didn't have much money at all. Faced with the same situation, what do you think most people would do with the money? Would they pay off their bills and get their accounts back in order? Would they use the money to supplement their income and get some relief? Or would they do what Barbara did when, in an inspired moment of clarity, she invested the money in real estate?

"My philosophy was survival," Barbara recalled. "If I could start buying real estate and build up enough to replace Tom's income, it wouldn't be so bad if he couldn't ever work again." Over the next six months she started buying rental properties. Eventually the rents began to add up until finally she could see light at the end of the tunnel. Today, because she placed no artificial limits on her potential, Barbara owns a real estate company and over $9 million in real estate. Because Barbara could imagine better possibilities and a bigger life, she was able to have them.

> *"One of the beauties of real estate is you don't need money. If you can find a great deal, people will throw money at you. But most people can't find a great deal and tie it up, and they can't do it because they start from a poor person's point of view: 'I'll invest when I have the money.'"*
>
> Robert Kiyosaki
> Best-selling author and millionaire investor
> Scottsdale, AZ

Be warned. Once people step over into possibility thinking and believe that they can achieve financial wealth, they often see a whole new set of obstacles. They quickly become certain that they will need more time, money, and investment knowledge than they currently have or could acquire easily. They think things like "It's too late, I don't have enough time," "There's no way; I just don't have enough money to start investing," or "I would if I could, but I have no idea what to do, and besides, I'm no good with money." What these individuals don't realize is that most big things start small. They mistakenly believe that big success at anything requires big and mysterious things they don't have, such as the following:

- Special natural abilities versus a little of some acquired abilities
- Lots of free time versus a little bit of well-spent time
- Massive amounts of money versus a little well-placed money

In the end, what you actually need to become a successful investor is a lot less than what you think you need.

Figure 5, on the facing page, graphically demonstrates how much ability (A), time (T), and money (M) a person needs to begin an investment career. While many people mistakenly believe they need a lot of all three, they actually need a little of each: the right abilities, well-spent time, and well-placed money. Beyond this they can accelerate their growth as an investor by picking one area to increase. They can choose to focus on acquiring more ability (through reading, seminars, or mentors), give it more time (seeking opportunities or networking with other investors), or attract more money (from family members, friends, other

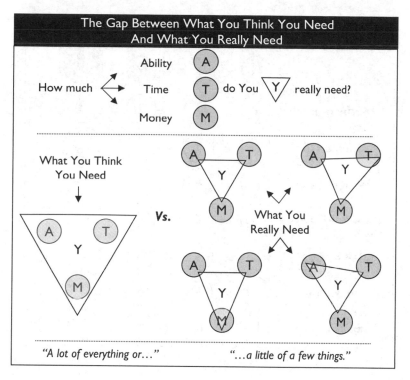

Figure 5

investors, or lenders). Over time, each of those three areas can grow and your power as an investor will increase.

The hidden secret is that the three factors are multipliers of each other. If you double your time, even if your ability and money remain the same, you double your current investment potential. If you double your ability *and* your time, you quadruple your current investment potential. If you double each of the three (2 × 2 × 2 = 8), you increase your current investment potential eightfold.

The investment game is played by beginning with a little of each and working to

> *"It takes patience and perseverance, but you can make it big on little deals. You're not going to get rich overnight, but you will slowly."*
> Will Stewart
> Millionaire Real Estate Investor
> Sugar Hill, GA

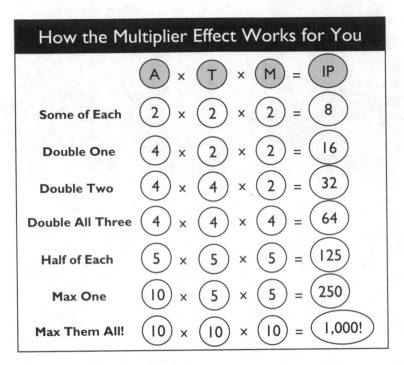

Figure 6

increase any one of the three. The chart above illustrates how this multiplier effect works when you increase your investing time, money, and ability.

Your self-assessment in these three areas often dictates your strategy. People who have the luxury of time but have limited financial resources can focus on amplifying their ability to achieve greater success. They also can earn sweat equity by doing much of the work other investors might contract out. In contrast, investors with more financial resources and less time can afford to employ experts and contractors to make up for their lack of time. Time and money often are strongly connected, in that time can be used to earn money and money can be spent to buy time. Similarly, ability can be had with time (think books and seminars) or bought with money (think consultants). Understanding how ability, time, and money combine to produce investment results is an important step

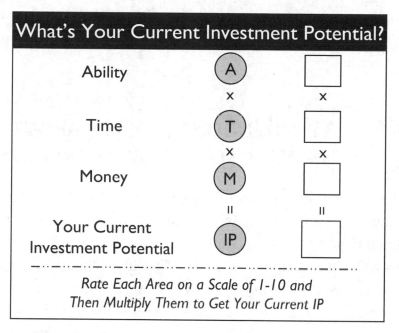

Figure 7

on the path to becoming a successful investor. The wonderful thing is this: Any extra ability, time, and money you have in the beginning speeds up the process.

When we interviewed best-selling author and Millionaire Real Estate Investor Robert Kiyosaki, he made an important observation: "People will believe what they want to believe. They find excuses that prevent them from taking a look at what might work. And when they find a reason, they make that reason their reality." He was talking about the power of personal myths and the way they serve as barriers to achievement in our lives.

The "Big Three" MythUnderstandings are some of the most power-ful limiting beliefs you can have, and we hope you're ready to step past them and discover your true financial possibilities. I'm hopeful that you now believe that your job is not your financial wealth, that you both need and want to pursue financial wealth, and that true financial wealth is possible for you no matter where you are in life. If that is the case and you have moved past these fundamental doubts and fears, you're ready to address the MythUnderstandings people commonly hold about investing.

THE FIVE MYTHUNDERSTANDINGS ABOUT THE WAY YOU LOOK AT INVESTING

Where did you get your earliest thoughts about money and investing? More important, what beliefs do you currently hold, and are they accurate? I'm intrigued by these questions mainly because over the years I've become convinced that most of the myths and misunderstandings I've encountered about investing and financial wealth building come from people who've never invested successfully or built financial wealth. Isn't it interesting that so many of us accept and believe the words of others without first verifying that they've earned the right to teach us?

In our research on these myths about investing we went straight to the source: We talked to more than 100 millionaire investors about these very issues. What emerged were five common MythUnderstandings about investing that can cause people to get off track. While these myths certainly apply to investing in real estate, they also transcend it and apply to investing as a whole. They can seep into any discussion about investing. They often are used as justifications for failure, and they are repeated widely in the form of cautionary tales. "Investing is complicated . . . hard to understand . . . risky . . . inaccessible . . . requires perfect timing." They circulate quietly, are taken on faith, and for the most part go unnoticed, which is why we call them the "Phantom Five."

> *"People get so trapped by fear that they never take the first step."*
>
> Rische Beeson
> Millionaire Real Estate Investor
> Lubbock, TX

Investing Myth 1: Investing Is Complicated

Truth: Investing Is Only As Complicated As You Make It

Here's the truth: Investing is complicated. But to be fair, almost anything, taken as a whole, can appear more complicated than it really is. Take your car. You don't have to be a mechanic or an engineer to drive it, right? Of course not. All you have to know are the basic rules of the road and how to drive. Investing is no different. The trick is to step back and identify the aspects that matter the most.

> *"People try to overcomplicate real estate investing. You can't pay $5,000 a month if you're not making $5,000 a month."*
>
> Jimmy Napier
> Millionaire Real Estate Investor
> Chipley, FL

In the end I think you'll come to understand that the fundamental things you need to know and do to be successful are simpler than you might have imagined. It's like Warren Buffett says: "You don't need to be a rocket scientist. Investing is not a game where the guy with 160 IQ beats the guy with 130 IQ."

Chris Hake, a Millionaire Real Estate Investor in Madison, Wisconsin, started out like most investors, with books, audiocassettes, and seminars. He freely admits that there was more knowledge available than he could digest at once. But instead of being overwhelmed, he found a way to deal with all the new information: "I just treated it like a buffet line. You use what you can. The rest of it may not apply today." I think he is absolutely right. What I've come to understand about learning is that it is always progressive. It builds on itself step by step. Fractions look like nonsense to a child who has not yet learned about them in school. That's why good teachers start by teaching the basics and then build on them over time. On a practical basis, what I know is that you never need to know everything in order to do something. You just need to know the right things to do at any given moment. Over time, given enough chances to study and experience something, you naturally and progressively will learn everything you need to know to do it well. That is how you become an expert.

Real estate investing is no different. When you learn things in the correct order, your knowledge will come more easily and more quickly. One of the core goals of *The Millionaire Real Estate Investor* is to provide the fundamental knowledge you need to get in the game correctly and lay a foundation for success. Like anything else in life, real estate investing is only as hard or as complicated as you make it. As Forrest Gump might say, "Complicated is as complicated does." Great investing can be learned if you take it slowly, start with the basics, and follow proven models.

INVESTING MYTH 2: THE BEST INVESTMENTS REQUIRE KNOWLEDGE MOST PEOPLE DON'T HAVE

TRUTH: *YOUR BEST INVESTMENTS WILL ALWAYS BE IN AREAS YOU CAN OR ALREADY DO UNDERSTAND*

One of the great lessons I've learned about investing is this: Investing in what you don't know or understand isn't investing at all. Doing that is like taking a shot in the dark, and you'll need luck to hit anything worthwhile, much less your intended target. To me, the real nature of investing is always to invest in what you know and fully understand. Choose an area that you already know or one that greatly interests you and commit yourself to becoming an expert in it over time.

I love the story legendary investor Warren Buffett tells about the technology stock boom of the late 1990s. Rather than jump on the bandwagon where thousands of amateurs were amassing small fortunes, Buffett chose to sit out the boom on the sidelines. He admitted that he just didn't know that industry, and without knowledge he'd essentially be gambling. I love that attitude. Here is an investor who absolutely, no matter what the apparent upside is, sticks to his criteria. Buffett is an amazing investor, and

> *"Real estate provides investors with a tangible investment that is easy for anyone to understand. If profits were lower than expected this quarter, was that because it was a colder-than-usual winter, driving up heating expenses? Or did a pipe burst? These are issues that any investor can understand."*
>
> Paul Morris
> Millionaire Real Estate Investor
> West Hollywood, CA

one reason for that is that he invests only in what he knows or can understand. I encourage you to do the same thing; if you don't have specialized knowledge, pick an area and start learning today. I think you'll discover that investing in real estate is one of the easiest areas of investing in which to acquire expert knowledge and understanding.

INVESTING MYTH 3: INVESTING IS RISKY— I'LL LOSE MY MONEY

TRUTH: INVESTING, BY DEFINITION, IS NOT RISKY

If you look up "invest" in the dictionary, this is what you'll find: "Invest—To commit (money or capital) in order to gain a financial return." You'll notice that the word "risk" doesn't appear anywhere in the definition. Why? Because risk is what people bring to the concept of investing. I don't want to sound like a Pollyanna, but the truth is that great investors don't think of investing as risky. For them it's not about ignoring risk; instead, it's about following sound investment principles and models. By doing that, they take the risk out of the game.

When I say investing, by definition, isn't risky, what I mean is that in investing you make your money going in. In most cases this means buying something of value for terms that immediately create a profit for you. This way investors go into the deal knowing they don't need the market to bail them out. These are the "no-risk" deals.

Jerry Clevenger, a Millionaire Real Estate Investor in Kansas City, Missouri, told us about a deal that perfectly illustrates how investors make their money going in. One evening a real estate agent called him at nine o'clock at night and said, "Hey, I've been following this property that's been listed by the bank for $65,000. Well, they just dropped the price to $39,000." Clevenger immediately wrote an offer of $42,000, and his agent faxed it to the owner sight unseen. He felt comfortable making this bold move because he understood what he was buying and what it was really worth. And he was right. He quickly sold the house for $54,000 and pocketed the difference. He later told us, "If I hadn't made that offer that night, I wouldn't have acquired the property, because the next day eight more offers came in . . . You gotta be able to pull the trigger immediately." And to do that you must know what you're doing.

Investing like a Millionaire Real Estate Investor isn't about taking risks. It is about having sound criteria, the patience to find the right opportunity, and a willingness to take the correct action quickly. The best investors know this and are dedicated to following this formula. As a result, they are always minimizing their risk while maximizing their return. Investing can never be absolutely risk-free, but it doesn't have to be risky.

Investing Myth 4: Successful Investors Are Able to Time the Market

Truth: In Successful Investing, the Timing Finds You

Timing is everything. But now that you know that, forget it, because you can't truly time anything.

Timing is one of the most misunderstood concepts in investing. When people say that timing is important, they are correct. Timing is not only important, it's critical to investment success. The economy is cyclical. Markets are cyclical. And buying and selling opportunities are created by the ebb and flow of the cycles. Finding the best time to buy or sell is called timing. What is misunderstood is the way timing actually is accomplished. Most people think timing is about active observation—sitting on the sidelines waiting for the moment when they should jump in and take action. It's a passive and then active approach. In other words, timing is about being reactive to opportunity. The truth, however, is that timing is all about being active—active all the time. I believe that the vast majority of opportunities cannot be observed from the sidelines—you must be in the game. The best deals come from the best opportunities,

> *"Generally, real estate is cyclical. You have to buy in a way that lets you afford the cycles. And you have to know where you are in the cycle."*
>
> Charles Brown
> Millionaire Real Estate Investor
> Austin, TX

and the best opportunities go fast. This is where the phrase "a window of opportunity" comes from. Investors recognize and seize these opportunities because they are always engaged in the game and close to the action.

Dyches Boddiford, a Millionaire Real Estate Investor from Marietta, Georgia, was watchful and engaged when he noticed that the day before a foreclosure sale a bank had lowered its opening bid on a property by more than $100,000. He knew this because, rather than taking the fore-closure information at face value, he called the bank to learn more about the property. Armed with that knowledge, he and a partner purchased the house at auction, put it back on the market priced to sell, and 90 days later made over $100,000 from the transaction. In retrospect, someone might say that Boddiford was lucky or had great timing, but Boddiford wasn't timing the foreclosure market. He was there every day, watchful for opportunity and ready to act on it when it arose. If you pursue opportunity in this way, you too can look like a timing genius.

> *"There is no crystal ball that tells you what the market will do. So you need to know the fundamentals of a property: what it will do in a good market, and what it will do in a bad market."*
>
> Robert Kiyosaki
> Best-selling author and millionaire investor
> Scottsdale, AZ

In fly fishing they say, "You can't catch a fish with your hook in the air." That's also true of timing the market.

Successful timing is made possible by time spent on the task over time. You have to keep your hook in the water. Being active and engaged doesn't mean you're always buying and selling. What it does mean is that you are consistently searching with your Criteria, watchful for the moment when opportunity surfaces. This is what I mean when I say that timing finds you. You can never know the absolute best time to act except after the fact. Hindsight is, as they say, 20/20. Better to look at it like this: Any time an opportunity meets your strict Criteria and you act, you have timed the market successfully.

> *"It doesn't matter what the market's doing. You're going to buy what the market gives you."*
>
> Bill O'Kane
> Millionaire Real Estate Investor
> Chicago, IL

Timing isn't about being in the right place at the right time; it's about being in the right place *all* the time.

INVESTING MYTH 5: ALL THE GOOD INVESTMENTS ARE TAKEN

TRUTH: EVERY MARKET, IN EVERY TIME, HAS ITS SHARE OF GOOD INVESTMENTS

Rest assured: All the good investments will be taken. The only question is by whom. As simple as it sounds, the truth is that those who take them are those who best understand the conditions that create them. By the way, this is the other and more subtle side of the timing issue. While the previously discussed myth was about timing the market, this myth addresses your timing as an investor. A lot of people say to me, "Okay, Gary, now that I've decided to become an investor, where are all the deals? It seems like the few opportunities I've been able to find are already taken." I understand what they're saying, and there are really two issues at work here: the idea that there aren't many deals and the idea that you're too late to get them.

Here's what I know about market forces and how they create investment opportunities. There are two fundamental forces at work—economic ones and personal ones—and they are always present, always at work, and always influencing the marketplace. Basic economic forces show up in the form of things such as job growth, interest rates, population shifts, and area revitalization. These are the things most people think of when they think of the forces that create investment opportunities. What is often overlooked, however, is a second set of human, or personal, forces that are always present and can create additional and significant investment opportunities. Some arise from positive circumstances such as relocation, marriage, and family growth. Others arise from negative conditions such as divorce, death, and debt. In my experience, those who declare that all the good deals are taken are almost always overlooking this second set of human forces and the unique opportunities they create.

> *"When markets go down, opportunities go up for smart real estate investors—if you know what you're doing. I would much rather play the downturn than the upturn."*
>
> Harry S. Dent, Jr.
> Best-selling author and economist
> Burlington, VT

What I most want you to understand is that opportunities are always there in every market and in every time. Sometimes there are a lot, and sometimes there are not. Some opportunities are the result of obvious economic forces. Others are the result of local and incidental personal forces. And you're never too late. Because personal forces are always at work, these opportunities are constantly being created. While yesterday's deals have indeed been taken, tomorrow's deals have not; nor are they destined to go automatically to someone else. But in time they will be taken by someone, and I want you to realize that that someone could be you. It's really a game of hide and seek, and if you choose, you are now "it" and must seek. The opportunities are gone only for those who assume they are. You're too late only if you believe you're too late.

THE LAW OF MOMENTUM: COMPOUNDING YOUR SUCCESS

In closing, let me encourage you to believe that everything big starts small. When most people consider investing for the first time, it is not uncommon for them to think, "It will take forever for my investments to amount to anything." When they consider their first investment, most people find it difficult to justify the time, money, and effort for the returns they can see. It can seem like madness to look so hard for a rental property that may yield only a couple of hundred dollars a month. These short-term benefits just don't seem to balance out the short-term sacrifices.

I strongly encourage you to step past that short-term thinking and look at the larger implications of small investments. What must be understood is that there is a

> *"There's room for the little fellow in this business. Houses are too small for big guys to get started in."*
> Jack Miller
> Millionaire Real Estate Investor
> Reno, NV

natural growth curve to momentum. Think of a ball rolling downhill that picks up mass and speed as it goes. It's what we commonly call the snowball effect. Although it may start out small or slow, it ends up growing quite big and fast. In the same way, money, once invested, has its own momentum, and the technical name for that is "compounding." What starts small and grows slowly builds in size and momentum over time.

My son discovered the power of compounding one Saturday afternoon when we were weeding the flower beds at our home. As we worked, we were listening to an audiotape about money and life I'd been listening to before he joined me. We were going along fine until I looked up and found myself alone in the backyard. My first thought was that he'd gone in for water and gotten sidetracked. When I went in to look for him, I found him at the kitchen counter adding up a series of numbers on a piece of scrap paper. He was trying to disprove a story he'd just heard and couldn't believe.

It was the classic story of the value of a penny doubled every day for 30 days that often is used to illustrate the idea of compound interest. In short, a worker is offered a reasonable daily wage for a month's work. Instead of taking the normal pay, the worker negotiates a compounding pay scale where his pay doubles every day but starts with just a penny. The employer quickly shakes on the agreement, thinking she's getting a great deal. Unfortunately for her, as the story later illustrates, the 30 days of doubled pay that began with a single penny end with a total invoice of $10.7 million.

A Penny Doubled for 30 Days	
	Daily Wage
Day 1	$ 0.01
Day 2	$ 0.02
Day 3	$ 0.04
Day 4	$ 0.08
Day 5	$ 0.16
Day 6	$ 0.32
Day 7	$ 0.64
Day 8	$ 1.28
Day 9	$ 2.56
Day 10	$ 5.12
Day 11	$ 10.24
Day 12	$ 20.48
Day 13	$ 40.96
Day 14	$ 81.92
Day 15	$ 163.84
Day 16	$ 327.68
Day 17	$ 655.36
Day 18	$ 1,310.72
Day 19	$ 2,621.44
Day 20	$ 5,242.88
Day 21	$ 10,485.76
Day 22	$ 20,971.52
Day 23	$ 41,943.04
Day 24	$ 83,886.08
Day 25	$ 167,772.16
Day 26	$ 335,544.32
Day 27	$ 671,088.64
Day 28	$ 1,342,177.28
Day 29	$ 2,684,354.56
Day 30	$ 5,368,709.12
Total Invoice	$ 10,737,418.23

Figure 8

I walked John through the numbers and assured him that the numbers told the truth. This led to a great discussion of money, and rates of return.

Any form of investing is about putting your money to work and letting it work for you over time. Real estate investing is no different. What distinguishes it from other investments is that the original value of your asset tends to be large and, through the magic of leverage, can be purchased for less. For example, if you bought a $100,000 investment house each year by putting $10,000 down and achieved only a modest 5 percent rate of return on the total value of the assets, you'd be a millionaire in less than a decade.

With each asset you add to your portfolio, your portfolio grows. As your investments grow, so do your buying power and your investment knowledge. That's the foundation for bigger and ever-increasing investments.

No matter what your current station in life is, financial wealth is available to you. No matter how little money or knowledge you have in the beginning, a great ending is possible for you. The trick is to get started and then let the power of growth on growth take you higher. The longest journeys are just an accumulation of small steps; the tallest buildings are built by placing block upon block. If you're ready to take the next step on your journey to financial wealth, if you believe that it is both possible and probable for you, it's time to leave your MythUnderstandings behind, turn the page, and begin thinking like a Millionaire Real Estate Investor.

POINTS TO REMEMBER

- Many high-achieving investors have faced fears or doubts about investing that ultimately proved unfounded. These common MythUnderstandings can stand between you and true financial wealth building. Examining them can ultimately free you to pursue your dreams.

- Yes, you do need to be an investor. Chances are, your current job income and savings plan will not be nearly enough to build true financial wealth. Your job is your job; building financial wealth is something else.

- Yes, you do need and want to be financially wealthy. Becoming an investor is about preparing for the minimums and maximums in your life. Instead of forgetting your dreams and living within your means, pursue the means to live your dreams!

- Yes, you can do it! Don't place limits on your financial potential. "I can't" is just a rationale for not trying. Believe that true financial wealth is possible for you no matter where you are in your life.

■ No, investing doesn't need to be complicated. It's only as complicated as you make it. Learn the basics and build on them over time. Great investing can be learned if you take it slow, start with the basics, and follow proven models.

■ Yes, you must invest in what you know. Pick an area and become an expert over time. Real estate investing is one of the easiest areas in which to acquire this expert knowledge and understanding.

■ Investing isn't about taking risks. It's about following sound investment principles and models, thereby taking the risk out of the game.

■ Yes, timing is important, but it's active not passive. Opportunities cannot be observed from the sidelines—you must be in the game. Timing isn't about being in the right place at the right time—it's about being in the right place all the time.

■ No, the good investments are not all taken. Opportunities are always there, in every market and in every time. Yes, they will all be taken by someone, but realize that that someone could be you.

■ Step past short-term thinking. Small investments can have extraordinary implications over time, thanks to the power of compounding.

Part Two:
THE FOUR STAGES

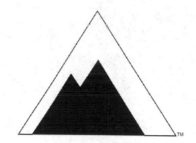

THINK A MILLION

I have about concluded that wealth is a state of mind, and that anyone can acquire a wealthy state of mind by thinking rich thoughts.

Andrew Young

THE SPIRITUAL JOURNEY OF WEALTH BUILDING

It's my belief that the pursuit of money is actually a spiritual journey. That's a statement most people wouldn't agree with—in fact, they might even argue against it—yet I know it's true. Would it surprise you to learn that the Bible has over 2,000 references to money, property, and wealth? That is more than twice the number of references to faith and prayer combined. In fact, money shows up as a prominent theme in every major religious text. No matter what your personal faith is, spirituality and money are always connected. It seems that God cares about how you think about money and wealth, and that makes perfect sense to me. Money—what you do to acquire it, how you hold onto it, and what you do with it—reflects your innermost values.

What you may not realize is that every time you open your wallet, endorse a check, or sign a credit card receipt, you're making a statement about your spiritual values. In other words, money spent is a personal testament—the receipts absolute proof of your priorities. Money in and of itself is neither good nor bad. It simply has the power to reflect and reveal. And whether money reveals you to be honest or dishonest, generous or greedy, it is *you*—not the money—who inherently own those values.

I've come to think of money as being about having choices. Typically, the more money you have, the more positive choices you have. The two go hand in hand. The spiritual journey of financial wealth builders begins when they understand that their choices define their lives, that having more positive choices is a good thing, and that pursuing more positive choices is an enlightened pursuit.

> *"I always hear people say, "God will provide." I say, God's already provided. Go out and do something with it."*
> Robert Kiyosaki
> Best-selling author and millionaire investor
> Scottsdale, AZ

The millionaire investors we interviewed understood this and had taken care to square their financial goals with their spiritual values. While most set out on the path to financial security and prosperity, they all came to understand that the way they earned their money mattered and that mutually beneficial deals, a reputation for honesty, and fair dealing were essential to the fulfilling pursuit of their financial goals. The further they progressed, the more generous they tended to be with their time, money, and financial wisdom. They talked about the satisfaction they received not only from successful deals but also from saving people from foreclosure, putting people in affordable homes, and turning downtrodden properties and even neighborhoods into places where anyone would want to live. They also related how the success of their personal investing had created income and opportunity for their colleagues and partners. To sum it up, they had no hang-ups about money or wealth. They were experiencing the power of money and realizing all the good it could do.

Over the years I too have come to understand that money is good for the good it can do. I encourage you to adopt that viewpoint as well—that money is good for the good it can do for you and for others.

Financial wealth building is also about personal growth. Along the way you'll discover that you have to acquire new skills and greater wisdom to keep moving forward. The simple truth is that if you don't grow personally with the growth of your fortunes, you're unlikely to enjoy them for long. In the end you can achieve a financial place of security and abundance that I call true financial wealth, where you have accumulated assets that deliver the passive income necessary to achieve your personal mission in life without having to work. To put it another way, you have financial wealth when you're finally free to stop working for a living and start living for your work—your life's work.

In the following pages we take a deeper look at some of the ways Millionaire Real Estate Investors think about money, their motivation for seeking financial wealth, and their understanding of how it's attained. If you can tap into their mindset and grasp the fundamental principles of how to build, hold, and employ wealth, you'll have achieved the first major goal of this book: thinking like a Millionaire Real Estate Investor.

THE SEVEN WAYS MILLIONAIRE REAL ESTATE INVESTORS THINK

Thinking is thinking. It takes just as much time and energy to think small as it does to think big. The only difference lies in the results you get. Most people don't truly realize this and as a result don't consciously choose the way they think. The millionaire mountain logo on the cover of this book is meant to symbolize the power of thinking big. It comes from a discussion of climbing Mount Everest I sometimes use to illustrate the path of high achievement—going after big audacious goals. People who set out to test the slopes of Mount Everest don't do so on a whim. It's a big goal, and it requires big thinking. They study, plan, and think strategically. Months, even years, of preparation are involved because there's a lot at stake. One major misstep can result in falling short of the summit or even in disaster.

There is just as much at stake in your financial life, and becoming financially wealthy represents an Everest of sorts in the world of money. The journey is big and can be long, sometimes trying, and often extremely difficult, but it is always worthwhile—always. The best way to prepare for a climb to the highest altitude is first to acquire the right mindset and attitude. It's even been said that your attitude determines your altitude. That's why a substantial section of this book is dedicated to the way you think. It's about building sound financial thinking as a foundation for building solid financial wealth—enriching your mind and enriching your life.

Consider this chapter, "Think a Million," as your financial base camp on the path to climbing the millionaire mountain. It's a place where even the most competent and confident climbers must pause and listen to the wisdom of those who have reached the summit before them. It's time to examine the Seven Ways Millionaire Real Estate Investors Think.

The Seven Ways Millionaire Real Estate Investors Think

1. Think Powered by a Big Why

2. Think Big Goals, Big Models, and Big Habits

3. Think Money Matters

4. Think Net Worth

5. Think Real Estate

6. Think Value, Opportunity and Deals

7. Think Action

Figure 1

1. THINK POWERED BY A BIG WHY

In *Think and Grow Rich*, Napoleon Hill wrote, "What a different story men would have to tell if only they would adopt a definite purpose, and stand by that purpose until it had time to become an all-consuming obsession." Motivation matters. Napoleon Hill believed it, and so do I. In fact, this is something I learned a long time ago, and ever since, I've made it my practice to study the lives of successful people to discover their motivation to achieve. I clip news articles, read biographies, and watch documentaries on their lives. What I try to decipher from their individual stories is a common pattern for achievement. What did these people do differently? Were they smarter or better educated? Did they come from high-achieving families? Were they exceptionally gifted or hardworking? The primary characteristic I've found in the lives of high achievers is that they had a strong drive to succeed. They had a compelling, personal reason to achieve. It's what I call a Big Why.

One of the many articles I clipped was from a management study in which the authors made an interesting discovery: "When tested in national surveys against such seemingly crucial factors as intelligence, ability, and salary, level of motivation proves to be a more significant component in predicting career success."[1] The authors went on to state that while the level of motivation was strongly correlated to individual success, it didn't matter where the motivation came from. In general, I've found this to be true so long as the motivation is powerful and lasting.

The Millionaire Real Estate Investors we spoke to while researching this book shared with us the fact that their motivation arose from a desire to be free from their jobs, have more choices in their lives, achieve self actualization, and gain the security that comes with abundance. They shared a similar drive to reach for their potential, asking questions like: "How much am I capable of?" and "What's possible for me?"

---

[1] Bashaw and Grant, *Journal of Personal Selling and Sales Management*, 1994.

High achievers—Millionaire Real Estate Investors—are powered by a Big Why. Striving to be your very best will have you following in their footsteps on the path to Big Success. A Big Why can redefine your life in ways you might not have imagined, but to qualify as a Big Why, your motivation should move you from thinking in terms of electives to acting in terms of imperatives. What I mean is that you stop thinking of success as something you *want* to achieve and start feeling that it's something you need to and in fact *have* to achieve. Life is very different when you move from want-tos to have-tos, and a truly significant Big Why causes you to make that transition.

> *"When someone is struggling financially, there are two things going on. They have limited financial training, and they have a weak spirit. The spirit has to be extremely strong if you're going to succeed. There are a lot of people with the right financial knowledge, but they lack guts."*
>
> Robert Kiyosaki
> Best-selling author and millionaire investor
> Scottsdale, AZ

Are you plugged into your Big Why? Are you tapping into the energy it can bring to your life? Chances are, you're reading this book for a reason. You probably have a strong motivation for seeking financial wealth. I encourage you to take a moment to reflect on the things in your life that motivate you the most. Try to think beyond material goals. You may be working hard to pay off college loans or credit card debt or maybe to get a new family car, but as big as those things seem now, they are really short-term sources of motivation. Any benefits you receive from a focus on them today are unlikely to outlive your achieving them tomorrow. Maybe your greater motivation is financial freedom.

Take a moment now and write down your thoughts. What are the big reasons that drive the choices you make? When you're finished, look for a natural hierarchy. Do some things motivate you more than others do? Is there a higher motivation beyond what you've written down? Ask yourself, what would that choice do for me? What would it mean to me to have that or do that? What would it allow me to become? Do your best to rank all these things in terms of their importance to you.

Hopefully, at the top there is something along the lines of "I want to be as financially wealthy as I can be" or "I want the largest life possible for me." Big Whys related to achieving your highest potential are in my experience the most powerful. Reaching one's personal financial potential is a limitless pursuit; after all, there's no cap on that potential. This is important because the power and reach of your motivation often dictate the level of your success. Having no motivation will lead you nowhere. A small source of motivation will bring you small success. Big Success, in contrast, requires much, much more. It requires a Big Why—an evergreen, ever-growing Big Why!

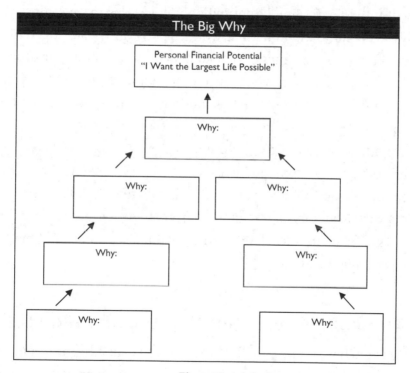

Figure 2

In the end, you shouldn't be too judgmental about your honest answers. Your highest and best calling is your highest and best calling—it's not comparative, and it's not competitive. Life isn't, and neither are your reasons for living it. The goal of this exercise is simply to look for and articulate the factors that drive you to take meaningful and persistent action. Once they are put on paper and written in your heart, they will become a powerful guiding force in your life. The natural next step is to ask yourself, "Do my professional goals line up with that vision? What's the best way to finance my Big Why? Are my relationships in line with these goals?" What you'll discover is that a Big Why brings clear answers to these probing questions and helps you see how the choices you're making help or hinder you on your quest.

Possibly the most tangible gift of a Big Why is that it requires and enables you to prioritize your needs as well as the choices and actions that will fulfill them. Simply put, when you say yes to one thing, you're clearly saying no to anything that works against it. If your Big Why is to seek the limitless opportunities that come with financial wealth, you soon may realize that some of your current spending decisions are working against your long-term financial aspirations. Keeping your focus on the big prize is a great way to avoid missteps or distractions. It's like the Olympic athlete who tapes a picture of a previous gold medal winner to her bathroom mirror to remind her why she is rising before dawn to train for hours while her friends are still in bed. All great achievements are the result of sustained focus over time—all of them. A Big Why brings incredible power and enormous stamina to your financial focus, and big financial success requires that.

2. THINK BIG GOALS, BIG MODELS, AND BIG HABITS

Life is too big to think small. If you want to lead a big life, your thinking has to lead the way. I can't tell you how many times in the course of our research we heard the refrain, "I wish I had started sooner, bought more, and sold less." Even our Millionaire Real Estate Investors realized that as big as their thinking had been, they could have thought even bigger. They understood that the size of their financial lives had been determined by the size of their thinking.

I believe in thinking big, but I also know that's not enough. Without Big Goals, Big Models, and Big Habits, big thinking may be wishful thinking, and by itself wishful thinking isn't that useful. There's only a small difference between living a great life in your head and living a great life in reality, but that small difference makes all the difference. People who lead great lives allow their big thinking to direct them to action. And countless big thinkers have lived before us—trails have been blazed and paths cleared, twigs have been broken and bread crumbs dropped, clues have been left and X marks the spot. The Big Models and Big Habits they discovered on the path to their Big Goals have been left for us to learn from. Not learning from their methods—reinventing the wheel—is a monumental waste of time. Life is too short to move slowly.

It's been said that if you don't know where you're going, any path will get you there. Interestingly, the opposite is equally true: If you know where you're going, there is a best path for getting there. The gift of discovering your Big Why is knowing your ultimate destination and being driven to reach it. However, the challenge of a Big Why lies in finding the best path to get there. For the Millionaire Real Estate Investor finding that path is about two things: establishing Big Goals and acquiring Big Models. Big Goals force you to restate your Big Why in specific and measurable terms, and Big Models represent the proven systems and activities that will get you to those Big Goals. If your Big Why is to achieve financial independence, you'll have to take that abstract concept and quantify it. Then, faced with a specific financial goal related to your Big Why, the question becomes, "How do I achieve that?" The answer is found in proven Big Models.

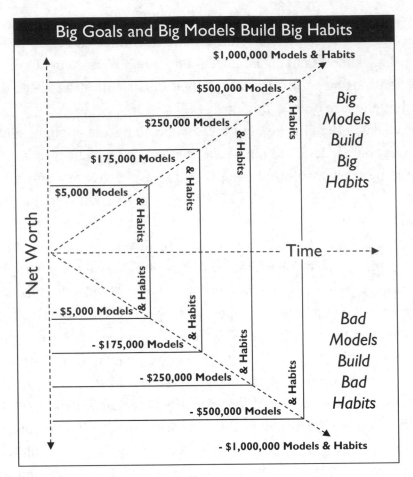

Figure 3

In the context of this book I'm advocating that you adopt the Big Goals and Big Models of a Millionaire Real Estate Investor. There are some subtle but powerful lessons in the chart above. If you follow the arrows that go through the different levels of achievement, it appears that the various levels are just milestones on the way to the models and habits of millionaires. Sadly, life doesn't work like that. The truth is that each level is more like a box created by thinking and habits that form an end rather than a means. And rather than being a stepping-stone to the next level, the box you're in becomes a barrier to higher achievement. You will have hit a dead end before you realize it. And unwittingly so—that's the danger of limited thinking and the box your habits will create.

Specifically, if you follow the models and actions that lead you to $5,000 in net worth, they are not likely to allow you to go beyond that goal to, say, $175,000. The things you would do to get to that higher level would be very different. In a sense, by following the $5,000 model, you have created for yourself a low ceiling, or at least a box with a very tight lid. It's the difference between long-term and short-term thinking. While most people would say they want a great life, they rarely plan beyond the current year. As a result, they choose a financial model that fits only their short-term goals, and that financial shortsightedness can be devastating to their long-term dreams.

Interestingly, those numbers aren't random. The 2001 Survey of Consumer Finances by the Federal Reserve documented that people who rent have a net worth of less than $5,000, while the typical home-owner has a net worth of a little less than $175,000. That illustrates the stark difference between the financial models and habits of renters and those of people who own their own home. In contrast, following the truly big financial models that can take you to $1 million in net worth will pull you through the lower levels—it's the power of future pull. It's the power that comes from following Big Models and developing the Big Habits to implement them. You're so focused on doing things in a manner that will get you to your Big Goal that you are pulled right past the smaller ones. This is the real magic of Big Goals and Big Models.

> "I love real estate investing. I know how much money is coming in and out, and I try to pay things off faster than I need to. I have my 5-year and 10-year goals; the first one is that I want to make sure right now that our investments will cover our monthly nut after my husband retires in five years."
>
> Mary McDonald
> Millionaire Real Estate Investor
> Coopersburg, PA

When you follow the Big Models of Millionaire Real Estate Investors, you will find your day-to-day activities begin to mirror those of high achievers. Over time those Big Models will cease being guidelines you follow and become the habits that power you through your day. Habits, as we all know, are hard to break, and so it's truly wise to build the best habits from the beginning. The Russian novelist Fyodor Dostoevsky wrote, "The second half of a man's life is made up of nothing but the habits he has acquired during the first half." The models in this book are about acquiring big financial wealth-building habits for your life.

Big Goals, Big Models & Big Habits

1. Big Goals—The specific, measurable targets that fulfill your Big Why.

2. Big Models—The proven systems and strategies for reaching your Big Goals.

3. Big Habits—The consistent actions and right choices that come from following Big Models.

Figure 4

There is no such thing as a neutral habit. Habits are either good or bad. They either lift you up or drag you down. In the financial world the models you follow and the habits they form are either additive or subtractive, which is why the chart we have been discussing includes negative net worth models and habits that are opposite to the positive ones. Good habits put money in your pocket, and bad ones take money out. But even good habits can be a handicap if they are small and box you into a certain level of accomplishment. Those who take the incremental approach and start with small habits will find that the real challenge lies not in adopting new goals and models but rather in breaking their old habits and forming bigger and better new ones.

Think Big Goals and Big Models from the start. The Big Habits you will have to build will serve you at every level of financial achievement along your journey. Not only will they guide you toward the most appropriate actions to achieve your goals, they tend to protect you from the mistakes people with lesser goals, models, and habits make. Would you rather make a millionaire mistake or a rookie mistake? There's a big difference, and in real estate investing a costly mistake in the beginning can knock you completely out of the game. Big Goals, Big Models, and Big Habits do more than just direct you—they also protect you! In addition to guiding you to do the right things, they keep you from doing the wrong things.

Millionaire Real Estate Investors have Big Goals; they seek out Big Models to attain them; and over time they enjoy the gift of Big Habits to drive them toward their financial destiny. And when this is all powered by a Big Why, there's little that can hold them back.

3. THINK MONEY MATTERS

We all have a fundamental choice in our financial lives: the path of earned income or the path of unearned income. In other words, you can work for money or money can work for you. On one path you get paid only for what you do; on the other you get paid no matter what you do. One path is well worn, and the other is largely undiscovered.

Somehow, some way the concept of building financial wealth—the path less traveled—has fallen through the cracks of our collective consciousness. As important as money is in our daily lives and as powerful as the concept of financial wealth building is, most people have not taken their financial education seriously. Millionaire Real Estate Investors, however, are different. For them, money matters. What is almost universally considered an elective is for them a prerequisite course for life. By choice, they're students of the financial wealth-building game.

At a certain point these investors grasped that understanding money paid dividends in their lives—big dividends. As soon as they made that connection, the pursuit of the knowledge of money—its history, its rules, and its disciplines—became a primary focus for them. They sought mentors, read books, listened to tapes, and attended seminars. They set out to get a superb home-school education in financial matters and received the equivalent of a master's degree in money.

Wendy Patton, a Millionaire Real Estate Investor from Detroit, MI, got her start when her mom gave her a set of real estate investment tapes. Later, a $39 course on lease options formed the basis of the investment strategy she's successfully used for 15 years. Now she collects them. "I bought every course I could find. I have at least $50,000 worth in my library."

> *"I never let anyone rain on my parade or wreck my day. I never listen to anything negative. I'm in charge of my attitude. I had a lot of energy, and I had a plan, so it took me only four years to become a millionaire."*
>
> Mary McDonald
> Millionaire Real Estate Investor
> Coopersburg, PA

The goal of this book is to get you on the positive, life-changing path to passive income as quickly as possible. At the end of that path is a place called financial wealth where you have enough money working for you that you no longer have to work for money. But that kind of passive income doesn't happen by accident. You first have to get educated and then make investing a priority in your life. That education begins with the Money Matrix.

THE MONEY MATRIX

Most people are in the dark about money. They live from paycheck to paycheck in a twilight world with only the dim candle of conventional financial thinking to light the way. As a result they have a kind of financial shortsightedness that prevents them from distinguishing between good and bad financial decisions. It's time to throw some light on the subject and illuminate the way wealthy people think about money.

The most powerful model for understanding the use of money and the building of financial wealth is the Money Matrix. It tells the story of how the rich get richer and the poor get poorer. It helps people identify whether they are investors or consumers and whether their money works for them or they work for money. The two pyramids in the Money Matrix—one pointing up and the other pointing down—reflect the contrasting financial priorities of investors and consumers. The essential difference between the two is the importance they place on the four roles of money:

■ *Capital*—money invested in anything expected to grow in value
■ *Cash Flow*—money generated from those investments
■ *Cash*—money held in reserve for security or future investments
■ *Consumption*—money spent on anything not expected to grow in value

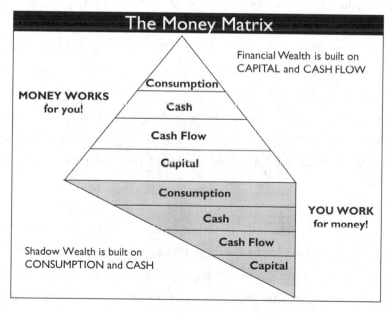

Figure 5

Investors build their financial lives on Capital, while consumers build theirs on Consumption. It's a little like the old Sunday school song about building your house on the rock instead of the sinking sand.

Investors understand that your first financial priority has a cascading effect on your financial life. In other words, what you do with your money in the beginning will dictate what you're able to do in the end. It's about your financial priorities—what you actually do when you receive money. While investors see money as an opportunity to invest, consumers see money primarily as an opportunity to spend. As a result, while investors are generating money from their investments, consumers are at best saving money for security. Later, while investors are setting aside more money for future investments, consumers are trying to wring some return out of their modest savings. Finally, while investors are free to spend all that's left, consumers are struggling to invest the little that is left.

When you invest in Capital first, an amazing thing happens: Slowly but surely your money starts to work for you. Amazingly, your money is now making you even more money. And each year, as you invest more of your income in Capital, the Cash Flow it creates grows in significance. Suddenly you find that you're well along the financial wealth-building Path of Passive Income (Figure 6 on the facing page) and an ever-increasing percentage of your income is being earned by your money, not by you. The game Millionaire Real Estate Investors play is to see how much unearned income they can generate from their investments.

In the end it all comes down to a person's ability to prioritize investing over spending, to value Capital more than Consumption. Many of the Millionaire Real Estate Investors we interviewed reported making some short-term sacrifices for long-term gains while they were building a foundation for financial wealth. Not only did they invest a relatively large percentage of their earned income, they also overcame the impulse to

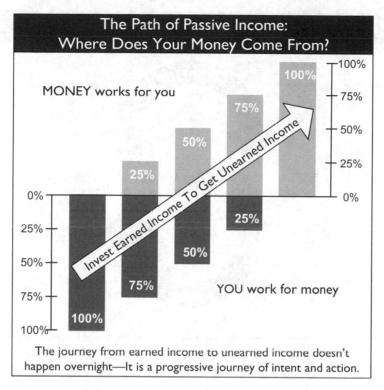

The Path of Passive Income:
Where Does Your Money Come From?

MONEY works for you

YOU work for money

Invest Earned Income To Get Unearned Income

The journey from earned income to unearned income doesn't happen overnight—It is a progressive journey of intent and action.

Figure 6

squander any extra income generated from their investments. Instead, they reinvested the lion's share of their Cash Flow in additional Capital to accelerate the financial wealth-building process (see Fig. 7 on the following page). That was when their investing process took on a life of its own. It seemed that the more Capital they owned, the more Capital they could afford. Reinvesting your Cash Flow creates a financial wealth-building machine that feeds itself and has the potential to grow exponentially over time.

Consumers, in contrast, have it all backward, and that is why they live for Shadow Wealth. We call it Shadow Wealth because when you live a life of consumption, it can give the appearance of wealth without any of the substance. It's what the authors of *The Millionaire Next Door*

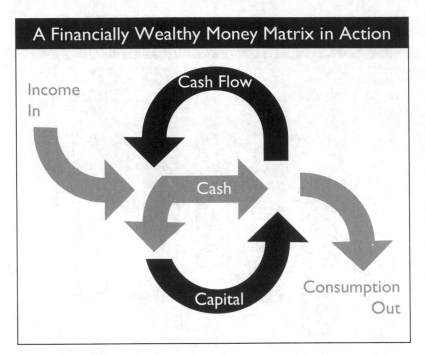

A Financially Wealthy Money Matrix in Action

Income In

Cash Flow

Cash

Capital

Consumption Out

Figure 7

referred to as "big hat—no cattle." In the context of this book, it's "big house—no investments" or, even worse, "big car—no house." These are the individuals who may have high-paying jobs but have failed to get their financial priorities in order. They see having money as an opportunity to spend first, spend second, and spend last. They get their values from the media and spend their money accordingly. In short, they allow Consumption to dominate their thinking (see Fig. 8 on facing page). And with no Capital to serve as a financial foundation, at the end of the day they are a pink slip away from financial distress and maybe financial disaster. Living life as an investor means first living a life of less Consumption than the media would have you believe you should. It requires listening to wisdom—not to the world.

Although an emphasis on Consumption hinders your ability to build financial wealth, Consumption is not entirely a bad thing. After all, the

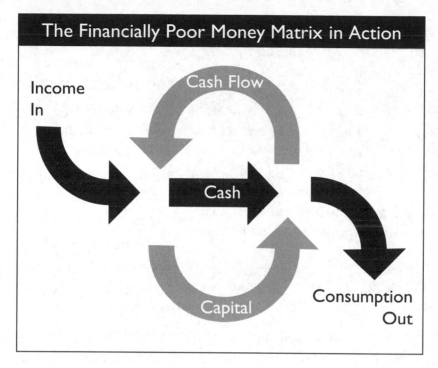

Income In

Cash Flow

Cash

Capital

Consumption Out

Figure 8

goal of wealth building is to create a big enough foundation of Capital and Cash Flow that your Consumption needs are met without your having to work. Consumption has two distinct forms. On the one hand you spend money on yourself to satisfy your needs and wants, but on the other hand you can spend money for the benefit of others. I'm talking about taking care of your loved ones and, of course, making contributions to charity, which in my mind is the highest and best use of money. Charity is a kind of capital investment for the soul that pays real dividends in your life and in the quality of *all life*.

When you view your financial decisions through the lens of the financially wealthy half of the Money Matrix, you start understanding where your money comes from and where it goes. You begin to recognize the natural cycle of growth on growth when earned income is invested in

> *"My truth is that money will be anything you want it to be. If you think money's hard to get, it will be. If you say you have to work real hard for money, you'll work real hard for it. If you say it takes money to make money, then that's the only world you'll live in. But if you say, there's plenty of money, I can make as much as I want of it, that is also true. Money is anything you want it to be."*
>
> Robert Kiyosaki
> Best-selling author and millionaire investor
> Scottsdale, AZ

Capital that creates Cash Flow, which can be reinvested in more Capital for more Cash Flow. It's like compound interest with a turbocharger.

Ask yourself this question: In which half of the Money Matrix have you been living? Does your income go straight out the door in the form of Consumption? Or do you always designate a substantial portion of your earned income for direct investment into Capital? I can't overemphasize how important it is to take a moment to understand the Money Matrix. Your financial priorities can make the difference between achieving true financial wealth and falling prey to the allure of living in the world of Shadow Wealth.

4. THINK NET WORTH

Every day an undeclared game is being played out. It is a serious game of individual achievement with both winners and losers. Whether you realize it or not, you are a player in this game. It's the personal game of financial wealth building. And if you want to win and win big, you have to know how to keep score. The question is: Do you know your score?

One of the great lessons I carried away from my breakfasts with Michael was the knowledge that the wealthy are conscious players of the financial wealth-building game, that they play it strategically and keep score by carefully watching their net worth. Each year, *Forbes* magazine devotes an issue to ranking the wealthiest people in the world. By the way, can you guess what they use as a yardstick for financial success? Interestingly, it's not annual income. They believe the best and most definitive measure of financial wealth is net worth: the sum total of an individual's assets and liabilities. In personal terms, your financial wealth is your net worth, which is what you own minus what you owe.

I didn't always understand this. In fact, like most people, I probably placed too much importance on my earned income when I should have been tracking my assets—Capital—and my unearned income—Cash Flow. I later learned that the trick to financial clarity is to look past your earned income to your unearned income and then beyond that to the underlying source of that unearned income. While almost everyone who talks about investing emphasizes Cash Flow, people probably don't place as much importance as they should on the origin of that Cash Flow. Without a doubt achieving positive Cash Flow from your investments is critical to long-term investment success. But let me ask you this: Do you know where your cash flows from? Cash Flow comes from Capital, which is the basis of your net worth. I would argue that the fundamental wealth-building number you should focus on and track is your net worth. It's the golden goose.

This insight changed the way I looked at my personal finances, and on Michael's advice I started keeping score. Together we took a standard bank loan application and used it to create a list of all the financially significant things I owned (stocks, bonds, real estate, furniture, car, etc.), and then we subtracted all my various debts and liabilities. The final number was my net worth. Each week I'd update my net worth worksheet, and when Michael and I met again, we would ask one simple but profound question: "What's the best way to make that number grow?"

Through this weekly process I discovered that knowing your net worth, while an eye-opening process,[2] is really only half the battle. The greatest clarity comes when you also track your net worth over time. When I did that, I started to notice which financial decisions had the greatest positive impact on my financial wealth. As a general rule, investing made my net worth go up and consumption made it go down. Sometimes, when I thought I was investing, I really wasn't. I discovered that not all assets are equal—some appreciate, while others depreciate. For example, when I purchased a car, even though it was an asset, it was a depreciating asset, and my net worth went down. In contrast, when I invested in real estate, an appreciating asset, although I incurred debt, my net worth went up. I started to take a closer look at all my assets to see whether they were true investments. What I discovered was that even my own home, which I hadn't originally treated like an investment, was in fact an appreciating asset. My home mortgage turned out to be a little like a forced investment plan in real estate, with each payment increasing my equity and lowering my debts.

> *"If you're going to be an investor, you'd better know your assets. There are depreciating assets and appreciating assets and some people don't know the difference."*
>
> Dave Fairweather
> Millionaire Real Estate Investor
> Bethesda, MD

Most people don't think of their homes as an investment when they buy them. It's only later, after a few years of appreciation and equity buildup, that they say, "My house was the best investment I ever made." I would make the case that owning a home might be the most important "accidental asset" most individuals will ever acquire. In fact, the data collected by the Federal Reserve in the last four Surveys of Consumer Finances reports (see Fig. 9) certainly support that argument.

---

[2] Later, in "Buy a Million," I'll walk you through the process of completing your own net worth worksheet and creating a simple monthly budget.

The Impact of Real Estate Ownership on Net Worth				
	1992	1995	1998	2001
Median Net Worth: Homeowner	$122,300	$120,200	$143,800	$171,700
Median Net Worth: Renter	$4,000	$5,600	$4,600	$4,800
The Real Estate Difference	$118,300	$114,600	$139,200	$166,900

From the 1992, 1995, 1998 and 2001 Survey of Consumer Finances compiled by the Federal Reserve.

Figure 9

The Millionaire Real Estate Investors we interviewed made Thinking Net Worth a habit. They also grasped the effect home ownership has on net worth and were compelled to ask the following questions: How much faster would my net worth grow if I owned more real estate? How fast would it grow if someone else paid down the mortgage? What if the rent they paid more than covered the property's expenses and generated positive Cash Flow? In answering those big questions about their wealth, they started down the path to becoming the committed real estate investors they are today. They began to live in a world of "intentional investments," not just "accidental assets." What became clear to them, and is clear to me, is that once you begin to Think Net Worth, it is only natural to begin to Think Real Estate.

5. THINK REAL ESTATE

Your government wants you to Think Real Estate. Actually, the government not only wants you to think real estate, it wants you to own it. In fact, it needs you to do that. This point was driven home for me during a taxicab ride in Florida. The driver was from Chile, and when he heard I was in real estate, he told me a remarkable story of how the

Chilean government had launched a housing program in the 1970s to revitalize the economy. The idea was to make housing affordable to more middle-income and low-income buyers, which would allow them over time to build equity. The program was based on the well-documented effects of housing affordability and ownership on the American economy. Home ownership and the resulting expenses of maintaining a home (fixing it up and furnishing it) are widely considered the largest and most important category of spending in the United States. That's not all: Home ownership also helps launch small businesses by allowing would-be entrepreneurs to borrow against the equity in their homes. My cabbie was articulating the economics of property ownership in a way that very few people do. I enjoyed the conversation and hated to see it end.

> *"It's impossible not to become wealthy over time in this business."*
> Stanley Armstrong
> Millionaire Real Estate Investor
> Washington, DC

When I got home, I looked it up and discovered that the story didn't end there. As it turns out, the housing reforms in Chile were so effective that Ecuador implemented a similar program in the 1990s. In a white paper on the subject the economist Hernando de Soto observed: "The critical difference between successful capitalist societies and those that are not is their ability to create wealth with private property, especially land and housing." It's a fact. Historically and globally, free-market societies foster and protect real estate ownership because it can underpin a society's ability to build financial wealth and prosperity. That is why Millionaire Real Estate Investors Think Real Estate for building their personal financial wealth and prosperity.

Our research and experience show that no other investment has had as consistent and powerful an effect on the average person's net worth as real estate ownership. In fact, as real estate historian Dana Lee Thomas revealed, "The oldest fortunes in America have come from the land. Unlike Europe, where most of the valuable acreage has been held and passed down by nobility for centuries, American real estate has been open to virtually anybody with the daring and the ingenuity to possess it."[3] With that powerful insight in mind, let's take a moment to run through some of the many advantages of investing in real estate that lead Millionaire Real Estate Investors to refer to real estate as a most "able" investment.

For starters, real estate is remarkably *accessible* to investors. Not only is it easy to understand and easy to find, more significantly, it's easy to finance. In addition to a wide variety of conventional and government-supported mortgage loan programs, there are many sources of private and owner financing. In the end, there are real estate financing options for every type of property and almost every type of buyer (low income to no income, poor credit to no credit, little down to nothing down—you name it). There are typically no insurmountable financial barriers to entry.

Real Estate — A Most "ABLE" Investment

1. Accessible – Anyone can buy it
2. Appreciable – Increases in value over time
3. Leverageable – Buy on margin & borrow against equity
4. Rentable – Cash Flow! Cash Flow! Cash Flow!
5. Improvable – Sweat equity
6. Deductible/Depreciable/Deferrable – Great tax benefits
7. Stable – Slow to rise & slow to fall
8. Liveable – Shelter in more ways than one....

Figure 10

---

[3] Dana Lee Thomas, *Lords of the Land: The Triumphs and Scandals of America's Real Estate Barons, from Early Times to the Present.* New York: Putnam, 1977.

The biggest reason for this is that real estate provides *significant insurable collateral* for any mortgage no matter who the lender is, institutional or individual. When loans are secured by real estate, lenders feel . . . well . . . secure. This is what you see when you look at the big picture of investing, and that's a huge reason why real estate remains so accessible to all.

The second thing that makes real estate an "able" investment is that it is *appreciable*—it increases in value over time. This is due to two primary factors: First, general inflation drives up the replacement cost of housing (construction materials and labor) and therefore the value of all real estate. Second, there is the influence of supply and demand. As the population increases,[4] so does the demand for housing (see figure 11).

> "*Real estate does cycle throughout history. But even if it's always up and down, the long-term trend is up.*"
> George Castleberry
> Millionaire Real Estate Investor
> Austin, TX

This makes sense because, as research shows, in the modern era real estate consistently has increased in value at a rate of about 6.1 percent a year,[5] outpacing inflation by an average of 33 percent a year (see figure 12).

Trammell Crow, one of the most successful real estate investors ever, once famously declared, "The way to wealth is debt." What he was bluntly describing is the third area that makes real estate an "able" investment: Real estate is *leverageable*. The 6.1 percent appreciation rate mentioned earlier may not seem like a lot, but that figure is actual-

---

[4] The U.S. Census Bureau reports that the U.S. population grew at an average rate of about 2.3 million a year (0.98 percent compounded annually) from 1970 to 2000 and is projected to grow at almost the same pace (0.82 percent compounded annually) from 2000 to 2030. At the same time, the percentage of home ownership has increased from approximately 64 percent to 69 percent; therefore, the number of homeowners has increased at a greater rate than has the population.

[5] U.S. Department of Housing and Urban Development data show that median home prices appreciated at an annual rate of 6.1 percent from 1972 to 2002. At the same time, the cost of living (inflation as measured by the Consumer Price Index) increased only 4.2 percent per year.

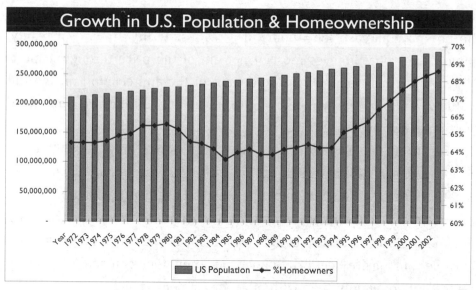

Figure 11

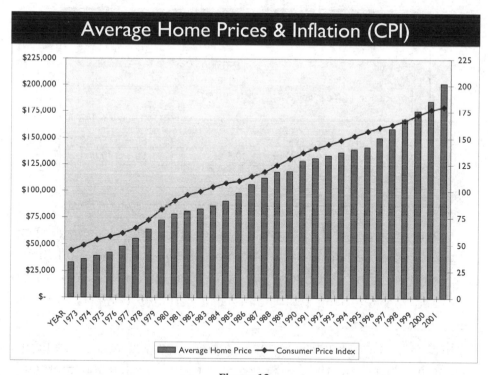

Figure 12

ly a little deceiving. It doesn't take into account the fact that practically no one pays all cash for a home or a real estate investment. In reality, almost everyone finances most, if not all, of the price through a mortgage. As a result, people get the benefit of the appreciation on the full value of the property while having to invest only a relatively small proportion of the purchase price.

For example, a person may have put down only $30,000 on a $150,000 house. If that leveraged property has appreciated 6.1 percent to $159,150, the $9,150 gain should be weighed against the $30,000 invested, not the $150,000 price. A gain of $9,150 on $30,000 translates to a 30.5 percent rate of return on the investment! Because real estate is leverageable, Millionaire Real Estate Investors know they can achieve rates of return not commonly seen with other investment vehicles.

The Power of Leverage on Rate of Return		
Price Paid	$150,000	
Down Payment	$30,000	
Appreciation (1 Year at 6.1%)	$159,150	
Gain	$9,150	($150,000 × 6.1%)
Rate of Return on Price	6.1%	($9,150 ÷ $150,000)
Rate of Return on Investment	30.5%	($9,150 ÷ $30,000)

Figure 13

When we talked real estate with the noted economist Harry S. Dent, Jr., this is what he had to say: "The most important thing about home ownership is that it's leveraged . . . When you look at your net investment and the return on that, homes can certainly compete with the stock market."

In 1936, Harry Helmsley, one of this country's largest landlords, bought his first property for $1,000 down and a $100,000 mortgage.

He sold it 10 years later for $165,000. Leveraging an investment doesn't get much better than that.

The concept of leverage doesn't work only when you purchase a property. Once you build up an equity position in an investment property, you can leverage that investment for cash in one of two ways: You can secure a secondary loan against the increased equity or refinance the original loan amount plus the increased equity.

"Where else are you going to make a small down payment, let somebody else pay for it, and you reap all the rewards? I can't find anything that beats that."

Will Stewart
Millionaire Real Estate Investor
Sugar Hill, GA

Remarkably, the leverage advantage can work two ways. You can buy a property for dimes on the dollar, and you can convert any equity gains into cash without selling the asset.

Leverage — Pull Cash Out Without Selling the Asset

Price Paid	$150,000
Down Payment	$30,000
Original Loan	$120,000
Appreciation (1 Year at 6.1%)	$159,150
Equity Gain	$9,150

Method 1: Borrow Against Equity	
Secondary Loan	$9,150
Cash Out	$9,150

Method 2: Refinance	
New Loan	$129,150
Cash Out	$9,150

The tax free cash you take out on both is the same. The method you choose will be dictated by the new monthly payment and terms each option offers.

Figure 14

The next major bonus of real estate is the Cash Flow it can generate: Real estate is *rentable*. It continually amazes me that I can purchase a property and then turn around and rent it to a person who will pay down my debt in exchange for living there. In reality, that's what renters do—they pay your mortgage, which builds your equity. If you bought the property right, they provide you with the opportunity to get unearned income in the form of positive Cash Flow. When you take a look at the total return from real estate investing, you have the opportunity for an investment "triple play"—appreciation, debt paydown, and positive Cash Flow. The last two come from your ability to rent the property. Interestingly, history has shown that despite local periods of fluctuation, over the long haul rents have increased. According to the U.S. Department of Housing and Urban Development, rents have been appreciating over the last 30 years at an annual rate of 5.3 percent.[6] Millionaire Real Estate Investors understand all this and know that although rents tend to be cyclical, they rise over time.

One of the unique and attractive advantages of real estate is that it is *improvable*. Because real estate is a tangible asset made of wood, brick, concrete, and glass, a Millionaire Real Estate Investor knows you can improve the value of any property with some tools and a little elbow grease. Whether the repairs are structural or cosmetic, whether you do it yourself or hire someone else, the principle is the same. It's called "sweat equity."

You also can increase the value of the property in a more subtle way by changing its zoning or use. Converting vacant lots into parking lots and converting apartments into condos are a couple of common examples of adding value through creativity. Actually, this is another form of sweat equity—it's just more mental than muscular.

---

[6] In the 30-year period from 1972 to 2002 the median rent rose at a compounded annual rate of 5.32 percent.

This is what Millionaire Real Estate Investors love about real estate. They can use their hands and use their minds. Their investing can even take on the aspects of a game in which with each property they attempt to discover its hidden value.

> "I bought a house in an owner-financed deal for $120,000. I only had to put $10,000 down, and then I put $10,000 into the house to remodel it. I ended up selling for $189,000. So in 58 days, I made $40,000."
>
> Carlos Rivero
> Millionaire Real Estate Investor
> Austin, TX

When they find that hidden value, they buy the property, improve it, and reap the financial reward. In the end, real estate offers investors a unique opportunity to affect their investments directly—this is an area where personal time and energy can really pay off.

If you ever needed proof that the government wants you to own real estate, look no further than the many tax benefits the government has given it. The three that stand out the most are that it's *deductible, depreciable*, and *deferrable*. Millionaire Real Estate Investors are well aware of these tax advantages and take advantage of them. You could say that they see real estate in 3D.

The first D, *deductible*, reflects the fact that tax law allows various deductions for the normal expenses incurred in owning real estate, such as property upkeep, maintenance, improvements, and even the interest paid on a mortgage. Millionaire Real Estate Investors use these deductions to offset their investment income and in some cases their personal income, thus reducing their overall taxes.

The most important of these deductions comes from the second D, *depreciable*. What's interesting is that not only does tax law *allow* you to depreciate your investments, it *requires* it. Simply put, things are presumed to wear out and lose value over time. The government expects you to account for that "wear and tear," whether it's actually happening or not, by claiming an annual decline in the value of the building, its contents, and any improvements. Millionaire Real Estate Investors love this tax break because it allows them to reduce their taxable income through depreciation even when a property is increasing in value through appreciation.

The third D is *deferrable*. Tax law allows you to use IRAs and 1031 exchanges to buy and sell investment real estate while deferring the tax hit to a more advantageous time. IRA funds can be invested in real estate, and as long as any profits from rental income or property sales remain in the IRA, those profits are tax-deferred. The 1031 exchanges give you a choice at the moment of sale either to realize the gain and pay taxes on it or to reinvest that gain in another property and defer the taxes. And when you choose to reinvest, the transaction is treated as if you simply exchanged equity in one property for equity in another. The government has established these tax-deferring vehicles as a way for investors to reinvest real estate profits without having to pay the taxes until later. Millionaire Real Estate Investors believe that taxes deferred until tomorrow are always better than taxes paid today. As a result, they make use of these programs to preserve their profits as they go, giving them more to reinvest and accelerating the growth of their real estate portfolios.

U.S. Appeals Court Judge Learned Hand once observed, "There are two systems of taxation in our country—one for the informed and one for the uninformed." I agree. When it comes to taxes, there are two kinds of people: consumers and investors. One group avoids planning for taxes, and the other plans for avoiding taxes. One sees doing their taxes as a painful chore that costs them money, and the other views their tax work as a necessary task that saves them money. Consumers think of tax refunds as found money they didn't have. Investors see tax refunds as evidence of money they overpaid. When you connect tax work to the money you save versus the money you pay, thinking about and working on your taxes cease being so painful. It's still work, but it doesn't have to be your work. Accountants will do it for you, because they're the only ones who think tax work is fun.

In the end the three Ds—deductible, depreciable, and deferrable—are about reducing your taxable income. No investment does that better than real estate, which offers unprecedented tax advantages both while you own it and when you sell it.

Millionaire Real Estate Investors also count on the fact that real estate is quite *stable*. It's slow to rise and slow to fall. It doesn't surprise you, and better yet, it doesn't shock you. Nicolas Retsinas, director of Harvard University's Joint Center for Housing Studies, noted:

> From 1975 to 1998, only 14 of the country's largest metro areas experienced price declines of 5% or more over a three-year period . . . Unless you overpaid walking in—if you're prepared to live through the cycle—you're probably not going to lose money over the long haul.

In other words, the real estate market is predictable for anyone who's paying attention—you can see it coming, and you can see it going.[7]

Statistically, economists rate the volatility of an investment through a measure called the "standard deviation," which in this case is the percentage an investment's value will go up or down on average in a given year. From 1973 to 2003, the standard deviation for real estate was 4.0 percent. In other words, real estate values have fluctuated up or down by only about 4.0 percent each year. On a graph, real estate values look like

---

[7] There have been two times since 1900 when the stability of real estate has been called into question, and both were ultimately the result of extraordinary government policy or tinkering. The first was the Great Depression of the 1930s, a time when any mortgage could be called due at any time. The second was the Tax Reform Act of 1986, when the tax laws regarding real estate were changed abruptly and retroactively.

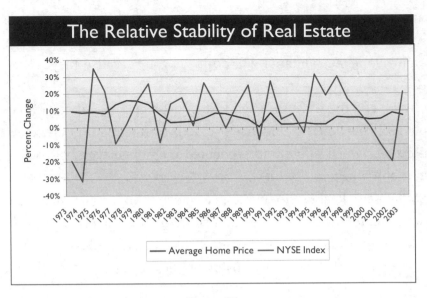

Figure 15

a series of gently rolling hills. In contrast, over the same period of time the stock market had a standard deviation of 16.8 percent, which looks more like a jagged electrocardiogram printout. The facts speak for themselves: Real estate is more stable.

But let's be clear. This is not a discussion about rates of return—it's about day-to-day risk. Figure 16, on the facing page, which illustrates the differences in various investment portfolio mixes, drives this point home. You can see that when real estate is included in the mix, the standard deviation (the volatility and the risk) is minimized. This happens because of the remarkable stability of real estate prices. While this doesn't mean you should avoid other investments, it does mean you should include real estate in your investment portfolio, and that's exactly what Millionaire Real Estate Investors do.

The last thing that makes real estate an "able" investment is that it is *livable*. It is quite literally the only investment vehicle that can put a roof over your head. This point is included not for the sake of cuteness but to

The Millionaire Real Estate Investor

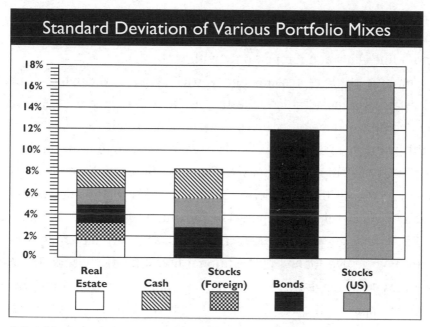

Standard Deviation of Various Portfolio Mixes

Figure 16

make a point that many Millionaire Real Estate Investors made to us. The home you live in can also be an investment—the second you start thinking of it as one. The trick is to start seeing your home for everything it can be. It's more than just shelter—it's a foundation piece of your financial wealth-building program. That's the way I looked at it when I bought my first property. I was in my early twenties and needed a roommate to afford it. Later I moved out, moved a tenant in, bought a second home, and moved my roommate with me. This was a great formula for me and one I could repeat. I was buying shelter and an investment. And because I understood the real estate game, I got both houses for no money down.

Many of our millionaire investors shared with us the fact that they also began their investment careers by moving into a home, fixing it up, and then renting it out when they moved to a second home. They took care of a life necessity while launching an investment career. It was a strategy they could use any time and as often as they wanted. Here's the bottom line—this can happen only with real estate.

Combine all these reasons and you will understand why we believe real estate is a most "able" investment. Note that this discussion is not intended to disparage other investment options. While I've created a lot of wealth through real estate, I've also made great money by investing in business ownership as well as traditional stocks and bonds. I am an investor. I use all these vehicles. But just like the Millionaire Real Estate Investors we interviewed, I appreciate the unique advantages of real estate.

The challenge you may face is that these many advantages of real estate may be overlooked by traditional investment advisors. For example, to my knowledge there is not a single popular financial magazine or business paper with a regular column dedicated to active ownership of investment real estate. Any real estate articles that appear in these publications tend to coincide with downturns in the stock market, which often push traditional investors into the real estate market. I don't fault these magazines. They are, after all, businesses, and as such they write for the investment markets that attract the most advertising dollars. The unfortunate net effect, however, is the marginalization of real estate investing. Because it's not commonly written about or discussed in financial publications, investors may not realize that real estate is a credible option for them. If you never considered real estate in the past, I hope you'll think about it now. Our Millionaire Real Estate Investors chose to Think Real Estate, and that's how they became millionaires.

6. THINK VALUE, OPPORTUNITY, AND DEALS

Almost anything worth doing has a process. What the Millionaire Real Estate Investors revealed to us was that their thinking followed a process that in the end instructed their actions. The truth we discovered was that

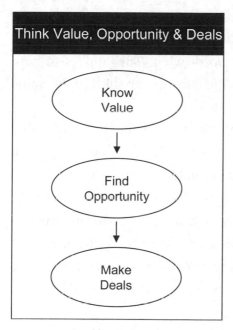

Think Value, Opportunity & Deals

Know Value

↓

Find Opportunity

↓

Make Deals

Figure 17

you have to know values in order to recognize opportunities and have to find opportunities before you can do deals. That makes sense because you don't just go out and do deals. You can't really make a deal until you've found an opportunity, and you can't really know if it's an opportunity until you understand value. It's that simple. The millionaires follow a simple process, and that process works.

Curiously, none of the investors we interviewed articulated these three important concepts as a detailed process. But as they described the way they went about their business and made their decisions, the process became apparent, and we began to see the simple wisdom and brilliance of it. We came to understand how it saved them time, reduced their risk, and kept them focused. That's why we need to emphasize it here. It is how they think, and it does make a difference in the results they achieve.

Successful real estate investing begins with identifying value. How do investors identify value? That's easy. They look at real estate. They look at a lot of real estate. They look very carefully at a lot of real estate. I wish I could tell you there was a shortcut, but there's not, and I caution you against trying to create one. When you are starting to learn the value of real estate in an area, you

> *"Beginning investors' biggest mistake is that they don't do their homework."*
>
> Dottie Bowe
> Millionaire Real Estate Investor
> Portland, ME

will need to look at a lot of real estate. And as you carefully begin to get a sense of what people are asking and what people are willing to pay, you gain a sense of market value—what's worth what. This applies to both sales prices and rental rates. These are the two big variables in the value equation.

The more you look at properties, the more your sense of value becomes accurate and internalized. This way, when you come upon an available property, you'll be able to determine quickly what price will make that property worth pursuing. This is where opportunity shows up.

Every opportunity is not necessarily a deal. What turns an opportunity into a deal is that the property meets your Criteria and the seller is willing to meet your Terms. Millionaire Real Estate Investor Dyches Boddiford put it very well when he said, "Deals aren't found. Opportunities are found. Deals are made."

In the "Buy a Million" section of this book we'll walk you through all the aspects of Criteria and Terms. But understand this: It is your growing awareness of values in the marketplace, the clarity of your Criteria, and the ability to obtain favorable Terms that make this process so powerful. The underlying key to your thinking is that you know there is a process that works—know value, find opportunity, and make deals.

7. THINK ACTION

My father was a good investor. A lifelong educator, he had a modest lifestyle and used his savings to invest carefully in rural land and residential real estate. However, after a while he became impatient for bigger returns on his investment of time and effort, and as a result he made his first speculative investment. It was also his last. He was invited to participate in an opportunity that involved converting an abandoned drive-in movie theater into a parking lot. The outcome hinged on the city adopting the site for its park-and-ride program, but soon after the purchase the deal went sour. The city opted for an alternative site, and the property continued to yield negative cash flow with no end in sight. Because my dad didn't have deep pockets, he couldn't hold on. In the end his partners released him from his obligations, but he lost his entire investment.

To his credit, he told me the whole story and didn't sugarcoat it. His early real estate investments paid my and my sister's way through private college, but this one bad deal knocked him out of the real estate investment game for life. It's a hard lesson all would-be investors should learn. Impatience or, worse, confusion can lead you down a path from which you may not be able to recover.

When it comes to making money, I think most people don't realize that they too are impatient and confused. What they're confused about is what it really means to be an investor. As a result, they may never take action, or if they do, they take the kind of confused action that can lead to financial disaster. Millionaire Real Estate Investors are not confused. They understand that investing requires action. More important, they also understand that successful investing requires the right action. That's what we mean when we say that Millionaire Real Estate Investors Think Action.

In the course of our research we talked to hundreds of would-be investors. Some were moving toward their goals, and others were still learning the game. It became clear that those who had become the most successful had at some point made a crucial decision—they decided to take action. They said to themselves, "I know enough to know I'm heading in the right direction. I need to get started and then keep learning as I go." Those investors understood that investing in real estate is without a doubt a game of acquired knowledge and, more important, a game of knowledge acquired over time. They also knew that no reading list and no seminar schedule could equip them for the task—some things are learned or refined through doing.

If you take a step back and look at this from a distance, you'll see that there are four basic ways people approach investing. Most are Observers, some are Speculators, others are Collectors, and a few are Investors. Observers love the idea of investing but, out of fear, buy nothing. Speculators love the action and, in their impatience, may buy anything. Collectors love ownership and, for self-gratification, buy something. Investors love opportunity and, in their wisdom, buy the right thing.

Observers can have all the mental qualities of a great investor, but without action they end up witnessing success instead of experiencing it. They are the bystanders on the sidewalk, the spectators in the stands, and the backseat drivers. I've known some incredibly knowledgeable Observers. Having read dozens of books on investing and having attended numerous seminars, they get investing. But what they don't get is that all the time, money, and energy they've invested in their learning will never earn them a financial return if they don't make investments. For some reason they haven't found the motivation to go out, take action, and become an Investor. This is the way it seems to go with Observers. Because they study it all the time, they think they are investing—but they're not.

Speculators aren't afraid to take action; in fact, they love action to a fault. These are the high rollers, the thrill seekers, the lottery lovers, the gamblers. They confuse risk taking with investing, and their risk tolerance may border on risk numbness as they pursue their dream of a big, fast

The Four Investment Profiles

INVESTOR
• Loves Opportunity
• Buys the Right Thing!

COLLECTOR
• Loves Ownership
• Buys Something

SPECULATOR
• Loves the Action
• Buys Anything

OBSERVER
• Loves Ideas
• Buys Nothing

Figure 18

payday. The trouble is that speculation is by definition a matter of taking above-average risks in the hope of achieving above-average returns. It's buying something on the basis of its *potential* selling price rather

> *"You've got to take action. I know people that study for years, but never buy a property. I don't know half of what I should know; I just go out and do it."*
>
> George Meidhof
> Millionaire Real Estate Investor
> Reston, VA

than its *actual* value. Look it up—Speculators bet on the come.

A classic example of Speculators in action was the 1636 Amsterdam tulip bulb craze. To make a long story short, imported tulip bulbs at that time were the exclusive province of Holland's wealthiest Collectors. Sometime around 1635 Speculators got involved and started buying the bulbs not for their gardens but for resale. That small amount of pressure on a market already short on supply soon forced legitimate tulip bulb vendors to bid against one another and drive up prices. Before long, a public market was created and prices of different bulb varieties were tracked publicly in taverns and meeting places. Soon more Speculators began to take advantage of the pinched market, further driving up prices. Then the market shifted from trading real bulbs (which can be pulled only in season) to trading promissory notes for bulbs that would be dug up at a later date. This is important because notes began to be bought on margin (10 percent down, 90 percent on delivery) and traded multiple times from origination to extraction. One could call this the "credit card" effect, since the notes buffered prospective buyers from having to fork over actual cash.

This opened up the tulip bulb market to everyone, and for a period of about two months in late 1636 the market exploded as the Dutch middle class dived into the fray, looking to make fast fortunes. Ordinary people mortgaged farms and homes to buy single bulbs worth as much as a year's income. But as quickly as the rush for riches began, it ended.

Frustrated merchants threw up their hands and stopped buying the over-priced bulbs. A full-on panic ensued, and in a matter of days bulb prices plummeted 90 percent. The financial damage was so widespread that the government had to declare all tulip bulb contracts written during the craze null and void.

> *"People use the word* investor *lightly. Everyone wants to be an investor. But a lot of them aren't really investors. They're absolute rank speculators hoping they can make money."*
>
> Jack Miller
> Millionaire Real Estate Investor
> Reno, NV

Change the commodity from tulip bulbs to land and you could rewrite this story as the great Florida land boom (and bust) of the 1920s. Make it stocks and you have the Internet boom (and bust) of the late 1990s.

The story has played out time and again in markets where prospects for quick and apparently endless appreciation have encouraged Speculators to put down real money for products with artificially inflated values they had no desire (or ability) to hold for the long term. This is the way it seems to go with Speculators. Because they might make money, they think they are investing—but they're not.

Collectors make up the third broad group we have identified. You don't have to have books of stamps in a drawer or fabulous art on your walls to be a Collector. A Collector is simply someone who buys things on the basis of their emotional value rather than their investment value. It's emotional value first and investment value second, if at all. Think Beanie Babies. Collectors buy for love, status, aesthetic gratification, and pleasure. As a result, any financial aspects of the deal become an afterthought. This is the way it seems to go with Collectors. Because their collections may go up in value, they think they are investing—but they're not.

Investors are a breed apart. Unlike Observers, they take action. Unlike Speculators, they minimize risk. Unlike Collectors, they buy on the basis of investment value. Investors are defined by their expectation for financial gain and the process they follow to minimize financial risk. They make it their practice to study and know market value, and then they go out to find assets priced below that value. They don't count on appreciation to bail them out; they make their money going in. Like a bargain hunter, they find as much joy in the search for a bargain as in the transaction itself. Because they think and act like Investors, they tend to achieve excellent returns on those investments while exposing themselves to little or no risk.

Investors follow a straight and narrow path—straight in that they move from knowledge to action and narrow in that they minimize risk and maximize return. It's a way of thinking and a way of acting. This is the true north of the financial wealth builder—the Investor.

So that you understand what happens over time, this path widens a bit. With a certain amount of wealth, your options increase; one sees this

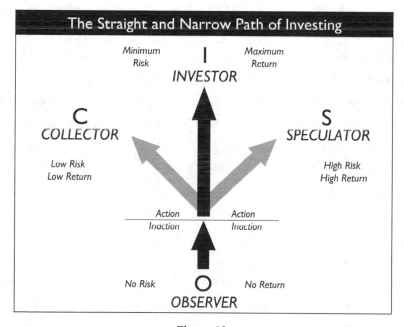

Figure 19

> *"For beginners, it's just important to start. Most people never start. It doesn't matter where you start because it's not going to be where you end up. With real estate, it's hard to make a bad decision. Unlike stocks, if you buy stocks on margin and it goes down you have to come up with a lot of cash immediately."*
>
> Mike Netzel
> Millionaire Real Estate Investor
> Pittsburgh, PA

with successful Investors. They may move a little to the left or right of the narrow investment path, but they've earned that right. They can afford to do a little speculating (to seek a greater return) and collecting (to store some wealth), but they never stray too far and never confuse speculating or collecting with investing. When Warren Buffett, having made his fortune, bought a corporate jet, he didn't try to hide the truth. He appropriately named it *The Indefensible*. He could afford it, he bought it, but he couldn't justify it as an investment. May we all have the clarity of Warren Buffett.

While I believe that everyone has the potential to become an Investor, the truth is that not everyone will. In my experience you can walk up to anyone and ask, "Would you like to be wealthy?" and I'm certain his or her answer will be yes. However, most people won't achieve it for the simple reason that they are *wishful* instead of *willful* in their thinking. This difference makes all the difference. While the wishful enjoy the idea of big financial success, the willful enjoy the actions that lead to real financial success. Some people have a great life just in their heads, and some people just have a great life. It all comes down to how you think and whether your thinking naturally leads you to take action. It's thinking for the sake of doing instead of thinking for thinking's sake.

Millionaire Real Estate Investors are not the kind to get lost on the sidelines. They watch the game unfold, and as soon as they feel they understand what's going on, they dive in and play: They Think Action. They Take Action.

NINA'S RULE: WATCH YOUR POSTURE

Nina, a good friend and a personal trainer, shared with me the fact that one of the first things she works on with her clients is their posture. That surprised me because I would have thought the first thing she'd teach them would be exercises. When I asked her to explain, her answer was remarkably simple: Posture is exercise, and our posture in daily life—the way we sit at a desk or stand in a line—has a bigger impact on our physical well-being than we could imagine. It is a more important exercise for our health, she explained, than the crunches we do or the weight we press. While the best of us work on our muscles a little each day, our posture is at work 24 hours a day. Medical research supports her point of view. Posture has a measurable and profound impact on a person's health.

The challenge is that posture is unconscious—it's a habit. Unless you're thinking about it actively, you aren't usually aware of whether you've got your shoulders square and your back straight. (If you just sat up straight in your chair after reading that last line, welcome to the club.) Thus, Nina's first job is to ask her clients to start paying more attention to their posture and in doing so build stronger, healthier bodies. Since habits, even physical ones, are the product of one's focus and thinking, one could say that an able body is the product of an able mind. Nina sold me on the principle, and I've come to think of it as Nina's Rule. What's surprising is how applicable it is to your financial health.

To restate Nina's Rule in the context of personal wealth, your ability to build financial wealth is determined as much by your everyday "financial posture" as by your not-everyday big financial decisions. I'm talking about the unconscious and seemingly inconsequential spending decisions you make on a daily basis. These little decisions set the stage

> *"Fall in love with the process, not the decision."*
>
> George Castleberry
> Millionaire Real Estate Investor
> Austin, TX

for your big decisions, and they're habit-forming. Most people don't make this connection. Warren Buffett put it best when he said, "There is a tendency with small decisions to think you can do them for not very good reasons." The truth is that as an investor, all your financial decisions, big or small, should be for good reasons.

In the context of this book you need to develop the financial posture of a Millionaire Real Estate Investor—the unconscious habits that guide you all day, every day. This doesn't necessarily mean you're actively working on your investments all the time; what it does mean is that you always have the mental habits of an investor. It shows up in how you manage your money and how you look for opportunity each and every day.

Here's what I want you to begin to do. In the grocery store, at the gas station, basically any time you find yourself with a credit card in hand, I want you to do two things: First, say to yourself, "I'm an investor, not a consumer." Second, ask yourself, "Is this the best use for my money? Am I using my money like an investor or like a consumer?" When you find yourself comparing price and value, hunting for the best buy, and being willing to walk away if you don't find it—congratulations, you're beginning to think like an investor. You're a shopper, not a buyer. You're treating your small financial decisions the same way you treat your big ones.

Nina's Rule not only applies to your spending habits—it's also about building the mental habit of always being on the lookout for opportunities for investment. This is not just a once-a-month or once-a-week activity. It's an everyday posture. It's always being alert for investment opportunities and consistently letting others know that you are. It's about top-of-the-mind awareness. It's about the everyday posture of an investor. Just as your physical posture leads to physical health, your financial posture will lead to financial wealth.

Developing the seven thinking habits of an investor and making them part of your everyday mindset is foundational to building financial wealth.

POINTS TO REMEMBER

- The pursuit of money is a spiritual journey. Money reflects your innermost values and has the power to reveal you.

- Money is also about choices. The more you have, the more positive choices you have.

- True financial wealth is a place of security and abundance, where you are finally free to stop working for a living and start living for your work—your life's work.

- Motivation matters. Discovering your Big Why enables you to prioritize your needs, as well as the choices and actions that will fulfill them. It brings power and stamina to your financial focus.

- Thinking big is not enough. You need Big Goals, Big Models and Big Habits to drive you towards your Big Why and protect you along the way.

- For Millionaire Real Estate Investors, money matters. They take their financial education seriously and make investing a priority, and so should you. Understanding money will pay dividends in your life.

- Understanding the Money Matrix is imperative to your education. Are you an Investor or a Consumer? Investors build their financial life on Capital, while Consumers build theirs on Consumption. In the end, either you work for your money or your money works for you.

- The best and most definitive measure of financial wealth is net worth. So in the game of financial wealth building, keep a scorecard. Track your net worth over time to see which investments have the greatest positive impact on financial wealth.

- No other investment has had such a consistent and powerful effect on the average person's net worth as real estate ownership. It's *attainable, appreciable, leverageable, rentable, improvable, deductible, depreciable, deferrable, stable,* and *livable*—real estate is a most "able" investment indeed!

■ Real estate investment thinking follows a process, a process that saves time, reduces risk, and keeps you focused. Simply put, you must know value to recognize opportunity, and you must find opportunities before you can do deals.

■ Investing requires Action. Successful investing requires the *right* Action. Observers, Speculators, and Collectors are not true Investors—Investors take action, minimize risk, and buy based on investment value; they are a breed apart.

■ Follow Nina's Rule and develop the financial posture of a Millionaire Real Estate Investor. Little decisions set the stage for big decisions, so build and be conscious of the right kind of mental habits, those that will lead to financial wealth.

BUY A MILLION

Under all is the land. Upon its wise utilization and widely allocated ownership depend the survival and growth of free institutions and of our civilization. . . .

From the Preamble to the National Association
of REALTORS® Code of Ethics

AMERICA'S FIRST MILLIONAIRE

It's a little-known fact that America's first millionaire was a real estate investor. A German immigrant and the son of a butcher, he was named John Jacob Astor. In the early 1800s Astor got rich trading in furs, tea, silk, and fine china, but that was not where his real fortune was made. Eventually he invested his trading profits in something that would prove to be even better: real estate. His most profitable investments were in New York City, and before long the man known as "Manhattan's Landlord" was widely acknowledged as the wealthiest person of his time. He had not only become America's first millionaire, he was now its first multimillionaire. Shortly before his death Astor reportedly said, "Could I begin life again, knowing what I now know, and had money to invest, I would buy every foot of land on the Island of Manhattan." Astor passed away in 1848, leaving over $20 million to his heirs.[1] This immigrant butcher's son not only was America's first millionaire and multimillionaire, he also was America's first Millionaire Real Estate Investor.

---

[1] $20 million may not seem like a great fortune now, but in 2005 dollars it would be the equivalent of about $458 billion.

I love the story of John Jacob Astor because it captures both the art and the science of investing. The art inspires us, and the science instructs us. The fact that an immigrant butcher's son could build America's first great fortune is the inspiration. The fact that he did it through real estate is the instruction. This is consistent with my experience. I believe there is an art and a science to achieving your highest potential in any endeavor, and building financial wealth is no exception. The art of real estate investing is about becoming inspired to overcome your MythUnderstandings and think like a Millionaire Real Estate Investor. The science is about learning and applying the models these successful investors use. Up to this point we've addressed the art. It's now time to address the science: the Five Models of the Millionaire Real Estate Investor.

> "The essence of investing is getting good value. And in real estate, that's much clearer than many other areas. It's common sense. It's intuitively obvious."
>
> Todd Tresidder
> Millionaire Real Estate Investor
> Reno, NV

THE FIVE MODELS OF THE MILLIONAIRE REAL ESTATE INVESTOR

Proven models replace the need for years of experience. In fact, it's a case of experience replacing experience—other people's experience replacing the need for yours. With proven models you get the benefit of learning from the mistakes of other people without having to make them yourself. You also get to build on their successes. Models inform your activities, help you get the most out of your efforts, and accelerate you toward your goals. Built with the clarity of hindsight, they answer the all-important question: "What's the best thing for me to do?"

In our research and experience five key models stand out in the world of real estate investing: the Net Worth Model, the Financial Model, the Network Model, the Lead Generation Model, and the Acquisition Model. These five models represent the "best practices" of our Millionaire Real Estate Investors. A few of those investors are experienced speakers and instructors with an amazing breadth of knowledge about investing, some are generalists who ably play whatever cards they have been dealt, and others are niche experts who are building their wealth through specialization. We took the best wisdom we could find in our research and built our models around the idea of a collective Millionaire Real Estate Investor who represents the best of them all. As a result, these five models accurately describe the most widely applicable and timeless intelligence on investing in real estate.

When we set out in search of these models, we were working from the idea that two heads are better than one. By interviewing over 100 Millionaire Real Estate Investors, we amplified that simple truth many times over. For us, then, a hundred heads are better than two. What we

The Five Models of the Millionaire Real Estate Investor

(1) **The Net Worth Model**—A three-part model for identifying the best investment vehicles for your goals; budgeting your money in order to have more to invest; and tracking your assets and liabilities to measure your progress towards financial wealth.

(2) **The Financial Model**—A model for understanding the three ways wealth is built through real estate ownership: cash flow, appreciation and debt pay down.

(3) **The Network Model**—A model for building and organizing a Network of investing relationships to mentor, advise and help you.

(4) **The Lead Generation Model**—A model for determining your real estate investment Criteria and then systematically prospecting and marketing for opportunities that match them.

(5) **The Acquisition Model**—A model for creating Terms that will minimize your risk and maximize your profits when making real estate investment deals.

Figure 1

were looking for was perspective drawn from a large enough group to gain collective wisdom.

Perspective is an amazing thing. The gift it gives us is better vision, the ability to see things as they are and as they are relative to everything else. Perspective gives you the full picture and clarity for your actions. It's our hope that the Five Models of the Millionaire Real Estate Investor will give you the best possible perspective and clarity to apply to your wealth-building career.

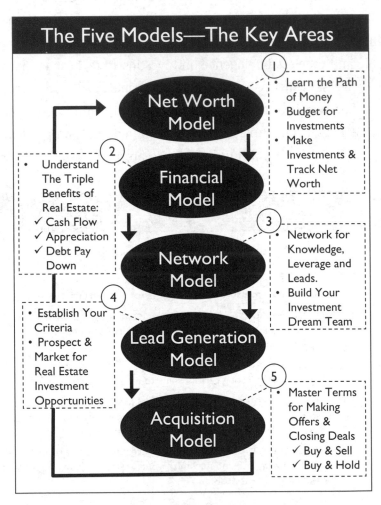

Figure 2

THE NET WORTH MODEL OF THE MILLIONAIRE REAL ESTATE INVESTOR

Your journey to becoming a Millionaire Real Estate Investor begins with your understanding of net worth and ends with your having a lot. Net worth is your worth—in *financial* terms. Practically speaking, it's what you own minus what you owe: your assets minus your liabilities. The Net Worth Model of the Millionaire Real Estate Investor is a proven plan of action for dramatically increasing your net worth over time. It's a simple three-step process:

1. Learn the path of money.
2. Manage a personal budget.
3. Track personal net worth.

For Millionaire Real Estate Investors these steps are sacred. Their knowledge of the path of money continuously reminds them that they must always make appropriate choices to maximize their returns. With this end in mind, they purposefully budget their money to maximize the amount they have to invest. Finally, after they've invested their money, they consistently measure and review the results they are getting to maximize their net worth.

My aunt and uncle were the perfect examples of how anyone can follow the Net Worth Model to financial freedom. Clem and Woody understood that their financial wealth probably wouldn't come from the modest income they earned from their barbershop in Galena Park, Texas. They worked hard doing what they loved, but they knew early on that they'd need income from additional sources to fulfill their financial goals. It was very clear to them that they would have to invest and let their money go to work for them. Therefore, they started budgeting aggressively, setting aside every dollar they could for investing. I grew up around Clem and Woody, and they cut the hair of everyone in my family each month. Even as a young child I was aware of their purposeful frugality, and that memory has stayed with me.

Thanks to years of thrifty living, planned savings, and careful investing, they were ready when an investor group from Austin, Texas, came to town to invite investors to buy land at the intersection of two major highways. The research showed that this was a terrific opportunity, really a no-brainer. My aunt and uncle didn't hesitate. They had the money, understood the opportunity, liked the terms, and invested in the deal. All their hard work and prudence soon paid off. A few short years later they were the richest people in my family—they had become millionaires. And because they kept investing, they went on to become multimillionaires.

PATH YOUR MONEY

My aunt and uncle realized that money has a path. Do you? Millionaires do—that's why they're millionaires. They know that when a dollar leaves their hands, it begins a critical journey down a path of choices and decisions, and they know that those decisions are the key to building their financial wealth. The map they follow and the guide they trust on this journey are called the Path of Money.

The Path of Money describes the ways money flows in and out of your life. You can think of it as a river with tributaries and distributaries, with inlets and outlets, with springs that feed it and sinkholes that drain it, getting channeled for strength or dispersed for weakness. Some rivers keep growing and flowing on their journey—some dry up.

The Path of Money works the same way. There are sources that start it down its path. Some are strong; others aren't. And the choices made as it flows will either feed and grow it, making it stronger, or drain and shrink it, making it weaker. Millionaires get this. They know that they have to direct their money purposefully. Some people let their money wander wherever it wants to go. Millionaires don't. They direct their money to the places that will bring them the greatest financial growth and the most substantial net worth.

Maybe it goes without saying, but to path money you first must have some. Equally obvious but just as important, the more money you path, the more you will have. Thus, getting as much money to path as you can is critical. There are only two ways to get money: You can earn money, and you can receive it. You can earn money from your work, and you can receive it from your assets. If you're like most people, while you'd like to have lots of assets that pay you money, you probably will have to start with the money you earn, and that will work fine. As long as you have some cash flow from one source or the other, you're in good shape. Why? Because income allows you to participate in the Path of Money game (see the chart below).

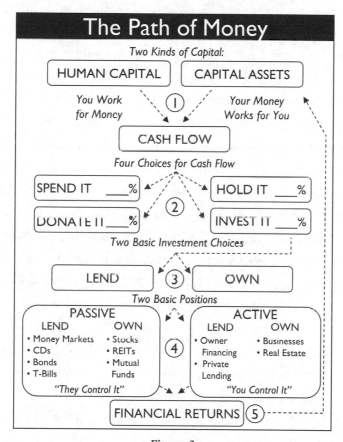

Figure 3

Here is how the game is played. Once you have cash, the path presents you with four basic choices:

1. You can consume it by spending it.
2. You can save it by holding it.
3. You can share it by donating it.
4. You can grow it by investing it.

Right here, at the very first crossroads, is where most people get knocked out of the game. They get knocked out so early that they believe they were never in it. What do they do with their money? They spend most of it, hold some of it, donate a little of it, and invest none of it. For them the game is over—the path ends right there. For millionaires, however, the game has just begun. They have a bigger end in mind and don't intend to be stopped here. Through intentional budgeting they make sure they always have ample money to invest. This enables them to stay in the game and move farther down the path.

This is where the game starts getting exciting. When you have money to invest, you have another choice—to loan or to own. You can lend your money to others for a predetermined rate of return, or you can buy an asset that could go up in value, pay you cash flow, or both. This is an interesting place in the path. To proceed wisely you must determine which season of your financial life you are in. Do you want to accumulate more wealth, or do you want to protect the wealth you already have? If you are in the wealth accumulation season of your life, you probably want to invest to own. If you are in the wealth protection season, you most likely want to invest to lend. With each of these choices there are two basic positions: You can lend or own passively, or you can lend or own actively. It's a critical set of decisions that can keep your money safe or make it soar.

Millionaires know that passive lending is mainly a money preservation strategy. The rates of return they can get from passive lending are comparatively low, because they usually are guaranteed and most of the borrowers will turn around and relend the money. When factored for inflation, passive lending usually does not lead to a significant increase in net worth.

Millionaires know that active lending, in which they lend their money directly to businesses or individuals, can bring them higher rates of return than passive lending can. However, it will require them to be able to lend significant amounts of capital and that they typically will not get the benefit of appreciation. Institutions and mature individual investors are usually best suited to take this path.

Asset ownership is on the other side of the path, and this is where big wealth is built. Millionaires know this and place most of their investment dollars here, buying and owning assets that can appreciate and give them cash flow. But when it comes to ownership, they know that the passive options (stocks for businesses and real estate investment trusts for real estate) usually don't build great wealth without insider positioning or great wealth having been invested. As a result they usually head straight for active investing in businesses or real estate. Millionaire Real Estate Investors choose real estate. Why? Because they like the big upside, the small downside, and the personal control it offers.

Here is the best news for investors on the Path of Money. The path never has to end. As money flows from your investments, you'll have more money to path—to reinvest and build more wealth. Millionaires know that at this point the Path of Money can become a most rewarding endless loop. If you want to become a Millionaire Real Estate Investor, learn the Path of Money game and play it.

BUDGET YOUR EXPENSES

Once you learn the Path of Money, get on it and stay on it. For most people this is easier said than done. Because they have an undisciplined approach to spending, they usually have more month left at the end of their money. This is a problem. People can't progress along the path if they spend all their income. To achieve your financial goals, you have to have some money left over at the end of every month. There has to be something left over to invest, and the best way to assure this is to budget for it.

We can thank the late nineteenth-century economist Thorstein Veblen for coining the phrase "conspicuous consumption." His study, *The Theory of the Leisure Class*, profiled a generation of newly rich Americans who abandoned the modesty of their Puritan forebearers in favor of an ostentatious display of wealth. Veblen described a kind of consumption "snowball effect" that ensues when individuals base their self-esteem on the possession of material goods: "As fast as a person makes new acquisitions, and becomes accustomed to the new standard of wealth, the new standard forthwith ceases to afford appreciably greater satisfaction than the earlier standard did."

> *"We knew we'd spend the money we were making if we didn't start doing something with it. So we started buying houses 20 percent down, and financing them over 10- or 15-year payouts. We had 15 percent automatically deducted from our checks, and put into a money market account. When we had enough money, we would buy another house."*
>
> Jimmy and Linda McKissack
> Millionaire Real Estate Investors
> Highland Village, TX

In other words, new stuff quickly becomes old stuff, creating the need for more new stuff . . . It's the nineteenth-century version of "keeping up with the Joneses." They were trapped in the financially self-destructive cycle where the spending never ends but the joy of it does.

Not a whole lot has changed. We still live in a consuming society—unrestrained and unbudgeted. Unlike the days of Veblen, we don't even need to *have* cash to spend it. Credit comes easy, and increasingly, people are willing to mortgage their financial future for the trappings of the rich today. To put this in perspective, a 2003 report by the Federal Reserve Board showed that while the median household income was just over

$43,000, those households carried almost $18,700 in consumer debt. That's high-interest, unsecured debt equaling 43 percent of their annual income. That means that even if they set aside 10 percent of their annual income to pay off that debt, it could take more than seven years to do so. It's a disturbing trend that appears to be getting worse. Instead of investing to finance their future, more and more people are spending on credit to finance their lifestyle. The hard truth is this: If you have to finance your lifestyle—you can't afford it.

Millionaire Real Estate Investors understand the temptation to live for today, but because they follow the Net Worth Model, they successfully and consistently keep their focus on their financial future. Through budgeting and thrift they manage to live a comfortable lifestyle while investing a sizable percentage of their disposable income. After all, a little less of today could mean a whole lot more of tomorrow.

Personal budgeting works. I do it, the Millionaire Real Estate Investors we interviewed do it, and you must do it. It is the only way wealth building gets launched and maintained.

Your ability to budget successfully is directly related to your ability to differentiate between discretionary spending and required spending. It's the priceless ability to distinguish between wants and needs. They are not the same. Investors can separate the two. There is no confusion; their required spending reflects their actual needs. Consumers don't have this financial clarity; their required spending reflects both their wants and their needs. The net result is that investors have money to invest and consumers don't.

The next four charts tell the story. The first two (Figures 4 and 5) illustrate the difference between consumers and investors in terms of the way they look at required spending. The third (Figure 6) shows how investors find money to invest, and the fourth (Figure 7) shows why millionaires are millionaires.

Consumers look at their monthly expenses and immediately come to the conclusion that they can't afford to invest. After all, by the time

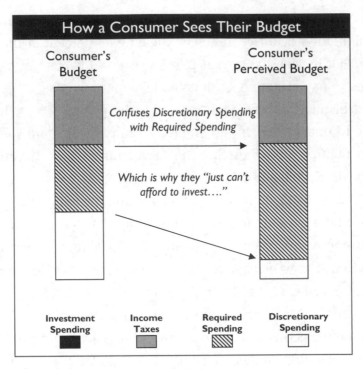

Figure 4

they've paid for their *necessities,* there doesn't seem to be anything left over for investing. Consumers often complain that they never have enough income to cover their needs when really *it's their spending, not their income,* that's the problem. In our experience the number one barrier to investing in real estate is a perceived lack of investment capital rather than a real one.

Investors, by contrast, see it as it really is. They take an honest look at their expenses and separate the discretionary from the required. Investors know that their daily, weekly, and monthly spending decisions can add up to a lot, and they are willing to make small sacrifices today in exchange for big rewards down the road. In the end investors see investment spending as required spending. That's why they always have money to invest.

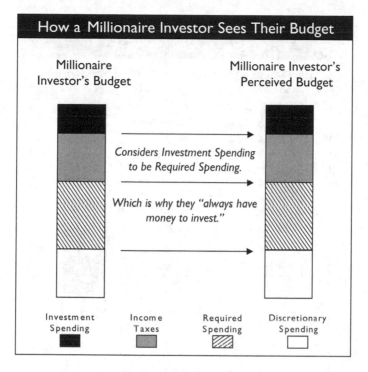

How a Millionaire Investor Sees Their Budget

Millionaire
Investor's Budget

Millionaire Investor's
Perceived Budget

*Considers Investment Spending
to be Required Spending.*

*Which is why they "always have
money to invest."*

Investment
Spending

Income
Taxes

Required
Spending

Discretionary
Spending

Figure 5

Investors want to invest and take every opportunity to set aside the money to do so. This is where the phrase "pay yourself first" comes from. They take investing so seriously that they start setting aside investment funds the moment money comes into their possession. Millionaire Real Estate Investors take this concept a step further: They pay themselves first, second, and last. They set aside money to invest before taxes, after taxes, and after all spending. Just like the legendary investor Sir John Templeton, who when he was young lived off just 50 percent of his income so that he could invest the rest, millionaires play a game to see how much money they can save for investing everywhere they can. Sacrifice can be fun when you connect it to a reward.

Make no mistake about it. Just as there are big differences between a consumer and an investor, there are big differences between an investor

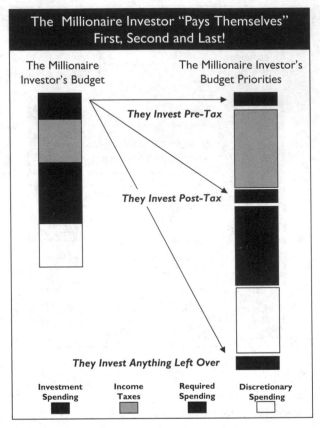

The Millionaire Investor "Pays Themselves" First, Second and Last!

| The Millionaire Investor's Budget | The Millionaire Investor's Budget Priorities |

They Invest Pre-Tax

They Invest Post-Tax

They Invest Anything Left Over

| Investment Spending | Income Taxes | Required Spending | Discretionary Spending |

Figure 6

and a millionaire investor. One of the biggest differences is the amount of money a person continually sets aside for investing. Millionaires believe in the Net Worth Model and budget to find more money to invest—a lot more.

Here's a simple and effective way to keep a personal budget and start behaving like a Millionaire Real Estate Investor: Using the Sample Personal Budget[2] form we've provided (see Figure 8 on page 138), start with your monthly income. Ideally, you're getting both earned income

---

[2] In Appendix A we've provided a full-size form as well as a worksheet for completing it. Look for downloadable forms on www.KellerINK.com.

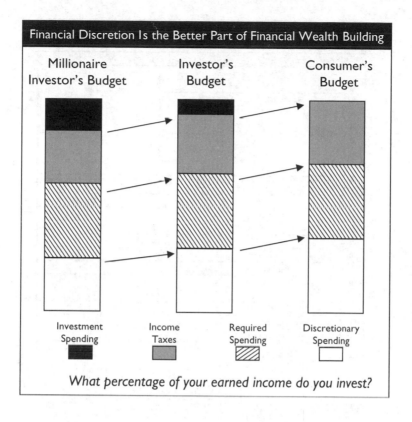

Figure 7

from your work and unearned income from your investments. (We separate the two because your goal will be to increase your monthly unearned income over time.) Total the two and you have your Gross Monthly Income.

Next, decide how much you will tithe to your charities or church, save for security and reserves, invest for the future, and hold back for taxes. What's left is your Net Spendable Income. The idea is to pay yourself first by taking care of your Big Goals up front. Therefore, charity, security, and investing always come first. Taxes, of course, also come first because it's the law.

Sample Personal Budget Worksheet

Monthly Income

(1)	Earned Income	$
(2)	Unearned Income	$
	Gross Monthly Income	$
(1)	Tithe ____%	$
(2)	Save ____%	$
(3)	Invest ____%	$
(4)	Tax ____%	$
	Net Spendable Income	$

Expenses

		Current	Required	Discretionary
(5)	Housing ____%	$	$	$
(6)	Food ____%	$	$	$
(7)	Automobile ____%	$	$	$
(8)	Insurance ____%	$	$	$
(9)	Entertainment ____%	$	$	$
(10)	Clothing ____%	$	$	$
(11)	Medical ____%	$	$	$
(12)	Debt Service ____%	$	$	$
(13)	School/Child Care ____%	$	$	$
(14)	Travel/Vacation ____%	$	$	$
(15)	Misc. ____%	$	$	$
	Total Current Expenses	$		
	Total Required Expenses	$		
	Total Discretionary Expenses	$		

Budget Analysis

Net Spendable Income	$
Less Required Expenses	$
Total Surplus/Deficit	$

Figure 8

Now it's time to figure out where your Net Spendable Income goes each month—your expenses. Using the Sample Personal Budget Work-sheet[3] (see the chart above), sort through your monthly bills and tally how much you spend on big expenses (housing, food, etc.) each month. Use the far left column. Once you get a grasp of your Current Expenses, it will take very little time to update this form periodically as your income and expenses change. This is where your goals meet your resolve, where you must hold yourself accountable to live within your prescribed means.

---

[3] A full-size version of the Sample Personal Budget Worksheet and subworksheets for various line items are provided in Appendix A.

You'll notice that we've added two extra columns (labeled "Required" and "Discretionary") to the Expenses section of the worksheet. Take a look at your actual spending and ask yourself whether a percentage of

those expenses might actually be discretionary. For example, if a monthly television bill (under "Housing") is $50, you might decide that the $35 basic monthly service is all you really need and free up $15 a month in discretionary income. We hope you'll be honest enough to admit that you could get by (and get by comfortably) spending less in one or more of these categories. None of us can be disciplined all the time. We all splurge a little on the things we love, and that's okay. What's not okay is to splurge unconsciously in all these areas all the time. This is where your personal resolve to meet your financial goals really comes into play. You must hold yourself accountable to live within your prescribed means—the amount of money you allow yourself to spend. It's the ongoing battle of budgeting for financial wealth. It's about always making sure you have money to invest.

Finally, at the bottom of the worksheet is your Budget Analysis, where you subtract Required Expenses from Net Spendable Income to arrive at any surplus or deficit in your monthly budget. If you show a deficit, you need to spend more time analyzing your required and discretionary spending priorities. A surplus is generally good news—that's money you can use for whatever you want.

Since high school I've kept a personal budget and tried to keep it as simple and uncomplicated as possible. From the beginning I always set my tithing, saving, and investing goals and knew what percentage of my income I planned to dedicate to each one. I also had a good grip on my monthly expenses and knew about how much was required to cover the necessities. When Mary and I got married, that knowledge allowed me to take our paychecks and efficiently divide them among three bank accounts. One was my investing, saving, and tithing account, into which a predetermined amount was deposited whenever we were paid. I then would transfer to my regular checking account enough to cover our required expenses. Everything that was left over, our surplus, went into Mary's bank account to handle the unplanned expenses and also for our fun, disposable income.

But a funny thing started happening. Each month Mary would announce that she'd saved an additional amount of money from her account that we could reinvest. Even though I told her that money was our fun money—it was meant to be spent—a lifetime of thrifty living was too hard to shake. We should all be like Mary.

Partitioning one's money into different accounts according to a predetermined budget works as a kind of fail-safe or alarm. Any time your actual spending exceeds your budget, you have to transfer money consciously from your reserves to cover it. It's about awareness. It's about adding an

---

Tip: Use Nina's Rule to Control Your Credit Card Spending

Next time you visit your bank, ask for a few of the protective sleeves they provide for ATM cards. Next, take a marker and write "I'm an Investor" on one side and "Remember Nina's Rule" on the other. Then put all the plastic you carry in one of these sleeves.

The idea is to make you pause and think before you spend. It's about your financial posture and credit card debt is a serious problem for would-be investors. Here's the facts:

• On average, consumers spend 112% more on a credit card purchase than when using cash. (The Center for a New American Dream)
• Over 40% of US families spend more than they earn. (Federal Reserve Board)
• An estimated 55%-60% of Americans carry credit card balances. (Massachusetts Public Interest Research Group)
• The average household with a credit card balance carries revolving debt of nearly $10,000. (Federal Reserve Board)

Figure 9

The Millionaire Real Estate Investor

extra step in the process to make you reconsider your spending decisions. When you have to think about it, you may think better about it.

The good news is that once you have a handle on this process, you don't have to think so much about your daily spending unless you find you're running a deficit in one of your accounts. All the money that ends up in your surplus account is by definition discretionary. That money is for fun. Although many of our Millionaire Real Estate Investors probably would say, "Investing that money is fun," ultimately, the choice is yours.

TRACK YOUR WORTH

The final step in the Net Worth Model of the Millionaire Real Estate Investor is to keep a personal balance sheet, a worksheet for tracking your net worth. The personal balance sheet is probably the greatest gift Michael gave me in our financial wealth-building breakfasts. He taught me to focus on my net worth and track it over time. Michael pointed out that businesses have three essential financial documents that are absent in most homes: a general ledger to record the details of business expenses, an income statement or profit and loss statement (P&L) for tracking income and expenses, and a balance sheet for a snapshot of the net worth of the business at a given time.

Michael didn't advocate keeping a general ledger for my household expenses. The general ledger is where a business records all its expenses in detail. For an individual, a general ledger would involve the tedious tracking of all his or her monthly receipts. (That's what most people think of when they think of budgeting and what I like to avoid.) The two documents Michael did advocate were the P&L and the balance sheet. A household P&L statement is just another name for a personal budget that tracks your income and expenses to show a net surplus or deficit or, in the case of a business, a profit or loss. At the time I was meeting with Michael I had a simple budget and adhered to it pretty well. Therefore, our focus was primarily on the personal balance sheet.

Using a bank loan application form as our guide, we crafted a one-page worksheet for calculating my net worth. We listed all my assets (stocks, real estate, businesses, collectibles, etc), subtracted my liabilities (the total debt I owed on those items), and calculated my net worth. That improvised worksheet went on to become the focus of our later meetings and ultimately a tool to which I credit a great deal of my current financial wealth. Michael and I started each breakfast by going over my updated personal

Sample Personal Balance Sheet

	January 1, Last Year	January 1, This Year	Annual % Increase	Current Total	YTD% Increase
ASSETS					
Retirement Accounts	$7,500.00	$8,250.00	10.0%	$9,000.00	9.1%
Equity Investments					
Businesses Private	$0.00	$0.00	NA	$0.00	NA
Businesses Public					
Stocks	$5,000.00	$5,357.00	7.1%	$5,897.00	10.1%
Bonds	$0.00	$0.00	NA	$0.00	NA
Annuities	$0.00	$0.00	NA	$0.00	NA
Total Equity Investments	$5,000.00	$5,357.00	7.1%	$5,897.00	10.1%
Cash/Savings	$2,500.00	$3,000.00	20.0%	$2,750.00	-8.3%
Insurance	$100,000.00	$100,000.00	0.0%	$100,000.00	0.0%
Collectibles	$0.00	$0.00	NA	$0.00	NA
Personal Property	$500.00	$500.00	0.0%	$525.00	5.0%
Real Estate Personal	$155,000.00	$163,000.00	5.2%	$171,500.00	5.2%
Real Estate Investments	$71,400.00	$83,500.00	16.9%	$98,120.00	17.5%
Notes Receivable	$0.00	$0.00	NA	$0.00	NA
Other Assets	$0.00	$0.00	NA	$0.00	NA
TOTAL ASSETS	$341,900.00	$363,607.00	6.3%	$387,792.00	6.7%
LIABILITIES					
Car Loans	($9,000.00)	($4,200.00)	-53.3%	($3,000.00)	-28.6%
Credit Card Debt	($2,500.00)	($3,250.00)	30.0%	($2,750.00)	-15.4%
Mortgage Debt	($181,120.00)	($178,500.00)	-1.4%	($176,020.00)	-1.4%
School Loans	($15,000.00)	($12,000.00)	-20.0%	($10,500.00)	-12.5%
Other Debt	$0.00	$0.00	NA	$0.00	NA
TOTAL LIABILITIES	($207,620.00)	($197,950.00)	-4.7%	($192,270.00)	-2.9%
NET WORTH	$134,280.00	$165,657.00	23.4%	$195,522.00	18.0%
ANNUAL CASH FLOW (EARNED)	$43,000.00	$45,000.00	4.7%	$46,500.00	3.3%
ANNUAL CASH FLOW (UNEARNED)	$1,200.00	$1,260.00	5.0%	$1,480.00	17.5%

Figure 10

balance sheet, and then Michael would underline the net worth total and ask the question: "Now, how can you make that grow?"

That document has evolved over the years, and I still use it. In fact, I keep a copy of my personal balance sheet with me at all times and update it every week. And I always ask that same question: "How can I make this grow?" It was by asking and answering that question over time that I began to get a real understanding of how wealth is built, and that understanding had a massive impact on my financial well-being. It gave me a great perspective on my evolving finances. Over the years I always knew exactly how far I'd progressed toward my financial wealth goals. I would look back at my records and calculate my year-over-year progress, and by updating the balance sheet regularly I would track year-to-date progress. All this added up to an awareness of where I was in relation to my financial goals, how fast I was getting there, and how far I still needed to go.

The Sample Personal Balance Sheet[4] provided on the next page can be completed on a quarterly, monthly, or even weekly basis. I think that monthly is the minimum frequency to keep a handle on your finances and that most individuals would benefit greatly from reviewing their finances, as I do, on a weekly basis.

Any time you make a major investment, you should update your balance sheet. It was by doing this that I began to understand the impact different choices I made with my money had on my net worth. Over time and with careful, consistent analysis, you'll see a familiar path emerge—the Path of Money.

Thus, with the Net Worth Model of the Millionaire Real Estate Investor, you begin with the Path of Money, and you end there as well. The insight gained from the Path of Money tends to lead investors to manage their budgets to maximize their investment dollars systematically. They then track their investments over time, using their balance sheets to determine

---

[4] In Appendix B we've provided a full-sized blank form. Look for downloadable worksheets on www.KellerINK.com.

Sample Personal Balance Sheet

	January 1, Last Year	January 1, This Year	Annual % Increase	Current Total	YTD% Increase
ASSETS					
Retirement Accounts	$	$	%	$	%
Equity Investments					
Businesses Private	$	$	%	$	%
Businesses Public					
Stocks	$	$	%	$	%
Bonds	$	$	%	$	%
Annuities	$	$	%	$	%
Total Equity Investments	$	$	%	$	%
Cash/Savings	$	$	%	$	%
Insurance	$	$	%	$	%
Collectibles	$	$	%	$	%
Personal Property	$	$	%	$	%
Real Estate Personal	$	$	%	$	%
Real Estate Investments	$	$	%	$	%
Notes Receivable	$	$	%	$	%
Other Assets	$	$	%	$	%
TOTAL ASSETS	$	$	%	$	%
LIABILITIES					
Car Loans	$	$	%	$	%
Credit Card Debt	$	$	%	$	%
Mortgage Debt	$	$	%	$	%
School Loans	$	$	%	$	%
Other Debt	$	$	%	$	%
TOTAL LIABILITIES	$	$	%	$	%
NET WORTH	$	$	%	$	%
ANNUAL CASH FLOW (EARNED)	$	$	%	$	%
ANNUAL CASH FLOW (UNEARNED)	$	$	%	$	%

Figure 11

how each investment affects their net worth. Finally, through their review and analysis of the budget sheet and investment performance, their personal Path of Money evolves and becomes clearer and clearer.

THE FINANCIAL MODEL OF THE MILLIONAIRE REAL ESTATE INVESTOR

There are two ways to build financial wealth by investing in real estate. I know that sounds way too simple, but it's true: There are just two. Within those two are a vast array of variations that can give the appearance of massive complexity, and by using those various options you can make real estate investing as complex as you want. Eventually most millionaires do, but not in the beginning. They always start with the basics and build from there. When you truly understand the two basic drivers of financial wealth, you begin to see the fundamental opportunities they present and know how to take advantage of them. If you are like me or any of our Millionaire Real Estate Investors, this is when you really get excited. That's the power of this financial model—it both guides you and motivates you.

The two ways to make money in real estate investing, the two drivers of financial wealth, are Equity Buildup and Cash Flow Growth. They can happen

> *"I invest in real estate to create cash flow, to build equity and to store wealth."*
>
> Todd Tresidder
> Millionaire Real Estate Investor
> Reno, NV

simultaneously, and so you can benefit from both at the same time. Equity Buildup increases your net worth in your real estate assets, while Cash Flow Growth provides a stream of unearned income. You can live on that income or reinvest it by paying down your debt or acquiring more real estate. If you keep your money in play by reinvesting the Cash Flow (my recommendation), you are accelerating your Equity Buildup and therefore the growth of your personal net worth. Remember, your net worth is the measure of your success—your score in the game of financial wealth building.

EQUITY BUILDUP

When you look at Equity Buildup closely (see the chart on the following page), you discover that it comes from two factors: price appreciation and debt paydown. If you buy it right (which we will clarify in the section on the Acquisition Model), your real estate investment will begin with a margin of equity right away. This means that your initial down payment (Investment) plus the mortgage loan you incur (Debt), when added together, will still be less than the price you could sell the property for (Market Value). That difference is your equity in the property.

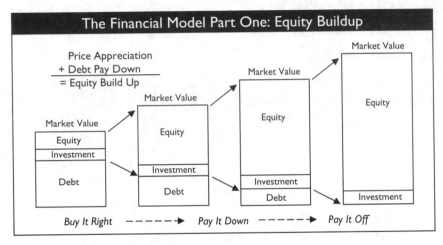

Figure 12

> *"Once I got really clear on the numbers in real estate, I realized that it was one of the best games in the world for building wealth."*
>
> Todd Tresidder
> Millionaire Real Estate Investor
> Reno, NV

Over time, as you rent the property, the two natural forces of price appreciation and debt paydown work together to increase your equity. Obviously, if the market value increases, your equity in the property goes up, but it also goes up because you are paying down the debt through the mortgage. Each monthly payment you make reduces the amount you owe on the loan. Thus, as the mortgage debt decreases over the term of the loan (30 years, 15 years, etc.), your equity increases consistently.

Let's take a real-life look at this process. If you had invested in a residential income property in 1988[5] at the then median home price of approximately $90,000, it would, 15 years later, in 2003, have been worth almost $170,000 (see the chart below). Price appreciation would have gained you $81,000 in equity. But that is only a part of the Equity Buildup picture. You also would have been paying off the mortgage and thereby reducing your debt.

This calculation of debt paydown requires some carefully considered assumptions. First, it assumes that you purchased the property at 20 percent below market value ($90,000 − 20 percent = $72,000); second, it

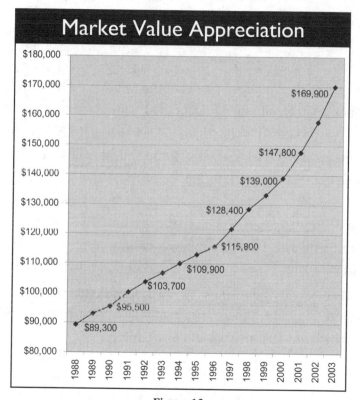

Figure 13

assumes that you made a 20 percent down payment (20 percent × $72,000 = $14,400). This means you would have gotten a mortgage loan of $57,600 ($72,000 − $14,400 = $57,600). As you make your monthly loan payments, covered by the rental income from your tenants, you are paying off some portion of the loan's remaining balance and therefore reducing your debt on the property. As you reduce the debt, you increase your equity.

In this real-life example, with a loan of $57,600 and a typical 30-year mortgage, you would have, during those 15 years, reduced the loan debt to $43,334 and therefore gained another $14,266 in equity buildup. The shorter the length of the loan is, the faster you will achieve debt paydown. In the example we are using, a 15-year mortgage would have reduced the debt to $0 and thereby increased the equity by the full $57,600 amount of the loan.

What makes the Financial Model of the Millionaire Real Estate Investor so compelling is the combined impact of all these factors. This is where the power of real estate to build financial wealth is fully revealed. In the investment we have analyzed, this is how it all adds up: Your $14,400 investment in 1988 turned into equity of more than $128,506 in just 15 years. This would be like putting your $14,400 in a bank account paying an annual compounded interest rate of 15.7 percent. If you had used a 15-year mortgage instead of a 30-year mortgage, your equity would have grown to more than $171,840. That's like an annual compounded interest rate of 17.9 percent. In either case this is a significant return on investment and not one you will find at a bank. And, those remarkable returns don't reflect what happens when you factor for Cash Flow Growth.

CASH FLOW GROWTH

As good as all this Equity Buildup is (and it is very good and very real to a Millionaire Real Estate Investor), it is not the whole story. There is the added benefit of Cash Flow Growth to consider (see Figure 14). Net

Cash Flow is achieved from a real estate investment when the rental income you receive is more than the costs you incur. The costs include your expenses, an allowance for vacancy, and debt service (the mortgage payment on the property). All this will be outlined in more detail in the section on the Acquisition Model.

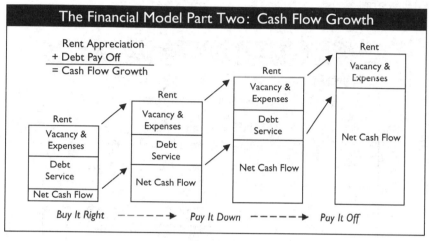

Figure 14

For now let's just say that if you buy it right, finance it wisely, and control your expenses, you can achieve a positive Net Cash Flow. As rents appreciate over time (historically, they increase at about the same rate as price appreciation), the cash flow will grow. Once the loan is paid off, the Net Cash Flow grows dramatically because your monthly mortgage loan payment goes away.

In our example of the $90,000 rental property purchased in 1988, we realistically could have received over the 15 years a total Net Cash Flow between $18,000 (if we had a 15-year mortgage) and $34,000 (using a 30-year mortgage). In 2004, our sixteenth year of ownership, the annual Net Cash Flow from the property would be about

> *"If I'm not going to make money, I won't buy it."*
>
> Jim Castagnari
> Millionaire Real Estate Investor
> Pittsburgh, PA

$4,600 with the 30-year mortgage. In the case of the 15-year loan, since it would be paid off, our annual Net Cash Flow would jump to over $9,400.

Let's add it all up. Beginning with an investment of only $14,400, the following chart reveals the financial outcomes we could have achieved in just 15 years.

Financial Model: Your Total Return

Example Property:
- Asking Price: $90,000 in 1988
- Discount: 20% ($18,000)
- Purchase Price: $72,000
- Down Payment: 20% ($14,400)
- Mortgage Loan Amount: 80% ($57,600)

	30-Year Mortgage	15-Year Mortgage
Total (1988-2004) Equity Buildup	$128,506	$171,840
Total (1988-2004) Net Cash Flow	$34,545	$18,327
Total Return	$163,051	$190,167
Annual Compounded Rate of Return	17.6%	18.8%

Figure 15

You would have increased your financial net worth by a significant amount in just 15 years with only one investment in real estate. What if you did more than one? What if you applied the power of this financial model many times? What if you made several real estate investments over the course of 15 or 20 years or more? You would become a millionaire—a Millionaire Real Estate Investor. That's the point. It's what the numbers show. It's what Millionaire Real Estate Investors know. It's where you want to go.

YOUR FINANCIAL JOURNEY

Let's see how the numbers play out. What happens when you make multiple real estate investments over a number of years? The clearest way to view this is to follow the path of a Millionaire Real Estate Investor who began to invest some years ago and then see what would have happened to those investments. Let's begin in 1983, track the progress over 20 years, and watch the numbers grow—both Equity Buildup and Cash Flow Growth.

This multiyear look at the Financial Model will tell a story about the journey of someone who began his or her real estate investing in 1983. For the sake of the story let's say that person was *you*. With you as our model real estate investor, we will observe what you did over 20 years and how it turned out. We're going to discover how you were able to turn an initial investment of $11,248 into an equity position of over $1.6 million and an annual net cash flow of over $50,000. How did you do this from 1983 to 2002? It is an intriguing and revealing story—a realistic and exciting journey of financial wealth building. It is the story of becoming a Millionaire Real Estate Investor.

It all began when you followed the wise advice of your mentor to "buy it right." With that advice as your guide, each of the 15 investments you made during those 20 years was in the "middle of the market," at about the median home price, purchased at 20 percent below market value.[6] Your first investment back in 1983 was at the U.S. median home price of $70,300. You paid $56,240 for the property, invested $11,248 (20 percent) as the down payment, and financed the remaining $44,992 with a 30-year mortgage loan. That became your fundamental formula—median price, 20 percent discount, 20 percent down, and a 30-year loan. You stayed true to that proven formula for the next 20 years. You knew that if

---

[6] This concept of "buy it right" will be explored in detail in the section on the Acquisition Model. Buying in the "middle of the market" is addressed in the discussion of Criteria in the section on the Lead Generation Model.

real estate prices and rents appreciated at an average of about 5 percent a year over the long haul and that if you used the best available financing (with a historical average interest rate of about 7.4 percent) and held your expenses to about 40 percent of your rents, your equity would build and so would your net cash flow. In fact, you predicted that your very first investment property would, after 20 years, have a market value of over $180,000 and your equity in the property would be more than $160,000. And you were right—that is in fact what happened.

But for you that was only the beginning. Your mentor told you about the compounding power of making several real estate investments over time. He said it would multiply both your net worth and your passive income exponentially. Therefore, you continued to invest in real estate carefully but consistently. Being realistic and needing time to accumulate some savings, you made your second investment two years later in 1985. The median price had risen to $75,500, and using your formula of a 20 percent discount and 20 percent down, you acquired the property with a down payment of $12,080 and financed $48,320 with another 30-year loan.

> "The basic plan is to start out small, and then upgrade. Start out by owning a house, and then another one, and then another one. When you have 10, you're in great shape. You can start paying them off and increasing your cash flow. Then you can start exchanging them into multi-family, and increase the cash flow even more. And then the problem you start to have is where to put all the money that comes in."
>
> Rische Beeson
> Millionaire Real Estate Investor
> Lubbock, TX

You continued implementing your real estate investment strategy by patiently saving some of your earned income and systematically searching for the next opportunity. You made it your goal to invest in another residential income property every two years, buying your third property in 1987, your fourth in 1989, and your fifth in 1991. Thus, in just 10 years you owned five properties. You had invested

$67,960 of your savings in five houses now worth over $537,000, and your equity had built up to over $280,000. Your net annual cash flow already exceeded $6,800—more than half of what you invested in your first house. You knew you could apply that cash flow toward your next acquisition. In fact, since you had accumulated over $33,297 in net cash flow over the first 10 years, you could now, if you chose, make *all* your future annual purchases from that accumulated cash flow. That accumulated money, when added to your ongoing annual cash flow, would more than cover all your future down payments![7]

Now your story really begins to get exciting. With your strong equity position and increasing annual cash flow, you began in 1993 to acquire an investment property each year for the next 10 years. Therefore, by the end of 2002, your twentieth full year as a real estate investor, you owned 15 residential income properties. They have a combined market value of over $2.5 million, and you have equity buildup of over $1.6 million. You have become a Millionaire Real Estate Investor with just 15 "buy it right" acquisitions in only 20 years. In fact, you actually became a net worth real estate millionaire three years before that, in 1999, with the 12 properties you owned then.

In addition to your $1.6 million in equity at the end of 2002, you would have earned more than $303,000 in accumulated cash flow. All that cash flow could have been used to make your ongoing real estate investments or to pay down your loans, converting the cash flow directly to equity. As you look back on your last 20 years (see Figure 16, below[8]), you realize that you have turned your total $271,800 of down

---

[7] If you look at year 11 (1993) in Figure 16, you will see that your down payment would have been $17,088 and you would have had $33,927 in accumulated cash flow to cover it. This would leave you with $16,209, and when that was added to the next year's annual cash flow of $10,316, you would have $26,525 to apply toward the next down payment of $17,584. This process continues, and your down payments in this example never exceed your accumulated cash flows.

[8] It should be noted that our Multiyear Financial Model does not factor in the tax benefits of these properties (depreciation) or the tax liabilities of the income (income taxes).

Multi-Year Financial Model Detailed Overview: 15 Properties Over 25 Years

Year	Median Price	Purchase Price	Down Payment	Total Investment	Total MV	30-Yr Loan Cum. Equity	30-Yr Loan Annual CF	30 -Yr Loan Cum. CF	30-Yr Loan Total ROI
1983	$70,300	$56,240	$11,248	$11,248	$73,816	$29,244	$300	$300	$29,545
1984				$11,248	$77,509	$33,390	$503	$803	$34,193
1985	$75,500	$60,400	$12,080	$23,328	$160,663	$69,164	$1,037	$1,840	$71,004
1986				$23,328	$168,702	$78,214	$1,478	$3,318	$81,532
1987	$85,600	$68,480	$13,696	$37,024	$267,027	$123,355	$2,306	$5,624	$128,979
1988				$37,024	$280,390	$138,443	$3,038	$8,662	$147,105
1989	$93,100	$74,480	$14,896	$51,920	$392,180	$193,063	$4,205	$12,867	$205,930
1990				$51,920	$411,809	$215,291	$5,280	$18,147	$233,438
1991	$100,300	$80,240	$16,048	$67,968	$537,740	$280,429	$6,838	$24,985	$305,413
1992				$67,968	$564,657	$311,006	$8,312	$33,297	$344,303
1993	$106,800	$85,440	$17,088	$85,056	$705,066	$387,643	$10,316	$43,613	$431,256
1994	$109,900	$87,920	$17,584	$102,640	$855,757	$473,588	$12,719	$56,332	$529,920
1995	$113,100	$90,480	$18,096	$120,736	$1,017,351	$569,494	$15,548	$71,881	$641,375
1996	$115,800	$92,640	$18,528	$139,264	$1,189,868	$675,803	$18,832	$90,713	$766,516
1997	$121,800	$97,440	$19,488	$158,752	$1,377,322	$794,544	$22,615	$113,327	$907,871
1998	$128,400	$102,720	$20,544	$179,296	$1,581,089	$926,853	$26,939	$140,266	$1,067,119
1999	$133,300	$106,640	$21,328	$200,624	$1,800,201	$1,072,993	$31,843	$172,109	$1,245,102
2000	$139,000	$111,200	$22,240	$222,864	$2,036,267	$1,234,218	$37,372	$209,481	$1,443,699
2001	$147,800	$118,240	$23,648	$246,512	$2,293,391	$1,412,838	$43,586	$253,067	$1,665,905
2002	$158,100	$126,480	$25,296	$271,808	$2,574,200	$1,610,735	$50,548	$303,616	$1,914,351
2003				$271,808	$2,703,060	$1,759,271	$57,606	$361,222	$2,120,493
2004				$271,808	$2,838,378	$1,915,778	$65,016	$426,238	$2,342,016
2005				$271,808	$2,980,477	$2,080,695	$72,797	$499,035	$2,579,729
2006				$271,808	$3,129,696	$2,254,486	$80,967	$580,001	$2,834,487
2007				$271,808	$3,286,391	$2,437,642	$89,545	$669,547	$3,107,189

Figure 16

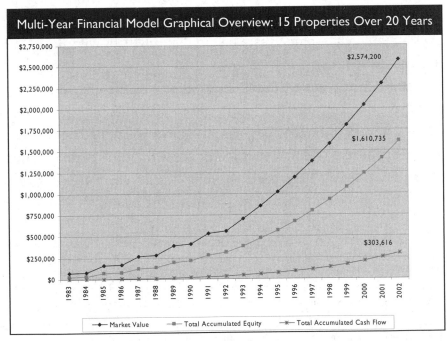

Figure 17

The Millionaire Real Estate Investor

payments into a return on investment (Equity Buildup plus accumulated Cash Flow) of more than $1.9 million. If you did no more investing over the next five years, those 15 properties would be worth nearly $3.3 million and your equity would exceed $2.4 million. As an added bonus, your annual net cash flow would be almost $90,000. Not bad: 25 years, 15 properties, $2.4 million net worth, and $90,000 annual cash flow.

Through this story you have experienced the power of the Millionaire Real Estate Investor's Financial Model. It is straightforward and real. In fact, we discovered an interesting truth in researching the actual financial positions of the more than 100 Millionaire Real Estate Investors we interviewed for this book. Their basic (median) financial numbers are strikingly similar to those we have just seen in the 20-year Financial Model (see the chart below).

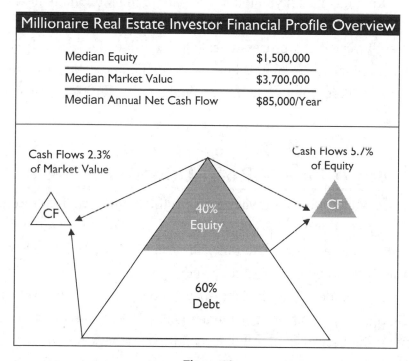

Figure 18

As you can see, these investors have a median market value of $3.7 million for their investment properties, an equity position of $1.5 million, and an annual net cash flow of $85,000. Our 20-year investment story, with 15 acquisitions from 1983 to 2002, generated $1.6 million in equity (virtually identical to the case for Millionaire Real Estate Investors) with a market value of $2.6 ($1 million less than those we interviewed) and an annual cash flow of $50,500 (also less than our real estate millionaires). The Millionaire Real Estate Investors we interviewed also had more debt in their investments (60 percent versus the 38 percent in our story). It would appear that they are buying larger properties, probably multifamily, and accruing more debt but greater cash flow. We have been more cautious and perhaps conservative in applying this financial model.

In the end, though, it's the equity that matters most and has the greatest direct impact on personal net worth. The lesson from our journey (your journey), is this: If you follow the path of the Millionaire Real Estate Investor, if you make real estate investments, if you buy them right, if you consistently repeat the process over time, you inevitably will become a net worth millionaire. May this journey of the Financial Model—the story we took the liberty to put you in—become your real life journey. Perhaps it already is!

BUY IT RIGHT—PAY IT DOWN—PAY IT OFF

This is the motto I want you to adopt, the litany I want you to repeat to yourself constantly. This is how I want you to build your financial wealth through real estate. All this will become clearer when we investigate the Acquisition Model, but for now I want you to internalize this three-part reminder: "Buy it right—pay it down—pay it off." When you "buy it right," you make your money going in—you assure yourself of achieving the best of Equity Buildup and Cash Flow Growth. When you "pay it down," you will be adding even more to your Equity Buildup.

When you "pay it off" and continue to own it and rent it, you will bring more and more Net Cash Flow into your financial life. You will have a growing stream of unearned income; your money will be working for you. This is the theme of the Millionaire Real Estate Investor's Financial Model: Buy It Right—Pay It Down—Pay It Off. We hope you will make this model yours.

THE NETWORK MODEL OF THE MILLIONAIRE REAL ESTATE INVESTOR

No one ever succeeds by himself or herself—no one. Behind every success story is another success story; behind every successful person is an equally successful person. While the term *self-made* is used commonly, the unspoken fact is that no one is self-made, whether biologically, spiritually, physically, personally, professionally, or financially. So, look around you and know this: Millionaire investors aren't succeeding without the help of others. For every Millionaire Real Estate Investor you might know, there is a group of people working behind the scenes who helped cause or support his or her success. They are the millionaire's Network—an intentionally recruited group of people who each play a key role in helping the Millionaire Real Estate Investor succeed. Investors couldn't succeed without this group. Neither can you.

A Millionaire Real Estate Investor's Network is an interconnected group of people with three things in common: They play an active professional role in real estate investments, they are the best at what they do, and they are willing to help you when you need help.

Don't confuse this with your Leads Network. This is your Work Network. Although over time you also will ask those people for leads and try to include them in your Leads Network, this is not your primary reason for building your Work Network. These are the people who give you advice, guidance, wisdom, information, instruction, intelligence, knowledge, mentoring, strategy, counsel, contacts, connections, leads, leadership, leverage, and labor. Some also provide partnering when you want it and honest feedback even when you don't. This Work Network is your personal and strategic wealth-building association with others. It is where you go to find all the people you need to find, learn all the things you need to know, and get done all the things you need to get done. In short, your Work Network is your investing lifeline.

> "Our mission and our vision is to create great networks of people wanting to help each other achieve success in life."
>
> Elmer Diaz
> Millionaire Real Estate Investor
> Houston, TX

But be careful: It isn't just anyone you need in your lifeline. If you have a dream, you will need a dream team. If you have a big dream, you will need a big dream team. If you have a big and powerful dream to achieve financial wealth through real estate investing, you will need a big and powerful dream team to achieve it. You need people, the right people, to help you get what you want. If you want to become a Millionaire Real Estate Investor, you must bring together a powerful group of people, a dream team, who can all play the right roles at the right times so that you can achieve your financial dreams. You need your own millionaire real estate investing Work Network.

The members of your Work Network will provide you a wide variety of important and interrelated things. They will help you from beginning to end with your transactions. They will inform and advise you about what to do and what not to do. They will provide the "best work" at the "best price" in the "best time." They will be there when you really need them—and no later.

If you don't have a Work Network, you'll be working alone. And if you ever need someone, you'll have to take whoever you can get at the moment. You won't know if you are getting the best advice, best work, best price, or best time. You'll just know you're in a pinch and can't do it by yourself. Contrast this with already having this Network set up. You'll know the best, know what they charge, know when they can do it, and know you can count on them. You'll be on the front end of good decisions instead of on the back end of desperate ones. You'll get what you need when you need it. You'll be able to make great decisions quickly because you won't have to slow down to go looking for people. You'll succeed instead of settle. Great Work Networks help make millionaires millionaires.

THE THREE CIRCLES OF YOUR WORK NETWORK

Do you want to be the best investor you can be? Then surround yourself with the very best Work Network you can. It's that simple. Take a look at the chart below. We've drawn it this way for two very important

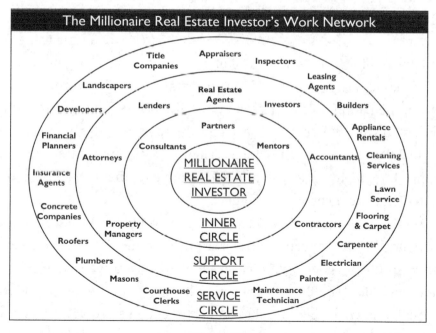

Figure 19

reasons: First, millionaires surround themselves with great people, and second, millionaires run in the right circles.

There is a practical reason why they do this and a scientific explanation for why it works. They surround themselves with great people because they mean to be great investors who intend to do more than one deal. They plan to duplicate their success many times over time. To do that, they have to actively, purposefully, and selectively build powerful working relationships that are long-term and mutually beneficial. They are creating a circle of influence with themselves at the center. Millionaires don't just seek influential people—they become influential.

> "Learning real estate is accelerated by finding a role model. Learn from someone who knows the business. Invest with someone who is willing to teach you. It's all been done before, so profit from the knowledge and mistakes of others."
>
> Paul Morris
> Millionaire Real Estate Investor
> West Hollywood, CA

There's a scientific reason why this works. When you are creating your own circles of influence, you're actually pulling people toward you and your goals. You're creating a true force of nature. It's called a centripetal force. The word *centripetal* is from the Latin for "center-seeking" and refers to any force that directs objects toward the center of a circle. In their world Millionaire Real Estate Investors are such a force. They intentionally attract the right people into their circles of influence and pull them in close around them. They are a center of influence.

With this in mind we want you to do two things: Visualize yourself surrounded by great people and start running in the right circles to attract and keep them. When you're clear about what you want your financial life to look like, you'll be clear about who you'll need to surround yourself with and what you'll need to do to attract those people. We want you to be intentional in your work relationships and never settle.

The Millionaire Real Estate Investor

The right people in the three circles of your investment life will provide you with important benefits:

1. Leadership and Advocacy
2. Advice and Management
3. Work and Results

You will need all three to take your investment life to its highest level. Each circle has its own function, and building a Work Network is about finding the right people to fulfill each of these functions.

The model for building a Work Network is quite simple, but the positive impact on your financial success is quite profound. The lines that separate the circles in the Work Network chart shown above are not hard lines but logical ones based on the roles people will play in your real estate investing. As a result, you will have three distinct groups in your Work Network: your Inner Circle, your Support Circle, and your Service Circle.

Your Inner Circle: Leadership and Advocacy

Your Inner Circle is composed of the key people who absolutely and truly care about your financial success. No ifs, ands, or buts about it—they are committed to you. These are the people closest to you, the select group you trust the most. All of them should have more investment knowledge, experience, and success than you have and be willing to mentor and guide you. Think of them as your informal board of directors for wealth-building and real estate investment decisions—your own personal Millionaire Mastermind.[9]

What separates the members of your Inner Circle from everyone else is not what they do for you professionally but what they do for you personally. If you don't know what to do, they'll tell you or find someone who can. If you need help, they will provide it or connect you with some-

---

[9] Napoleon Hill introduced the concept of the Mastermind in his classic *Think and Grow Rich*. He described the Mastermind principle as "the coordination of knowledge and effort of two or more people, who work toward a definite purpose, in the spirit of harmony . . . No two minds ever come together without thereby creating a third, invisible, intangible force, which may be likened to a third mind."

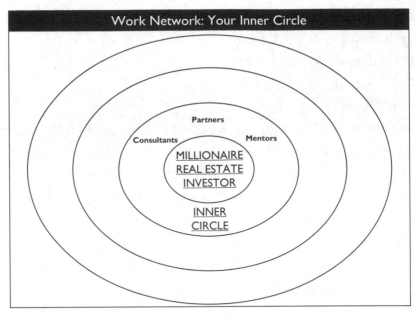

Work Network: Your Inner Circle

Partners

Consultants   Mentors

MILLIONAIRE
REAL ESTATE
INVESTOR

INNER
CIRCLE

Figure 20

one who will. If you need a partner, they'll become one or find one. This willingness to go out of their way to provide you with leadership and advocacy pulls them close to you—into your Inner Circle. While they also might be in your Support or Service Circle because of their professions, it's their active role in your personal investing success that makes them special. For example, they may be contractors, property managers, or real estate agents, but now, for you, they're that and more. They are your mentors, consultants, and partners, and you will touch them at least once a month.

> *"Partner with someone who knows what he's doing."*
>
> Allen Leone
> Millionaire Real Estate Investor
> LaPlace, LA

Your Support Circle: Advice and Management

Your Support Circle is composed of the key fiduciary people in your real estate investment life. As fiduciaries, they are always looking out for your best interest. They are the professionals you rely on to advise you on both the details of specific transactions and the people you will need to complete them. If need be, they will even contract and manage some of those relationships for you. They are the real estate agents, lenders, accountants, and others who are brought in on every opportunity in an important way and are key to almost every transaction in some way. These are your transaction advisors and managers—your "transactioneers."

Think of your Support Circle as investment company executives who are not on the payroll. They have the ability to manage any of the transaction pieces for you and, if need be, can manage all of them. For example, your contractor may refer a landscaper to you or hire one for you. Your real estate agent may connect you with a property manager or provide one as a service. It is the businesses they are in that will determine their primary role in the transaction. Your Support Circle forms the foun-

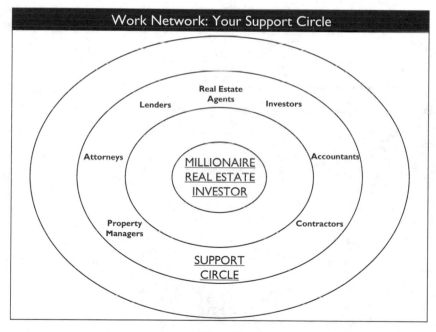

Figure 21

dation of the professional team you rely on, and you touch these people on every transaction.

Your Service Circle: Work and Results

Your Service Circle is composed of specialized independent contractors and freelancers. These service providers will perform specific functions for a particular property or transaction. They are the inspectors, electricians, painters, and others you may need depending on the situation. But their scope is limited. What they touch in a transaction usually is confined to what they specifically do or the special service they provide. You will personally direct them in the work they do, or your support team will manage them. In the end, the details of the transaction will dictate which service professionals you will need.

These are the foot soldiers on the front line of your wealth building, and you cannot succeed without them. They are the skilled professionals

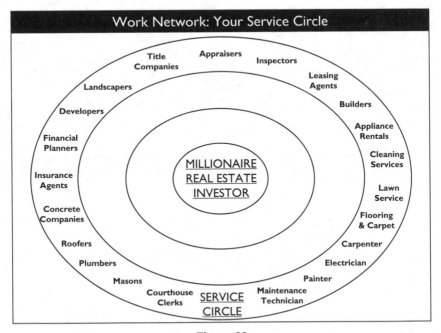

Figure 22

who physically touch the transaction and the investment. Remember: What they do, how well they do it, how fast they do it, and what they charge for doing it can

make or break any deal. Your Service Circle provides the specific work you need for any particular situation, and you will touch these people whenever their services are required.

WORKING YOUR WORK NETWORK

One of the biggest challenges for most investors is knowing when to ask for help. Most wait until they actually need it and as a result end up taking the help they can get instead of getting the help they need. This is what separates millionaires from everyone else. Millionaires don't wait. In fact, they understand this issue so well that they make getting into relationships with the right people before they need them their number one priority.

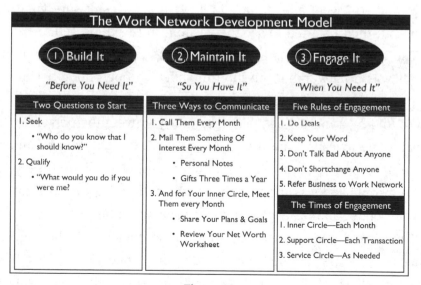

Figure 23

Working with this Network is the easy part; finding the right people and building it are not so easy. It's not that it's actually hard—it's that it will take time. If you intend to be very successful, only very successful individuals will qualify to be in your Work Network. That is why it takes time. You will have to turn over a lot of stones to find your Network treasures. As challenging as this may seem, it is not that difficult to do. It's simply an issue of time on the task. To build a quality Work Network, you must put in the time necessary to accomplish it.

Build Your Work Network

When I first got into the real estate business, I read an article on building a business that gave me direction and set me on a strong course. The advice boiled down to calling on industry professionals and asking them two questions:

1. "Who do you know that I should know?"
2. "What would you do if you were me?"

It sounded so simple that I almost didn't do it. However, since I was just getting started and needed to get moving, I was willing to do anything, and so I went ahead and did it. At first I wasn't sure what I was doing, but then I started to see the wisdom in this approach.

The first question was a pure Support Circle or Service Circle question. It was a networking question intended to open doors I would not have been able to open on my own. By calling someone up and saying, "I was told by a mutual acquaintance that you were the person to know in real estate investing, and I was wondering if I might drop by and meet you in the next few days." With that question I was able to meet a lot of quality people and was soon on the inside track to building a great Work Network better and faster than I could have any other way.

The second question was an Inner Circle question. If the suggestion someone gave me sounded halfway decent, I followed it. Then I went back and asked, "I did it, and here's what happened. What would you

Build Your Work Network with Two Questions
1. Seek: "Who do you know that I should know?"
2. Qualify: "What would you do if you were me?"

Figure 24

suggest I do next?" Anyone who was willing to be in my Inner Circle would warm up to this, give me additional suggestions, and over time, if I wanted, begin to mentor me. The quality of their advice was a qualifying factor. The better the advice was, the harder I would try to move a person into my Inner Circle.

The process worked, and over time I developed a millionaire's Work Network. This process will work for you too, if you are willing to work the process. It is simple and to the point and gets you in the Work Network–building game fast. All it takes is to ask these two questions to enough people.

Maintain Your Work Network

However, once you have someone in one of your circles, you're far from done. You don't just want to build a Work Network—you want to maintain it for the rest of your investing life. Maintaining your Network is about building solid relationships and a reputation people can trust. Over and over in our research, we heard the phrase "relationship and reputation equal deals," to the point where we realized we were hearing a mantra. We were hearing about the two Rs of networking: Relationship and Reputation. Relationships are built by communication, and Reputations are built by track record.

> *"Don't try to do everything by yourself because it gets overwhelming. I don't think you can be good at it all. You have to choose."*
>
> Peggy Rollins
> Millionaire Real Estate Investor
> Dalton, GA

The simple one-two-three plan for maintaining solid relationships goes like this: Call Them—Mail Them—See Them. Each step represents a unique way to contact your Work Network, or what we sometimes refer to in lead generation as a "touch."

Maintain Your Work Relationships
1. Call Them Every Month
2. Mail Them Something of Interest Every Month
3. And, for Your Inner Circle, Meet Them Every Month

Figure 25

First, call them every month. Find out how they are doing, share how you're doing, and talk about real estate investing. Just two or three calls a day will allow you to touch virtually everyone in your Work Network every month.

Second, mail them something of interest and value every month. Create a mailing list of your Work Network members in your contact database (see the section on the Lead Generation Model, page 198) and send them a news article, an interesting story, or advice on real estate investing. Include a handwritten note. One mailing a month is all it will take.

Third, for the people in your Inner Circle, see them every month and do one additional thing: Pay them a personal visit each month. Breakfast, lunch, dinner, or just a cup of coffee will do. Your goal is to tell them what you're doing, review your Net Worth Worksheet with them, and ask for their advice and guidance. You probably will have no more than three to five true mentors, so this is a matter of only one or two meetings a week.

Maintaining your Work Network boils down to three simple questions you ask yourself: Who am I calling today? Who am I seeing this week? Who am I mailing to this month? That is all it takes. Time does the rest.

ENGAGE YOUR WORK NETWORK

Reputation will take a little longer to build. It is who you are and what you stand for in their minds, and it takes time and interaction for that to become clear. That means you will have to engage your Network on a regular basis and in the right way. Here are the five things you must do over time to develop a track record that will cause the people in your Work Network to respect and trust you. We call them the Five Rules of Engagement.

The Five Rules of Engagement
1. Do Deals
2. Keep Your Word
3. Don't Talk Bad About Anyone
4. Don't Shortchange Anyone
5. Refer Business to Your Work Network

Figure 26

The First Rule of Engagement is to *do deals*. You must be a player in the real estate investment game. Look for real estate opportunities, make offers, and do deals. Otherwise, you're not really an investor. You're not taking the advice you're being given, and you're not hiring your Network. In other words, you could be wasting their time.

The Second Rule of Engagement is to *keep your word*. Always say what you mean and mean what you say. Walk your talk. Underpromise and overdeliver. You want to become known as someone who is reliable, someone people can trust. Don't miss appointments or show up late. Fulfill your obligations. It's about being where you say you'll be and doing what you say you'll do.

The Third Rule of Engagement is *not to talk bad about anyone*. This is about keeping your negative thoughts about others to yourself. People will believe that if you talk about others to them, you'll talk about them to others. No one trusts a gossip.

The Fourth Rule of Engagement is *not to shortchange anyone*. Give people the time you promised and the money you agreed to pay. Trying to get out of paying people the attention or money they deserve is the fastest way there is to ruin your reputation.

The Fifth Rule of Engagement is *to refer business to your Work Network*. Go out of your way to get others to use your Work Network. The quickest way to show you trust and care about people is to recommend them to others. When you refer members of your network to others, you're building their businesses and sending them a powerful message.

You will engage the different circles of your Network at different times. Your Inner Circle—your mentors, consultants, and partners—accounts for your most valued working relationships. You'll see these people every month whether you have ongoing work or not. These are the individuals who help set your vision, your goals, and your strategies for achieving them. Those in your Support Circle are called into action with almost every transaction. These professionals will provide invaluable service and advice in the course of working out a deal. Your Service Circle is engaged on an "as-needed" basis. Every transaction will be different and will dictate the qualified specialists you'll need. Working with these individuals will solidify your reputation and over time deepen these relationships.

The Times of Engagement
1. Inner Circle – Engage Them Each Month
2. Support Circle– Engage Them Each Transaction
3. Service Circle– Engage Them As Needed

Figure 27

Your Work Network can become what you want it to become and ultimately mirror your vision for your life. If you have ambition and goals, it will reflect them. If you don't, it will reflect that. To achieve your personal financial dreams you will need to surround yourself with mentors, support advisors, and service providers who match your financial dreams.

THE LEAD GENERATION MODEL OF THE MILLIONAIRE REAL ESTATE INVESTOR

Probably the most common question on the tip of every new investor's tongue is "Now that I'm ready to invest, how do I find great investment properties?" The Lead Generation Model of the Millionaire Real Estate Investor answers that question. Without leads—prospective properties that look like great opportunities—your investment plan can't be accomplished. To be successful, you need leads—lots of them; in fact, the more, the better. With more leads you get more opportunities, and with more opportunities you get to pick the very best among them. This is what millionaires do. They get the most leads and as a result get the best properties. You could say it's quantity of opportunities first and quality of picks second. This is why millionaires take lead generation seriously and take it big. They know that finding great investment properties is a numbers game and that "the quality is in the quantity."

Finding investment properties isn't easy, but it isn't complicated either. It's about knowing what you're looking for and looking for it. Often, investors aren't clear enough about what they want to find and therefore aren't sure how to find it. Or worse, this lack of clarity leads them to find the

> *"The deals are out there. But you spend time looking for them. Out of all the houses for sale, only 7 percent are our market."*
>
> Elmer Diaz
> Millionaire Real Estate Investor
> Houston, TX

wrong property and mistake it for the *right* one. This is where the Lead Generation Model of the Millionaire Real Estate Investor comes in. It bridges the gap between your investment goals and the investment properties that will help you achieve them. It not only will inform your property search but also power it. A lot of people confuse doing the wrong thing with bad luck. The Lead Generation Model shows you how to

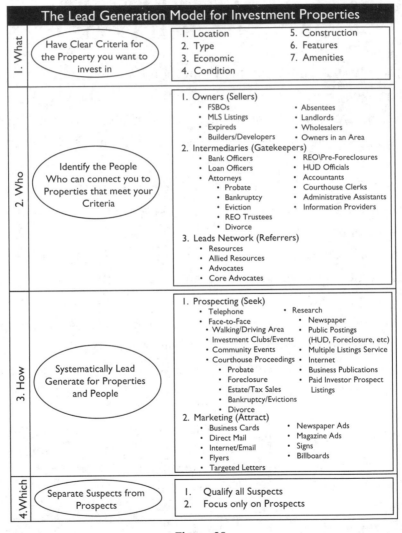

Figure 28

prospect and market for investment leads and is one of the main ways you can take luck out of the investment game.

THE FOUR KEY AREAS OF YOUR LEAD GENERATION MODEL

The Millionaire Real Estate Investor's Lead Generation Model is built around four core questions:

1. *What* am I looking for?
2. *Who* can help me find it?
3. *How* will I find the property or the people connected to it?
4. *Which* properties are the real opportunities?

When you can answer these four questions and take action, you're well on your way to doing deals.

QUESTION 1: *WHAT* AM I LOOKING FOR?

Your Lead Generation Model is driven by your Criteria—the economic and physical details of a property that would best meet your investing goals. As Millionaire Real Estate Investor George Meidoff put it, "Your Criteria form the operational base from which you make all your investment decisions."

Your Criteria provide you with as precise a picture as possible of your ideal investment property, and the clearer that picture is, the better the odds are that you'll recognize it when you see it. Knowing *exactly* what you're looking for helps you sift through large numbers of leads effi-

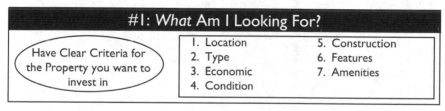

Figure 29

Buy a Million

173

ciently and has the added benefit of helping you make offers quickly and confidently once you find a match. Clear Criteria serve as a wanted poster, a missing property report you circulate through your prospecting and marketing efforts. The quality of your Criteria and how clearly you communicate them ultimately can determine the quality of the leads you get from your lead generation efforts. It will pay great dividends to build your Criteria carefully in the beginning and revise them over time as experience dictates.

Simply put, if you don't know what you're looking for, how will you know when you've found it? Maybe even more important, how will someone help you find it? It's easy to say you're looking for undervalued properties that will appreciate and cash flow, but what does that really

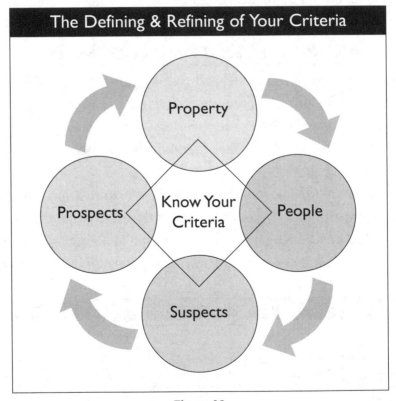

Figure 30

mean? It's the difference between saying you're looking for an "investment property" and saying you're looking for a "well-kept three-bedroom, two-bathroom single-story brick house with a two-car garage that was built in the last 10 years and that can be bought below market value." If you're going to invest in real estate, you need to be clear about what you want to invest in—that's your Criteria.

Having no Criteria leads you anywhere and everywhere but in the end leaves you nowhere. Having Criteria leads you where you want to

> *"You need to set parameters and treat your business like a business."*
>
> Anna Mills
> Millionaire Real Estate Investor
> Toledo, OH

go. Having specific Criteria allows you to narrow your search and develop expertise about the kinds of property you want to invest in. Millionaire Real Estate Investors have clearly defined Criteria. In fact, they have two sets of Criteria: what they will consider and what they will buy. The first is somewhat general, and the second is very specific.

The great thing about your Criteria for what you'll consider is that you can use them to narrow your search in two different ways. You can put them at the front end of your lead generation, thereby receiving fewer but better leads, or put them at the back end and thereby receive more leads but of less quality. Either way will work, so experiment to see which works best for you. In the first instance your "what you'll consider" Criteria serve as your filter on the front end, and in the second those Criteria serve as your filter on the back end.

Two Kinds of Criteria
1. Criteria for "What You'll Consider"
2. Criteria for "What You'll Buy"

Figure 31

Here is where your Criteria for what you will buy kick in. Because some of your leads will be suspects (unqualified leads) and some will be prospects (qualified leads), having well-defined Criteria for what you will buy allows you to reject suspects and focus on prospects quickly. You will learn that working with suspects instead of prospects costs time and money and for the most part is not very productive. Thus, your lead generation in the end must include a qualification and elimination process, and that's what your "what you'll buy" Criteria will do for you: filter and eliminate the suspects and identify and qualify the prospects. The reason you would rarely do lead generation with your "what I'll buy" Criteria is that your search could be so narrow that you'd miss some great opportunities. That's why you start with the general announcement "I buy houses" and then narrow it down with "I buy houses that meet my specific Criteria."

This sorting process is one of the best ways to develop expertise in the kinds of properties you've targeted. Every property you see, every suspect you eliminate, every prospect you investigate, and every deal you ultimately make increases your knowledge and refines your Criteria. Think of it as "on-the-job training." But in the end your best deals usually will be those that most tightly conform to your strict Criteria. You might even say, "The deal is in the details."

> *"I think one of the very first things people have to do, and then periodically review to see if it's still true, is determine what kind of property they want. They need to establish their Criteria and hold them in mind while they search. Then when a good deal comes along, they'll recognize it as a deal because it meets their Criteria."*
> Dyches Boddiford,
> Millionaire Real Estate Investor
> Marietta, GA

There are seven major categories you must make decisions about to define your investment property Criteria: Location, Type, Economic, Condition, Construction, Features, and Amenities. The first three—Location, Type, and Economic—are foundational and are the most important. Let's take a look at those three.

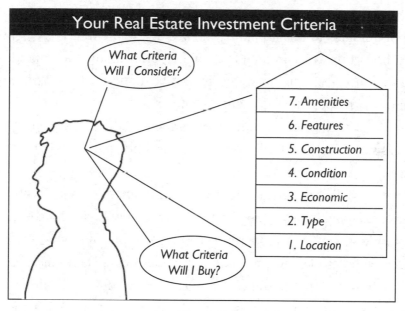

Figure 32

1. Location

The first area where Millionaire Real Estate Investors narrow their search is location. Picking a geographic area not only keeps the process manageable and affordable, it also allows you to become an expert quickly. It's about focus. It's about specializing in a neighborhood, subdivision, or area of town until you have a clear understanding of all the factors that determine local property values and rental rates. Those values and rates are ultimately comparative. If an area consists primarily of single-family brick homes with three bedrooms and two baths, it's important to know if a house with two bedrooms and one bath with siding tends to sell or rent for less. This kind of comparative pricing runs all the way from major features such as bedrooms, bathrooms, and square footage to smaller details such as vaulted ceilings and desirable landscaping. Picking an area helps you master this information more quickly so that you can make informed decisions about the properties you find there.

The physical location may be one of the most important factors in the value of a home. To put it plainly, the average home in a great neighborhood almost always commands a higher price than does an identical home in a less desirable area. "Location, location, location" is the oldest cliché in the real estate book, but it remains valid. Don't ever forget it or get tired of saying it, because location is the one thing about any property that is impossible to duplicate; location is what gives each piece of real estate its true uniqueness

For the Millionaire Real Estate Investor, finding a great location is a process of zeroing in. Obviously, you need to start with a great country that allows for and supports property ownership. From there you take a great city that isn't completely overbuilt and has growing economic prospects, and start looking for real estate. You're looking for desirable and emerging neighborhoods or communities. Historically, these tend to be the areas close to work, retail, and recreational centers that either have established reputations for great quality of life and great schools or are emerging.[10] Transitional neighborhoods on the rise can be ideal for investors. It can be very hard to find opportunities in established neighborhoods because everyone wants to live there and so prices tend to get pushed up. But in transitional neighborhoods homes are often overlooked and undervalued.

Within a great neighborhood location becomes even more precise; you're looking for the best streets and lots. It's fairly intuitive. People like privacy but also like access. A house in a small cove often brings a higher rent or sales price than does a similar house on an adjoining but highly trafficked street. Likewise, a house on a residential street will fare better for the investor than will one across the street from a shopping mall. Deeply wooded lots are better than small treeless ones. Big lots, corner lots, cul-de-sac lots, and secluded lots are all desirable to a potential

---

[10] Many investors, including Harry Dent, Jr., are watching a new trend that is likely to play out from 2010 through 2020: the move of baby boomers to exurbia. The members of this huge demographic group are heading for retirement and have shown signs they'd like to own homes in smaller towns outside large metropolitan cities. It's about a change of pace and a change of scale.

renter or home buyer. Don't forget the zoning. Some of the best deals I've done, and many of those our investors shared with us, hinged on zoning issues. Lots that are zoned commercial or multi-

> *"Most people understand real estate. They understand what makes an area attractive."*
>
> Harry S. Dent, Jr.
> Best-selling author and economist
> Burlington, VT

family, even those adjacent to or near yours, can affect value favorably or unfavorably depending on conditions.

A real estate agent once brought me an excellent deal. It was for a $460,000 commercial lot on a corner of a major thoroughfare in my community. Commercial developers were just beginning to develop the area, and we knew the real estate would quickly be in demand as the limited space was built out. But in investigating the lot, my agent picked up on a zoning detail of an adjoining lot that made the one we'd targeted

Figure 33

extremely valuable: My property had access to utilities, while my neighbor's did not. The current owner had more real estate than he could afford to hold, and to keep the rest, he needed to sell this property quickly. We bought it and began negotiating with the owner of the adjoining lot to trade access to my utilities for some of his land. It would have been a great deal for both of us, but unfortunately, it fell through at the eleventh hour. Forced to rethink our strategy, we rezoned to include retail development in addition to office. The lot still had access to utilities and was now even more desirable because retail property usually sells for more than office. A bank ended up buying the lot for about $1.1 million, netting me $640,000.[11] This transaction was made possible by one factor—location, location, location.

2. Type

The second essential area of Criteria is property type. Are you looking for single-family homes or multifamily properties, urban or suburban, resort or ranch, new construction or resale, lots or land? Since we've focused on investing in residential real estate—properties people live in— let's take a closer look at the single-family and multifamily properties.

You can acquire houses, condos, and apartments individually or buy them in bunches by purchasing duplexes, triplexes, fourplexes, and even larger condo and apartment complexes. The conventional wisdom is that single-family homes offer the most reliable demand and appreciation while multifamily properties offer the best opportunities for cash flow. On the surface this plays out. In most markets, the majority of buyers want to own a home, and so this demand tends to keep prices moving upward over time. Also, by and large, the market for single-family homes is set by noninvestors. These individuals are buying a *home,* and emotional factors play into their willingness to buy at a certain price. Multifamily prop-

---

[11] Actually, I netted $690,000 if you count the $50,000 nonrefundable earnest money I made when another buyer made an offer and subsequently walked away when he couldn't arrange financing and close.

erties, in contrast, are bought and sold largely by investors, and this means that their prices are determined dispassionately by the value of the rents they represent.[12]

However, rents appreciate over time at almost the same pace as home appreciation.[13] Thus, by default, both single-family and multifamily properties go up in price over time. The two tend to be countercyclical. When housing is affordable, rents go down and vacancies go up; this means houses are appreciating in value while rental properties and rents decline. But when housing becomes less affordable, the opposite tends to be true: Vacancies go down, and rents rise. Neither option—single-family or multifamily—is intrinsically better than the other. They both offer strong benefits to an investor over time.

> "Multifamily is difficult for smaller investors to get into unless they have a lot of capital on hand. If you start out with single-family houses, banks will incrementally grow with you into multifamily. Plus, single-families involve a lot less risk."
>
> Rische Beeson
> Millionaire Real Estate Investor
> Lubbock, TX

The decision to include single-family or multifamily properties in your Criteria ultimately depends on your goals. You can buy single-family homes for appreciation and relative stability—building your net worth—or you can emphasize multifamily properties that offer multiple streams of income—building your cash flow.

3. Economic

To put it plainly, you can't build your Economic Criteria unless you have a firm idea of what properties are really worth. Any successful

---

[12] Investors are buying cash flow when they purchase rental properties. In the section on the Acquisition Model we'll walk you through the process of how investors determine a property's value from Net Operating Income (NOI), which is gross rent minus expenses.

[13] From 1972 to 2002, a period that fairly represents rising and declining real estate markets, the median home price rose at an annual compounded rate of 6.11 percent and median rents rose at an annual compounded rate of 5.32 percent.

investor will tell you that it *pays* to know property values and rental rates. Actually, it's essential. You have to understand current market prices for property sales and current market rental rates to know what your Economic Criteria should be. Your Economic Criteria break down into four distinct parts:

1. The *price range* in which you want to buy
2. The *discount* you will require
3. The *cash flow* you expect to receive
4. The *appreciation* you hope to make

Basically, the price you pay (after your discount) will go a long way toward determining your cash flow and appreciation. If we add the two issues of *hassle* (the time and work involved in dealing with typical tenants for that price range) and *liquidity* (how quickly you might be able to sell the property) to *cash flow* and *appreciation,* we get four broad categories we must consider in determining the price range in which we might want to buy.

In the final analysis it's best to build your Economic Criteria toward the middle of the market. The chart just below shows how the four broad

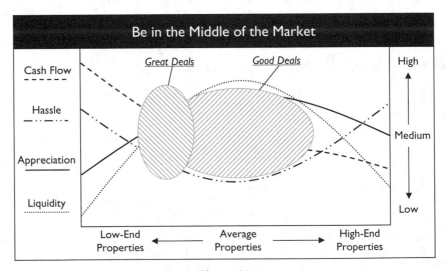

Figure 34

factors—cash flow, appreciation, hassle, and liquidity—tend to work at various price points. Our research shows that the best combination of these four factors—the sweet spot, if you will—lies on *the low end of the middle* of any market. That's where the great deals are found and made. Cash flow can be best at the low end of the market, but these properties can represent the most work for investors, don't tend to appreciate as well, and aren't as liquid. High-end properties tend to appreciate well, but their cash flow is usually the worst. It takes longer to sell them, and so their liquidity factor is low, and because of the expectations of typical high-end renters and buyers, they can represent a hassle for the investor. Especially in the beginning, we'd advise taking the solid cash flow, strong appreciation, and low hassle offered by midmarket properties. It's about identifying these "bread and butter" properties in your chosen location.

In general, it's best to be where the largest market is, and generally speaking, the majority of renters and buyers will be in the average-priced properties. In this market segment larger numbers of renters and buyers can increase demand and drive appreciation. You're playing the averages to have the greatest odds for success.

With your location and property type in hand, spend some time getting to know property values and rental rates. You want to get in the habit of browsing newspaper and Internet listings and taking notes. If you drive or walk through your target

> *"Typically the more expensive the house, the worse rental deal it makes. There's probably exceptions to that, but as a rule, as you get into a higher-priced home, the prices go up faster than the rental value of that house."*
> Bill O'Kane
> Millionaire Real Estate Investor
> Chicago, IL

area, set aside time to drop in on open houses and inspect rentals. If you see a "for rent" sign, call the number on it. Whether you're talking to a real estate agent, an owner, or a property manager, ask a few pointed questions: Why is the property priced the way it is? How does it compare to similar properties in the neighborhood? What kind of person typically buys or rents this property? The more you research, inspect, and ask questions about the properties in your target area, the better your understanding of value will be and the easier it will be to formulate your Economic Criteria. For Millionaire Real Estate Investors, this Criteria-building process begins with determining their foundational Criteria of Location, Type, and Economic, and it doesn't end there.

Let's turn our attention to the Millionaire Real Estate Investor's Criteria Worksheet (see part one below) and look at all the Criteria you need to consider. This worksheet is designed to walk you through the thought process of building your Criteria from beginning to end. By

The Millionaire Real Estate Investor's Criteria Worksheet (1 of 2)

1) LOCATION
- ❑ Country
- ❑ State/Province
  - ❑ Taxes
  - ❑ Rentals Laws
  - ❑ Weather
- ❑ County/Parish
- ❑ City/Town
  - ❑ Taxes
  - ❑ Services
- ❑ Neighborhood
  - ❑ School District
  - ❑ Crime
  - ❑ Transportation
  - ❑ Shopping/Recreation
- ❑ Street
  - ❑ Traffic
  - ❑ Size
- ❑ Lot
  - ❑ Zoning
  - ❑ Adjoining Lots
  - ❑ Lot Size
  - ❑ Trees
  - ❑ Privacy
  - ❑ Landscaping
  - ❑ Orientation/View

2) TYPE
- ❑ Single Family
  - ❑ Home
  - ❑ Condo
  - ❑ Town Home
  - ❑ Mobile Home
  - ❑ Zero Lot/Garden
- ❑ Small Multi Family
  - ❑ Duplex
  - ❑ Fourplex
- ❑ Large Multifamily/Commercial
- ❑ Land/Lot
- ❑ New/Preconstruction
- ❑ Resale
- ❑ Urban
- ❑ Suburban
- ❑ Exurban
- ❑ Rural
- ❑ Resort/Vacation
- ❑ Farm/Ranch

3) ECONOMIC
- ❑ Price Range
  - ❑ From $_____
  - ❑ To $_____
- ❑ Discount ___%
- ❑ Cash Flow $_____ / Mo
- ❑ Appreciation ___% /Yr

Figure 35

The Millionaire Real Estate Investor

checking the categories and filling in the blanks in the seven principal areas, you should get a tight, bullet-point description of your ideal real estate investment opportunity.

Location is the first principal area of your Criteria Worksheet. The subcategories listed here are meant to be reminders to investigate all the particulars of your prospective location. Are there favorable rental laws there? Does this neighborhood have a great school that will attract families year after year? What is the crime rate? Do work, retail, and recreational centers nearby make the property more marketable? Only by bearing in mind these many factors can you make an informed decision about location, and in the process of considering them, you'll also develop a great sense of who your eventual renter or buyer might be. Remember that real estate is always ultimately a game of local comparative values, so the location you choose and the selections you make will affect the number of opportunities available to you and their relative value as investments.

The second area on the Criteria Worksheet is *Type*. Do you want to invest in urban or rural properties, new construction or resale properties? These are broad classifications that can dictate the overall nature of the property. This is also where you decide whether your properties will be single-family or multifamily or even vacant lots.

Your *Economic* Criteria make up the third area on your worksheet. The first and most obvious category here is price range. You'll need to evaluate your buying power and pick a price point you can afford. Moreover, you'll need to be financially positioned to act quickly when properties become available, and so you'll want to stay within your current cash and financing means.

When you buy a property, you have two choices to make regarding the price: You can buy at market price and expect the price to rise or buy at a discount and have the option of later selling at current market prices or higher. Millionaires look for properties they believe will appreciate at above-average rates and then buy them at a discount. The discount is important because it represents built-in profit and equity; it's how you make your money going in. Successful investors label this their "margin of safety" and consider any investment without it to be speculative. Experienced investors assign a value to the work of acquiring an investment property either as a percentage or as a dollar value. For example, they may not acquire a property if they can't reasonably expect 20 to 30 percent (or $20,000 to $30,000 for higher price points) of built-in profit by buying it at a discount. Others set the bar higher or lower depending on their personal financial goals. How much cash flow you seek works the same way. How much monthly cash flow do you need to achieve from a property to make it worth your while? For some a single dollar is enough (they don't currently need the income or are focused on appreciation); others won't accept less than $200 or more each month per rental unit.

In the end, how much discount or cash flow you expect to achieve will be a factor in what you've experienced up to that point. Millionaire Real Estate Investor Carlos Rivero discovered a formula for maximizing his rents by making his properties available to government rental assistance programs. Having found a way to achieve $500 a month in positive cash flow (and having duplicated that success), he won't settle for anything less.

> *"When we started out, we decided our basic formula was to put down 20 percent cash, buy at least 10 percent below market value, and cash flow of a minimum of $200 a month after taxes, insurance, principal and interest, and property management fees. And it had to do that on a 15-year payout."*
> Jimmy & Linda McKissack
> Millionaire Real Estate Investors
> Highland Village, TX

The *Condition* of the property is the fourth principal area of your Criteria (see part two of the Criteria Worksheet on the facing page). Answers to the following questions can have a significant impact on your profit or loss:

The Millionaire Real Estate Investor's Criteria Worksheet (2 of 2)

4) CONDITION
- ❑ Needs No Repair
- ❑ Needs Minor Cosmetic
- ❑ Needs Major Cosmetic
- ❑ Needs Structural
- ❑ Needs Demolition

5) CONSTRUCTION
- ❑ Roof
- ❑ Walls (Exterior)
- ❑ Foundation
- ❑ Plumbing
- ❑ Water/Waste
- ❑ Wiring
- ❑ Insulation
- ❑ Heating/AC

6) FEATURES
- ❑ Age/Year Built ____
- ❑ Beds ____
- ❑ Baths ____
- ❑ Living ____
- ❑ Dining ____
- ❑ Stories ____
- ❑ Square Feet ____
- ❑ Ceilings ____ ft.
- ❑ Parking/Garage
- ❑ Kitchen
- ❑ Closets/Storage
- ❑ Appliances (Gas/Electric)
- ❑ Floor Plan (Open, In-law)
- ❑ Patio/Deck
- ❑ Basement
- ❑ Attic
- ❑ Lighting
- ❑ Walls (Interior)
- ❑ Laundry Room

7) AMENITIES
- ❑ Office
- ❑ Play/Exercise Room
- ❑ Security System
- ❑ Furniture/Furnishings
- ❑ Sprinkler System
- ❑ Workshop/Studio
- ❑ In-Law Suite
- ❑ Fireplace(s)
- ❑ Pool
- ❑ Hot Tub
- ❑ Ceiling Fans
- ❑ Window Treatments
- ❑ Satellite Dish
- ❑ Internet (Broadband)
- ❑ Sidewalk
- ❑ Energy Efficient Features
- ❑ Other:
  - ❑ _____
  - ❑ _____
  - ❑ _____
  - ❑ _____
  - ❑ _____
  - ❑ _____

Figure 36

1. How much cash will you need to make any repairs?

2. How long will it take to put the property in rentable or sellable condition?

3. For big projects, how much risk is involved?

Ideally, you want to find a discounted property that needs no repair, but that is quite rare. Generally, discounts come from fixing other people's problems. The seller doesn't have the cash, the time, or the inclination to handle the repairs himself or herself and then put the property up for sale at a higher asking price. That's where the investor comes in.

While we'll discuss this in detail in the section on the Acquisition Model, a general rule is that the more repairs a property requires, the greater the discount is. Major cosmetic repairs such as updating kitchens, bathrooms, and appliances can net investors big returns if they are willing to tackle them. Structural repairs such as fixing a bad foundation bring the biggest discounts but also entail risk. When you start moving or adding walls, there are often unpleasant discoveries (finding dated or dangerous wiring) or collateral damage (broken pipes) that will cost you time and profits. We recommend that beginning investors start with properties that will require only minor repairs unless they have significant construction experience.

As part of their research for this book I encouraged the rest of our writing team to buy, improve, and sell an investment house, using the millionaire models and worksheets. Through the seller disclosure and on-site inspections, Dave, Jay, and our researcher, Heather, learned that the property had a bad foundation and needed major cosmetic repairs. Everything went by the numbers, and their cost estimates were within 2 percent of the actual expenses except for one big problem: During the foundation repairs the main sewer line was broken about 20 feet under the slab. That amounted to a repair bill of over $10,000, as workers had to hammer through the slab to repair the line. That surprise expense added over a month to their holding costs and cut their profits substantially. But—and this is very important—because they were able to purchase the property at a deep discount by strictly following the models, they still earned a profit from their investment.

Bob Guest, a local Millionaire Real Estate Investor who advised them on the property, remarked that "they had the good fortune of having their education paid for by the property." He was absolutely right. By following the models they got a great education on Condition Criteria and made some money too.

The fifth principal area of your Criteria is *Construction*. This is an important consideration for real estate investors because a property's construction often has a big impact on maintenance and expenses. Roofs have to be replaced, siding has to be repaired, and septic tanks need periodic treatment. These are all costs that will affect net cash flow if you plan to hold the property or your selling price if potential buyers are sensitive to these issues. Millionaire Real Estate Investors Jimmy and Linda McKissack only buy homes with brick exteriors because they know that that's what people in their Denton, Texas, market want. They also understand that solid construction is more affordable to maintain over time.

Features and *Amenities* are the final principal areas of your Criteria. Features include such basics as the number of stories, bedrooms, bathrooms, and living areas a property has. Consider important features in your target area to be prerequisites for any property you purchase. If all the properties in your target location have two-car garages, your properties should too. Anything less and you'll probably have to discount the rent or price. Amenities are the unexpected extras a property may have. You may not include any of them in your Criteria, but you should always bear them in mind. A property that's missing a key feature may still be worthwhile if the amenities offset this deficit. For example, the two-car garage may have been converted to an extra bedroom that might be just as attractive to a prospective renter or buyer. Think of features as your minimums and amenities as your maximums.

> *"Theory and philosophy are great, but you must put in the work necessary to understand the market in which you intend to invest. Knowing a specific market is more powerful than any theory you could learn. Never try to shortchange the effort that is required to learn a market."*
> Paul Morris
> Millionaire Real Estate Investor
> West Hollywood, CA

Completing the Millionaire Real Estate Investor's Criteria Worksheet[14] should give you a clear picture of the type of property you hope to find. Over time, as you invest more and more, you may end up with several sets of real estate investment Criteria. While you may be in the market primarily for single-family homes in a certain area of town, you may have another set of Criteria for vacant lots you'd develop or even fixer-uppers you'd sell for a quick profit. The point of the Criteria Worksheet is that investors must always have a clear, detailed understanding of their current targeted properties. You must know what you hope to find if you are to have any hope of finding it.

Your All Properties Bulletin

Your completed Criteria Worksheet has a second and equally important function beyond building your Criteria. Once completed, the form provides a template for your All Properties Bulletin (APB). Your APB is a script. It's the basic description of the real estate investment for which you'll be prospecting and marketing (lead generating).

For example, if you pulled out only the categories you completed, your APB might go something like this: "I need your help. I'm looking for two-bedroom, two-bathroom duplexes priced between $125,000 and $150,000. Ideally, I'd like them to be close to downtown off Opportunity Square or on the main bus line in Overlook Hills. I don't mind some cosmetic repairs, but nothing serious. I prefer brick construction if possible, and it would be great if there was a privacy fence. Please let me know if you see any properties that meet that description."

If you're communicating this to an investment partner, scout, or real estate agent, you might consider including your discount and cash flow criteria, as that person most likely will be qualified to estimate those details when looking for opportunities to tell you about.

---

[14] A blank copy of the full worksheet is provided in Appendix C. Feel free to photocopy this worksheet to work on your personal real estate investment Criteria.

Criteria are unique to each investor and each market. There is no secret formula or magic bullet that works for everyone everywhere. Real estate investing is a limited-supply game within any price range, because there are only so many undervalued properties in any market at any given time, and competition can be fierce. Supply and demand always dictate price and value, and when too many investors seek the same kinds of properties in a market, it can be very difficult to find opportunities that are not already spoken for. As a result, we've observed that Millionaire Real Estate Investors tend to specialize in a niche (a narrowly defined set of Criteria) that they can learn well and identify fast—they niche to get rich. They master a set of specific Criteria and work them relentlessly. That's why there are investors who specialize in single-family, multifamily, land, new homes, rehabs, foreclosures, REOs (foreclosures reclaimed by the bank and named for their row on the bank's P&L—"Real Estate Owned"), and many, many more. You also may need to identify a niche so that you can acquire properties within it without undue competition. With time and experience you may even develop more than one Criteria mode in which you are highly competent so that you can switch gears whenever opportunities in one area become scarce.

QUESTION 2: *WHO* CAN HELP ME FIND IT?

Now that you know what you want, it's time to take the logical next step in the Lead Generation Model of the Millionaire Real Estate Investor: It's time to identify the people who can connect you to the properties that meet your Criteria. The chart below illustrates how the process works. This section of the Lead Generation Model is about the *who* of lead generating for investment opportunities. Let's look at the chart quickly, and in the following section we'll look at the ways in which we can connect with or contact them.

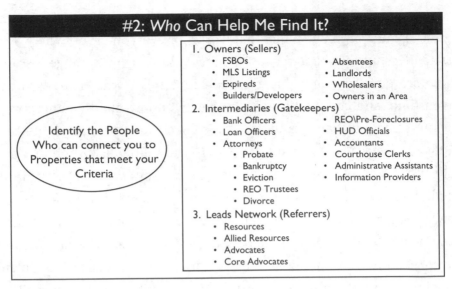

Figure 37

"It's a 'who you know' world. I happened to be on the inside track with a university that was selling some properties. I knew the people that were interested in selling them, so I was able to negotiate a deal before they were put on the general market. I think that's always where you buy your best deals. Now, people are calling to say, 'We understand you buy properties. We've got one to sell. Are you interested in looking at it?' And we always say, 'Absolutely.'"

Anna Mills
Millionaire Real Estate Investor
Toledo, OH

You can divide the people you may want to contact to generate leads for real estate investment properties into three distinct groups: Owners, Intermediaries, and members of your Leads Network. Millionaires sometimes call them sellers, gatekeepers, and referrers. Together, these three groups represent all the people who can connect you to investment real estate. Chosen specifically on the basis of who they are or what they do professionally, they can represent the exact group you will want to lead-generate to when looking for properties that meet your Criteria.

Owners (Sellers)

These are your sellers. They are the owners of the properties you might want to buy. Some have identified themselves as sellers or own real estate in an area in which you'd like to invest. If they are currently sellers, they're likely to be For Sale by Owners (FSBOs) sellers, active Multiple Listings Service (MLS) sellers, expired MLS sellers (Expireds), or new home sellers (Builders/Developers). If they are owners who are not currently sellers but are likely to be at some point, they are likely to be owners who live out of town (Absentees), owners who rent the property (Landlords), or owners who just acquired the property in order to resell it quickly (Wholesalers). There are also owners you'll target because they own property in an area that matches your Criteria (Owners in an Area).

Intermediaries (Gatekeepers)

These are the individuals who through their professions are directly in contact with people who may need to sell their property quickly. This list includes attorneys specializing in niche areas of law such as probate or divorce, bank or loan officers, and accountants.

Gloria Pfluger, my stepmother-in-law, was able to parlay her job as a former executive assistant (Gatekeeper) to a bank president into a percentage of ownership in a real estate limited partnership by introducing a wealthy bank client to a group of real estate investors. That client became the group's most active and important member, and when they formed a new investment partnership Gloria was given a piece of it in the process. Over time that opportunity netted her over $500,000. Don't underestimate the power of gatekeepers—for you and for the gatekeeper.

Leads Network (Referrers)

These are the individuals whom you have met, whom you've entered into your lead generation database, and with whom you are in regular communication throughout the year. Your goal is to have them refer investments to you. They can be divided into four categories:

1. *Resources*—people whom you've met and *who might* send you leads
2. *Allied Resources*—people whom you've met and *who can and probably will* send you leads
3. *Advocates*—people whom you've met and *who absolutely will* send you leads
4. *Core Advocates*—people whom you've met and *who are well placed and absolutely will* send you leads

Remember, just because you know people and they know you doesn't mean they all deserve equal status in your Leads Network. They don't. Your ultimate goal is advocacy, and advocacy isn't something that just happens. You make it happen. Through your ongoing communications with the people in your Leads Network, you soon discover who might and who will be an advocate for you. Core advocates are the people who are in situations that regularly generate investment leads and who absolutely will give them to you.

In the real estate investment world the people in your Leads Network often are called scouts (or in some cases bird dogs) because they are good at tracking down opportunities. Some scouts expect to be paid for their referrals; others do not. The choice is always yours, so do what feels appropriate.

QUESTION 3: *HOW* WILL I FIND THE PROPERTY OR THE PEOPLE CONNECTED TO IT?

So, now you've defined your Criteria—*what* you're looking for—and you've identified the key people who will help you find those opportunities—*who* you will prospect and market to. The third step is to execute your prospecting and marketing in order to reach those people and find

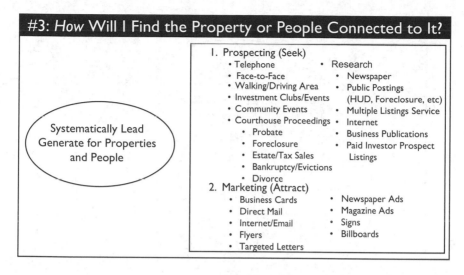

#3: *How* Will I Find the Property or People Connected to It?

1. Prospecting (Seek)
   - Telephone
   - Face-to-Face
   - Walking/Driving Area
   - Investment Clubs/Events
   - Community Events
   - Courthouse Proceedings
     - Probate
     - Foreclosure
     - Estate/Tax Sales
     - Bankruptcy/Evictions
     - Divorce
   - Research
     - Newspaper
     - Public Postings (HUD, Foreclosure, etc)
     - Multiple Listings Service
     - Internet
     - Business Publications
     - Paid Investor Prospect Listings

2. Marketing (Attract)
   - Business Cards
   - Direct Mail
   - Internet/Email
   - Flyers
   - Targeted Letters
   - Newspaper Ads
   - Magazine Ads
   - Signs
   - Billboards

Systematically Lead Generate for Properties and People

Figure 38

the opportunities you seek. This part of the Lead Generation Model is about the *how* of lead generating for investment opportunities.

A simple way to view lead generation is demonstrated in the chart on the following page, "Generating Leads and Moving People into Your Network Circles." It is helpful to view people as being in one of two categories: They're either people you Haven't Met or people you've Met. The people in the Haven't Met category consist of the general public at large or a targeted group you've specifically identified as a good group on which to focus your lead generation. The people you have Met are those in your Leads Network. The two methods you will use to generate leads from these groups are called prospecting and marketing.

Prospecting is about seeking opportunity. It's the process of personally calling and contacting targeted people you Haven't Met or people in your Leads Network to share your Criteria and ask for investment leads. You're sharing your APB and asking if anyone has seen properties that match it. It's also the process of researching neighborhoods, papers, the Internet, and public databases for properties. But whether you're calling

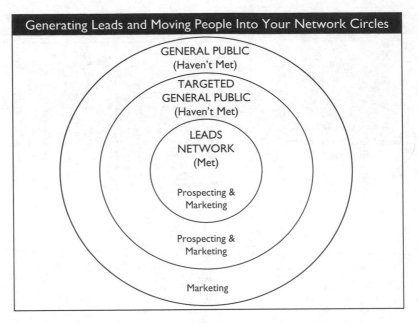

Figure 39

people, meeting them face to face, or researching alone, the challenge is that prospecting is always limited by the hours you can give it. This is why Millionaires utilize marketing in their lead generation.

Marketing is the opposite of prospecting. Instead of seeking opportunities, marketing is about attracting them. This is the process of putting up signs and billboards, mailing newsletters and postcards, and advertising in papers and periodicals. With marketing you don't have to be present or even awake for lead generating to be working for you—it's truly a leveraged activity.

It's important to remember that two fundamental forces—economic and personal—are constantly at work creating great real estate investment opportunities. Economic forces tend to affect the market as a whole. These forces include factors such as changing interest rates, job growth or recession, overbuilding or undersupply, and area revitalization. Personal forces are very specific to the owner and the property the owner represents. Personal forces, both positive and negative, include relocations, marriage or divorce, bankruptcy or good fortune, and even death or family growth. Millionaire Real Estate Investors never focus on only one but instead lead generate for both *properties* that meet their criteria and *sellers* who are motivated to sell.

Here's how this plays out with your prospecting and marketing. With prospecting you tend to be referred to or find properties that match your Criteria. The next step is to locate the seller and see if he or she is motivated to sell at your terms. Marketing tends to work in the opposite direction—it tends to attract motivated sellers. The next necessary step for the investor is to inspect the seller's property to see if it matches his or her Criteria. It may sound oversimplified, but you generally will be prospecting for properties and marketing for motivated sellers.

While the prospecting and marketing options we use to illustrate this step of the model may appear overwhelming, the truth is that our list is far from comprehensive. Millionaire investors are an unusually creative group of people and constantly innovate and improve on their lead generation methods. But none of the investors we interviewed felt obliged to attempt them all. Instead, most stuck to the three or four methods that they discovered worked best for them. The point is to pick a couple of methods and see if they work for you. The key is to get started. Over time and with experience you'll get a good sense of what works best for you and in your market.

When we surveyed our Millionaire Real Estate Investors, we asked for the top five ways they found real estate opportunities. The results are displayed in Figure 40, below. Clearly, these successful investors relied on their Leads Networks to send them opportunities. They built their Leads Networks purposefully and prospected and marketed to them relentlessly. You'll notice that we chose to break out real estate agents even though they are actually one of the groups of people you'll be Networking with (the number one category). They simply constituted too large a subset of

How Millionaire Real Estate Investors Find Opportunity

Networking	32%
Real Estate Agents/MLS	28%
Driving/Walking	10%
Newspaper & Ads	9%
Foreclosure Listings	7%
For Sale By Owners	4%
Internet/Database Research	3%
Targeted Marketing	2%
Other	5%

Figure 40

this category to remain anonymous. Together, the two categories—networking and working with real estate agents—account for as much as 60 percent of the lead generation results our Millionaire Real Estate Investors achieved. When you add in driving or walking in neighborhoods, culling leads from the newspapers or running ads in them, and tracking foreclosure properties, you approach 86 percent of all leads being generated by just five sources. These are the five we suggest you focus on.

Build a Database and Work It

The engine that drives all successful long-term lead generation programs is a contact database. The contacts in it are the fuel. Your job as the investor is to fuel the engine (put contacts in the database) and drive your lead generation program forward. The interesting thing is that the quality of your results is more a matter of the quality of your fuel (contacts) than a product of your driving skill (prospecting and marketing ability). What goes in has a direct effect on what comes out.

The chart below, "The Lead Generation Database Model," explains how you can use your database to generate leads. Your database will be built from two groups—people you Haven't Met and people you have Met. If you haven't met them, they are targeted sellers who live in a geographic area in which you'd like to own property or are a particular type of seller who may need to sell (FSBOs, expireds, absentees, landlords, builders, etc). You will record their contact information in your database and then categorize them for easy reference (e.g., "Local Absentee Owner Mailing List" or "Multiple Property Owner Mailing List"). Once they are in the database, you can contact them (prospect and market) with appropriate messages to encourage them to consider calling you when they are ready to sell.

If you have met these individuals, you record them in your database and categorize them in your Work Network, your Leads Network, or both. Then, as with your Haven't Met group, you will prospect and mar-

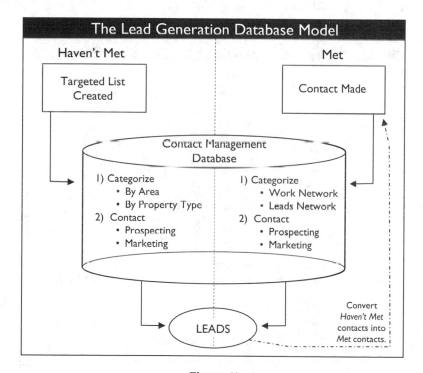

Figure 41

ket to them with appropriate messages to encourage them to consider contacting you if they know of a property or a seller who might constitute an investment opportunity.

The Met half of your contact database will include two basic kinds of contacts: all the people who help and advise you on investing (your Work Network) and all the people who might or will send you leads (your Leads Network). The Network Model is designed to help you build the first. The Lead Generation Model is designed to help you build the second. Over time the two should become deeply intertwined.

As the chart below, "Merging Your Work Network with Your Leads Network," shows, your goal as an investor is to achieve as much concentricity as possible between your Work Network and your Leads Network. When you stop to think about it, this makes perfect sense. Who is better qualified to send you real estate investment opportunities that match your Criteria than the people who work with you on those invest-

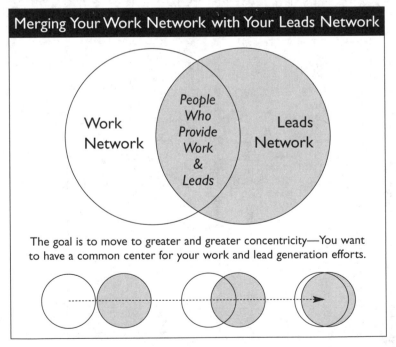

Figure 42

ments? The real estate agent you may have used to find your home or your first rental property will have a strong sense of your Criteria and can be on the lookout for properties that match them. The contractor you employed to repair that property may know another owner who would rather sell than make similar repairs. As a general rule, the people in your Work Network will be well positioned to send you leads. After all, they're in the real estate investment business too.

The individuals in your Work Network increasingly should make up the heart of your contact database, but along the way you'll add other names as well. Your family, friends, neighbors, and coworkers can send you leads if you include them consistently in your prospecting and marketing activities. You just have to educate them about your Criteria. In the end everyone you meet should know you're an investor (you'll tell them) and be added to this database. Once you have a target area, you can purchase mailing lists so that you can contact large numbers of people by e-mail with a click of a mouse or by mail using printed mailing labels. Your database powers these efforts and keeps you organized.

Your database doesn't have to be an expensive software package. The vast majority of our Millionaire Real Estate Investors used Microsoft Outlook as their primary database. They used this simple, ubiquitous program to its fullest extent,

> "In 1982, I saved up $4,000 and bought my first investment property. It was all the money I had in the world, and I spent it on a shack on 19 acres. I bought it for $24,000 — I put my $4,000 down, and the owner financed the rest. My payment was $170 a month and I rented it for $100, so I had negative cash flow, which is not what most investors would call a great investment. But, three years later I sold it for $45,000. In the meantime I had spent $3,000 because of the negative cash flow, but I still netted $17,000. In other words, I quadrupled my $4,000 investment."
>
> Mike Tavener
> Millionaire Real Estate Investor
> Asheville, NC

adding detailed notes to their contacts and creating categories (both are basic functions of the program) to keep records of previous interactions and prioritize their contacts. Just under 10 percent of the investors we surveyed used more than one database. In almost every case they used Outlook to build their databases and later, as their investing grew, incorporated one of the powerful specialized contact management programs to help them track their prospecting and marketing efforts. The graph in the chart below details the databases our investors used.

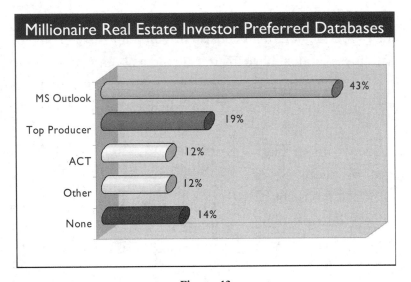

Figure 43

Categorizing your contacts is vital. As people emerge as key lead generators in your Leads Network, you'll want to earmark their contact records to show that. I like to think of this as a game of concentric circles (see the chart on the facing page). You want to move people from the outside to the inside, where they count the most. Remember, the four broad categories I recommend are Resources, people who might send you leads; Allied Resources, people who can and probably will send you leads; Advocates, people who absolutely will send you leads; and Core

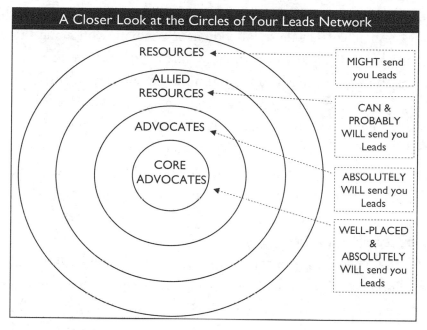

Figure 44

Advocates, people who are well placed to find investment opportunities and who absolutely will send you leads.

The process of converting these contacts from Resources to Allied Resources and then to Advocates and Core Advocates is about your reputation. That's the simplest way to put it. Because you touch them regularly and systematically (by meeting face to face, by telephone, and by e-mail and mail) and are always reminding them that you're an investor, they think of you when they come across real estate investment opportunities. You're building a reputation as an investor, and because you consistently share your Criteria, they know what kind of properties you're looking for.

You'll also be building your reputation by the way you respond to their referrals. You want to be known as an investor who respects the referrer by being decisive and prepared and who, when appropriate, rewards the referrer. When someone sends you a lead that matches your Criteria, show your gratitude. This can be as simple as a handwritten note or a small gift or as substantive as a finder's fee or a piece of the action. Always remember that these individuals are moving you along the path to financial wealth, and you should not look a gift horse in the mouth. Be grateful and express that gratitude in no uncertain terms. You also have to be decisive and prepared. When you are handed an opportunity that matches your Criteria, you need to be mentally and financially prepared to leap into action. There is no better way to discourage referrers than to sit on or squander the leads they give you. Build a reputation as an investor who rewards leads and is great to work with.

Prospect for Properties

In the beginning your lead generation program will be mainly prospecting-driven; later it will be marketing-enhanced. In terms of learning the game and perfecting your Criteria, nothing replaces calling and

---

Prospecting for Leads

1. Telephone
2. Face-to-Face
   - Walking/Driving Area
   - Seminars & Investment Clubs
   - Community Events
   - Courthouse Proceedings
     - Probate
     - Foreclosure
     - Estate/Tax Sales
     - Bankruptcy
     - Evictions
     - Divorce
3. Research
   - Newspaper
   - Public Postings (HUD, Foreclosure, etc)
   - Multiple Listings Service (MLS)
   - Internet
   - Business Publications
   - Paid Investor Prospect Listings

Figure 45

meeting people, looking at properties, and doing the required research. Prospecting is a vital element in the learning curve of a Millionaire Real Estate Investor. Don't skip it.

There are three basic ways to Prospect for real estate opportunities: telephone, face to face, and research. The first two involve your database, and the last involves your eyes.

A great place to start is the telephone. Flip through the contacts in your database and pick a certain number of people to contact each week. Then set aside some time and start dialing. With your All Properties Bulletin at hand, introduce yourself as an investor and share your Criteria. It's a simple seven-step process that begins with an introduction and ends with a thank you (see the chart below). It's a simple scripted conversation designed to build your reputation as an investor, deliver your Criteria to your Leads Network, and generate leads.

This conversation won't vary a lot even when you're meeting people face to face. For example, if you're walking in a neighborhood and spot

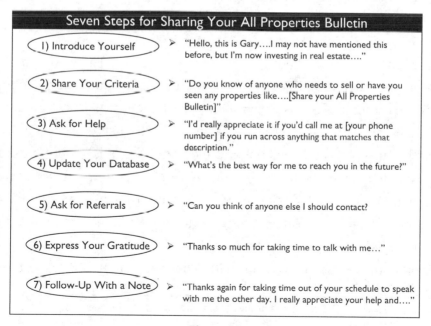

Figure 46

someone working in the yard, you might introduce yourself as an investor interested in buying a property in that area and ask if that person knows anyone who might be planning to sell his or her home in the future. You might leave people like that your "I Buy Real Estate" business card[15] or jot down their contact information so that you can follow up with a note or phone call.

This is a numbers game, and the majority of these conversations will not amount to much. But each time you personally engage someone and share your goals, you're making contact and planting a seed for potential real estate opportunity leads in the future. Time makes this pay off. You never know who your Core Advocates will be until they announce themselves, and this usually happens over time, not immediately. The individual you meet outside his or her home may be an attorney who serves as a trustee for bank foreclosures. That person may be a courthouse clerk with access to valuable information. Or that person may be an investor like you who would love to find a way to marry strengths and work together someday. You never know, so never stop.

One unbelievable opportunity I missed happened right next door to me. Years ago, right after we were married, our next-door neighbor's house was sold for tax liens on the courthouse steps. The buyer got it for a song and later resold it for a huge profit. My neighbor never told me about his troubles because even though he knew I was in real estate, he didn't know I was an investor. The lesson: tell everyone you know or meet because a tremendous opportunity could be right under your nose.

The final method of prospecting is research, in which you search information sources for investment opportunities. This can include the local newspaper's real estate listings, Internet sites, and the public property records at the local courthouse. With the help of a real estate agent you probably can search your local MLS online; it should have a complete

---

[15] Always carry a business card for your investment business. It is a wonderful way to build credibility and break the ice with people you encounter.

and detailed inventory of properties on the market. You may be able to get automated e-mail alerts to let you know when properties that meet your Criteria come on the market in your target area. The courthouse is another huge potential source for foreclosure property opportunities. There is a mini-industry of paid information providers who supply detailed listings of upcoming foreclosure properties; seek them out in the areas where you might want to invest.

Prospecting is a powerful way to find investment opportunities since it directly involves you and your growing expertise. The more you do, the better you get at it. Soon, in conversations and your research, you'll start recognizing important clues that others might miss and pursue them. Interestingly, prospecting's greatest benefit (that it involves you) is also its Achilles' heel: Your prospecting efforts will always be limited in that there are limits to the amount of time and energy you're able and willing to give to them. Nevertheless, prospecting can put you on the path to prosperity, especially when you are prospecting within your well-placed Leads Network. It is the work that must be done if you are to reach your investment goals.

Market for Sellers

One of the important lessons I've learned in business is that most big businesses happen as a result of big lead generation. That means that successful businesspersons leave no method out unless they have to. They both prospect and market for leads. There are limits to your reach with prospecting that don't exist with marketing. Prospecting is something you do; marketing is something you unleash. Once you've set it loose, it works without your having to be there to drive and power it. When you put

Marketing for Leads

- Business Cards
- Direct Mail
- Internet/Email
- Flyers
- Targeted Letters
- Newspaper Ads
- Magazine Ads
- Signs
- Billboards

Figure 47

up a sign on the side of a busy thoroughfare or tack a flyer to a pole, it does lead generating 24 hours a day, relaying your message to everyone who drives past. Prospecting stops when you do, but marketing lives on and on.

A great example of the awesome power marketing can unleash is HomeVestors of America, Inc., a real estate investing franchise company. Ken D'Angelo was a real estate investor in Dallas, Texas, who specialized in fixing and flipping properties. He had a well-proven strategy, and in 1995 he actually (and amazingly) flipped over 170 properties. That was when he knew that he was onto something significant and that it was time to take his model nationwide. The next year D'Angelo parlayed his unique, simple, and highly effective real estate investment marketing program—bright yellow billboards that read "We Buy Ugly Homes" and "Ugly's OK"—into a Top 100 franchise business.[16] His great little investing business became a great big investing business because of great marketing that really worked.

What D'Angelo understood was that to find big financial success through investing in real estate, he would have to have a big lead generation program. Many new and even experienced investors miss this point. For some reason they overlook marketing as a way to find real estate investment opportunities. Millionaires don't overlook it, and neither should you.

In the world of real estate investing marketing is all about attracting motivated sellers. It's a game of problems and solutions. Like the "We Buy Ugly Homes" billboards, you want your marketing to announce to the world that you're an investor and are prepared to solve someone's problem. People have situations that sometimes translate into a need to sell their property and sell it quickly. Maybe the property was inherited and needs more repairs than the owner wants to deal with. Maybe the owner's job or family situation has changed and he needs to move quickly to a larger or smaller home. The owner's problem could arise from a

---

[16] As ranked in 2004 by *Entrepreneur* magazine.

The Millionaire Real Estate Investor

positive circumstance such as a new job opportunity in another town or a negative circumstance such as a company going out of business that has left her short on cash. Regardless of the circumstances, you must realize that you are not the cause of those situations. You are not the problem. You do, however, represent a possible solution if the seller is willing and able to meet your Terms.

Millionaire Real Estate Investor Barbara Mattson shared a story that illustrates this point. A gentleman she had never met came to her one day and asked her to take over six properties he owned that were on the verge of foreclosure. He had approached other real estate professionals, but they had passed on the opportunity; he wanted to keep his credit and was at the end of his choices. Barbara, unlike the others, was thinking like an investor and saw an opportunity for a win-win deal. She agreed to take over the properties and assume responsibility for their debt and payments by using a simple quitclaim deed. Six weeks later Barbara sold the properties for a net profit of $85,000, and although the seller only wanted to avoid foreclosure and asked for no money, Barbara gave him $15,000 in addition to saving his credit. Here was an individual with nowhere else to turn who was helped by a real estate investor who cared enough to help and who understood how to solve people's real estate problems. He won. She won. Everyone won.

Contrary to what some people think, this type of circumstance is not a predator and prey situation. I don't believe in or advocate for dishonesty or deception of any kind to anyone. You want to help, but you're an investor, and by definition your goal is to remove risk from the transaction. You have to get an appropriate discount or Terms on the property, or you can't do the deal. I even encourage you to let the seller know you're an investor and do not plan to live in the property. It's an investment, and although you'd love to help out, it must meet your strict Criteria and Terms. The rest is up to the seller. You have plenty to offer in this type of situation: you're a willing and reliable buyer who is prepared to act quickly and solve the problem. The solution you offer may not be exactly what the seller wants, but it may be the best option he or she has.

The rule of thumb for marketing is that you should always send your message about being a solution to other people's property problems. There are many ways to get the word out. We talked to investors who did massive targeted mailings to subdivisions and neighborhoods. Others advertised in newspapers and real estate journals. Some distributed flyers, put up signs and billboards, or handed out their real estate investor business cards everywhere they went. A few obtained courthouse or publicly available lists of out-of-town property owners, local landlords, and even, in one case, minority owners in companies that held real estate. However, no matter which approach was used, these groups were all sent carefully tailored messages designed to announce a solution to their potential problems and attract motivated sellers.

For example, out-of-town homeowners were sent messages that highlighted the problems of managing a property long-distance, such as screening renters, managing maintenance contractors, and dealing with routine upkeep. All those things can present challenges to out-of-town owners. If your marketing represents you as someone who can solve this problem, maybe two or three out of every hundred people you mail to will inquire about your Terms. That's when the opportunity to make a deal shows up.

Remember to keep the message straightforward and simple. You buy properties, pay cash, and can close quickly. These are the three things someone with a property problem hopes to find—a quick cash solution to his or her troubles. By the way, when investors advertise that they pay cash, they aren't talking about a suitcase of money. They mean that they have set up lines of credit and quick private financing so that in a matter of days or even hours they can have a cashier's check ready for closing. That's what they mean when they say they will pay cash for properties. It's about how quickly you can supply "good as cash" funds to pay for a property.

QUESTION 4: *WHICH* PROPERTIES ARE THE REAL OPPORTUNITIES?

Your lead generation activities are working, and you have investment opportunity leads. Now what? The number one cause of disillusionment and lost momentum is chasing too many leads that look like opportunities but aren't. Although there is no foolproof way to avoid wasting some time with these "suspects," there is a way to avoid wasting a lot of time. It's called qualifying your leads. All this means is that you always must ask a few qualifying questions of the seller or the referrer to make sure the property falls within your Criteria for what you're willing to consider. In other words, they qualify as "prospects."

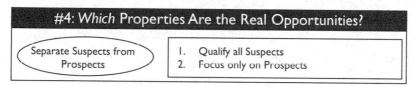

Figure 48

The way to convert suspects to prospects is to write down the broad Criteria that are most important to you and then make sure the property meets them. Properties that do—true prospects—are worth inspecting in greater detail. You still will end up talking to a lot of sellers and seeing a fair amount of property in this qualification process. Some aspect of your Criteria may demand that you get personally involved to get the details you need to make a sound investment decision. There also will be times when individuals in the Support Circle of your Work Network can step in on your behalf and help you qualify properties. Your real estate agent or contractor may be happy to take a look at a property for you and give you his or her opinion. These people are in your Support Circle because they are good at what they do and because you trust their professional judgment. If the suspect turns out to be a true prospect, one way you can reward those people is by involving them professionally in the deal.

The presiding wisdom when you're asking the question *"Which* properties are the real opportunities?" is to bear in mind your strict Criteria and never violate them. Great Criteria act like a safety valve and protect both your time and your money. The truth is that building great lead generation Criteria requires focus over time. If you're looking at single-family homes in a certain part of town, you can get a rough idea of what they sell for and rent for by looking at the current area listings. However, the more suspects you investigate, the better your sense will be of which ones represent true prospects. You'll start to understand which aspects of your Criteria count the most toward market values and rental rates. You need to understand why a certain property sells for the market average while another sells for $15,000 more or why a certain property rents for the average rent while one down the street rents for $150 more. Each time you look, you get a snapshot of how your Criteria perform in specific circumstances. Different factors affect value differently in your targeted areas, but your focus over time will give you insight into this process. Millionaire Real Estate Investors are always refining their Criteria; they want the tremendous advantages that come with truly understanding their market.

> *"When you buy a property, you want it to be worth more that day than what you pay for it."*
>
> Marshall Redder
> Millionaire Real Estate Investor
> Grandville, MI

LIVE THE FIVE LAWS OF LEAD GENERATION

They say that beauty is in the eye of the beholder, and that is certainly true in the game of real estate investing. Millionaire Real Estate Investors approach lead generation with a posture and perspective that allows them to recognize legitimate opportunities and disregard properties that might be trouble. It's a posture and perspective of the watchful investor, and it's built on the Five Laws of Lead Generation.

The Five Laws of Lead Generation

1) Never compromise—You're only looking for properties that meet your Criteria and motivated sellers who will meet your Terms.
2) Be a shopper not a buyer—It's better to miss a good one than buy a bad one.
3) Timing matters—Be the first or last person to make an offer.
4) It's a numbers game—The quality is in the quantity.
5) Be organized and systematic—Protect your time and your money.

Figure 49

Law 1: Never Compromise—You're Only Looking for Properties that Meet Your Criteria and Motivated Sellers Who Will Meet Your Terms

This law is about standards and the patience and persistence it takes to fulfill them. Finding real estate investing opportunities that meet the tough, unyielding standards of a successful investor takes time, patience, and persistence, especially in the beginning. It can take weeks, months, or even longer to find a deal that is right for you. After looking at property after property, many new investors start compromising their Criteria or their Terms.

For an investor the answer to the question "Is this a great deal?" is black and white, a yes or no answer. It is a great deal or it is not. For investors there is no "might be." That is the exclusive territory of speculators.

Properties either meet your strict Criteria or they do not. Sellers are either motivated to accept your strict Terms or they are not. The strong desire to do a deal, to get in the game, can lead to trouble. Never compromise.

Law 2: Be a Shopper, Not a Buyer—It's Better to Miss a Good One Than Buy a Bad One

Investors live for the hunt, the thrill of the chase. They are as attached to the process of searching for investment opportunities as they are to the act of buying them. They are shoppers, not buyers. In our interviews with Millionaire Real Estate Investors, the way they talked about their investments made this very clear. They were as proud of the effort they made in finding a deal and making it happen as they were of the profit they made.

These investors understand that being a shopper instead of a buyer yields two significant advantages. First, they get to enjoy the part of investing they do the most—the ongoing quest for great opportunities. Investing is cyclic. There are times of plenty and times of scarcity, but because they are shoppers, abundance never leads to recklessness and scarcity never leads to impatience. That leads to the second great advantage of this posture: It protects them. These investors never feel the urge to compromise their standards.

> *"It's a lot easier to get into a deal than to get out of one."*
>
> Charles Brown
> Millionaire Real Estate Investor
> Austin, TX

They treat every potential deal with a healthy dose of skepticism. They see properties first as suspects, and only after a thorough examination will they consider them prospects. It's the qualification process. The property must meet their Criteria, and the seller must meet their Terms. Nothing else will do. They believe it is as great a day when they say no as it is when they say yes. While a buyer never leaves the store empty-handed, a shopper will do so happily. Shoppers understand that it is far better to lose a good one than buy a bad one.

Most people think buying is investing, but they're wrong. Buying doesn't make you an investor any more than buying groceries makes you a chef. Making decisions on the basis of sound investment Criteria and Terms makes you an investor. Buying isn't the decisive factor; it's just the result of a decision. If you're looking at property, talking to sellers, and saying no, you're investing. Great investors celebrate the decision-making process first and the outcome second. They know that their success is based not on doing deals but rather on doing *great* deals. They love to shop and decide—not look and buy. In the end the great deals go to the great decision makers. They go to the shoppers.

Law 3: Timing Matters—Be the First or Last Person to Make an Offer

An essential component of finding a seller who will meet your Terms is timing. If at all possible, you want to try to represent the seller's first or last chance to sell. You're looking for the advantage of an uncompetitive environment. When other investors are vying for the same property, the very nature of competitive offers can make it difficult to achieve your Terms.

The lead generation programs of many Millionaire Real Estate Investors are designed to put them in the best possible position to be a seller's first chance to sell. They market and prospect for sellers who do not yet know they are sellers. They are competition-averse and love to ask the question "Have you ever considered selling that property?" They also have a hair trigger when it comes to properties that meet their Criteria.

They don't hesitate to take action and make the right offer. While time will tell if the seller will accept their Terms, they would rather have the offer fall through than risk competitive offers that almost certainly will drive up the price. There is no risk in this decisive action. The property meets their Criteria, and they only make offers that meet their Terms. The very nature of real estate offers is that what the investors are buying is an option to buy the property. If during the property inspection the realities of the property no longer meet their expectations, they can walk away.

If you've participated in an auction, you've seen how the law of being last plays out. Serious investors rarely bid before the auctioneer counts down with "going once, going twice . . ." They understand that most of their competition has been weeded out, and if their price terms can still be met, they make their offer. Also, they rarely stay in the bidding process for long. Great investors pick their moments, and when they can, they choose to be first or last.

Law 4: It's a Numbers Game—The Quality Is in the Quantity

Great lead generation in any business is about overkill over time. The more properties you look at and the more sellers you interview, the greater the odds are that you'll find something great. Millionaire Real Estate Investors understand this, and they cast a wide net for opportunity. The quality is in the quantity.

We surveyed our investors to get a sense of the number of opportunities they investigated to find and make a deal. Statistically it broke down like this: For every 30 properties they found that met their basic Criteria and were worth investigating (suspects), about 10 warranted serious investigation (prospects). Of those 10, only about 3 were worth making an offer on. And because their Terms were as strict as their Criteria, only one of those offers turned into a done deal. Call it the "30:10:3:1 lead generation ratio" for experienced investors.

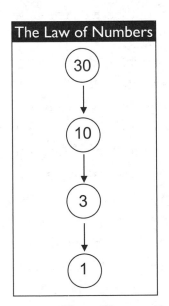

Figure 50

Beginning investors probably will have to look at three to five times as many properties (90 to 150) to find legitimate prospects. Why so many? Millionaire investor George Meidhof says that it's about "developing the knowledge you need to make good decisions." Your Criteria are developed and refined through the process of looking at properties—lots of them—that meet your basic standards. Over time, your sense of what constitutes a great opportunity becomes more precise and the numbers start to turn in your favor. With clear Criteria your marketing and prospecting will yield increasingly qualified leads. Whatever your personal lead generation ratio is, one thing is certain: Lead generation for real estate investments is a numbers game. If you cast a wide net, your chances of netting a winner will improve.

Law 5: Be Organized and Systematic—Protect Your Time and Your Money

The final law of lead generation is about treating it like a business. It's about protecting your time and money by being systematic and organized. When you're looking at real estate investment opportunities or prospecting for them, what's at risk is your time. Considering all the things you could do instead, your time is a precious commodity. Moreover, when you're marketing for opportunities, something even more tangible is at risk: the money you spend on promotions and advertising. That's precious, too.

The key difference between the top performers and the rest lies in their approaches to lead generation. The best sales professionals are systematic. They dedicate a set amount of time each week to lead generation and block their time so that nothing prevents them from pursuing this key business activity. For real estate investing, I've discovered that it takes the same kind of focus. You have to set aside dedicated time systematically each week to prospect for leads, implement your marketing plan, and track the results.

Being organized is about tracking and sourcing leads. When people call you with an opportunity, ask them how they heard about you. When you get the answer, record it. Whether it is the result of your local market or your personal talents, some of your prospecting and marketing efforts will yield better results than others will. The people who

> *"Have checklists for everything that you do."*
>
> Sharon Restrepo
> Millionaire Real Estate Investor
> DelRay Beach, FL

send you opportunities most often should get a disproportionate amount of your attention. Those are the first people you contact and the ones you touch regularly. Similarly, the marketing efforts that generate the most legitimate leads should get a disproportionate amount of your time and money. Unless you're tracking your efforts and recording the results, you may never know how best to spend your time and money to find great investment opportunities.

Think of it as "connecting the dots." Many people don't make the connection between the time and money they spend looking for opportunity and the financial results they achieve. As a result, blocking their time and setting aside money for lead generation can feel like a waste of time and resources and the process of tracking their lead generation efforts can feel boring. Therefore, these things don't get the attention they deserve.

If you make the commitment to being very systematic in your lead generation (and just a little organized), the connections will become clear and exciting. You begin to see not just the time and money you save but also the gains. That's when your efforts take on a different aura. That's when you realize you're not just prospecting, marketing, and tracking the results—you're actually engaged in a fundamental wealth-building activity that is changing your life.

THE FLOW OF YOUR LEAD GENERATION MODEL

When you take a step back and look at all the pieces, you can see the natural flow of how lead generation works (see the chart on the facing page). It's a game of moving around the four circles and constantly engaging your Work Network and Leads Network with only one goal in mind: finding a property that meets your Criteria. Once you find one, you will be ready to follow the Acquisition Model to see if you can acquire it on your Terms.

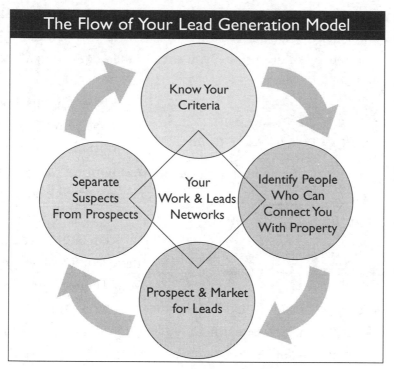

The Flow of Your Lead Generation Model

Know Your Criteria

Identify People Who Can Connect You With Property

Prospect & Market for Leads

Separate Suspects From Prospects

Your Work & Leads Networks

Figure 51

THE ACQUISITION MODEL OF THE MILLIONAIRE REAL ESTATE INVESTOR

Up to this point you've invested your time; now it's time to invest your money. You're at the real estate investor's moment of truth, the place where dreams come true or not, the place where financial wealth is made or lost. It's time to make money.

How do millionaires make money? It's simple: They make their money going in. By following the Acquisition Model and buying right, they virtually guarantee the success of their investments. That is what you want to do: You want to learn to follow the Acquisition Model of the Millionaire Real Estate Investor. If you can purchase property with enough profit built in, you will have ensured, at the time you buy, that your investments will make you money. This is important because once you begin to make real estate acquisitions, your performance will be recorded permanently and forever—no replays or do-overs. If you stick to the Acquisition Model, you won't need any.

> "The advice I give to my students is there's a million ways to make a million dollars in this business. Start by picking one. Learn one way to buy, and get good at it. Only then learn a second way, and then a third."
>
> Don Derosa
> Millionaire Real Estate Investor
> Alpharetta, GA

Earlier in this book we used the phrase "persistent effort, patient money." This moment of acquisition is where we were pointing you. If you have been persistent in your efforts, you can be more confident in investing your money; your patience will have paid off. Many would-be investors do not get this. They are so eager to be real estate investors that they just hop in and buy something. They attempt acquisitions before they know enough to buy wisely or safely. They put their money in play too soon and put themselves at risk.

By sharing the well-earned wisdom and real-life experiences of our Millionaire Real Estate Investors, we have been both preparing your mind and informing your actions to get your investment plans launched. You now understand the Path of Money, you've budgeted so that you have money to invest, and you've set up your Personal Balance Sheet so that you can track your progress. You know how real estate investing can increase your net worth through equity buildup and cash flow growth. You've begun to build your Work Network so that you will have the team you need to mentor you, support you, and service your investments. You've developed your Criteria, and you're lead-generating for it. Now you have leads, prospective opportunities to invest in, and you will have to start making decisions. The decisions you make and the actions you take in these critical moments can have a profound impact on your financial wealth building. Our fifth model, the Acquisition Model, gives you the framework and readiness to analyze these investment opportunities and make great deals.

CASH OR CASH FLOW AND EQUITY

In real estate investing there are only two fundamental acquisition strategies: buy for cash and buy for cash flow and equity buildup. There are many specializations and variations within each of these basic strategies, and they often are referred to by various names, such as optioning, assuming, rehabbing, long-term investing, quick-turn investing, wholesaling, wrapping, lease optioning, and fixing and flipping. However, all those names just complicate the picture. No matter what you call them, these strategies boil down to one simple fact—investors invest for Cash or invest for Cash Flow and Equity. One is a cash-building strategy, and the other is a wealth-building one. All you need to do is decide which of these two strategies you want or need to use and then follow the model for it.

Experienced Millionaire Real Estate Investors often make their investment decision making seem easy. They can look at a property, do some quick calculations on the back of an envelope or in their heads, and tell you whether it could be a good deal or not, along with how they'd do it. This is somewhat frustrating to observe because you can't really follow their thought process and the way they arrive at their answers. At times it can look like they don't have a process at all.

What we came to understand was that millionaires

> *"Buying and selling makes you rich Buying and holding makes you wealthy. We know lots of people who make over a million dollars a year buying and selling. But while having a lot of income means you're rich, it doesn't mean you're wealthy. You won't be really wealthy until you buy and hold and pay them off and let them appreciate."*
>
> Jack Miller
> Millionaire Real Estate Investor
> Reno, NV

do have a method of analysis they follow without fail. It's based on their experience, and they apply it intuitively. It's like a rule of thumb, except with lots of thumbs all working together. You could call it a rule of hand that sometimes seems like sleight of hand, a trick casual observers can't follow. But it's there, and when you put it on paper you begin to see the detailed, step-by-step process they follow. It tells them what to do and allows them to make good decisions quickly and efficiently. The fundamental process they follow is the Acquisition Model of the Millionaire Real Estate Investor (see the chart below).

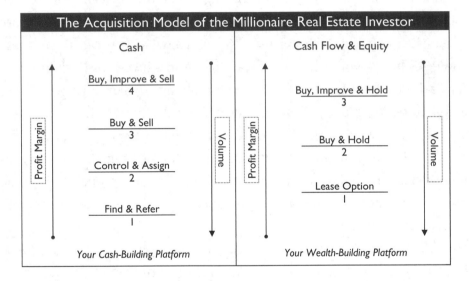

Figure 52

Cash

For some investors, because of their goals or current circumstances, cash is king. If you want cash, you have four basic options for accumulating it: Find & Refer, Control & Assign, Buy & Sell, and Buy, Improve, & Sell.

If you are looking for cash and don't want to invest any money or even write a contract, you can accomplish that through Find & Refer. You can become a scout. As a scout, you seek out good investment opportunities and then bring them to investors who are ready and willing to acquire those properties. In many cases they will be willing to pay you a "finder's fee" if the opportunities are good and they would not have located them otherwise. This is probably the fastest way to earn cash and by far the option you can do the most of in terms of numbers. The drawback is that the money paid per transaction is the least among the four options.

The second fastest option to earn cash is Control & Assign. This means you gain an option or an assignable contract on an investment property and then find someone else to acquire it. Since you control the property, you have negotiation power. This method has a little better margin than Find & Refer, but the volume potential is a little less.

The third option is Buy & Sell, in which you acquire the property, make no improvements, and put it back on the market at a higher price. Your profit margin begins to improve with this option. The issue now is that you will have to spend more time to do these deals and the volume will be less. The payoff is the profit.

> *"When I flip, I want to put at least $15,000 in my pocket. For example, my first flip was a property I bought for $40,000 at a bank auction. I put $40,000 into it and sold it for $125,000. I learned a lot of my fixer-up skills by managing other people's properties: first a six-unit and then a 16-unit building."*
>
> Mary McDonald
> Millionaire Real Estate Investor
> Coopersburg, PA

The fourth option is Buy, Improve, & Sell. This cash-building method can offer even better margins than Buy & Sell, but it takes considerably more time and money and there will likely be even fewer deals to do.

You can see from the Acquisition Model shown in the chart on the facing page that Find & Refer can provide you with lots of fast cash deals but usually pays the least per deal, whereas Buy, Improve, & Sell can pay the most per deal but usually requires considerably more of your investment money to do. There are rare cases where Control & Assign can pay off big, but those deals are extremely hard to find. The truth is that you always should be on the lookout for opportunities, and when a property matches up with one of the four cash-building methods, you should consider moving forward to make some cash from it.

"I always suggest either a long-term or short-term thought process. There are some properties you don't want to keep long-term. If you see some undervalued property but it doesn't really fit into your long-term holding, you can buy it and flip it and make your money."

Bill O'Kane
Millionaire Real Estate Investor
Chicago, IL

In the end the primary purpose of the four cash-building strategies is to generate immediate cash, income which can be used as earned income or put back into play along the Path of Money. Many of the investors we talked with at one time or another used all these methods to launch their real estate investing careers. When they did them right, which they will warn you is not as easy as it often is made out to be, they were able to build up some cash savings, which they could use as down payments on income properties. They were taking cash and reinvesting it for cash flow and equity: long-term financial wealth building.

Cash Flow and Equity

If you want cash flow and equity, you have three options for building and attaining them: Lease Option, Buy & Hold, and Buy, Improve, & Hold.

In the game of cash flow and equity, an option that requires little or no money is the Lease Option. By the way, you can Lease Option In, Lease Option Out, or do both. Lease Option In is when you negotiate to lease a property from the seller (usually for two to five years) with the option to buy at the end of the period at a prenegotiated price. You may or may not have to put money down. As a part of your Lease Option contract agreement, you've secured the right to lease this property to a lease-to-own buyer, and that's exactly what you do, except that you lease the property to a tenant for more than the original lease. The difference between the rent you collect and the lease payment you make is your cash flow. Any difference between the prenegotiated sales price and the market value at the end of the option period is your equity if you choose to buy the property. This is essentially a Lease Option In wrapped inside your Lease Option. The key is to have a renter lined up before you agree to lease option the property.

Lease Option Out is when you rent a property you own to a tenant (possibly someone who needs a few years to clean up his or her credit) with an option to buy at the end of the lease period. You may gain increased cash flow during the lease period and, depending on the pre-negotiated price, gain equity. As you can see, if you Lease Option In and at the same time enter into a Lease Option Out with your renter, you're doing both at once.

The second way to create cash flow and equity is to Buy & Hold. In this case you simply buy the property and lease it out. In some cases you may purchase a property that already has tenants who have signed lease agreements. This can be less complicated than Lease Option In, but you are now actually the owner of the property, and that brings both risk and reward. Also, you no longer are bound to a predetermined sales price and may choose to sell the property at any time or hold it for cash flow and equity buildup as long as you like.

The last and possibly best way to build cash flow and equity is to Buy, Improve, & Hold. This looks just like Buy & Hold, but because improvements must or can be made, there is an opportunity for an additional upside in terms of higher rents and better equity buildup. Some improve-

> *"The first rule is that every property has a surprise."*
>
> George Meidhof
> Millionaire Real Estate Investor
> Reston, VA

ments will be physical, in the sense that you repair the property or add features or amenities. You can also improve it through zoning or use (such as converting residential zoning to commercial or apartments to condos). Because some of your physical improvements may be classified as capital improvements by the IRS, they may effectively reduce the taxes you pay on the cash flow you earn from the property.

In the end the three cash flow and equity-building strategies all work to generate unearned income and increased net worth. Many of the millionaire investors we talked with were very clear about a few things regarding cash, cash flow, and equity buildup. They were very clear that the opportunity in real estate to generate cash is great but that it's also a job. The moment you stop buying and selling, your income goes away. They also believed that building equity and generating cash flow were the ways to create wealth. They also were very clear that each strategy has a formula that cannot be violated. They knew that the dollars are in the details and the profits are in the pennies. They understood that if they didn't manage the process tightly, the big money might escape them. They were right on all counts.

When you take a step back and look at all the ways you can earn cash or build cash flow and equity, the two fundamental ways that stand out above all the others are Buy & Sell and Buy & Hold, especially when they include improvements. They are foundational strategies that, once learned, open the doors to understanding all the other strategies. Let's take a closer look at each one.

TERMS FOR BUY & SELL

In the Buy & Sell strategy you are looking for one thing—cash. The goal is to ensure a net profit payoff within weeks or at most months by buying a property and then turning around and selling it. Although this method usually has the biggest payoffs, it comes with one big challenge: You must know your numbers, lots of them. And if you are going to Buy, Improve, & Sell, there are even more numbers you need to know and understand.

Your numbers have to be accurate going in. You are making a series of predictions, all of which have to turn out pretty much as forecast for the deal to be a success. You better be right or you better have built in a serious margin for error.

The Terms Worksheet for the Buy & Sell (on the next page) allows you to do this in as systematic a way as possible. It is your checklist for making a good investment: Each transaction is unique, and you will have to deal with its quirks on a very short-term basis. With Buy & Sell you need the ability to assess the situation as it unfolds and respond quickly to the contingencies.

> *"I do some deals where I flip properties to make money right away. But I know that that's just to create cash flow. It doesn't create wealth."*
>
> Steve Chader
> Millionaire Real Estate Investor
> Mesa, AZ

Take a moment and read through this worksheet. You'll notice that there are many acronyms with Buy & Sell: ARV, FARV, COP, COR, CC, and COS. Each one represents a number you will need to estimate with great accuracy, and they all will factor into your actual purchase offer. These are the details that when done right yield the dollars you're after. You can see in this worksheet that there is a primary purchase terms section that shows what you will offer for the property and what investment you will make. Then there are four subworksheets that constitute the operating terms section. Each subworksheet is used to determine a key number that will be carried up to the purchase terms and used to determine what will have to happen for this to be a "buy it right" deal.

There are two very important safety margins or factors that must be determined as you use the Buy & Sell investment strategy. First, think Quick Sale! Rick Villani is the founder of Austin-based HomeFixers, the

Terms Worksheet: Buy & Sell

Terms Worksheet			
After Repair Value (ARV)	$ _____		
Fast Sell Factor	− $ _____	%	
Fast After Repair Value (FARV)	= $ _____		
Discount/Profit	− $ _____	%	
1 — Cost of Purchase (COP)	− $ _____		
2 — Cost of Repair (COR)	− $ _____		
3 — Carrying Costs (CC)	− $ _____		
4 — Cost of Sale (COS)	− $ _____		
Purchase Price	= $ _____		
Amount Financed	− $ _____		
Total Investment	= $ _____		

1 — Cost of Purchase Sub-Worksheet	
Finder's Fee	$ _____
Inspection	+ $ _____
Closing Costs	+ $ _____
Total Cost of Purchase	= $ _____

2 — Cost of Repair Sub-Worksheet		
Cosmetic Minor	+ $ _____	
Cosmetic Major	+ $ _____	
Structural	+ $ _____	
Fixtures/Appliances	+ $ _____	
Landscaping	+ $ _____	
Contingency Factor	+ $ _____	%
Total Cost of Repair	= $ _____	

3 — Carrying Costs Sub-Worksheet	
Taxes	+ $ _____
Fees/Insurance	+ $ _____
Utilities/Services	+ $ _____
Debt Service	+ $ _____
Property Upkeep	+ $ _____
Total Carrying Cost	= $ _____

4 — Cost of Sale Sub-Worksheet	
Agent Commissions	+ $ _____
Home Warranty	+ $ _____
Title Insurance & Fees	+ $ _____
Buyer Closing Costs	+ $ _____
Total Cost of Sales	= $ _____

Purchase Terms (rows: After Repair Value through Total Investment)
Operating Terms (Cost of Purchase, Cost of Repair, Carrying Costs, and Cost of Sale Sub-Worksheets)

Figure 53

national contracting company for the real estate investment industry. In any given market, HomeFixers consults with dozens of investors each month and sees first-hand the painful experience of investors who over-estimate the selling price. Rick told us, "Overestimating the market and asking too high a sales price can add weeks, even months, to your selling time. The price a property *might* sell for versus the price it will 'quickly' sell for can be the difference in controlling your carrying costs and, most importantly, making an accurate initial calculation about expected profits. The expected profits establish the initial offer price on the house. So, when forecasting your sell price don't just consider the after repair value (ARV), consider also the 'fast' after repair value (FARV)."

Rick's formula for FARV is two weeks—what will the house sell for within the first two weeks on the market. The difference between ARV (what the house might sell for) and FARV (what the house will sell for within the first two weeks on the market) is the "Fast Sell Factor."

The second safety factor is called your Discount/Profit Margin and is the actual margin from which you will make your profit on the investment. This number is critical because it also has to give you breathing room—your margin for error—in case something unforeseen happens. This could include hidden repairs, unexpected bad weather, contractor delays, and any number of examples of Murphy's Law: What can go wrong will go wrong. Those with the most experience in this method of real estate investing feel that the Discount/Profit Margin needs to be as high as 30 percent of your property price. As the price of the property increases, they believe that this margin usually becomes a flat dollar amount such as $30,000 or $40,000, since the 30 percent figure may not hold up for properties

> *"Based on my experience of working with hundreds of real estate investors across the nation, my advice about the Buy, Improve & Sell strategy is: One, stick to your buying Criteria— resist the pressure to buy an overpriced property especially when you've gone a very long time without buying something. Two, don't underestimate the repair cost. If they've shot themselves in the foot because they bought it too high, many investors will drive the final nail in the coffin by wrongly assuming that 'it just needs paint and carpet.'"*
>
> Rick Villani
> Millionaire Real Estate Investor
> Austin, TX

costing in excess of $150,000. In either case, they agree that you must establish this margin going in. You have to be accurate and conservative in all your cost estimates, assessment of eventual market value, and estimate of the price point that would sell the property quickly.

The subworksheets are fairly self-explanatory. As much as anything they are meant to be reminders so that you never omit these important costs in your thinking. For example, the Cost of Purchase subworksheet reminds you to account for the costs of potentially rewarding the scout who brought you the deal, paying your inspector to walk through the property with you, and any other closing costs you might incur as the buyer.

Using the Cost of Repair subworksheet instantly transforms your Terms Worksheet: Buy & Sell into a Terms Worksheet: Buy, Improve, & Sell—an entirely different kind of transaction. The Cost of Repair subworksheet is also slightly different in that it is a summary worksheet as well. The five main repair categories—Cosmetic Minor, Cosmetic Major, Structural, Fixtures/Appliances, and Landscaping—have detailed subworksheets of their own. (See Appendix D for a detailed version of this worksheet). For example, for Cosmetic Minor repairs you might include everything from carpets and paint to adding new hardware to the cabinets and crown molding to the living room. Because there are so many things to consider, it pays to have a detailed checklist. It also pays to account for a contingency factor here. One of our favorite and most helpful investors, Bob Guest, was very fond of reminding us that "every house has a surprise," and he was absolutely right. The Cost of Repairs subworksheet is where you account for that contingency factor as it relates to repairs.

> *"Rehabbing can be an extraordinarily risky venture. The goal is to finish the house off to homeowner standards. You have to know what you're doing, and you can't do it halfway."*
>
> Vena Jones-Cox
> Millionaire Real Estate Investor
> Cincinnati, OH

The Carrying Costs subworksheet is where you'll estimate the taxes, fees, utilities, debt service, and upkeep you'll have to pay for from the time you buy the property to the time you sell it. Remember that these are all time-based estimates. You'll need your contractor to tell you how quickly he or she can complete the expected repairs and then pad that time frame to account for bad weather, worker unavailability, and any other potential delays. This is your repair time. Next, you have to account for the time it will take to show, sell, and close on the property. Many of the good investors we talked with conservatively budgeted for three to four months of carrying costs for homes with only minor repairs. Repairing and selling can take much longer than you might expect.

Many of the homes targeted by Buy & Sell investors are often at the high low end or lower middle market. This means you're not always selling to buyers with lots of cash for closing and perfect credit. The great offer you accept may fall through because of financing or credit issues. This could mean starting over, and that means time.

The Costs of Sale subworksheet is appropriately last. This is where you must account for any real estate agent commissions if you enlist the help of an agent to market and sell the property. You'll probably want to include a home warranty for a few hundred dollars since it can give both you and your buyer security against the unknown. Other costs of sale include title insurance, origination fees, and the like—all the typical closing costs associated with traditional financing. A real estate agent, title officer, or mortgage loan officer can help you calculate these costs correctly. This can be a big "gotcha" for a Buy & Sell investor who doesn't prepare for the right type of buyer. Because you could be dealing in homes on the lower end of the market, you may be asked to pay the buyer's closing costs. Your buyer may have great credit and be willing to meet your asking price but have no cash for closing costs; account for that and you'll be protected in the long run.

Buy, Improve & Sell for Maximum Return

Finally, when it comes to Buy, Improve, & Sell, you should be aware that you have a window of opportunity to achieve a Maximum Return (see the chart below). Understanding this window makes you an expert in maximizing your returns when improving real estate investments.[17]

On the front end you know that you will have to invest a certain amount of money and make a certain amount of improvements just to break even. As you begin to invest money in improvements, even with your Discount/Profit Margin taken into account, you may reach a point

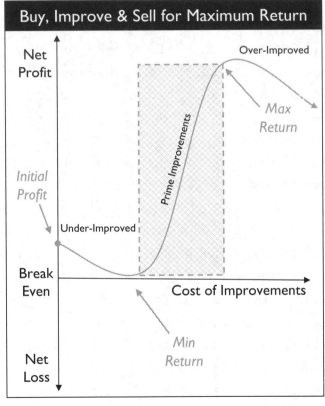

Figure 54

---

[17] Maximum Return is used by permission of HomeFixers. Thanks, Rick!

where the costs of improvement have chewed away your margin. Selling before this point (while the property is under-improved and not yet ready for resale) will lower your profit margin or even cost you money. At a certain point, you realize that your improvements reach critical mass—the point of your minimum return (or maximum loss)—and subsequent improvements will earn you more than they cost.

From this point on, as you make additional improvements (if they are the right improvements), you will increase the market value of the property. You are in the prime improvement zone. However, be aware that this increase in value has a practical limit: what the market will bear. From here on any additional investment in improvements will not add much, if any, market value to the property. You have reached the point of Maximum Return on Investment. It is now time to avoid over-improving the property and put it on the resale market fast, cash in on your profit margin, and move on to the next investment.

Knowing which improvements, at what cost, will bring the Maximum Return is the ultimate skill in this game. It's the game of getting the highest return from the least investment in improvements. Investors with construction experience and those with do-it-yourself skills and a solid knowledge of repair work can do well with Buy, Improve, & Sell. Not only do they enter the game with an informed idea of the costs and time needed to do common repairs, they are capable of doing many of those repairs themselves. This sweat equity allows them to exchange their time and labor for reduced expenses and larger profit margins. Most people, however, will need the advice of an experienced contractor and the help of a solid team of repair and remodeling professionals to optimize this strategy.

> *"Beginners often make the mistake of fixing a property as though they were going to move into it. That's the wrong way to do it."*
>
> Judy Cook
> Millionaire Real Estate Investor
> Ronan, MT

Terms for Buy & Hold

We are now ready to consider the true financial wealth-building strategic option of the real estate investor: Buy & Hold. This is the long-term strategy that can bring you maximum equity and personal net worth. Ultimately, it's the strategy you will want to use and master. Buy & Hold epitomizes what we learned in the Financial Model about the power of real estate investments to create Equity Buildup and Cash Flow Growth.

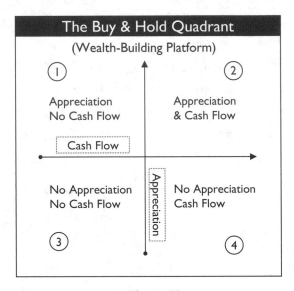

Figure 55

The Buy & Hold illustration above highlights the primary financial considerations to bear in mind for your long-term acquisition strategy. You're buying properties for Appreciation, Cash Flow, or, preferably, both. You can give primary emphasis to Appreciation (quadrant 1) or Cash Flow (quadrant 4) or both (quadrant 2). What you want to avoid is any investment that falls in quadrant 3—low or no cash flow and low or no appreciation. This is not the path of the Millionaire Real Estate Investor, because the risks are way too high. Millionaires buy quadrant 2 properties and avoid quadrant 3.

Remember, a great real estate investment carries almost no risk. It is based on the underlying fundamentals of attaining price and rent appreciation. Buy it right going in and those fundamentals will work relentlessly in your favor.

> "I'd rather buy homes to keep than sell because I don't want to lose the income."
>
> Marshall Redder
> Millionaire Real Estate Investor
> Grandville, MI

Buy & Hold is just as much a numbers game as Buy & Sell is, but you're letting the results happen over a longer, more predictable period of time. Doing it right at the beginning—making your money going in—is just as critical here, and there is a process to follow to help make this happen: a preinvestment checklist. We call it the Term Worksheet: Buy & Hold (see the chart on the next page). Just as with Buy & Sell, there is a purchase terms section and an operating terms section. The four subsections of the operating terms guide you in estimating and calculating the numbers that will be placed in the purchase terms section. This will determine what you can offer for the property and what you will accept. Once again, these terms are financial, and you must become a master of the financial terms that make a real estate investment work.

For openers, you must have an accurate figure for the current market value of the property as well as some well-supported evidence that home price appreciation will continue for that price range in that area. Next, you must establish your Discount/Profit Margin up front. This is your basic foundation for "buy it right." The margin we recommend is at least 20 percent, more if you can get it. Just as with Buy & Sell, for investments over about $150,000, you'll want to pick a dollar amount ($20,000 to $25,000 is the typical range) since this percentage will be hard to attain in middle and high-end properties. Purchasing the property with this margin gives you security and often means that you will achieve positive net cash flow from the very beginning.

Terms Worksheet: Buy & Hold

Terms Worksheet

<table>
<tr><td rowspan="14">Purchase Terms</td><td></td><td>Market Value (MV)</td><td>$</td><td></td><td></td></tr>
<tr><td></td><td>Discount/Profit</td><td>– $</td><td></td><td>%</td></tr>
<tr><td></td><td>Purchase Price</td><td>= $</td><td></td><td></td></tr>
<tr><td></td><td>Amount Financed</td><td>– $</td><td></td><td></td></tr>
<tr><td></td><td>Down Payment</td><td>= $</td><td></td><td>%</td></tr>
<tr><td>1</td><td>Cost of Purchase (COP)</td><td>+ $</td><td></td><td></td></tr>
<tr><td>2</td><td>Cost of Repair (COR)</td><td>+ $</td><td></td><td></td></tr>
<tr><td></td><td>Total Investment</td><td>= $</td><td></td><td></td></tr>
<tr><td>3</td><td>Net Operating Income (NOI)</td><td>$</td><td></td><td></td></tr>
<tr><td>4</td><td>Principal & Interest</td><td>– $</td><td></td><td></td></tr>
<tr><td></td><td>Cash Flow Monthly/ Annual</td><td>= $</td><td>-</td><td>= $</td></tr>
</table>

1 — Cost of Purchase Sub-Worksheet

Finder's Fee	$	
Inspection	+ $	
Closing Costs	+ $	
Total Cost of Purchase	= $	

2 — Cost of Repair Sub-Worksheet

Cosmetic Minor	$	
Cosmetic Major	+ $	
Structural	+ $	
Fixtures/Appliances	+ $	
Landscaping	+ $	
Contingency Factor	+ $	%
Total Cost of Repair	= $	

3 — Net Operating Income Sub-Worksheet

Gross Rental Income	$	% of MV
Vacancy	– $	
Net Rental Income	= $	
Expenses		
Property Management	– $	
Leasing Costs (Annual/12)	– $	
Maintenance (Annual Reserve/12)	– $	
Utilities	– $	
Property Taxes	– $	% of MV
Insurance	– $	% of MV
Other	– $	
Net Operating Income	= $	

4 — Principal & Interest Sub-Worksheet

30-Year Mortgage		
30-Year Mortgage Rate		%
30-Year Principal & Interest	$	
15-Year Mortgage Rate		
15-Year Mortgage Rate		%
15-Year Principal & Interest	$	

Figure 56

The vast majority of Millionaire Real Estate Investors believe that having positive cash flow is critical. Some are willing to do without discounts or even deal with short-term negative cash flow if they can get solid appreciation. It happens all the time but requires a lot of knowledge and skill to successfully pull off. However, in the overwhelming majority of cases millionaire investors go for both, and we recommend that you do the same thing.

The second big decision in the purchase terms section is the down payment. In some cases the lender on a mortgage for an investment property will require you, the investor, to put down 20 percent. They want to be sure that you have your money as well as theirs at risk. Because you won't be living in the property, they want extra assurance that you are equally committed to the investment. If you are going to be living in the home, even though you are doing it as part of your investment strategy (we call this Buy & Live), you may be able to purchase it with little or no money down.

The same calculations for Cost of Purchase and Cost of Repair are done here that were done with Buy & Sell. They are straightforward, and you can use the same detailed repair estimate worksheet that is in Appendix D.

> *"I have a rule. I will walk away from a hundred marginal deals to get one good one. In other words, I'm a very picky buyer. I never buy negative cash flow. Positive cash flow gives you an unlimited holding period."*
>
> Todd Tresidder
> Millionaire Real Estate Investor
> Reno, NV

What is unique to the Buy & Hold Worksheet is the Net Operating Income Subworksheet. This is where you will come to know the numbers that make a residential income property work for you. You will have to determine the current monthly rental rates in your local area for the type of property you are considering. That's what you put on the line for Gross Rental Income. While many longtime investors use a 1 percent rule of thumb (you will get as your monthly rent an amount equal to 1 percent of the property's market value), if you must guess, we recommend a more conservative ratio of 0.8 percent. Instead of counting on a $100,000 home to rent for $1,000 per month, you conservatively use $800 for your rental estimation.

No rule of thumb is good enough for estimating this critical number in your acquisition worksheet. You need to *know* what that particular property has rented for in the past or what similar properties rent for in the neighborhood. While you are doing your due diligence on the property, ask for copies of the lease, call the numbers on area rental signs, and research the Internet, an MLS, and newspapers for market rents. Your ballpark estimate using our 0.8 percent rule may have been fine for making an initial evaluation or even an offer, but the real rental value, which is determined through due diligence and market research, will be a deal-breaking factor in your ongoing negotiations.

Having established your best projection for Gross Rental Income, you must allow for vacancies: times when the property is unoccupied and you are not receiving rental income. We have used 6 to 8 percent (or about three to four weeks annually) as a Vacancy factor in our model, but you will have to determine this locally and take into account current rental market conditions. When you subtract your Vacancy factor from the Gross Rental Income, you have your Net Rental Income. From that you will subtract all your Expenses (your monthly operating costs), which will leave you with your Net Operating Income (NOI). What you now have is a number that will tell you what you will be able to pay in debt service (the monthly principal and interest on your mortgage loan) and what Cash Flow you will have left.

This is a critical point in the Buy & Hold acquisition model. If the property does not produce cash flow with the numbers you have, you will have to lower your offer appropriately or seek special financing. The right terms on your loan (interest rate and length of payback) can often make a significant difference. The investors we talked to were extremely creative in their financing solutions. They understood how to take advantage of variable-rate and adjustable-rate conventional mortgages to get immediate cash flow on the deal. Often they sought seller financing, which allowed them to set terms that were unique to each deal. All these strategies may require trade-offs, so be aware of this at all times. Shortcuts that get you Cash Flow often take away from your Equity Buildup.

As a simple way to illustrate this, we created a chart to illustrate the dramatic difference in Equity Buildup using a 15-year conventional loan versus a 30-year loan (see chart). In general, shorter terms on your mortgage loans will lead to higher monthly loan payments that have a direct negative impact on your Cash Flow but a major positive impact on your Equity Buildup. As you can see, after 16 years the 15-year loan is completely paid off (which means you'll experience a big jump in Cash Flow). In contrast, at year 16 the 30-year loan still has 75 percent of the principal debt remaining.

Millionaire Real Estate Investor Ron Garber adopted a strategy of acquiring a single property and then aggressively paying down the principal by using any income he and his wife had. Together, they acquired foreclosure properties in California and effectively turned 30-year mort-

Percentage of Annual Debt Paid Down by Mortgage Term				
Year	15 Year Note	Debt Remaining	30-Year Note	Debt Remaining
1	3.9%	96.1%	0.9%	99.1%
2	4.2%	91.9%	1.0%	98.1%
3	4.5%	87.4%	1.1%	97.0%
4	4.8%	82.5%	1.2%	95.8%
5	5.2%	77.4%	1.3%	94.6%
6	5.5%	71.8%	1.4%	93.2%
7	5.9%	65.9%	1.5%	91.7%
8	6.4%	59.5%	1.6%	90.2%
9	6.8%	52.7%	1.7%	88.5%
10	7.3%	45.3%	1.8%	86.7%
11	7.9%	37.5%	2.0%	84.7%
12	8.4%	29.1%	2.1%	82.6%
13	9.0%	20.0%	2.3%	80.3%
14	9.7%	10.4%	2.4%	77.9%
15	10.4%	0.0%	2.6%	75.2%
16			2.8%	72.4%
17			3.1%	69.3%
18			3.3%	66.0%
19			3.5%	62.5%
20			3.8%	58.7%
21			4.1%	54.6%
22			4.4%	50.1%
23			4.8%	45.4%
24			5.1%	40.2%
25			5.5%	34.7%
26			6.0%	28.8%
27			6.4%	22.3%
28			6.9%	15.4%
29			7.4%	8.0%
30			8.0%	0.0%

* Based on average mortgage rates from 1992 to 2003: 6.97% for 15-year and 7.43% for 30-year.

Figure 57

gages into 12- and 24-month mortgages. Admittedly, the first few houses were the most difficult and required the strictest personal budgeting. But they stuck to the strategy because they "couldn't stand having debt." They wanted their assets free and clear, and so only when they had paid off one property fully would they acquire another and then apply all the cash flow from all the paid-off properties to the new one. Each property that was paid off accelerated the process, and in a matter of years the Garbers assembled an impressive portfolio of investment properties that generated big Cash Flow with almost no financial liabilities.

While these debt-averse investors represent an extreme version of Equity Buildup, their aggressive strategy made them Millionaire Real Estate Investors and gave them financial freedom. As we discussed in the section on the Financial Model, if you don't need the cash flow today, why not reinvest it for tomorrow? Reinvestment can put you on the fast track to financial freedom.

With your Net Operating Income and Principal and Interest sub-worksheets completed, you're now able to plug in the final pieces of your purchase terms at the top. This is where you are considering four things at once: the best purchase price, what kind of loan to use, how the seller might provide additional help with the financing, and whether you want to do this deal. If the Terms Worksheet shows you that the numbers will work with conventional (15-year or 30-year) financing, you will be willing to make an offer. If the seller is unwilling to meet these terms or if you need additional, low-cost owner financing to make it work and the seller is not willing to do that, you will not be able to accept the deal. With your options exhausted, you will, with no attachment to this property, move on in your Criteria-based lead generation. If the seller agrees to what you have offered (based on your thorough analysis of the numbers on the Terms Worksheet), you have a deal and will make the investment.

ACQUISITION WORKSHEETS: REAL-LIFE EXAMPLES

To see how the Acquisition Worksheets can be used in your investment decision making, let's look at two real-life examples. We will be dealing with the same property, but from two different investment points of view. In the first case we will be using the Buy & Sell Worksheet, and in the second case the Buy & Hold Worksheet. Our target property is a $125,000 single-family home. Whether we use Buy & Sell or Buy & Hold, this example will involve Costs of Purchase and Costs of Repairs. In the Buy & Sell analysis (case 1), we will be focusing on our Fast After-Repair Value, Carrying Costs, and Costs of Sale. In the Buy & Hold analysis (case 2), we will be focusing on our Net Operating Income and our Principal & Income (debt service). In both cases we will be looking for and factoring in a Discount/Profit Margin of 30 percent for the Buy & Sell and 20 percent for the Buy & Hold. Finally, we are going to assume that we have about $28,000 to put toward either investment.

The Buy & Sell Worksheet in Action

First, let's look at this property using the Terms Worksheet: Buy & Sell (see the chart on the next page). The purchase terms are described at the top of the worksheet, with subworksheets below to get the primary numbers. We have estimated the market value of the property to be $125,000. The Cost of Purchase (the expenses incurred at closing, excluding the sales price) is $925, which includes the inspector's fee and the closing costs.

The Cost of Repair subworksheet details the work you will need to have done for the house to sell for the maximum return on your investment. The house's interior needs new paint, new carpeting throughout, and a good cleaning ($3,200). The roof needs to be repaired, which you manage to do for $1,800. The kitchen is also a mess, and so you install new composite countertops ($300), repaint the cabinets, and update the pulls and hinges ($250); to top it all off, you install a new oven and dish-

Terms Worksheet: Buy & Sell

Terms Worksheet			
After Repair Value (ARV)	$	125,000.00	
Fast Sell Factor	− $	12,500.00	10 %
Fast After Repair Value (FARV)	= $	112,500.00	
Discount/Profit	− $	33,750.00	30 %
1 Cost of Purchase (COP)	− $	925.00	
2 Cost of Repair (COR)	− $	7,095.00	
3 Carrying Costs (CC)	− $	2,420.00	
4 Cost of Sale (COS)	− $	10,360.00	
Purchase Price	= $	57,950.00	
Amount Financed	− $	30,000.00	
Total Investment	= $	27,950.00	

1 Cost of Purchase Sub-Worksheet		
Finder's Fee	$	0.00
Inspection	+ $	125.00
Closing Costs	+ $	800.00
Total Cost of Purchase	= $	925.00

2 Cost of Repair Sub-Worksheet		
Cosmetic Minor	+ $	3,200.00
Cosmetic Major	+ $	0.00
Structural	+ $	1,800.00
Fixtures/Appliances	+ $	1,250.00
Landscaping	+ $	200.00
Contingency Factor	+ $	645.00 10 %
Total Cost of Repair	= $	7,095.00

3 Carrying Costs Sub-Worksheet		
Taxes	+ $	750.00
Fees/Insurance	+ $	350.00
Utilities/Services	+ $	300.00
Debt Service	+ $	900.00
Property Upkeep	+ $	120.00
Total Carrying Cost	= $	2,420.00

4 Cost of Sale Sub-Worksheet		
Agent Commissions	+ $	6,750.00
Home Warranty	+ $	485.00
Title Insurance & Fees	+ $	1,125.00
Buyer Closing Costs	+ $	2,000.00
Total Cost of Sales	= $	10,360.00

Purchase Terms

Operating Terms

Figure 58

washer ($700). The yard needs work, and so you hire a local lawn company to mow and edge, trim the trees out front, and plant some perennials in the front beds ($200). So far the repairs will cost you $6,450, but to be safe you add 10 percent ($645) as a contingency factor. The Total Cost of Repair is $7,095.

In the Carrying Costs subworksheet we are allowing for three months' worth of these expenses. You have estimated that all the repair work can be done in a month and that it will take a month to sell and another month to close. Therefore, you are allowing for three months of taxes at $250 per month ($750 total), the cost of your insurance policy ($350), and three months of utilities at $100 per month ($300 total). Since you have $28,000 to invest, you will need to borrow $30,000. Your private lending source is going to charge you 1 percent a month interest, which will total $900 for the three months. The total Carrying Costs thus will be $2,420. You can see that any additional carrying time will cost you $800 a month, so getting it sold quickly is important.

> "One time, I found out the day before a foreclosure sale that the bank had decided to reduce their opening bid by over $100,000. With this knowledge, a partner and I purchased the house at foreclosure and were able to sell it in less than 90 days and pocket the $100,000. Not too shabby!"
>
> Dyches Boddiford
> Millionaire Real Estate Investor
> Marietta, GA

Finally, you will look at the Cost of Sale subworksheet to be certain that you have planned for these expenses. You allow for a 6 percent agent commission on the planned $112,500 sale price ($6,750), a home warranty of $485, title insurance and related fees of $1,125 (about 1 percent), and an allowance for buyer closing costs of $2,000. While you may be able to close the sale without incurring all these expenses, you need to allow for them. If it costs less to repair, carry, or sell the property, you make more.

As you now look closely at the Terms Worksheet: Buy & Sell, you see that you will be able to offer $58,000 for the property. If the seller accepts this, you have a deal. If not, you will have to move on. There is little wiggle room in your calculations. While you have allowed for some contingencies, this is the only price at which you can be confident of getting the proper return on investment. You are putting in almost $28,000 of your own money and the liability of an additional $30,000 loan to achieve a net profit of $33,750. If anything goes wrong and any of your costs go up, that profit margin can be reduced quickly. Since you are a disciplined real estate investor who knows your numbers, the purchase price will be $57,950 or it won't be a deal.

The Buy & Hold Worksheet in Action

Let's look at the same $125,000 property using the Terms Worksheet: Buy & Hold (see the chart on the facing page). Again, the purchase terms are described at the top of the worksheet, with subworksheets below to get the primary numbers. Since you are following the Millionaire Real Estate Investors' guidance, you will need to get a 20 percent discount on the property ($25,000) and therefore will offer $100,000 to buy it. You have $28,000 to invest, and so you will be able to put 20 percent down ($20,000) and finance 80 percent ($80,000).

As in the Buy & Sell Model, your Cost of Purchase is $925 and your Cost of Repair is $7,095. Since you will be holding the property and renting it, you will not be dealing with either closing costs for a resale or carrying costs for the holding period. You will have ongoing carrying costs, but they will be paid from the rental income.

The Net Operating Income Subworksheet is the place where your analysis of the investment must be sharp. A quick glance reveals that

Terms Worksheet: Buy & Hold

Terms Worksheet

Market Value (MV)		$	125,000.00	
Discount/Profit	−	$	25,000.00	20%
Purchase Price	=	$	100,000.00	
Amount Financed	−	$	80,000.00	
Down Payment	=	$	20,000.00	20%
1 Cost of Purchase (COP)	+	$	925.00	
2 Cost of Repair (COR)	+	$	7,095.00	
Total Investment	=	$	28,020.00	
3 Net Operating Income (NOI)		$	563.33	
4 Principal & Interest	−	$	555.54	
Cash Flow Monthly/ Annual	=	$	7.79	= $ 93.52

Purchase Terms

1 Cost of Purchase Sub-Worksheet

Finder's Fee		$	0.00
Inspection	+	$	125.00
Closing Costs	+	$	800.00
Total Cost of Purchase	=	$	925.00

2 Cost of Repair Sub-Worksheet

Cosmetic Minor		$	3,200.00	
Cosmetic Major	+	$	0.00	
Structural	+	$	1,800.00	
Fixtures/Appliances	+	$	1,250.00	
Landscaping	+	$	200.00	
Contingency Factor	+	$	645.00	10%
Total Cost of Repair	=	$	7,095.00	

3 Net Operating Income Sub-Worksheet

Gross Rental Income		$	1,000.00	0.8%	of MV
Vacancy	−	$	60.00		
Net Rental Income	=	$	940.00		
Expenses					
Property Management	−	$	0.00		
Leasing Costs (Annual/12)	−	$	16.67		
Maintenance (Annual Reserve/12)	−	$	20.00		
Utilities	−	$	0.00		
Property Taxes	−	$	250.00	0.20%	of MV
Insurance	−	$	75.00	0.06%	of MV
Other	−	$	15.00		
Net Operating Income	=	$	563.33		

4 Principal & Interest Sub-Worksheet

30-Year Mortgage		
30-Year Mortgage Rate		7.43%
30-Year Principal & Interest	$	555.54
15-Year Mortgage Rate		
15-Year Mortgage Rate		6.97%
15-Year Principal & Interest	$	717.72

Operating Terms

Figure 59

the three biggest expenses are property taxes, insurance, and vacancy. The first is impossible to avoid or control. Tax rates vary greatly from municipality to municipality. Ask your local tax assessor's office or your real estate agent for the local taxation rates. Insurance also fluctuates greatly depending on the type and location of a property. When you call to get quotes, remember to indicate that the property will be an investment property since that will affect the rates.[18] These costs should be factored into the rent you charge. Vacancy is something you can manage by making both the property and the rent attractive to renters. We'll discuss this, along with maximizing your rents, in "Own a Million." For now you need to realize that these three expenses can cost as much as 40 percent of your gross rental income. You need to be aware of them and manage what you can control to maximize your NOI.

Your NOI is really what dictates the kind of financing you can afford to select. In our example, the 30-year mortgage loan is the only one that actually will generate Cash Flow. Even then, this sample property will net the investor only $7.79 a month, or less than $100 a year. These numbers are sobering indeed, and they illustrate how difficult it can be to find the kinds of great deals that generate cash flow of $200, $300, or even $500 a month. Rent, as we'll explain in "Own a Million," is your most powerful lever in this equation. If you rented this property for just 0.02 percent of the market price more (the frequently talked about but not easily achieved 1 percent rule), you'd net $242.79 a month and $2,913.52 a year the very first year.

We have looked at this real estate investment using each of the two terms worksheets, using real numbers. If you want to Buy, Improve, & Sell, you can pay about $58,000. If you want to Buy, Improve, & Hold, you can pay about $100,000. This is assuming that *all* your numbers are correct. If any of the numbers change, so does your offer or your return.

---

[18] Your occupants should be required to provide their own renter's insurance, and so you're just insuring the property itself and possibly seeking liability insurance if you don't have an umbrella policy or your personal homeowner's insurance won't protect you. Be a shopper, not a buyer. You're trying to minimize your number two expense!

The Millionaire Real Estate Investor

In the beginning it will take time and discipline to complete this analysis for each investment opportunity you investigate. Until you know how much it costs to get carpets installed, you have to call vendors and get quotes. Until you know market rents, you have to research them. But with some practice and experience, more and more of these numbers will be readily available to you. Either you already have the numbers or you know someone who can supply them quickly. This is how two Millionaire Real Estate Investors we know were able to estimate the total repairs on a property they purchased within 5 percent of the final costs with nothing more than a notepad and a 10-minute walk-through. Over time the process will get easier, but it never should be dropped. It will always inform and protect you.

BUY A MILLION: YOU HAVE THE POWER

If knowledge is power, you now have more power. You should feel ready, willing, and more able than ever before to make real estate investments—to take your financial wealth building to the next level. All that remains is to get into action—informed, purposeful action. There are two very practical steps to take—first, to understand value, and second, to get perspective—before you explore your acquisition strategies.

By that we mean you must study your target marketplace and know the prices for properties that meet your criteria and know the trends of those prices. Is the market appreciating? At what rate? What makes you think it will continue to appreciate? What are the economic and demographic forces driving the prices both in the area and in specific neighborhoods? In addition, you will need to study rental rates. What are the expected rental rates for the properties that meet your criteria? Are they

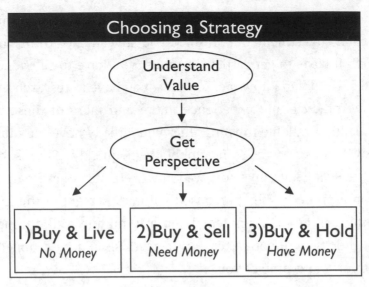

Figure 60

going up, going down, or staying flat? What has been the trend over time, and what is predicted? What are renters looking for that might allow for higher rental rates?

As you look at more and more properties, check what they are selling for, and learn what rental rates they are getting, you will build confidence as an investor and be able to calculate the numbers you will put in your terms worksheets accurately. This will empower you to identify the best investment opportunities, make intelligent offers, and "buy it right" when you acquire a property. You eventually will become a value expert for your type of investment properties in your targeted areas.

The second step is to get perspective on where you are on your path as an investor. You will have three choices for your primary short-term strategy: Buy & Live, Buy & Sell, and Buy & Hold. If you are just beginning and have little or no capital to invest, your best bet is Buy & Live. This means you will treat your own residence as an investment. You will buy it like an investment with the added advantage of being able to get the kinds of financing and minimum down payments that are available to owner-occupant buyers. You can add your own sweat equity while you are living in the house and thereby increase its value. In the future you can move on to another residence (also purchased using an investor mindset) and sell the first one for a profit or hold it for equity buildup and cash flow. Many investors have used this financially sound strategy of buying, living, moving, and holding.

If you currently have your own residence, want to invest in more real estate, but don't have money to invest, the Buy & Sell strategy is a great way to build up your investment capital. By acquiring properties under market value, fixing them up (if they need it), and quickly reselling them, you can make a net profit. While you usually will have to pay taxes on that profit, you can use the remaining money to make your next investment. As you do more of these deals, you can increase the amount of money you have available for investing. There are Millionaire Real Estate Investors who have used some of this cash flow for their living expenses. In this case they are buying and selling real estate as both a job and a way to earn cash for future investing. Eventually, though, they will be investing the greater proportion of the cash they receive.

In the end all roads lead to Buy & Hold. This is where true financial wealth is built. You know this from studying the Financial Model. When you have the money from your savings or your net cash proceeds, you will look to acquire properties that you can rent and hold for the long term, maximizing your Equity Buildup and Cash Flow Growth. No matter where you are on the path, pick the best strategy and then follow the models of the Millionaire Real Estate Investor. Stick to your Criteria, be systematic in your lead generation, use the worksheets, insist on getting your Terms, engage your Network, and be a shopper, not a buyer—in fact, shop till you drop. Your financial Net Worth will rise, perhaps to a level you never imagined.

■ Proven models allow you to learn from the mistakes of others as well as build on their successes. The five key models in real estate investing are the Net Worth, Financial, Network, Lead Generation, and Acquisition models.

■ *Net Worth Model:*

- Learn the *Path of Money*—Money has a path and you must guide it to the places that will yield the greatest financial growth and most substantial net worth.

- *Budget* for Investments—Stay on the Path, differentiating between what you want and what you need. Make a personal budget and hone the discipline to stick to it.

- *Track* personal net worth—Keep a household P&L and balance sheet to track net worth over time. Examine your total often, and ask yourself, "How can I make it grow?"

■ *Financial Model:*

- There are two ways to build wealth by investing in real estate: Equity Buildup and Cash Flow Growth.

- *Equity Buildup*: increases your net worth in your real estate assets and comes from the twin forces of price appreciation and debt paydown.

- *Cash Flow Growth:* provides a stream of unearned income, possible when you buy it right, finance wisely and control your expenses.

- Adopt the motto *"Buy it right—Pay it down—Pay it off!"*

  ◆ *"Buy It Right"*—make your money going in, assuring yourself the best of Equity Buildup and Cash Flow Growth.

  ◆ *"Pay It Down"*—as you do so, you add significantly to your Equity Buildup

  ◆ *"Pay It Off"*—thus ensuring a growing stream of unearned income, where your money starts to work for you.

- *Network Model:*
  - Your *Work Network* is your investing lifeline. Build it by bringing together a powerful group of people, a *dream team*, who can play the right roles at the right times so you can achieve your financial dreams.
  - The *Three Circles of Your Work Network*
    - *Inner Circle*: the select group you trust the most. They are your mentors, consultants, partners, your "informal board of directors."
    - *Support Circle:* the key fiduciary people in your real estate investment life. They are the professionals you rely on to advise you on both the details of specific transactions and the people you will need to complete them.
    - *Service Circle*: the specialized independent contractors and freelancers who perform specific functions for a particular property or transaction.
  - Work your Work Network—*Build it, Maintain it, Engage it.*
- *Lead Generation Model:*
  - To find great investment properties, you need leads, lots of them. The Lead Generation Model informs your property search and powers it, and is one of the main ways you can take luck out of the investment game.
  - The Lead Generation Model is built around four core questions:
    - What *am I looking for?* Establish your Criteria: location, type, economic, condition, construction, features, amenities. Then devise an APB describing the real estate investment for which you'll be prospecting and marketing.
    - Who *can help me find it?* Identify the people who can connect you to properties that meet your Criteria (Owners, Intermediaries, Leads Network)
    - How *will I find the property or the people connected to it?* Systematically prospect and market for real estate investment opportunities.

- Which *properties are the real opportunities?* Separate the suspects from the prospects.
- Build your investing posture on the *Five Laws of Lead Generation*:
  - Never compromise.
  - Be a shopper, not a buyer.
  - Timing matters.
  - It's a numbers game.
  - Be organized and systematic.

■ *Acquisition Model:*
- By following the Acquisition Model and buying right, you virtually guarantee the success of your investments. The key? Make your money going in.
- There are two fundamental acquisition strategies: Buy for Cash or Buy for Cash Flow and Equity Buildup.
  - Buy for *Cash*: Use one of the four cash-building strategies (Find & Refer; Control & Assign; Buy & Sell; Buy, Improve & Sell)
  - Buy for *Cash Flow and Equity*: Explore the three options for building and attaining them (Lease Option; Buy & Hold; Buy, Improve & Hold).
- Of all these strategies, the two that stand above the others are Buy & Sell and Buy and Hold:
  - *Buy & Sell*: With this strategy you are looking for one thing, cash, ensuring a fast net profit payoff by quickly buying and selling. But you *must* know your numbers going in, so work them carefully with a *Terms Worksheet: Buy & Sell*.
  - *Buy and Hold*: This the true financial wealth-building option, a long-term strategy employing the twin forces of Equity Buildup and Cash Flow Growth. It's still a numbers game, but over the longer term, so vigilantly employ the *Term Worksheet: Buy and Hold* as your guide.

OWN A MILLION

Dealing with complexity is an inefficient and unnecessary waste of time, attention and mental energy. There is never any justification for things being complex when they could be simple.

Edward de Bono

THE LABYRINTH AT CHARTRES

Sometimes life feels amazing and sometimes it just feels like a maze, filled with dead ends, double-back loops, and places that look alike but aren't. Real estate investing can present a similar set of challenges, and so the symbol of the labyrinth at Chartres may be an appropriate place to begin our Own a Million discussion. That famous walk-through maze is located on the sanctuary floor of the Chartres Cathedral in France, which was built in AD 1235. It was created so that parishioners could walk the maze as a substitute for making a pilgrimage to Jerusalem. In some cases they had to shuffle along on their knees as a penance. The key to making it through the maze is to stay focused and stay on the path. You see, in the Chartres maze there are no wrong turns, just a long winding path to the center. Sometimes the path takes you away from the center, but if you carefully watch where you are going and stay on the marked path, you will make it to the end. The curious thing about these types of mazes is that they always look more complicated than they really are.

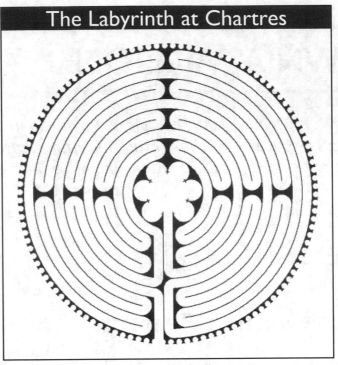

The Labyrinth at Chartres

Figure 1

That's what I want to talk about here. I want to take the complexity out of the maze of investing in and owning investment properties. The fact is that anything taken to its most sophisticated level usually becomes complex. Even the cars we drive, the TVs we watch, and the computers we use are at some level very complicated. However, using them to our advantage can be as simple as turning the key in the ignition, operating a remote, and pointing and clicking with a mouse. The question to ask about anything we do is this: "How much of the complexity must I know in order to get what I want from it?"

Based on what we have covered already, you now understand how to acquire real estate investment properties and therefore know how to Buy a Million (acquire a million dollars in property market value). What is different about looking at how to Own a Million (amass a million dollars of

The Millionaire Real Estate Investor

equity)? The real difference is a shift in your focus from trying to "buy it right" to now attempting to "grow it right." It's about turning acquired market value into realized equity gain. It's about turning your real estate investments into actual net worth that shows up on the balance sheet. From the very beginning of this book this is the game you set out to play. It is the real estate investing wealth-building game.

But let me be very clear about one thing. You already have covered everything you need to know to become a net worth Millionaire Real Estate Investor with a million dollars in equity in your investments. It's all in the Financial Model, the Lead Generation Model, and the Acquisition Model. If you follow those models, you won't go wrong and inevitably will become an Own a Million real estate investor. Here you will be shifting your focus to a Buy & Hold investment strategy. While you can always do a Buy & Sell if the opportunity is right and you want to generate some cash, it's Buy & Hold that brings real financial wealth. The Buy & Hold strategy is all about maximizing and accelerating Equity Buildup and Cash Flow Growth.

A word of caution before we continue. Up to this point we have kept things simple and straightforward. Now we are going to cross that line. It's unavoidable. Everyone who pursues financial wealth-building will, over time, be forced to deal with these nuances of the game. Just remember that as complex as it may first appear, if you stick with it and stay on the path, it will become increasingly uncomplicated for you. And knowing how to deal with them can make a positive difference in your investing life.

Veteran investors love this part of the real estate game. They love to be creative and enthusiastically dive into the complexity like little kids in a mud puddle. They can spend hours debating cash flow versus equity. The can sit on the porch and "spit and whittle" about rents, repairs, and property management. They can go on and on about 1031s, tax loopholes, and the calculation of returns on investment. Lease options, nonqual lending, and owner financing are to them the frosting on the cake. They love to tell the stories and share the details of their deals: the good, the bad, and the ugly. And they love to use insider language and shortcut phrases that no one except a few people even remotely understands to describe their favorite deals and transactions. As you become one of those investors, getting into the creativity of real estate investing may not be necessary, but it is likely. In time you too will come to understand the maze of creative options available to you and become fascinated by variations of this amazing game.

> *"Don't try to do everything at once because it gets overwhelming. I don't think you can be good at it all. You have to choose."*
>
> Peggy Rollins
> Millionaire Real Estate Investor
> Dalton, GA

However, when it comes to reaching your long-term goals, this world of creativity and complexity can be as dangerous as it is compelling. Many of our Millionaire Real Estate Investors warned us about these dangers. They told stories of how they got bored with the things they were doing that were working for them and began to get creative in their real estate investments. Then they told us what went wrong: how their financial wealth building got sidetracked or went off-track. Looking back, they would say, "I wish I had stayed with what was working. I wish I'd bought more of those basic good deals and not sold the good ones I had."

THE SEVENTEEN ISSUES OF OWN A MILLION

With that wisdom in hand, let's focus on the 17 issues you are likely to encounter in the Own a Million stage of your financial wealth-building journey. They fall in to five principal areas: Criteria, Terms, Network, Money, and You.

The Seventeen Issues of Own a Million

- **Criteria**—Always the Guiding Light
    1. Stick or Switch
    2. Become an Expert
    3. Think in Units

- **Terms**—Hold Them Dear
    Acquisition Terms
    4. Control the Property and Negotiate Everything
    5. Finance Creatively
    Operating Terms
    6. Max Your NOI
    Disposition Terms
    7. Know Your Options for Property Disposition

- **Network**—Together Everyone Achieves More
    8. Make Associating with Talent Your #1 Priority
    9. Top-Grade for Ever-Increasing Leverage
    10. Always Work from Written Proposals & Contracts
    11. Protect Your Reputation & Operate with Confidence

- **Money**—Give It a Work Ethic
    12. Hold Your Money Accountable to Work For You
    13. Minimize Your Tax Exposure

- **You**—Your Primary Asset
    14. Protect Your Time
    15. Protect Your Assets
    16. Be Learning-Based
    17. Be Accountable

Figure 2

CRITERIA: ALWAYS THE GUIDING LIGHT

As tight as your Criteria are now, they are not as tight as they're going to be. As you continue to acquire more real estate, you will become even more certain about your Criteria for both considering an opportunity and making an offer. The experience you gain in looking at properties, the insights you get from tracking local values, and the results you achieve from your earlier investments will inform your current thinking and decisions. You will be able to sort out the prospects from the suspects much more quickly and ever more precisely let your Lead Generation Network know what you are looking for.

ISSUE 1: STICK OR SWITCH

Once you've begun to acquire good, basic residential real estate investments, don't let your need for greed, speed, or novelty take you off track. Don't cash out too quickly even if you'd like to have the money right now. Don't begin to take risks because someone says you can get rich faster with other kinds of investments. Don't change your Criteria simply because you're bored with looking at the same kinds of opportunities and deals again and again. Repetition is the mother of mastery—and of skill. When you connect to the results you are achieving the activities you are repeating, you'll get excited about the activities. The power is in the repetition.

Here's the basic wisdom: Pick a niche to get rich. Learn the niche, master the niche, and eventually own the niche. Stick to it and maximize your financial growth from it. Your Criteria will define your niche: It may be geographic, or a type of property. It usually will be focused on a price range and the condition of the property. It also may involve a type of financing or a particular clientele of renters. Once you have that niche and you're getting good results, stick with it; ride it for all it's worth.

There may come a time when your niche is maxed out and there are no more good deals in it, or you may find that economic conditions or governmental regulations have put a hold on growth in that niche. Then you will be faced with a dilemma I call the dilemma of Stick or Switch. Do I stick with my Criteria and switch my market, or do I stick with my market and switch my Criteria? Think about this carefully. Don't do it as a knee-jerk reflex. Be sure the switch is necessary and think about what you would prefer to master: a new market or a new set of Criteria.

In either case you will need to put in the time and do the work to master your new niche. Our millionaires told us that when they changed strategies, they did it carefully and purposefully. They took enough time to gain confidence in the new niche before ramping up their acquisitions.

In a sense, they kept a beginner's mind, willing to learn before taking action. For them the phrase "persistent effort and patient money" is a lifelong working principle.

> *"There's a time to buy, and there's a time when it doesn't make sense to compete to buy."*
>
> Todd Tresidder
> Millionaire Real Estate Investor
> Reno, NV

ISSUE 2: BECOME AN EXPERT

How does an investor become an expert in his or her niche? Once you've picked a specific geographic area, a type of property, and a set of economic standards, you focus on the details and issues of that real estate investment profile. You must uncover all the information sources you can, find out who else is working that area (get to know them), and set up your lead generation program. There are three ways to master your niche:

1. Study and observation
2. Experience and doing
3. Asking and listening

Study and Observation

You already know that you must be able to determine market values and rental values accurately. In your target area you will track these two factors continuously and be able to apply them to any particular property. But you also will want to follow the local trends that affect those values. You will keep track of business growth, new construction, zoning changes, highway construction, recreational development, and any other factors that might indicate increased population, employment, and housing demand.

Millionaire Real Estate Investors are students and observers. That is how they become confident about predicting average time on the market for property sales, future home sale prices, vacancy rates, and the likelihood of continued price and rent appreciation. When they factor appreciation into their acquisition evaluations, they aren't guessing or being hopeful. They know because they take the time and make the effort to become experts in that type of property, in that price range, in that kind of condition, in that location. They know their Criteria in great detail, and they do enough research to know whether a property is worth pursuing or a deal worth doing. Many of them even keep their own databases of real estate activities, listings, rents, and recent closings.

They know that they need to know, so, they notice and take note. They search out reports and review the facts. You will too.

Experience and Doing

You can't play the game from the sidelines, and you certainly can't do it from the stands. So, as much as you learned from observing and tracking trends, your real estate investment education has really just begun. To be a true expert, you have to get in the game, mix it up, get dirty, take your lumps, and learn from your miscues. Millionaire Real Estate Investors know what they know because they know how it works in the real world, the multivariable, interactive world of action and reaction, cause and effect. In the end, real wisdom comes from taking action and learning from what happens.

I have come to see learning as having four stages: understanding, knowledge, wisdom, and power. Understanding means you are aware of something; you get it mentally. Knowledge means you have studied it and see how you could do it. Wisdom means you have experienced it and know how it works. Power means it has become a part of you and you do it habitually. You are now unconsciously competent. There is no difference between you

> *"The bottom line is that if you do your homework, you too can be a 'genius.' It's just not that difficult."*
>
> Paul Morris
> Millionaire Real Estate Investor
> West Hollywood, CA

and what you know. It is reflexive; you act on it virtually without thinking about it. You make it look simple.

The true masters of anything are like this. Their knowledge and wisdom are deep. However, this level of learning has a price. It comes from doing. While the masters remain students of the game, they are first and foremost players of the game. That is the place I want to point you toward: becoming a master of the real estate investment game. Be willing to get in the arena and learn by doing. Mistakes are okay; in fact, they are great teachers. Don't fear them; embrace them. Do this not because mistakes are your goal but because they are inevitable in achieving any goal. Take action and learn to enjoy the challenges and lessons of the game.

Asking and Listening

It's not just the formal or institutional sources of information that matter. It's the locals at the café and the retirees shooting the breeze on the porch. There's a wealth of useful local information that comes from the spittin' and whittlin' and the neighborhood gossip. Don't overlook it, underestimate it, or prejudge it. You want access to that kind of unpublished insider information. It can give you an advantage in finding hidden opportunities, avoiding unknown dangers, and negotiating from strength. What these people know can make you wealthy.

Locals know who may need to sell and why (death, divorce, lost jobs, family changes, etc.). They know the history of a property and its neighborhood (fires, floods, repairs, crime, etc.). They may know people who would like to rent the property, help you maintain it, and even keep an eye on it for you. Remember that all real estate is local. It is tied to the community and what is happening in the community. The principles for real estate investing may be universal, but the conditions are always local. You must know your niche intellectually, experientially, and socially. Your knowledge, your experience, and your relationships are what can make you a financially wealthy expert.

ISSUE 3: THINK IN UNITS

There is one trend that is so pervasive among our Millionaire Real Estate Investors that it seems to be a truth. We've come to call it the Think in Units Truth. It's about how many units you own, and it's really a double think: rental units and management units. To understand this truth graphically, look at the chart below. As the number of dollars invested in real estate increases (you can see more dollar signs as you move down the left-hand column), so does the number of rental units (each of the circles represents a rental unit). However, our research shows that there is at the same time a decrease in the number of management units (the shaded rectangles). In other words, as you invest in more and more real estate, you begin to "think in units": the number of management units that contain your rental units.

If all you owned were single-family houses, you would have one management unit for each rental unit. But when you acquire a duplex, you

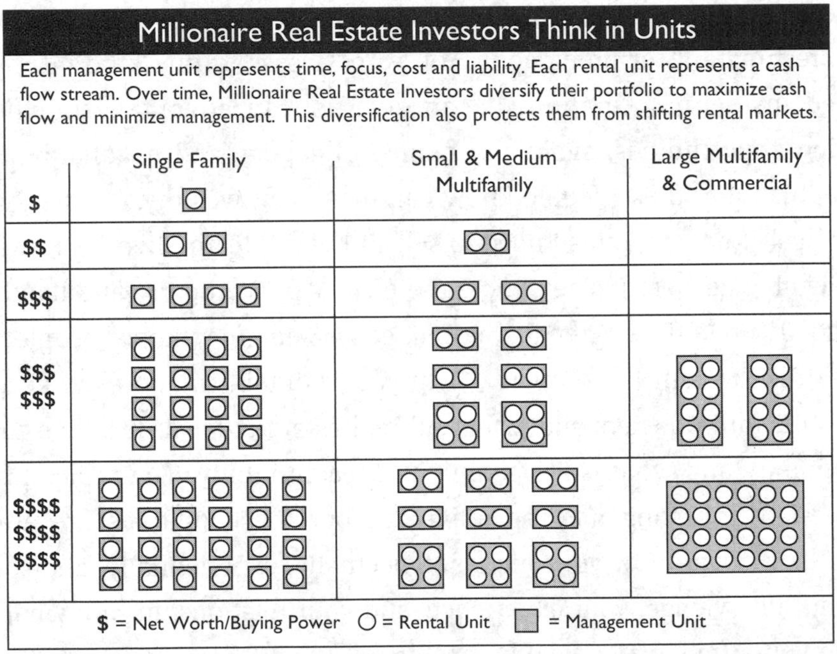

Figure 3

now have two rental units in one management unit. In a fourplex you have four rentals in one management unit, and in an apartment building there can be many rentals within just one management unit. This trend toward multiunit properties makes sense for at least two reasons: simplicity of management and limitation of losses.

Since each building will require both property management and leasing services, it is usually easier and more efficient to have fewer of them. Handling one large apartment building with a hundred rental units is easier than managing and leasing a hundred separate single-family houses. Thus, consolidating management costs can increase the profitability (net cash flow) of the investment. The second reason for doing this is that it can limit potential losses on individual management units. If you have one vacant apartment in a 20-unit building, you are still receiving 95 percent of your rental income from that property. You're unlikely to go into default on your debt service, and you probably still will have positive cash flow. When your single-family rental house is vacant, you don't have any income from that property, and that presents a big problem for that management unit. If you own 20 single-family homes, your total income loss is the same (just 5 percent) as it is in the 20-unit building, but you may incur more hassle and paperwork as you move cash flow from other properties to protect your vacant home, especially if you've got your homes separated into different legal entities.

That brings up another important factor that leads investors to Think in Units. Each management unit also entails entity protection, insurance policies, a tax return, and probably a separate property management person. The consolidation of your units under one roof, so to speak, saves on all these costs and, when you must be involved, probably will save you a lot of driving time. This is certainly a case where you can take complexity out of the game.

Multiunit properties also can increase your ratio of rents to value. This means that you are receiving more monthly income for each dollar's worth of market value of the property. You can see this easily with a duplex, triplex, or fourplex. In most areas, based on our research, you will be able to get between 0.7 percent and 1 percent of the property's value as a monthly rent. In our Acquisition Model we recommended using 0.8 percent. As you'll recall, this means that if the property has a market value of $100,000, you can expect to rent it for $800 per month. Typically, you will find that the rental income from a duplex (with two rental units) is greater. It won't be double, but it is usually 25 to 50 percent more. Thus, if the $100,000 property is a duplex, you may have two units that each rent for $600, thereby getting you a total of $1,200 per month (1.2 percent).

The downside of large multifamily buildings is that they may not get the same level of appreciation in value that is possible for single-family properties. Also, there is a more limited market for those who will or can buy them. If you sell, it will be to other investors, and they will base their offers strictly on your cash flow numbers. No emotional buyers here. Therefore, most of our Millionaire Real Estate Investors told us they kept some single-family properties in their portfolios. They liked the flexibility (the ability to sell or refinance one or two for immediate cash) and the increased appreciation (if there was ongoing buyer demand in the market).

TERMS: HOLD THEM DEAR

As you become a master of Terms on your path to Own a Million (and beyond), you will learn more and more about four things: controlling the property before you make the deal, using creative financing to finance the deal, maximizing your net operating income to get more cash flow out of the deal, and knowing your options for property disposition to get maximum cash out of the deal. Controlling the deal, getting in for less, generating greater cash flow and maximizing cash you get when you sell will become for you "terms of endearment." Remember, while your Criteria drive your lead generation and help you identify an investment opportunity, it is the Terms that make a deal worth doing. Your long-term success as a real estate investor will come down to your ability to master (and get) the right terms, so always hold them dear.

There are really three kinds of terms: acquisition, operating, and disposition. Each one of them can affect the overall financial performance of your invest-

> *"There are two matters to consider: the price of property and the price of money."*
>
> Mike Brodie
> Millionaire Real Estate Investor
> Plano, TX

ments. Making the Terms work for your money is how you get your money to work for you. I recommend that you master the Terms Worksheet: Buy & Hold. Each area of the worksheet represents a place where you can improve the way your money works for you. If you use it as a guide, you will learn to control it, buy it right, operate it right, and, when it's time, sell it right.

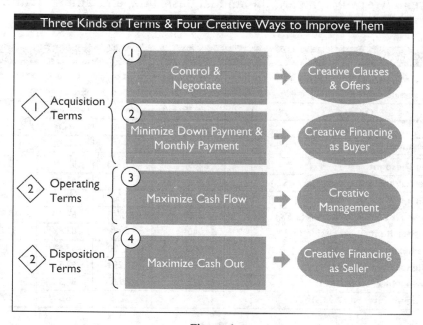

Figure 4

Buying, operating, and selling is a dynamic process. What you do at one point in the process will affect many other parts of your investment picture. Successful investors understand the way all the parts affect each other and the results that are achieved. If you can understand this, you will make more informed decisions and more positive choices along your path to becoming a millionaire.

The first step in getting clarity is to have a standard model to use for comparison. Then, as you make changes from that standard model, you can see what the impact is on your cash flow and your return on investment and see how great that impact is. Let's now look at how Terms can affect your cash flow and ROI by isolating the variables.

Our standard model looks like this: $100,000 current market value, 20 percent discounted purchase price, 20 percent down payment, 5 percent annual appreciation in market value, 5 percent annual appreciation in rents, initial monthly rents at 0.8 percent of market value, expenses and vacancy at 40 percent of rental income, and a 30-year loan at 7.43 percent. We will compare the annual cash flow and annual return on

Standard Model Investment Comparisons				
($100,000 price, 20% discount, 20% down payment, 5% annual appreciation of value and rent, initial rent at 0.8% of value, expenses/vacancy at 40% of rental income, 30 year loan with interest rate of 7.43%)				
	Performance in the 10th Year			
	Annual Cash Flow	Change	ROI	% Change
1. Standard Model	$3,602	--	78.3%	--
2. No Discount	$2,269	-$1,333	57.4%	-20.9%
3. Lower Value Appreciation (2.5%)	$3,602	$0	49.3%	-29.0%
4. Higher Value Appreciation (7.5%)	$3,602	$0	119.7%	41.4%
5. Lower Rent Appreciation (2.5%)	$1,860	-$1,742	67.4%	-10.9%
6. Higher Rent Appreciation (7.5%)	$4,940	$1,338	83.8%	5.5%
7. Reduced Expenses/Vacancy (30%)	$5,092	$1,490	87.6%	9.3%
8. Higher Rent (1% of MV)	$5,836	$2,234	92.3%	14.0%
9. Lower Interest (6.93%)	$3,862	$260	80.3%	2.0%
10. Higher Interest (7.93%)	$3,337	-$265	76.3%	-2.0%

Figure 5

investment we achieve in year 10. You can see the results of this analysis in the chart below. For our standard model we would achieve at year 10 an annual cash flow of $3,602 and a total return on investment (for that year) of 78.3 percent ($12,526 divided by $16,000). This return on investment (ROI) is a total ($12,526) of annual appreciation ($7,759) plus annual principal paydown ($1,165) plus annual net cash flow ($3,602), divided by the initial down payment ($16,000). This is not the only way to calculate return, as we will discuss later, but it provides a standard for comparison.

What we see from the Standard Model chart is that if we don't buy with a discount, both our cash flow and our return will go down. Lower market value appreciation doesn't really affect cash flow but seriously reduces ROI (by 29.0 percent). Higher market value appreciation doesn't change the projected cash flow but increases ROI by 41.4 percent. Lower rent appreciation reduces cash flow and ROI. Higher rent appreciation is very positive for anticipated cash flow and also increases ROI. Holding expenses to 30 percent causes a dramatic increase in cash flow ($1,490 over the Standard Model). Getting rents up from 0.8 percent to 1 percent of property value increases cash flow by a whopping $2,234 annually. Doing this also increases ROI. Finally, a 0.5 percent increase or decrease in loan interest rates doesn't seriously affect either cash flow or ROI. Even a full 1 percent reduction in the interest rate (not shown in this chart) increases ROI only by 5 percent—nowhere near as dramatic an impact as having higher market appreciation or getting a higher rental rate.

As you acquire and operate your income properties, you now know where to focus your efforts to improve your Terms. Depending on whether your current goals concern maximizing the cash flow from your properties or the ROI of your investments, let these numbers direct your focus. If you want increased cash flow, do these three things:

1. Get higher rents, for a 62% increase over the standard model.
2. Reduce expenses, for a 41% increase over the standard model.
3. Invest in areas where rents are appreciating, for a 37% increase over the standard model.

If your goal is to maximize ROI, do these three things:

1. Invest in areas where values are appreciating, for a 53% increase over the standard model.
2. Get higher rents, for a 18% increase over the standard model.
3. Reduce expenses, for a 12% increase over the standard model.

Investing in areas with strong rent or value appreciation is really about Criteria. The two areas impacted by Terms that have a strong impact on both cash flow and ROI are higher rents and reduced expenses (see the chart below).

Impact on Real Estate Investments		
	Annual Cash Flow	**ROI**
Higher Rents	+62%	+18%
Reduced Expenses/Vacancy	+41%	+12%

Figure 6

Millionaire Real Estate Investors at the Own a Million stage understand the impact their acquisition, operation and disposition Terms can have on their cash flow and ROI. They are continually exploring new, creative ways to impact the profitability of their investments through Terms. So let's explore in detail the four principal ways millionaire investors do this:

1. They control the property and negotiate everything.
2. They take full advantage of creative financing.
3. They max their NOI.
4. They know their options for disposition.

Issue 4: Control the Property and Negotiate Everything

In real estate, as in almost everything in life, the advantage goes to the one in control. Putting a property under contract even before all the details are worked out gets you into the driver's seat. And that's where you need to be. When you find an opportunity that looks good, always think about quickly getting it under contract. The contract gives you control and will always have clauses that allow you to exit the deal if your due diligence (inspections, conveyances, zoning research, etc.) shows that you need to get out. In some cases you might need to invest in an option or a nonrefundable deposit, but this may be a small consideration in return for the advantage of controlling the sale. If you determine that you do not want the property, you can still sell and assign your contract to another investor and be paid for it.

Control the Property & Include Escape Clauses In Your Offer

1. Escape Based on Condition at Inspection
2. Escape Based on Results of Feasibility Study
3. Escape Based on Financing
4. Escape Based on Repairs
5. Escape Based on Other Party Approval

Figure 7

Here is some advice from our Millionaire Real Estate Investors: Negotiate everything and anything. You do this when you make your initial offer and later with counteroffers. Of course, you will be sure to get your price with your discount, but in many ways that is only the beginning. Look at the property and see what could be conveyed with the sale.

Valuable conveyances might include the washer and dryer, the drapes or blinds, the gas grill, some of the furniture. When appropriate, ask for needed repairs or for the seller to cover part or all of your closing costs. You never know what you can get until you ask. Think outside the box; think outside the house!

Negotiate Everything!

1. Price
2. Financing Costs
3. Closing Costs
4. Possession Date
5. Conveyances
6. Ability to Rent Prior to Closing
7. Ability to Start Repairs Prior to Closing
8. Ability to Assign Contract

Figure 8

I've seen it all in the thousands of transactions that have come across my desk as a broker. From the buyer who said he would do the deal if the seller would throw in all the lawn equipment to another who said she'd buy at the seller's price if it included the classic Mercedes in the garage. In both cases the sellers said yes. But it's not just about personal property and conveyances; it also can be about the financial numbers. When my coauthor Dave bought a property six years ago, he offered to pay the sellers the full asking price if they would contribute $7,000 toward his closing costs. They said yes without making a counteroffer. He knew that they had been out of the house for several months and already had had one purchase contract fall through. Rather than lowball his offer on a house he really wanted, he guessed that a full-price offer with his financing preapproved and in writing would be very attractive to them. The contribution to his closing costs would seem incidental to getting it sold and closed quickly. He was right, but he wouldn't have known if he hadn't asked.

The key is to find out what is important to the sellers. Offer them what they want and then ask for what you want. If it doesn't work, it doesn't work. Find out what will. Great negotiators are great investigators. They know that every transaction needs to be a win-win. You need to make it a win for you for sure, but also look for the best way to make it a win for the other party. Always be curious; always ask. Find out what is important to the seller and know what is important to you. Negotiate everything and anything.

> *"The longer you can tie up the property for little or no money before you actually have to buy it, the more flexibility you'll have."*
>
> Charles Brown
> Millionaire Real Estate Investor
> Austin, TX

ISSUE 5: FINANCE CREATIVELY

As you do more investing, you will want to master creative financing. Your ability to construct creative financial Terms might get you into deals you might not otherwise be able to do. In some markets, as I experienced in the late 1970s and again in the late 1980s, creative financing may be the only way to get transactions done. There comes a time when conventional and institutional financing can be overly expensive or not available. This situation may be caused by general economic conditions or your personal financial position. Once you have a number of properties, institutional lenders may place limits on what they will lend you as an investor. You may have to wait until you have the equity in or positive cash flow from your properties that they require in order to lend you more. Finally, sometimes sellers have specific situations that may require or allow creative financing. This presents a unique opportunity to construct a creative transaction that meets the seller's goals and still works for you.

Creative financing is the way around these binds. It also can help you get into properties with less of your own money used as a down payment and lower your monthly debt service. Thus, you will want to master such concepts as:

1. Owner financing—where the seller carries the mortgage for you.
2. Assumptions—taking responsibility for the seller's mortgage when this is allowed by the seller's mortgage lender.
3. Wraps—where the owner offers you a new loan while keeping and paying down their original loan (the new loan "wraps" the original).
4. Lease options—Leasing the property from the seller until you have the equity or cash to buy it.
5. Private seconds—where you obtain a second loan to cover your down payment on a primary mortgage loan.
6. Syndications—where you involve other investors and partners in your acquisitions.

Millionaire investors use all the tools in their toolbox to get the deal done. The chart on the facing page illustrates how the numbers might work in a scenario where the investor attempts to take ownership of a $100,000 property through creative financing. You'll note that conventional financing (column 1) is included as a point of reference for these creative variations.

In all four of the ownership scenarios (columns 1–4), it is important you understand that a private second loan can also come from the seller. Just know that secondary liens in general carry less favorable terms for the buyer—it's about collateral. First liens are generally secured against the property and first in line if the deal goes sour and the property must be liquidated to pay back the loan. Secondary lenders account for this in

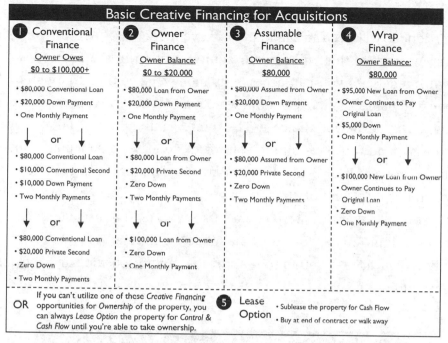

Figure 9

the terms they offer. Also, any of these scenarios can be syndicated if you are unable or unwilling to provide cash or collateral to make these deals happen. In each case, you would negotiate the deal and bring in other partners and investors.

Your ability to borrow the money will go through three stages: Credit, Equity, and Cash Flow. At first lenders will look to your creditworthiness as reflected in your credit score. Therefore, having little or no credit card debt, paying your bills on time, and having a history of paying back loans (mortgage, auto, student, etc.) in a timely, responsible way will contribute to a strong credit rating. It also matters that you have some savings available for down payments. Although you may be able to purchase your own residence with little or no money down, when it comes to conventional financing for Buy & Hold investment real estate, you usually will need to put your own money into it. The lenders will expect it, and it gives you instant equity.

At some point you will need credibility as well as a credit rating. The lender will need to see that you have made wise investments. The first measure of this will be your equity position in the properties you own. Sometimes you can access this money by getting a home equity loan and using it to make your down payment. In fact, you may become your own "lender of choice"—The interest rate is right, the approvals are easy, and you have all the control. Beyond self-financing, many of our Millionaire Real Estate Investors took advantage of private lending or established a line of credit, using the equity in one or more of their investment properties as collateral. In any case, if you have reached a lender's limit on borrowing, that lender will consider you for more only if you have a very strong, provable equity position in your current holdings.

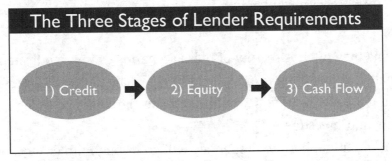

Figure 10

Finally, particularly for larger multifamily acquisitions, the amount of the loan will be based strictly on the Cash Flow of the property. An institutional lender will require a detailed analysis based on recent and verifiable financial reports of the rental income, expenses, vacancies, and net cash flow of the property. Those lenders are looking to minimize their risks, and so they will be very cautious when considering a large loan on an income property. Your track record and reputation will be as important as the specific numbers on the building. At this stage of your investing *you* are likely to be the major factor in people's willingness to lend you money. In a sense your creditability is always with you, and it can be one of your most valuable assets.

ISSUE 6: MAXIMIZE YOUR NOI

The third area of Terms you will need to master is maximizing your Net Operating Income (NOI). In a sense this is the ability to run your real estate investments at a profit. NOI is what you have left from your Gross Rental Income after you have covered your vacancies and paid your operating expenses. This is detailed in the Terms Worksheet: Buy & Hold (see the chart on page 236). Actually, from an operating point of view there are only rental income and expenses. Vacancies simply reduce your rental income. Thus, there are three things you can do to maximize your Net Operating Income: increase gross rental income, control expenses, and minimize vacancies. Let's take them in that order.

Figure 11

Increase Gross Rental Income

Millionaire Real Estate Investors achieve higher rents than others. Most of the millionaires in our research group followed the 1 percent rule of thumb for rents, getting 1 percent of the property's market value as the monthly rent (i.e., a $100,000 house would rent for $1,000 per month). When we looked at rents and values in a large number of markets, that rule of thumb seemed too optimistic, particularly for single-family homes. We determined that 0.8 percent for single-family properties was probably more realistic as a rule of thumb, and that is what we used for the examples in the "Buy a Million" section of the book. But that rule of thumb didn't hold up: Our millionaire investors consistently achieved higher-than-average rents. How do they do that? As a group they do five specific things to maximize rents (see illustration below.)

First, they used rent escalators in their contracts so that the rent would increase year by year without question, negotiation, or notice. It

Maxing Your Rents

1. Contractual Rent Escalators

2. Strategic Improvements

3. Government Subsidies

4. Targeted Tenants

5. Other Income

   - Non-refundable deposits and fees

   - Charge for parking and storage

   - Lawn service

   - Cleaning services

   - Coin-operated laundry facilities

   - Etc.

Figure 12

would happen automatically, and the renters would know that they had preagreed to it; thus, it didn't feel arbitrary. While this preset rent increase might not keep up with the actual rental trends, it at least meant that there was some increase even when the same renters were in place for a long time.

Second, they made the kinds of improvements that were attractive to local renters and made their properties stand out. What they discovered was that within reason people will pay more if they believe they are getting more. Cosmetic improvements and certain amenities can make your rentals uniquely better than the competitions's and bring more gross income. Remember from our earlier discussion that raising rents even a few tenths of a percent can have a big positive impact on your net cash flow and returns.

> *"I put automatic 10% rent increases in the contract. Then at the first of the year, when I say the increase won't actually be that high, the tenants are ecstatic because they think I've saved them some money."*
>
> Anna Mills
> Millionaire Real Estate Investor
> Toledo, OH

Third, some of our investors specialized in government-subsidized housing called Section 8 subsidies. They knew which houses in which areas would qualify for the subsidies, and that allowed them to market this advantage and achieve premium rents. Their net positive cash flow became virtually automatic.

Some of those we interviewed were very good at targeting their tenants. They would work with local real estate agents or apartment locators to attract the right renters: those willing to pay a premium for the right place. They would highlight the quality, features, and amenities of their units. In a sense they would work to lead generate their tenants in the same way they lead generated for their investment opportunities. They would get testimonials from current renters and would ask those good renters for additional rental leads. In some cases they would target people with short-term needs (those new to the area or those waiting for a custom home to be built) and give them flexibility in the length of the lease in order to maximize the rental income.

The fourth method for increasing revenue was to gain other income from the tenants. Coin-operated laundry and fees for pets, storage, parking, and lawn care could all be additional sources of income. It was highly recommended to have the tenants take care of all their own utilities, with direct, personal responsibility for payment to the utility providers.

Control Expenses

Controlling operating expenses is a great way to increase your NOI and is only a matter of record keeping and attention to details. Many investors we interviewed set up well-organized systems of bookkeeping and cost accounting. Several set up their own property management businesses. Whether you do it yourself or have a management service do it for you, it is important to watch your expense trends and question anything that seems out of line. Rob Harrington from Boston says that he compares his costs sheets from month to month, notes the trends, and looks for unusual changes. Over the years he has discovered water leaks and faulty electrical units that if let go for a long enough period of time could have cost him hundreds and even thousands of dollars. If you have the right record-keeping system in place and set aside a regular time slot each month to do your review, he says, this will not take very much time and you will be paid well for doing it. Expenses saved are profits earned.

Another consideration in maximizing your NOI by controlling expenses has to do with repairs and improvements. We've looked at this in the Buy & Sell area, and we've discussed the concept of Maximum Return (see the chart on page 232). The most astute investors know that repairs and improvements are not just an issue for Buy & Sell or fix and flip. They are a major part of the NOI equation. There are three moments of truth for improvements:

1. After you buy but before you rent
2. While you own and operate
3. Before you sell

Repairs and improvements involve making cost-benefit calculations. The right improvements may allow you to get higher rents and a better price when you sell. The wrong improvements may accomplish neither. The right improvements may represent a great use of your cash flow. The wrong ones may not. Improvements are a tax-deductible expense, and the right ones can add value to your property, thereby increasing equity. The wrong ones are just deductions. There are four kinds of improvements:

1. Improvements that are *necessary* and *add value*, such as a new roof or flooring
2. Improvements that are *unnecessary* but *add value*, such as landscaping and cosmetic enhancements
3. Improvements that are *necessary* but *don't add value*, such as plumbing repair, rewiring to code, and foundation work
4. Improvements that are *unnecessary* and *don't add value*, such as adding expensive fixtures or amenities

The last category is a judgment call and is essentially a matter of whether the costs of the improvements will bring about an equivalent increase in market or rental value. Your Support and Service Network specialists will be able to consult with you on this, so seek them out and listen hard to their advice.

The wisest landlords know that repairs and improvements are an NOI financial game. They know that it is not always wise to minimize operating costs at the expense of income and equity gains. They understand these operating costs are in fact another form of investing.

Minimize Vacancies

Reducing vacancies and the time it takes to rerent the property are also important ways to improve net operating income. The key is to anticipate vacancies and have a game plan to market the properties to new tenants. Get ahead of your vacancies—not behind them. When a unit goes vacant, be ready to rehab, clean, prep, and market it quickly. (Note: The more units you own, the more cost-effective it becomes to have staff or service providers perform this service for you.) While it may seem obvious that keeping your tenants for a long time reduces vacancies and is a good thing, Rob Harrington says that many landlords are so eager to raise rents that they may alienate good tenants. "Remember," he points out, "it may take you a very long time, even at a higher rent, to make up for the lost income from a vacancy."

ISSUE 7: KNOW YOUR OPTIONS FOR PROPERTY DISPOSITION

Selling a property right is just as important as buying it right, and this goes beyond getting the highest price. Beyond staging the home for sale and marketing for buyers, what do Millionaire Real Estate Investors do that maximizes their returns from selling? The first thing they do is determine why they are selling. If it's to get immediate cash then they are like any motivated seller. What they now get to decide is which property to sell and why. For example, they may have to choose between a property that is underperforming as an investment or one that can command an unusually good price in the current market. Making this decision simply takes some thoughtful analysis that includes value and rent forecasting.

Now, before you decide to actually sell a property, you should always review your options. There are other ways to get cash out of a property than selling it. It may meet all your needs to simply refinance the property and pull some of your equity out in the form of cash. Millionaire Real Estate Investor Cathy Manchester took advantage of her strong equity position in a high-end vacation rental to use it as a "$250,000 equity line of credit." She taps into this amazing cash resource regularly for short-

Options for Property Disposition
1. Lease Option Out
2. Refinance
3. Tax-Deferred 1031 Exchange
4. Sell

Figure 13

term Buy, Improve & Sell investments and then quickly puts the money back into her home.

If you are looking for a way to maximize your price, you can use the Lease Option Out strategy by finding a renter who wants to buy but cannot qualify for traditional lending. In the lease option contract, you can offer to apply some of the rent toward the purchase, agree on a higher-than-market rental rate, and negotiate the terms of the future sale at a precise point in time. With this approach, you should have a higher NOI and usually a higher sale price. If the renter does not exercise the purchase option when the contract expires, you can do it again with the next renter. In a lease option or any sale you also can opt to be the lender. Many nonqualifying buyers will pay a premium in both price and interest rate because you are their last or only source of financing. If they default, you get to do it again, probably at a higher price.

One of millionaire investor Bob Guest's best deals was on a lease option. The woman who leased his home for a period of two years took amazing care of the property. She landscaped, painted, and improved. As with many lease option tenants, she considered herself the owner of the property even though she had not exercised her option. At the end of the contract she decided not to purchase and control of the property reverted to Bob. In the end, he had two years of strong cash flow from a great tenant and a more valuable property that had been cared for lovingly.

Your next option would be the tax-deferred 1031 exchange, where you sell one property and buy another without incurring capital gains taxes. The fundamental requirement from the IRS is that you reinvest all your profits into the next property (or properties) within a specific timeline.

We will talk later, in the Money section, about the opportunities to do tax-deferred 1031 exchanges.

Lastly, there is always the option of just selling the property. Millionaire investors consider this their *last* option, since they are always seeking to minimize taxes paid on the net proceeds of a sale. They know that the other options present better ways of preserving their capital and, when necessary, providing them with cash.

NETWORK: TOGETHER EVERYONE ACHIEVES MORE

In all businesses teamwork is one of the fundamental operating principles. For us it's not just a feel-good, warm, fuzzy concept—it's about synergy and achieving the best results. That happens only when everyone is pulling for one another and, whenever possible, pulling together toward a common goal. Anything worth doing is more likely to succeed at the highest level when we synergize with others. This fact was made real for us by our Millionaire Real Estate Investors. They not only pointed out how others had helped them get started but told us how important it was all along the way to have a group of trusted partners, mentors, supporters, and providers.

I made this point earlier when I talked about your Work Network and Lead Generation Network. What I want to say here is that your networks must grow as your investments and financial wealth grow. In fact, there will be a direct correlation between the two: Your network will reflect your net worth.

Here are the four things you should do in your network as you grow your financial wealth:

1. Make associating with talent your number one priority.
2. Top-grade for ever-increasing leverage.
3. Always work from written proposals and contracts.
4. Protect your reputation and operate with confidence.

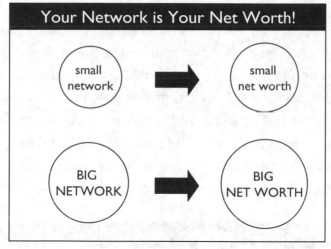

Figure 14

ISSUE 8: MAKE ASSOCIATING WITH TALENT YOUR NUMBER ONE PRIORITY

Your success will be determined in large part by those around you. As a result, you must proactively surround yourself with highly talented people. You are the social engineer of your own people matrix, the architect of your personal mastermind. Whether you are contracting for labor or employing it, talent is always the key.

What is talent? Talent is the intelligence, behavior, motivation, attitude, abilities and experience of a person that make that person uniquely suited to do what he or she is doing. That person is a natural "fit" for the task or venture. Talent is not a measure of someone's worth; it is not a generalized label for a person. It is always related to the role a person will be playing. Talent is role and task specific.

You want to find talented people who do what they do well and love doing it. More than that, you want talent that is fiduciary, not just functionary. This means that the people you choose go beyond doing the job they were hired or assigned to do: They look out for your interest and protect it. I had an insurance agent who was doing an underwriting inspection of an investment property that I was in the process of buying and that his company was going to insure for me. He called me back to tell me he had completed his report and gotten the approval for my insurance. Then he told me that he was aware that his company had dealt with a number of foundation issues in that neighborhood recently and that I might want to have it checked out. I did, and while there wasn't a problem with my property, I valued the extra effort by my fiduciary insurance agent in warning me about this. Always work with fiduciary talent. They will make a significant difference in your investment success over time.

Functionary vs. Fiduciary	
FUNCTIONARY	FIDUCIARY
• Completes the Task	• Owns the Result
• Other-Directed	• Self-Directed
• Narrow Focus	• Big Picture
• Delivers Information	• Advises and Consults
• Responds to Needs	• Anticipates Needs
• Adequate Skill	• Exceptional Skill
• Low Service	• High Service
• Low-Level Thinking	• High-Level Thinking
• Meets Expectations	• Exceeds Expectations
• Replaceable	• Irreplaceable

Figure 15

Getting the right people in your Work Network doesn't happen by accident; it is a matter of intention and process. Finding talent and establishing a relationship with talent must be purposeful, so you must have a process. A simple process I recommend involves three steps: behavior, references, and track record.

Determine people's natural behavior by asking behavior-based questions. Actually, if I'm hiring someone, I always use a behavioral assessment. The DISC test, for example, is a proven low-cost assessment that is widely available on the Internet. It can be taken online, with a report sent to you. An assessment will help you understand what people are good at and how they tend to act. Are they aggressive or not? Do they work well with people? Are they systematic in their approach? Do they follow rules and procedures? The key is to know what you're looking for and then decide if they measure up.

You can sharpen your observational skills when you know what you are looking for. I recently needed some handyman work done on a property. Since I was in a hurry and my repairman was tied up, I called a guy who had a small handyman-for-hire ad in our neighborhood paper. I could tell after five sentences that he was not the man for the job. He had all the verbal energy and emotional expressiveness of a telemarketer—he was selling me from the get-go. I know that good detail workers on physical projects don't behave that way. I wanted a handyman, a craftsman, not a salesman pretending to be a craftsman. Remember that talent means the person's behavior fits the work to be done. Learn to read people's behavior. Find the person who's the right fit and you're less likely to end up having one.

Next, always check references and do second- and third-level reference checks. In other words, I ask each of the provided references who else I might talk with who could give me insight into this person. For example, the reference may know a neighbor who also used the contractor in question. When I am two or three levels away from the direct references, I usually get the whole picture: the person's weaknesses as well as their strengths.

Finally, probe for the track record from that person and from independent sources. I have found that a person usually continues to operate in the way he or she has before, with similar results. This is particularly true with important things such as attitude, work ethic, integrity and quality of work. Get to know people; make it your business. Success leaves clues, so look at their track record until you find the clues you're looking for. Determine who is talent, and then make having those people close to you a high priority. Your net worth ultimately depends on the talent you bring into your life.

ISSUE 9: TOP-GRADE FOR EVER-INCREASING LEVERAGE

Ultimately, you can't do everything yourself—not if you want to get a lot done in your life. Thus, you need leverage: people who do things with and for you. Every business owner knows this, and all the investors we interviewed told us this. You can't do it all alone, and you'll do better if you don't try, particularly when it comes to investing in real estate. Get leverage. Find out which people get it done, which ones do what they say they'll do, and which ones are the best. Use them, contract with them, and hire them. Always be upgrading and never settle. Find the best, expect the best and continue to work only with those who deliver the best. Those people will help make your real estate investments grow and enrich your life.

We'll talk more about building your employed staff when we cover the 7th Level in the "Receive a Million" section (see page 324). For now I encourage you to have the courage to top-grade those who are close to you in your investing. Whether it's an advisor, a professional associate, or a service provider, do not be afraid to replace that person. You have the right, and if you care about how things turn out in your investing business, you have the obligation.

How things turn out will be a function of who you bring in and, more important, who you keep in. I don't know why people are afraid to say "no" or "no more," but they are. Some people stay in bad relationships, and others put up with less than quality work and not getting what they paid for. Don't do that! Care about people and treat them fairly. However, when people don't do what they say they'll do or don't care about doing

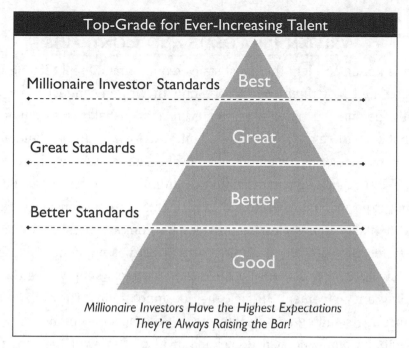

Figure 16

it well, move on to those who do care. Don't do it in a mean manner; in fact, always try to let these people know that you care for them as a person. Encourage them in their future work, give them any personal support you can, and then start working with people who you believe will do a better job. To ensure you can always judge a person's work fairly, you follow this mantra in your professional relationships: Work first, friends second, and social maybe.

It's an approach that works. If you're going to the top, if you want your real estate investments to go to the top, you must top-grade the people on your team. The best athletic teams do this, college or professional, and their fans expect it. Recruit the best players and play the best players. Some good players may be left on the bench when the best ones take the field. That's what those coaches get paid to do—top-grade—and so do you.

ISSUE 10: ALWAYS WORK FROM WRITTEN PROPOSALS AND CONTRACTS

It is not an accident that most states require that all real estate transactions be done by written contract and only by written contract. No word of mouth, no inferred agreement, not even a handshake is as enforceable when it comes to a real estate transaction. A written contract is binding, but only its written terms are enforceable. Real estate transactions have a long-standing and honored legal tradition regarding the written word. Besides, putting expectations in writing is fundamental to good business transactions. It makes things clear, it provides for consequences, and it can be interpreted and enforced by a third party. Paper has no memory lapses.

Many people mistakenly believe that contracts simply create understanding and agreement. In fact, they do much more: They also provide for misunderstanding and disagreement. Contracts outline not only what will happen and who will do what but also what will happen if they don't. Good contracts provide for clear and straightforward consequences for default or breach and for a prescribed manner of dispute resolution (mediation and arbitration). In a sense, good written contracts cover contingencies so that if worse comes to worst, all parties know in advance what will happen.

For me, contracts are agreements for disagreement. When everyone is in agreement, no one looks at the contract. It's only when there is disagreement that it gets pulled out and gone over with a fine-tooth comb. As a rule, write agreements to resolve any possible disagreements as agreeably as possible.

Do everything in writing. Get your bids in writing, get your proposals in writing, and work from written work orders and job descriptions. Even when it is not a purchase or sale of a property, any agreement you make with someone to do something for you or for you to do something for another person should be in writing. The costs, the fees, the specs, the plans, the options, the deadlines, the penalties, and the method for dispute resolution should all be there, in writing and signed by all parties. It's a pay me now or pay me later deal. You do the tough negotiating and agreement reaching up front or pay with misunderstanding and contention later. I encourage you to be tough up front and get it in writing every time.

Issue 11: Protect Your Reputation and Operate with Confidence

Your reputation is perhaps the most important asset you have. It is amazing how many people misunderstand this or get it reversed. They believe that reputation is important only when you are just beginning and when you clearly need the cooperation of others. Then, when you are successful and financially independent, you can be arrogant and difficult to work with. They seem to believe that power comes from success and money. In my experience, those with the most success and money are usually the most cooperative and responsible. Of course, there are always exceptions. There are a few successful investors who are egocentric and difficult to work with. Perhaps they have created an erroneous stereotype for the financially wealthy.

Your reputation for honesty, responsibility, and cooperation is foundational for your success. Since this reputation was earned over time, it is unlikely that it will change suddenly. The habits you built and demonstrated along the way will be sustained for the long haul. Begin with the end in mind: Treat your reputation as the precious asset it is. Develop it wisely and protect it fiercely. Follow the Five Rules of Engagement (see the chart on page 169), and become a person others want to be around, support, and cooperate with. That reputation will bring you many opportunities and cost you none.

Beyond that, your reputation may reduce the problems you have to deal with. First, people will be there for you when you need them. They will help you find solutions. Second, a good reputation may prevent problems from arising. I experienced this once with dramatic results. A problem had arisen as the result of a transaction. The buyer involved in the deal called me. He said that he had been so upset with what had happened in his real estate purchase that he planned to sue me. When he talked with several attorneys about it, each one told him that I always did the right thing. Turns out, these attorneys were all in my Network and knew me very well. As a result, the buyer decided to call me rather than sue me. We resolved the problem, and he was very pleased with the way it was handled. When it was all over, what stuck for me was that other people's opinions of me (my reputation) had prevented a lawsuit against me. The same can happen for you, too.

In your role as an investor, your reputation will come from the way you make offers and do deals. Always do this with respect for the other person and an understanding of his or her needs. One of the most important is honest and straightforward communication. Since your acquisitions will have to meet both your Criteria and your Terms, you usually will be making below-market offers and negotiating for everything you can. It will be important for the seller not to take any of this personally or have the sense that you are trying to steal the property. Let the seller know, and be sure your real estate agent lets them know, that you are trying to help them get their property sold—you are an investor, and you can buy the property only if it is a good investment. If the numbers don't work for the seller, that's okay. You are only looking to do win-win deals. It has to work for the seller and for you as an investor.

> *"The job of a real estate investor is not to buy or sell real estate, but to solve people's real estate problems."*
> Bill Cook
> Millionaire Real Estate Investor
> Adairsville, GA

You are looking for "deals, not steals." You want to be the one who helps the seller solve his or her need to be out from under the property. The only way you can do this as an investor is to have the numbers work; you must get the right terms. You need to operate with confidence, knowing that you are providing solutions to other people's problems while staying true to your path as a real estate investor. When it works for both sides, it's a true "win-win." When it doesn't, it's a "move on–move on," and that's okay too.

MONEY: GIVE IT A WORK ETHIC

Own a Million is about building equity. Along with equity comes the opportunity for the cash flow it can generate. If we have stayed true to our Criteria and met our Terms, our real estate investments should be achieving Equity Buildup and Cash Flow Growth. But are they? That is the question you will be asking continually, and those are the numbers you will be tracking consistently. In the end, investing is a numbers game, a financial numbers game. You must hold your money accountable. You must count it and see if it's working for you. Is it, in fact and by the numbers, building your net worth and your financial wealth?

ISSUE 12: HOLD YOUR MONEY ACCOUNTABLE TO WORK FOR YOU

Throughout your investing career, you want to be sure that your money is healthy or wealthy. I call this the Wise Money Rule: For me to be financially wealthy, my money must at least be healthy. After many years of business and investment experience, I've come to understand that there are four conditions of money: dead, safe, healthy, and wealthy. I began to understand this in my breakfasts with Michael. Whenever I would show him the money I had in the bank, he would say, "That's just dead money, Gary; you can't become financially independent with dead money." He taught me that my money needed to be alive and working for me. How much additional money it was returning to me each year was crucially important. That was my return on investment, my ROI, and it was something I needed to measure and hold my invested money accountable for.

Over the years, as I've become more financially educated, I came to define the four conditions in the following way:

1. *Dead:* money that earns interest below the inflation rate
2. *Safe:* money that earns interest at or just above the inflation rate
3. *Healthy:* money that earns interest that is well above the inflation rate
4. *Wealthy:* money that earns interest that is above that for healthy money

To put this into more specific financial terms, in today's economic market Dead Money would be earning 4 percent or less, Safe Money would be earning from 5 to 8 percent, Healthy Money would be earning from 9 to 12 percent, and Wealthy Money would be earning above 12 percent. Money earns wages just as people do, and for money to become wealthy, it must be paid high wages. The interest or return your money is earning tells you what it is getting paid as it works for you. Your money is gainfully employed or it isn't. If it isn't, it's unemployed (dead). If it's gainfully employed, it's now a matter of how much it's being paid for its work. From the beginning of your financial wealth-building career you want your money to be earning high wages: healthy or, better yet, wealthy.

Some people don't understand interest rates or returns on investment. They know that higher is better, but they may not see how much better. Here's an easy way to understand this. Let's assume that you invested $100 every month for

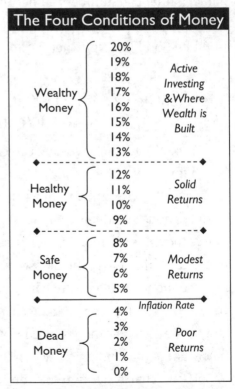

Figure 17

The Millionaire Real Estate Investor

30 years. For simplicity's sake, let's say you put it in an interest-bearing account and kept it there along with any interest you earned. The chart below shows what your total compounded value would be over those 30 years at various rates of interest.

The Impact of Various Interest Rates over Time						
Years	0%	4%	8%	12%	16%	20%
1	$1,200	$1,226	$1,253	$1,281	$1,309	$1,338
5	$6,000	$6,652	$7,397	$8,249	$9,225	$10,345
10	$12,000	$14,774	$18,417	$23,234	$29,647	$38,236
20	$24,000	$36,800	$59,259	$99,915	$174,946	$316,148
30	$36,000	$69,636	$150,030	$352,991	$887,048	$2,336,080
$100 Invested Every Month with Interest Rates Compounded Monthly						

Figure 18

What a difference a few percentage points can make over time. At $100 a month for 30 years we've invested $36,000 of our earned income. At 4 percent (Dead Money) we've turned that into $69,636, which probably represents no gain against inflation. At 8 percent (Safe Money) we've turned it into $150,030, and that feels a little better. With Healthy Money earning 12 percent we've grown our $36,000 into nearly $353,000, almost 10 times what we put in. Our money has been getting paid good wages. But look what happens when our money earns wealthy wages. At 16 percent it grows to over $887,000—Wealthy Money for sure. And at 20 percent it goes through the roof to over $2 million.[1]

Keep track of what is happening with your money. Know what condition it's in and how well it is being paid. You need to keep track of your ROI for each of your properties and for your entire portfolio. You will see what annual return you are receiving on the money you have invested (your return on investment) and will track the annual return you are receiving on your equity. I call this second number your ROE (return on equity). You

---

[1] Since the beginning of his investment career, Warren Buffett has reportedly averaged over 20 percent compounded annually. Is it any wonder he is widely considered the greatest investor ever?

want to know both your ROI and your ROE. The difference is that ROI shows what you are earning annually on the money you initially invested, while ROE shows what you are earning annually on all the equity you have.

In essence, your equity is your capital. You could take it out and invest it somewhere else through an equity loan or by refinancing the property. You also could do that by selling the property and exchanging it for another, larger property. We'll talk more about that in a while. For now, be clear about equity: It's your money, it's your capital, and you want to know how hard it is working for you.

Let's put some real-life real estate numbers to this idea of tracking ROI and ROE. We begin with our earlier example of investing in a single-family property that was worth $70,300 in 1983 (see page 151). Remember, we acquired this property with a 20 percent discount and a 20 percent down payment of $11,248 (this is our investment). In this example we assumed a 5 percent annual appreciation in both market value and rent. Let's look first at our investment performance using a 30-year loan at 7.43 percent (see the chart below).

	Tracking Your Return on Investment and Return on Equity over Time (30-Year Mortgage)							
Year	Start of Year Market Value	Annual Price Appreciation	Year End Appreciated Market Value	Annual Principal Debt Pay Down	Year End Accumulated Equity	Annual Cash Flow	Return On Investment	Return On Equity
1	$70,300	$3,515	$73,816	$420	$29,244	$300	37.7%	16.7%
2	$73,816	$3,691	$77,509	$453	$33,390	$503	41.3%	15.9%
3	$77,509	$3,875	$81,387	$488	$37,756	$715	45.1%	15.2%
4	$81,387	$4,069	$85,461	$525	$42,355	$938	49.2%	14.7%
5	$85,461	$4,273	$89,739	$565	$47,198	$1,173	53.4%	14.2%
6	$89,739	$4,487	$94,232	$609	$52,300	$1,419	57.9%	13.8%
7	$94,232	$4,712	$98,950	$656	$57,674	$1,677	62.6%	13.5%
8	$98,950	$4,948	$103,906	$706	$63,336	$1,949	67.6%	13.2%
9	$103,906	$5,195	$109,110	$760	$69,301	$2,233	72.8%	12.9%
10	$109,110	$5,455	$114,575	$819	$75,585	$2,533	78.3%	12.7%
11	$114,575	$5,729	$120,315	$882	$82,207	$2,847	84.1%	12.5%
12	$120,315	$6,016	$126,343	$950	$89,184	$3,176	90.2%	12.3%
13	$126,343	$6,317	$132,673	$1,023	$96,537	$3,523	96.6%	12.2%
14	$132,673	$6,634	$139,321	$1,101	$104,286	$3,886	103.3%	12.0%
15	$139,321	$6,966	$146,302	$1,186	$112,453	$4,268	110.4%	11.9%
16	$146,302	$7,315	$153,633	$1,277	$121,061	$4,669	117.9%	11.8%
17	$153,633	$7,682	$161,332	$1,375	$130,135	$5,090	125.8%	11.7%
18	$161,332	$8,067	$169,416	$1,481	$139,701	$5,532	134.1%	11.6%
19	$169,416	$8,471	$177,906	$1,595	$149,786	$5,996	142.8%	11.5%
20	$177,906	$8,895	$186,821	$1,718	$186,821	$6,483	152.0%	11.4%

Figure 19

The Millionaire Real Estate Investor

As we noted before, after 15 years our $11,248 investment is worth $112,453 (the accumulated equity). We have been achieving this Equity Buildup from the property's appreciation (it now has a Market Value of $146,302) and Debt Paydown (we have paid down the loan principal by $11,143). In addition, we are achieving an annual positive Cash Flow. To determine our ROI during the fifteenth year, we add up the annual appreciation ($6,966) plus the annual principal paid ($1,186) plus the annual cash flow ($4,268), which gives us a total annual return of $12,420. To calculate the ROI, we divide that total by the initial investment of $11,248 and get 110.4 percent. This means that during the fifteenth year of our investment we received an annual return of over 110 percent on our money. You can see in the chart that our annual ROI has grown from 37.7 percent in the first year to over 110 percent in the fifteenth year. You can see that in five more years that annual ROI will increase to 152 percent.

This is just part of the picture. It isn't the whole story about how hard your money is working for you. We know your initial investment is working very hard and getting paid very well, and we know that comes from the leverage power of real estate investing. In just this one property you have gained a very strong equity position. As you can see from the chart, at the end of the fifteenth year your accumulated equity stands at $112,453. That is your money too. It can and should be working for you. If you keep it where it is, you can calculate how hard it is working: what it is getting paid. We call this your return on equity, and all we do to calculate it is divide your total annual return ($12,420) by your equity ($112,453). Therefore, in the fifteenth year of this investment your ROE is 11.9 percent. It is still healthy money, and that's a good thing.

However, it's not working as hard for you as it once was. In fact, your ROE has been dropping since you made the investment. It was 16.7 percent in the first year and has been going down ever since. In the next few years it probably will drop to near 11 percent. What is happening, of course, is that as you increase your equity position in the investment, your rate of return on that equity decreases even though you continue to get appreciation, debt paydown, and cash flow.

This phenomenon is what causes Millionaire Real Estate Investors to tap into their accrued equity, pull it out, and reinvest it for greater returns. They want their money, both earned and unearned, to work as hard as possible and get paid as much as it can. Therefore, they continue to leverage that equity back into additional real estate investments, always buying it right with clear Criteria and favorable Terms. Our survey of our millionaires showed that they had a 40 percent equity position in their holdings. Most admitted that they could have used cash flow to pay down more debt and increased their equity more rapidly over time. But they chose to keep building their financial wealth by putting that money back to work at a higher wage. You may be wise to do the same thing. Not only will it get you to the Own a Million level, it can build up an unstoppable momentum that can carry you to the Own Multimillions level.

In our example, let's now reinvest some of the equity and see what happens to the return on equity. Let's say that at the end of year 14 you refinanced your debt and took out some of the equity. You had $104,286 in accumulated equity, which meant you had a 75 percent equity position ($104,286 divided by $139,321). Let's say you wanted to keep a 40 percent equity position ($55, 728) and therefore pulled out $48,558 through refinancing. You now owe $83,592. When we again calculate your return on equity for the fifteenth year, we will use $55,728 as the denominator. With the added debt, your cash flow will be reduced, but you still will achieve a total annual return of $10,004. Your ROE on this property is now back up to 18 percent ($10,004 divided by $55,728). If you also reinvested the $48,558 by acquiring one or two more properties using our Standard Model for investment, that money too would be working at a higher rate of return (16 percent or more). All this equity (capital) is now in the Wealthy Money condition.

The return on investment (or on equity) is similar if you use a 15-year loan (see the chart below). The ROI goes up over time, and the ROE comes down. In this case, equity builds up faster and cash flow is reduced until the loan is paid off in year 15, and then it goes up dramatically. As we said earlier, 30-year loans are safer in that you are more likely to get positive cash flow. Also, you can always make additional payments, reduce the remaining balance of the loan, and accelerate the payoff.

	Tracking Your Return on Investment and Return on Equity over Time (15-Year Mortgage)								
Year	Start of Year Market Value	Annual Price Appreciation	Year End Appreciated Market Value	Annual Principal Debt Pay Down	Year End Accumulated Equity	Annual Cash Flow	Return On Investment	Return On Equity
1	$ 70,300	$ 3,515	$ 73,816	$ 1,763	$ 30,587	$ (794)	39.9%	17.7%
2	$ 73,816	$ 3,691	$ 77,509	$ 1,890	$ 36,171	$ (592)	44.4%	16.3%
3	$ 77,509	$ 3,875	$ 81,387	$ 2,026	$ 42,075	$ (379)	49.1%	15.3%
4	$ 81,387	$ 4,069	$ 85,461	$ 2,172	$ 48,321	$ (156)	54.1%	14.5%
5	$ 85,461	$ 4,273	$ 89,739	$ 2,329	$ 54,928	$ 78	59.4%	13.8%
6	$ 89,739	$ 4,487	$ 94,232	$ 2,496	$ 61,917	$ 324	65.0%	13.3%
7	$ 94,232	$ 4,712	$ 98,950	$ 2,676	$ 69,311	$ 583	70.9%	12.9%
8	$ 98,950	$ 4,948	$ 103,906	$ 2,868	$ 77,135	$ 854	77.1%	12.5%
9	$ 103,906	$ 5,195	$ 109,110	$ 3,075	$ 85,414	$ 1,139	83.7%	12.2%
10	$ 109,110	$ 5,455	$ 114,575	$ 3,296	$ 94,176	$ 1,438	90.6%	11.9%
11	$ 114,575	$ 5,729	$ 120,315	$ 3,533	$ 103,449	$ 1,752	97.9%	11.7%
12	$ 120,315	$ 6,016	$ 126,343	$ 3,788	$ 113,264	$ 2,082	105.7%	11.5%
13	$ 126,343	$ 6,317	$ 132,673	$ 4,060	$ 123,655	$ 2,428	113.8%	11.3%
14	$ 132,673	$ 6,634	$ 139,321	$ 4,352	$ 134,655	$ 2,792	122.5%	11.1%
15	$ 139,321	$ 6,966	$ 146,302	$ 4,663	$ 146,302	$ 3,176	131.6%	11.0%
16	$ 146,302	$ 7,315	$ 153,633	$ -	$ 153,633	$ 8,418	139.9%	10.8%
17	$ 153,633	$ 7,682	$ 161,332	$ -	$ 161,332	$ 8,839	146.9%	10.8%
18	$ 161,332	$ 8,067	$ 169,416	$ -	$ 169,416	$ 9,281	154.2%	10.8%
19	$ 169,416	$ 8,471	$ 177,906	$ -	$ 177,906	$ 9,745	161.9%	10.8%
20	$ 177,906	$ 8,895	$ 186,821	$ -	$ 186,821	$ 10,232	170.1%	10.8%

Figure 20

Fifteen-year loans act more like a forced savings program: You have to make the payments and therefore build equity more quickly. We observed that once they had a solid financial foundation (a good equity position), most of our Millionaire Real Estate Investors tended to favor shorter-term loans. However, they continued to refinance, take out the equity, and add more income properties to their investment portfolios.

ISSUE 13: MINIMIZE YOUR TAX EXPOSURE

In addition to making your money accountable by tracking your ROI and ROE, you want to minimize your tax exposure. This is a fundamental operating principle for all millionaire investors. They understand that taxes are an obligation but not a mandate: The government wants you to pay what you owe but gives you many ways not to pay, at least not right away. It is really saying: "We will charge you less if you do these things." Looking at it another way, it is saying: "We will invest in you if you do what we want you to do." The government wants you to invest in real estate, hold those investments, or move into bigger ones. In a sense, the government is your coinvestor. You are wise to take advantage of what it wants you to do, particularly since that is very advantageous to you as a real estate investor.

The first thing you want to do is keep a detailed and comprehensive accounting of all your expenses, including the costs you incur in lead generation and property evaluation. Almost everything you do during your acquisitions (inspections, finder's fees, real estate commissions, etc.) represents costs you can use to offset your rental income. Most of those costs can be recaptured even years after they were incurred, at the time when you have begun to achieve positive cash flow. You certainly need to keep track of all your operating expenses while you own the properties. In addition, you can make property repairs and improvements, especially those which add value to the investment, and these expenses are also deductible against current or future income. Beyond all this you can depreciate the property; in fact, the government requires you to. It is well worth the expense to retain a great tax accountant who specializes in real estate investment. This person will be a key member of your Work

Network. If he or she is not in your Inner Circle, your Inner Circle will help you find the best person to be your tax advisor.

The first step has been to reduce the realized income on which you will pay taxes. The second step is to reduce capital gains taxes: the amount you pay the government when you realize a profit (gain) on the sale of a property. While this profit already is taxed at a rate below most income tax rates, you can delay paying it for a very long time. The two primary ways to do this are through IRAs and 1031 exchanges. You can use your Individual Retirement Account or other tax-deferred saving plans to make and hold your real estate investments. As long as you don't take the money out of those accounts, you do not have to pay taxes even if you achieve large amounts of equity. You can, if you choose, take that money out later, when you need the income.

In the end it's the tax-deferred 1031 exchange that gets massive use by Millionaire Real Estate Investors. This program in the IRS tax code allows you to sell and buy properties without having to declare capital gains or pay those taxes. It's a very straightforward procedure, but it takes some planning. First, you need to hire a 1031 Qualified Intermediary before you close on the sale of one of your prop-

> "An out-of-town owner called me wanting to sell four properties. They were all in great condition, just needing a little paint and one new roof, and they were all fully occupied. But he had happened to get my postcard at the time he was trying to get the tenants out so he could sell them and do a 1031 exchange into an apartment building in Florida. So he told me that if I bought all four by the date he needed to sell, he'd take 90% of their value. I negotiated him down to 82% of what they were worth, and I bought them for basically no cash out of pocket. That is, I had two people in lease-option agreements who refinanced at about that time, so I used the $130,000 I got out of those two lower-end properties as down payments on four occupied properties worth $360,000. And it was a 1031 exchange, so I didn't pay taxes on anything."
>
> Vena Jones-Cox
> Millionaire Real Estate Investor
> Cincinnati, OH

erties. That person will act as your guide and escrow agent as you move through the sale of one property and the purchase of the next. After the sale of your "relinquished property" you have 45 days to identify the "replacement property" and a total of 180 days to close on that second property. You want to be looking for the replacement property before or during the marketing of the property you are selling. If you find a good opportunity, you can enter into a contract with a right to assign clause if your first property does not sell or with a 1031 clause in the purchase agreement if it does.

Many people have the mistaken notion that you are exchanging your property with someone else: You take theirs, and they take yours. In some cases that can be done, but it is neither the purpose nor the requirement of a 1031 exchange. A 1031 exchange is designed for you to "exchange" one property in your portfolio (sell it) and replace it with another one that you wish to buy. It allows you to keep purchasing larger, more expensive properties without having to pay capital gains taxes on the ones you sell. This is a wonderful way to keep your money working for you.

YOU: YOUR PRIMARY ASSET

Don't underestimate what's possible and don't underestimate yourself. Invest in yourself. Stay plugged in. Seek out role models and mentors. Invest in your personal development and education. Learn everything you can as soon as you can and never stop learning. Never stop asking questions; stay into curiosity and out of the need to know it all now. Remember that you are your most important asset. That's not a selfish point of view. Shakespeare was reflecting this when he said, "To thine own self be true." The degree to which you develop yourself and achieve your financial wealth-building goals will be the degree to which you can leave a legacy. In the end others will benefit from what you do for yourself.

ISSUE 14: PROTECT YOUR TIME

Arguably, the most valuable asset anyone has is his or her time, and so it pays to value it, protect it and invest it wisely. In the game of real estate investing at the Own a Million level, this becomes vital.

From start to finish the best use of your time will always be in generating leads, looking at real estate and in doing deals. At the Own a Million stage you'll have two new issues that you would be wise to include on your short list. First, you'll want to watch your finances with an eye toward maximizing your returns, which was described in the Money section. Second, you'll be holding others accountable to keep your time free.

Your growing portfolio of rental properties will need someone's attention; it doesn't have to be your responsibility alone. Things break. Toilets and furnaces cease to function on Fridays as often as they do on Mondays. Properties have to be shown. Tenants sometimes need to be reminded to pay the rent. These problems and situations are the stuff of the "war stories" experienced investors tell, the stories that frighten many new investors away. What our investors made all too clear was that while owning real estate investment properties does make you a landlord, it doesn't mean you have to do the work of one. Therefore, don't act like one—hire one.

> *"Give 10% of your gross income to buying investment properties, and spend a tenth of your time each week watching your money and your property. You have to learn to invest time in your properties. If it digs into your work day, you need to start earlier."*
>
> Marshall Redder
> Millionaire Real Estate Investor
> Grandville, MI

I'm talking about property managers, and there are increasingly more options for investors, large and small, to contract with property management firms for single-family residential, multifamily, and commercial rentals. You simply account for it in your expenses (a typical fee is 10 percent of gross rents) and make sure the properties you acquire have enough gross rent to handle this cost and still generate positive cash flow. If your portfolio is large enough to support this, you may be able to let the economies of scale work in your favor by hiring a full-time property manager as an employee to manage all your properties.

This is another area where investors have been quite creative. To protect their time, they not only budget for property management independent contractors or employees but also cut deals with responsible tenants. In return for free or reduced rents these model tenants often will manage small multifamily properties on the owner's behalf. Many single-family investors sidestep the issue through home warranties and lease agreements. For example, they purchase a warranty for their property that covers common repairs with a $50 deductible. They then write into the lease that all repairs are the tenant's responsibility, along with the deductible. This can be marketed as a win for both the owner and the occupant, since the renter can call for any repairs at any time for a small out-of-pocket cost, while the owner doesn't have to book repairs around the tenant's schedule.

There are innumerable solutions to the problem of the day-to-day management of your holdings. As your wealth grows make sure you're holding someone besides yourself accountable to tend to these daily tasks. Your time is too valuable and your life is too short to collect late rents or fix leaky faucets.

ISSUE 15: PROTECT YOUR ASSETS

I encourage you to do entity and estate planning as early in the game as you can. I waited too long and had to pay a high price when I finally got the right advice. I cost myself money and opportunities because I wasn't thinking big enough soon enough. I thought I didn't need it in the beginning, and it seemed like an unnecessary expense. I was wrong. If you fail you need it, and if you succeed you need it. And if you succeed big and don't have it, not only will it be expensive but you may have made mistakes you can't undo. My advice is this: Do it right and do it right away.

Very early in your investment career you should meet with a qualified lawyer and estate planner with experience in real estate. Your network will be a good source of people to contact and interview. Once you find the right one or two people, ask all your questions, answer theirs, and make decisions. First, you want to make sure that you and your assets are protected from any liabilities that may arise from your ownership or your position as a landlord. This is the right time to be sure you have proper insurance in place. Second, you want to be sure that your estate is handled properly and that you have minimized the tax consequences for your family and heirs. You want to maximize the amount you can give (tax free) while you are alive as well as minimize the tax burdens on your estate. If you get to work on this early, it will inform some of your investment and acquisition decisions.

ISSUE 16: BE LEARNING BASED

First you learn, and then you earn. This old adage continues to be true even for those who have acquired an enormous number of investment properties. Investing is a lifelong learning endeavor. Even the most experienced Millionaire Real Estate Investors told us how much they were still learning and how much of an advantage their increased awareness was bringing them. They told us to remind you always to be a student of the game, and that's what I'm telling you now: Never stop learning. To put a twist on the old adage, the more you learn, the more you'll earn.

> *"Earn and learn your way."*
>
> Jack Miller
> Millionaire Real Estate Investor
> Reno, NV

The learning curve is a scientific and research-based concept. It has a real shape (see the chart below) and a real impact on everyone. What it says is that at the beginning of every venture, when you are a novice, you will put in a lot of time on the task (learning or skill building) without much apparent increase in your skill (ability to be effective). But don't be discouraged by this! After a certain amount of learning, your skills will begin to show some improvement. Just after that there comes a very important and exciting time: a period of accelerated growth in both awareness and skill. Suddenly it all comes together. You get the whole picture and see how every piece fits into that picture. Your judgment is sharper, your confidence is higher, and as a result you are even more motivated. You're now in the game.

The key to getting good at real estate investing is to stay with it long enough to reach this accelerated "zone of skill attainment." Many people quit too early, sometimes just before entering the zone. Others never put

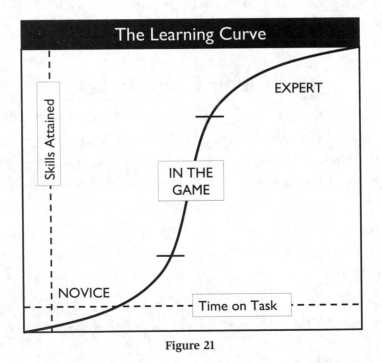

Figure 21

The Millionaire Real Estate Investor

in the time it takes to get there: They remain novices and therefore make novice mistakes throughout their investment career.

At the top end of the learning curve is the place where the experts dwell—those uniquely motivated people who enjoy mastering the game. Even at their level of expertise, they continue to learn and fine-tune their knowledge and ability. However, as the curve shows, they do not gain a massive increase in ability for the time they put in. But for them that little difference makes all the difference, and a 1 percent improvement in an area can translate to big, meaningful returns. They are at the top of their game, and while it isn't always a competitive game they play, no one plays it better.

There is an important reason why I have introduced this concept at this point in our discussion. I want you to understand that learning is the game we play when it comes to investing and financial wealth building. Knowledge is power, particularly in financial matters, and it is worth taking the time and having the patience to reach the "zone of skill attainment" in any area you want to master. There is a second point I want you to appreciate: Every time you undertake a new area of knowledge, you again will go back to the beginning of the learning curve—you will, in that area, be a novice.

This is the real problem with changing your real estate investment strategy again and again: You will move backward before you can move forward confidently. There will be some carryover from your general learning about real estate, but if you move your investment strategy from residential single-family houses to mini-warehouses, from urban to exurban properties, or from existing rental units to raw land, you will have to start

> *"Keep going to seminars and keep learning, because that's what keeps you enthused. Even if you just do two deals in a year, that will get you enthused."*
>
> Peggy Rollins
> Millionaire Real Estate Investor
> Dalton, GA

over and learn both the basics and the nuances of a new area of real estate.

Become the master of one approach, not the jack of all approaches or even many. Once you pick your primary investment strategy, learn it and begin to employ it. Don't switch out of boredom or for the promise of some magical, no-one's-ever-thought-of-this get-rich-quick scheme. Follow a proven path, use the fundamental models, and learn the ropes for yourself. Let any aggressiveness or sense of urgency drive you first to learn and then to stay tenaciously focused on working your chosen strategy. Master your niche before you ever consider a switch.

ISSUE 17: BE ACCOUNTABLE

Few people understand the concept or the power of accountability. Most confuse it with discipline, evaluation, and criticism. The truth is that accountability is a very powerful and personally enabling process. The greatest successes and the highest achievements almost always are due to accountability. For me, big success comes 10 percent from having a goal (specific and written), 10 percent from having an action plan (predetermined strategies and activities), and 80 percent from having accountability. As important as goals and plans are, accountability is even more important. Accountability means having someone else with whom you review what you have done, evaluate the results you have gotten, and commit to the next things you are going to do. This process must involve another person: a mentor, a coach, a consultant, or a peer-partner. You can be more or less disciplined by yourself, but you cannot hold yourself accountable over the long haul. There must be another person. That's what makes it work and makes it powerful.

> *"You need the education and the experience, but first you need the heart."*
> Robert Kiyosaki
> Best-selling author and millionaire investor
> Scottsdale, AZ

Almost every great athlete or artistic performer has a coach. Many have more than one. Tiger Woods is reported to have had five at one time. Who holds you accountable is important; those people should know you and what you are trying to accomplish, and you must trust and respect them. But they do not need to be better than you at what you are doing. Their role is to keep you on track, to make sure that you are doing what you set out to do and are looking at the results you are getting. Always remember that "feedback is the breakfast of champions." Accountability is about getting feedback and using it to inform and motivate our future actions. It's about not letting ourselves get too far off track or out of balance. Find the best accountability partner you can, and allow the accountability process to work for you. Once you experience the life-altering power of accountability, you will never stop using it.

It All Comes Down to This

Our goal with Own a Million was to touch on the complexity of investing without getting lost in it. Surprisingly, all this apparent complexity can remain simple if you keep the right perspective. All the complexity you will encounter in the real estate investment game boils down to trying to accomplish four simple things:

1. Getting in for less (little or no down payment)
2. Maximizing cash flow (increasing rents and reducing debt service and expenses)
3. Avoiding taxes (reducing or delaying them)
4. Increasing return on investment (and on equity)

Don't let new names for things or more complicated ways of doing them distract or disorient you. Keep it simple, keep your focus, and avoid getting lost in the labyrinth of complexity. Your path is straighter and far

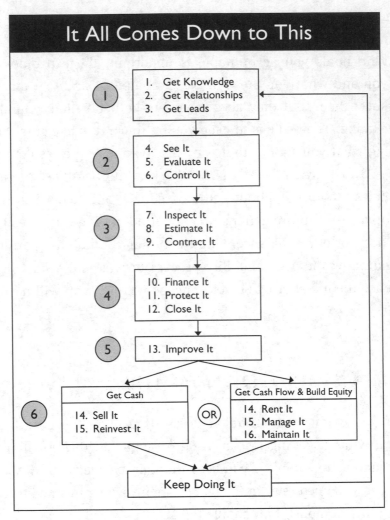

It All Comes Down to This

1
1. Get Knowledge
2. Get Relationships
3. Get Leads

2
4. See It
5. Evaluate It
6. Control It

3
7. Inspect It
8. Estimate It
9. Contract It

4
10. Finance It
11. Protect It
12. Close It

5
13. Improve It

6
Get Cash
14. Sell It
15. Reinvest It

OR

Get Cash Flow & Build Equity
14. Rent It
15. Manage It
16. Maintain It

Keep Doing It

Figure 22

less complicated than you might think. Almost everything we've learned to this point can be readily distilled into a short, memorable form (see the chart above). When you take a step back and put things in their simplest terms, it all comes down to this.

■ Owning a million is about turning your investments into actual net worth that shows up on your balance sheet. To do so, you must concentrate on the Buy and Hold strategy, maximizing and accelerating your Equity Buildup.

■ Along the journey, you are likely to encounter issues in five principal areas:

- *Criteria: The Guiding Light*

  ◆ Stick or Switch—Pick a niche, learn it and master it. Repetition is the mother of mastery.

  ◆ Become an Expert—Learn your niche through study and observation, experience and doing, asking and listening.

  ◆ Think in Units—Consolidating management costs and limiting potential losses on individual units is efficient, and can increase the net cash flow of your investment.

- *Terms: Hold Them Dear*

  ◆ Acquisition Terms—Put the property under contract quickly, negotiate everything, and master creative financing.

  ◆ Operating Terms—Maximize your NOI by increasing gross rental income, controlling expenses and minimizing vacancies.

  ◆ Disposition Terms—Knowing *why* you are selling determines your strategy. Remember, selling only makes sense when you can maximize the cash you take out and then put it into another investment that brings a better return.

- *Network: Together Everyone Achieves More*

  ◆ Associate with Talent—Hire carefully and have a process to do so.

  ◆ Top-Grade—Find the best and demand the best.

- Work from Written Proposals and Contracts—"Get it in writing" every time.
- Protect Your Reputation—It's your most precious asset.

- *Money: Give It a Work Ethic*
  - Hold It Accountable—To be wealthy, your money must be healthy, so know what condition it's in (dead, safe, healthy, wealthy) and how well it is being paid.
  - Minimize Tax Exposure—Reduce realized income on which you pay taxes, and reduce Capital Gains taxes (through IRAs or 1031s)

- *You: Your Primary Asset*
  - Protect Your Time—Hire others, like property managers, to tend to daily tasks.
  - Protect Your Assets—Prioritize entity and estate planning.
  - Be Learning Based—Knowledge is power, so endeavor to be at the top end of the Learning Curve.
  - Be Accountable—Get feedback and use it to inform and motivate your future actions.

RECEIVE A MILLION

Don't simply retire from something—
have something to retire to.

Harry Emerson Fosdick

REACHING FOR THE LIGHT

In his award-winning book *The Trees in My Forest,* Bernd Heinrich describes how trees in his part of the Maine woods individually manage their growth and resources to compete for light. The choices are simple: They can take the nutrients they absorb and focus their growth upward or focus it outward. To reach the light some trees attempt to be taller than those around them. Think of the tall forest pines that are mostly bare except at the highest reaches; those trees are racing upward for the light. Other trees grow wide in hopes of drowning competitors in their shadows, like an oak spreading out in a clearing. Last is the curious case of running ground pines that sprout up wherever the light pokes down through the upper canopy. An opportunist like this can have a root system the size of a football field and is often mistaken for many separate plants. Each tree in its own way manages growth upward or outward or some combination of the two to strive, thrive, and reach for the light.

The journey of the Millionaire Real Estate Investor is no different. On the path from Buy a Million to Own a Million investors must manage their primary resources of cash flow and equity buildup to reach their net worth goals. Some choose to apply cash flow to paying down debt and therefore accelerate their equity buildup. Others tap into their equity or save their cash flow to reinvest in other properties. A few take the cash flow as it comes, leave their equity where it is, and let time do its thing. None is right or wrong—these are different paths to the same goal of increased net worth. Now it's time to turn our focus from net worth growth to annual unearned income growth.

Receive a Million is founded on the idea that you can, if you choose, reach a place in your investment life where you can step out of the day-to-day work of investing and receive $1 million in annual pretax income. It's about amassing the capital assets that can provide you with that kind of unearned income; it's about knowing the ways to convert those capital assets to cash flow; and it's about building an organization that ensures that your money will continue to work for you even when you are no longer working for your money. That's one of the Big Questions we want you to be able to answer—the ultimate destination we want you to strive for. We know that if you can reason a path to that *big* income goal, you can learn how to step out of your investment business some day and receive more unearned income than many would ever dream of or need: $1 million in annual unearned income.

THE CHALLENGE OF UNEARNED INCOME

One of the things I've found to be almost universally true is that most people do not know what it takes to generate meaningful amounts of unearned income. Before you can invest money, you generally have to earn it and pay taxes on it. Only then are you able to take your net income and invest a portion of it for a passive return.

If you were working at a job to earn $1 million in annual after-tax net income, you'd have to earn over $1.5 million to compensate for taxes.

Think about it. Today the highest tax rate for ordinary earned income is 35 percent. That means you'd have to earn $1,538,461 to net an even $1,000,000. That's one year of amazing earnings that goes away the moment you stop working.

How Much Money Would You Have to Earn to Net $1 Million in Annual Income?			
Gross Earned	Tax Rate	Tax Paid	Annual Pretax Income
$ 1,538,461.54	35%	$ 538,461.54	$ 1,000,000.00

Figure 1

Investing for $1 million isn't much easier, and it takes a lot of after-tax income to generate $1 million in interest. The chart below tells the story. Working from left to right, you can trace the amount of income you'd have to earn before taxes to have enough money left to invest after taxes to reach your big income goal. If you could achieve 5 percent annual interest on your investment, you'd have to earn over $30.7 million to net the after-tax $20 million you'd need to invest to receive a million dollars in pretax income.[1] At a 10 percent annual rate of return you'd still have to earn over $15.3 million to invest $10 million after taxes to receive a million dollars in cash flow. Even at a 15 percent annual rate of return an investor would have to earn over $10.2 million to invest $6.6 million and reach his or her big passive income goal.

How Much Money Would You Have to Earn to Invest for $1 Million in Annual Income?					
Gross Earned	Tax Rate	Tax Paid	Net Invested	Annual ROI	Annual Pretax Income
$ 61,538,461.54	35%	$ 21,538,461.54	$ 40,000,000.00	2.5%	$ 1,000,000.00
$ 30,769,230.77	35%	$ 10,769,230.77	$ 20,000,000.00	5.0%	$ 1,000,000.00
$ 20,512,820.51	35%	$ 7,179,487.18	$ 13,333,333.33	7.5%	$ 1,000,000.00
$ 15,384,615.38	35%	$ 5,384,615.38	$ 10,000,000.00	10.0%	$ 1,000,000.00
$ 12,307,692.31	35%	$ 4,307,692.31	$ 8,000,000.00	12.5%	$ 1,000,000.00
$ 10,256,410.26	35%	$ 3,589,743.59	$ 6,666,666.67	15.0%	$ 1,000,000.00

Figure 2

---

[1] Remember, almost all investment vehicles require you to pay tax on the cash flow you receive. Whether that is capital gains tax or ordinary income tax depends on the investment vehicle.

Honestly, it doesn't have to be this difficult. Receiving $1 million in annual income is very possible with real estate; it can be comparatively easy for those who are willing to Think, Buy, and Own like Millionaire Real Estate Investors and put their money to work for them over time. Let's take a close look at what it takes to receive $1 million in annual pre-tax income from investments in real estate.

ACHIEVE $1 MILLION IN ANNUAL CASH FLOW THROUGH INVESTING IN REAL ESTATE

The interesting thing about investing in real estate is that you have many options for achieving your big income goal. As one of our millionaire investors put it, "There are many roads to Rome." For the purposes of this discussion, let's narrow our focus to single-family residential investment homes and attack the issue from four distinct angles:

1. How much real estate would an investor need to acquire *today* to receive $1 million in annual cash flow *now*?
2. How much real estate would an investor need to acquire *today* to receive $1 million in annual cash flow *in the future*?
3. How much real estate would an investor need to acquire *over time* to receive $1 million in annual cash flow *in the future*?
4. How much real estate would an investor need to acquire *over time* to receive $1 million in annual cash flow and equity pullout *in the future*?

In all four models we'll work with the understanding that an average single-family home costs about $170,000 with a gross monthly rent of $1,360 (based on our conservative 0.8 percent of market value formula). To account for vacancy and other expenses we used a conservative figure of 40 percent for our calculations, and where appropriate we used mortgage interest rates of 6.97 percent for 15-year loans and 7.43 percent for 30-year loans.[2] Rent and the value of our properties will appreciate at 5 percent annually, which is slightly below historical averages. Finally, we'll work from the assumption that properties are acquired at a 20 percent investor's discount with a 20 percent down payment.

Don't forget that your choices and your abilities can improve the results with all these models. If you choose to reinvest cash flow to acquire more real estate or pay down debt, you may achieve your goals faster. If you consistently achieve higher rent rates, lower your expenses, or reduce your vacancies, you'll be accelerated along the path to your net income goal. With that in mind, let's look at the first way to receive a million in real estate.

> *"Make sure you understand what you want your portfolio to look like at the end. My future portfolio will be 250 houses. If all paid off, that would be $1.4 million in annual gross rental income, and when I'm 60 or 65 I can sell them and hold the notes. You want to get to a point where you have a business."*
>
> Marshall Redder
> Millionaire Real Estate Investor
> Grandville, MI

1. How Much Real Estate Would an Investor Need to Acquire Today to Receive $1 Million in Annual Cash Flow Now?

To receive $1 million in annual pretax income now, an investor would need to acquire 102 single-family rentals at once and own them *free and clear*. Anything less than a 100 percent equity position requires a substantial increase in property ownership as well as a greater investment of cash. For instance, if an investor chooses to close with 50 percent down payments, he or she will have to acquire more than 240 homes for a total investment of over $16.3 million.

---

[2] Mortgage interest rates are based on the average recorded rates from 1992 to 2003.

As illustrated in the chart below, to achieve this goal immediately an investor needs to invest $13.8 million to gain a 100 percent equity position in the properties and save $3.5 million by acquiring properties at a 20 percent discount. Achieving a million dollars in cash flow today requires a substantial up-front investment. The good news is that most people don't need to Receive a Million immediately. Most people have at least some time to let the advantages of investing in real estate work in their favor.

$1 Million in Annual Pre-Tax Income Buy It Now—Receive It Now			
Residential Home Profile			
Market Value	$ 170,000.00		
Rent Rate (0.8%)	$ 1,360.00		
Vacancy & Expenses (40%)	$ 544.00		
Monthly Cash Flow	$ 816.00		
Annual Cash Flow Per Home	$ 9,792.00		
Number of Units Owned	102		
Total Investment at 20% Discount		Annual ROI	Annual Pretax Income
$ 13,888,888.89		7.2%	$ 1,000,000.00

Figure 3

2. HOW MUCH REAL ESTATE WOULD AN INVESTOR NEED TO ACQUIRE TODAY TO RECEIVE $1 MILLION IN ANNUAL CASH FLOW IN THE FUTURE?

Factoring for time works in an investor's favor because it allows the investor to account for appreciation in real estate values and rents, both of which historically tend to appreciate at around 5 percent a year. Using the same assumptions but this time including our regular 20 percent down payment for 15-year or 30-year mortgages, let's examine how much real estate an investor would have to acquire today to achieve $1 million in unearned income in 10, 20, or 30 years. This time we'll allow our hypothetical investor to let the market forces work in her or his favor. The chart below depicts six different scenarios in which this could play out. Three are for 15-year mortgages, and three are for 30-year mortgages. Pick a quadrant that matches your time line and take a moment to consider the numbers.

$1 Million in Annual Pre-Tax Income					
Buy It Now—Receive It in the Future					
10 Years on a 15-Year Mortgage			10 Years on a 30-Year Mortgage		
Annual Cash Flow Per Home	Number of Homes Owned	Total Annual Pre-Tax Income	Annual Cash Flow Per Home	Number of Homes Owned	Total Annual Pre-Tax Income
$ 3,477.39	288	$ 1,000,000.00	$ 6,124.16	163	$ 1,000,000.00
Total Investment	Annual Rate of Return		Total Investment	Annual Rate of Return	
$ 6,901,726.18	14.5%		$ 3,918,904.63	25.5%	
20 Years on a 15-Year Mortgage			20 Years on a 30-Year Mortgage		
Annual Cash Flow Per Home	Number of Homes Owned	Total Annual Pre-Tax Income	Annual Cash Flow Per Home	Number of Homes Owned	Total Annual Pre-Tax Income
$ 24,743.90	40	$ 1,000,000.00	$ 15,677.45	64	$ 1,000,000.00
Total Investment	Annual Rate of Return		Total Investment	Annual Rate of Return	
$ 969,936.17	103.1%		$ 1,530,861.14	65.3%	
30 Years on a 15-Year Mortgage			30 Years on a 30-Year Mortgage		
Annual Cash Flow Per Home	Number of Homes Owned	Total Annual Pre-Tax Income	Annual Cash Flow Per Home	Number of Homes Owned	Total Annual Pre-Tax Income
$ 40,305.20	25	$ 1,000,000.00	$ 31,238.75	32	$ 1,000,000.00
Total Investment	Annual Rate of Return		Total Investment	Annual Rate of Return	
$ 595,456.67	167.9%		$ 768,276.48	130.2%	

Figure 4

In this model the numbers take an astounding turn to the investor's advantage. With a 10-year window, the investor would need to invest $6.9 million with 15-year mortgages or $3.9 million with 30-year mortgages to achieve $1 million in pretax income. With a 20-year window the investor would have to invest just under $1 million with 15-year mortgages or $1.5 million with 30-year mortgages. Finally, given a 30-year time frame, one would need to invest between $595,000 and $768,000. All these scenarios produce strong and in some cases remarkable rates of return on investment that would satisfy most Millionaire Real Estate Investors. What keeps this scenario in the realm of the hypothetical for most individuals is the necessity of buying all those properties in just one year. Let's look at our third model, where the investor can purchase properties over time to achieve $1 million in unearned income in the future.

3. How Much Real Estate Would an Investor Need to Acquire over Time to Receive $1 Million in Annual Cash Flow in the Future?

In this model we'll factor for both time in the market and the time it takes to acquire the portfolio of a cash flow millionaire. What's instructive about this model is that it shows investors the average number and market value of the homes they will have to buy each year to meet their unearned income goal. Furthermore, it shows the amount of money an

$1 Million in Annual Pre-Tax Income					
Buy It Over Time—Receive It in the Future (Cash Flow Only)					
10 Years on a 15-Year Mortgage			10 Years on a 30-Year Mortgage		
Average Market Value of Annual Acquisitions	Average Number of Annual Acquisitions	Average Annual Investment	Average Market Value of Annual Acquisitions	Average Number of Annual Acquisitions	Average Annual Investment
$ 8,522,891.59	39.9	$ 1,363,662.65	$ 586,030.39	17.1	$ 586,030.39
Total Market Value of Acquisitions	Total Number of Homes Owned	Total Annual Pre-Tax Income	Total Market Value of Acquisitions	Total Number of Homes Owned	Total Annual Pre-Tax Income
$ 112,581,054.01	398.6	$ 1,000,000.00	$ 48,381,407.53	171.3	$ 1,000,000.00
20 Years on a 15-Year Mortgage			20 Years on a 30-Year Mortgage		
Average Market Value of Annual Acquisitions	Average Number of Annual Acquisitions	Average Annual Investment	Average Market Value of Annual Acquisitions	Average Number of Annual Acquisitions	Average Annual Investment
$ 784,401.23	2.8	$ 125,504.20	$ 935,055.46	3.3	$ 149,608.87
Total Market Value of Acquisitions	Total Number of Homes Owned	Total Annual Pre-Tax Income	Total Market Value of Acquisitions	Total Number of Homes Owned	Total Annual Pre-Tax Income
$ 27,249,371.23	55.8	$ 1,000,000.00	$ 32,482,959.48	66.5	$ 1,000,000.00
30 Years on a 15-Year Mortgage			30 Years on a 30-Year Mortgage		
Average Market Value of Annual Acquisitions	Average Number of Annual Acquisitions	Average Annual Investment	Average Market Value of Annual Acquisitions	Average Number of Annual Acquisitions	Average Annual Investment
$ 357,987.73	1.0	$ 57,278.04	$ 449,045.87	1.2	$ 71,847.34
Total Market Value of Acquisitions	Total Number of Homes Owned	Total Annual Pre-Tax Income	Total Market Value of Acquisitions	Total Number of Homes Owned	Total Annual Pre-Tax Income
$ 24,999,996.43	28.5	$ 1,000,000.00	$ 31,359,022.08	35.8	$ 1,000,000.00

Figure 5

investor will have to invest on average each year, a key driver in setting one's budgeting and savings goals. Again, the model (see the chart on the facing page) depicts six scenarios that are based on the mortgage loan selected and the time frame. Take a moment to review each scenario and the numbers they represent.

What immediately jumps off the page in this analysis is the growth of net cash flow over time. In the 10-year scenario there is a marked benefit to choosing the increased cash flow of the 30-year mortgage (17.1 homes purchased each year) over the equity buildup of the 15-year mortgage (39.9 homes purchased each year). In fact, the investor's acquisitions are more than cut in half. However, this is reversed once the 15-year mortgage has been paid off in the 20-year and 30-year scenarios. If you're looking for cash flow and have time to grow it, accelerated debt paydown may get you there faster and with fewer overall acquisitions.

4. How Much Real Estate Would an Investor Need to Acquire over Time to Receive $1 Million in Annual Cash Flow and Equity Pullout in the Future?

In the last and most comprehensive model we're going to accelerate the process by factoring in the fact that equity buildup can be used as a source of income. As you know, there are two ways to achieve income from investment real estate. First, investors can receive cash flow from their investments; second, they have the additional option of tapping into and pulling out their equity buildup. Equity buildup—the combination of value appreciation and debt paydown—is very real. In fact, until the mortgage debt is completely paid off, there will be greater average annual returns from equity buildup than from cash flow in almost any scenario.

As we discussed in "Own a Million," Millionaire Real Estate Investors who are in the growth phase of their investing always manage their return on equity to keep their money working hard for them. Thus, they rarely look for a 100 percent equity position in their properties, much less their portfolios. Our research and experience show that the best, most prudent investors will manage this to range from a minimum of 20 percent to a maximum of around 70 percent before pulling some equity out. In the beginning equity pullout often is used for reinvestment in more property to accelerate the process.

The beautiful thing about equity pulled out periodically through refinancing is that this equity income is tax-free. The IRS sees this income for what it is: a liability incurred. These investors count on appreciation and their tenants to pay down their debt and build up their equity so that they can repeat this process. This equity pullout can be periodic or all at once, with the primary considerations being the investor's desired ratio

$1 Million in Annual Pre-Tax Income					
Buy It Over Time—Receive It in the Future (Cash Flow + Equity Pullout)					
10 Years on a 15-Year Mortgage			10 Years on a 30-Year Mortgage		
Average Market Value of Annual Acquisitions	Average Number of Annual Acquisitions	Average Annual Investment	Average Market Value of Annual Acquisitions	Average Number of Annual Acquisitions	Average Annual Investment
$ 985,919.46	4.6	$ 157,747.11	$ 1,562,649.73	7.3	$ 250,023.96
Total Market Value of Acquisitions	Total Number of Homes Owned	Total Annual Pre-Tax Income	Total Market Value of Acquisitions	Total Number of Homes Owned	Total Annual Pre-Tax Income
$ 13,023,262.15	46.1	$ 1,000,000.00	$ 20,641,439.76	73.1	$ 1,000,000.00
20 Years on a 15-Year Mortgage			20 Years on a 30-Year Mortgage		
Average Market Value of Annual Acquisitions	Average Number of Annual Acquisitions	Average Annual Investment	Average Market Value of Annual Acquisitions	Average Number of Annual Acquisitions	Average Annual Investment
$ 315,933.65	1.1	$ 50,549.38	$ 506,603.90	1.8	$ 81,056.62
Total Market Value of Acquisitions	Total Number of Homes Owned	Total Annual Pre-Tax Income	Total Market Value of Acquisitions	Total Number of Homes Owned	Total Annual Pre-Tax Income
$ 10,975,242.07	22.5	$ 1,000,000.00	$ 17,598,949.87	36.0	$ 1,000,000.00
30 Years on a 15-Year Mortgage			30 Years on a 30-Year Mortgage		
Average Market Value of Annual Acquisitions	Average Number of Annual Acquisitions	Average Annual Investment	Average Market Value of Annual Acquisitions	Average Number of Annual Acquisitions	Average Annual Investment
$ 147,959.57	0.4	$ 23,673.53	$ 231,645.35	0.6	$ 37,063.26
Total Market Value of Acquisitions	Total Number of Homes Owned	Total Annual Pre-Tax Income	Total Market Value of Acquisitions	Total Number of Homes Owned	Total Annual Pre-Tax Income
$ 10,332,724.58	11.8	$ 1,000,000.00	$ 16,176,903.29	18.5	$ 1,000,000.00

Figure 6

of equity to debt and the cost of refinancing. However, any time an investor reaches the $20 million equity mark and is achieving at least 5 percent annual appreciation, that investor is in effect getting $1 million a year in tax-free income if he or she chooses to pull it out.

In all the scenarios of this fourth and final model, the investor buys fewer properties and invests less to reach his or her net income goal. As the time frame of the investment plans lengthens, the investor has the extra bonus of having to lead generate for fewer and fewer genuinely great investment prospects each year. In fact, in the 30-year scenario the investor must find an average of only one outstanding property every two years.

Whether your goals are for today, 10 years from now, 20 years from now, or even 30 years in the future, we hope you're motivated to do your own math. It's about asking the $1 million unearned income question in a personal way. Will your Criteria allow you to buy for less and achieve more? How will the real estate and rental values in your market affect your personal equation? Where is your comfort level with your leverage? Do you want to keep a high equity position in your properties for security, or would you prefer a lower one for greater rates of return?

One of the things we discussed in "Own a Million" was the concept that millionaire investors Think in Units. Interestingly, when you apply the powerful leverage of trading up to larger multifamily investment properties to this equation, $1 million in unearned annual income becomes far more approachable. As we've learned, by consolidating property management and leasing into fewer properties, investors can lay claim to higher rental rates than the 0.8 percent we've considered for single-family rentals here while having fewer management issues with which to deal. In fact, one of the investors we interviewed built an amazing investment business by buying and selling real estate for investment income and then reinvesting in larger multifamily and commercial properties that now generate $12 million in annual profits. That, by the way, is $1 million a month!

$1 Million a Month: The Inspirational Story of Investor 34

One of my favorite stories is that of a millionaire investor we interviewed in California who built a remarkable real estate investment business that generates $12 million in annual profits. Since he was our thirty-fourth interview and out of respect for his wish to remain anonymous, we'll call him Investor 34.

Investor 34 started his investment business on savings and credit cards, and for the first six months he and his wife worked from their kitchen table. By that measure his success should feel repeatable to most people. He didn't have the advantage of beginning his investment career with large sums of money. The niche he latched onto was buying limited partnership interests in real estate. He and his wife would obtain lists of the limited partners from the general partners (which, by law, they were required to share) and then mail those investors a marketing piece offering to buy their interest. At the time they would offer as little as $50 for shares that were valued at about $100, and roughly 5 percent of the people they mailed to would take them up on their offer. But then a rising tide in the California real estate market swept them up and helped them turn as much as $150 in profit on each share they acquired.

As this investor said, "Our goal is not to be the biggest company around; it's to be the most profitable. So we would rather do a lot of small transactions that are highly profitable than a big transaction that generates the same amount of net income."

Their business success was limited by how much time they could devote to the mailings. A big breakthrough came when this investor's wife called the printer and asked, "Can you print, address, and stuff these for us?" All of the sudden they went from mailing 1,000 marketing pieces a month to 5,000 and then 10,000, 20,000, and 30,000.

"Our response rates and our profit margins were the same whether we mailed 1,000 or 100,000," he told us. "So the profitability of the company went way up."

Rather than treat the money as income and consume it, they reinvested directly in real estate—apartment buildings and storage facilities—to build a stable platform of residual income. Today Investor 34 owns over 4,000 apartment units and more than 1 million square feet of storage rentals. Amazingly, he nets over $12 million annually from $45 million in gross revenues. His little investment business has grown into a big investment business, obviously more than he and his wife could maintain at their kitchen table. Currently, he has over 60 direct employees divided among five investment companies and another 100 independent contractors who manage his apartment buildings. What I love about Investor 34's story isn't that he built his multimillion-dollar investment business so cleverly in little increments of $100 and $150 reinvested in real estate; it's that he discovered a powerful way to take him farther while working less: people leverage.

"It really wasn't about the money," he told us. "I wanted to set my own schedule, and mostly I wanted to be able to spend more time with my family."

Investor 34 works about 20 hours a week. He doesn't carry a cell phone or a pager because "I want to be connected when I want to be connected." He spends more and more time with his family. In our language, Investor 34 is well down the path of Receive a Million. In fact, he's at a point on the path where it's possible to receive $1 million a month. But no matter what amount of unearned income he receives at the end of his journey, be it more or less, I know he's already discovering the amazing freedom that comes when you can step out of your daily investment business without losing your income. It's what we call the 7th Level: The Path to People Leverage.

THE 7TH LEVEL: THE PATH TO PEOPLE LEVERAGE

If you're like Investor 34 or any of the other Millionaire Real Estate Investors we interviewed, you'll find that as your investment business grows, you will rely increasingly on others to perform the day-to-day tasks of investing while you manage the process. This is the natural evolution of a growing business. One day you'll discover that you're doing all you can and look for help. Sometime later you'll realize that even with the help you have you're hitting a ceiling of achievement because there are more opportunities than you have time to explore. You'll seek more help and continue to grow, and the cycle will repeat as your investment business expands along with your mastery of it. In our observations and experience there will be seven distinct and separate levels you will pass through on the path to becoming a Receive a Million Millionaire Real Estate Investor.

> *"We made the mistake of assuming the more properties we bought, the easier it would be to have positive cash flow. We kept thinking, 'We're making $200 a month per unit. We get enough of those and it's got to equal positive cash flow.' The problem with that is you've got to have somebody to manage them, and as you grow you've got to add more people."*
>
> Anna Mills
> Millionaire Real Estate Investor
> Toledo, OH

Although the exact organizational makeup of your investing operation may vary slightly, the 7th and final level of investment business is sure to include one commonality: One day you'll remove yourself from the routine daily business and allow a preselected, highly qualified individual or individuals to run your investment business for you. It's the place where you get to enjoy the financial wealth you've built without having to manage it actively.

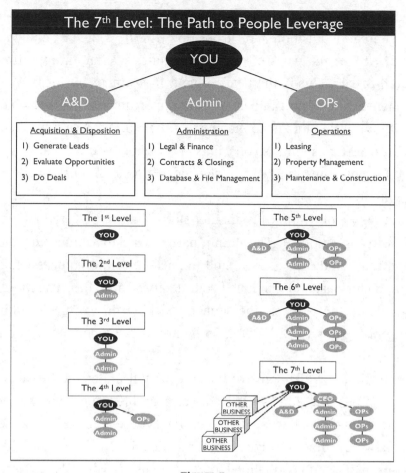

Figure 7

There are three basic components to the investment business of a Millionaire Real Estate Investor: There will be one part of your business dedicated to Acquisition and Disposition, one committed to Administration, and one that handles your Operations. In the beginning you will run all three departments and either do all the work yourself or manage independent contractors from your Work Network who do these functions for you. But over time, as your investment portfolio grows and you increasingly rely on your Work Network, you will see the wisdom in hiring an employee to do these jobs for you and only you.

Let's take a quick look at the three areas of your investment business. The first area, Acquisition and Disposition (A&D), is the last one you will give up. A&D is the work of generating leads, evaluating opportunities, and doing deals. This is the heart of your investment business. Without leads there are no opportunities; without opportunities there are no deals; and without deals there is no income. It's that simple. You'll want to stay active in A&D for as long as you can. This is where you will earn the most money for your time, and so it makes good financial sense to spend the most time there.

Administration (Admin) is another story. This is the very first area we advise you to relinquish. The Admin part of your investment business is the part that handles your legal and financial work, organizes your contracts and closings, and maintains your database and files. The more clerical in nature the work is, the sooner you may find yourself willing to farm it out to your Work Network and later hire someone to tackle these tasks for you.

Interestingly, while some of these tasks fall under the broad title of Admin, many are highly specialized. For example, unless you happen to be an accountant or lawyer by profession, you're probably best served not to advise yourself on complex tax or legal issues. You should contract this work out to qualified professionals in your Work Network. However, you may find that it saves you money to pay for the advice of these professionals and then file your own tax returns with the IRS or record the minutes of the investment business meetings you keep for your legal entities.

The last area is Operations (OPS), and it covers the broad area from leasing and property management to maintenance and construction. Whether you, someone in your network, or someone you hire does these tasks, you probably will have to develop expertise in these areas to become a Millionaire Real Estate Investor. Since these tasks are tied directly to your vacancies and expenses, leasing and property management can have a big impact on your bottom line. When we discussed maximizing your NOI in "Own a Million," we were pointing you toward the moment when you might hire contractors or employees to do this important work on your behalf.

Maintenance and construction are similar in that strong knowledge in these areas can both save and make you lots of money. The good news is that your continued work in A&D, particularly the estimation of repair costs for your acquisitions, will help keep you abreast of standard costs in these areas.

For many investors a property manager is the first non-Admin employee they hire. Arguably, other than a full-time A&D person, no other position will save you as much time and energy. The moment you contract with or hire a property manager is the moment you cease to function as a full-time managing landlord. This means someone else is taking the call for the broken toilet, the wobbly ceiling fan, or the broken furnace. Someone else is collecting rents and calling past-dues. Someone else is freeing you up in a massive way to pursue A&D and build your business.

As you can see in the chart above, the investors we interviewed first made the important decision to stop doing it themselves and hire part- or full-time administrative help. Every business has a certain amount of work (filing, record keeping, organization, and errands) that can be ignored for periods of time but not forgotten. At some point those tasks must be done for your business to stay on track, but they can steal valuable lead generation time from your critical A&D work. That's why Admin help almost always comes first. A highly focused investor probably can generate enough Admin work to keep more than one person busy while the investor pursues opportunities and deals.

If the 1st Level is where you do everything, then the 2nd Level and the 3rd Level are where Admin employees help you do more. The 4th Level is really about bringing in a property manager. In our research and experience that's almost always the first person hired for OPS. A few of our investors chose a maintenance employee first, but those instances were rare and usually were the result of larger multifamily ownership.

The 5th and 6th Levels represent your growing investment business with ever-increasing needs for Admin and OPS employees and one significant addition: your first A&D hire. This is a person who gets the game of investing. It may be someone from within your organization or your network who seems to have a knack for finding opportunities or doing deals. You will want to find a fair way to compensate this person, whether through base salary, bonuses, or percentage splits, for doing this for you full-time.

The final and most important stage is the 7th Level, where you hand over the day-to-day operations of your investment business to another person. Up to this point, as your organization grew, you were acting not only as the owner and principal investor but also as the company's CEO. It's now time to hire a CEO to replace you.

By this time the people in your organization with the gift of leadership should be revealing themselves to you. It's likely that one person already is largely responsible for your Admin functions and manages the other employees in that area for you. Similarly, another person probably is in charge of your OPS. If multiple employees have joined you in your ongoing A&D efforts, it's possible that a leader is emerging in that area as well. (Remember, A&D is the last area you should relinquish, and so it is just as likely that you are still providing primary daily leadership and accountability for your company's A&D.) These talented individuals have demonstrated that they are committed to the goals of your investment business and have risen to leadership positions within it. You still manage them, but they skillfully manage many people and projects on your behalf. These emerging leaders probably will be the best candidates to slide into the role of CEO.

The sobering truth about this transition is twofold. For one thing, no one will be able to do everything you do as well as you do, especially in the beginning. After all, you've spent years perfecting your investment models and the systems you use to manage your investment business. You know your models so well and are so good at implementing them because they most likely were built to match your natural strengths and compensate for your natural weaknesses. The talented individuals you've hired were brought in to complement, not replace, your skills. You can expect your CEO to stumble and struggle a bit in the beginning. You won't be freed right away but most likely will have to manage and mentor your CEO until both of you are confident that that person can do the job without supervision or safety nets. That's sobering truth number one.

Sobering truth number two is that your new CEO probably will be much better at some aspects of the job than you ever were. This is where you will have to rein in the natural competitiveness that helped you build your investment business in the first place. Because your CEO brings new strengths to the position, he or she may earn the right over time to change and even improve some of your systems. Your new role as business owner will be to monitor that person's progression from duplicating the success you created to being allowed to tinker with it. Remember, you built your investment business on proven models. You should expect your CEO to do the same thing.

The interesting thing about building a real estate investment business is that you have two distinct choices. On the one hand you can build a large, active business, as Investor 34 did. On the other hand you can choose to hire sparingly and count on your extensive Work Network for leverage. Both methods are valid. The big difference shows up at the 7th Level.

> "There are downsides of being a landlord: the phone ringing when you don't really feel like going and checking somebody's water heater. But I have someone managing my properties now, so it's mostly headache-free."
>
> Carlos Rivero
> Millionaire Real Estate Investor
> Austin, TX

Investors who build bona fide businesses tend to be better positioned to step out and count on their unearned income. Businesses are about cash flow and rarely have caps on their growth: They can remain active and agile even when the primary investor steps away.

Investors who build their investment enterprises primarily through their Work Networks are aiming toward a pseudo-7th Level. To fully achieve the 7th Level, you will have to hire your replacement. This path never leads to total leverage. Even though, through outside property management, the investor may be far removed from the day-to-day work, he or she still will need to give the investments considerable attention. Those investments won't continue to grow your investment portfolio the way your replacement CEO would. This is really the path of preserving and maintaining wealth. Many of our investors selected this option. With the help of key partners and a property manager, they built large real estate portfolios that required less and less of their time. They knew how much they needed and didn't mind that their portfolios were unlikely to grow once they turned their attention elsewhere. They achieved a pseudo-7th Level with lots of freedom and great rewards.

Over time you will be able to remove yourself from the day-to-day work of your investment business and focus on managing your CEO and key leaders. Instead of working in your business each day, you'll be able to work on it as little as a few hours a week. If you've ever wondered how entrepreneurs manage to run multiple businesses simultaneously, this explains it. They work on their businesses—managing key leaders—rather than working in the business every day.

MOVING FROM MANAGING YOUR TIME TO MANAGING OTHERS

Reaching the 7th Level will involve an entirely new set of skills for a prospective millionaire investor: business and management skills. Instead of creating a pro forma system for a transaction, you'll be reviewing one made by someone who works for you. Instead of inspecting real estate, you'll be inspecting reports made by someone who looked at a property for you. The good news is that from the moment you began developing your Work Network, you were building the foundational skills necessary to make this transition from investor to business owner.

That's what you did with every independent contractor you hired to fix your property, file your taxes, or manage a renovation. You had to tell them what you expected and then inspect their work to make sure it met your expectations. It's about communicating your standards and then inspecting to make sure you got what you expected.

The decision to keep for yourself or assign to others the A&D, Admin, and OPS functions of your business always lies with where your time and their time are most valuably spent. Not only do you want to stay focused on your most dollar-productive activities, you want the talented members of your growing organization to do the same thing. If the bookkeeper who saves you thousands in accounting fees each year could save you tens of thousands as a property manager or make you even more money scouting for opportunities, you may find yourself looking for a replacement bookkeeper.

Choosing whether to contract with this person from your Work Network or to employ this person outright involves the same financial common sense. The main difference lies in the length of time you pay the person. You engage contractors from job to job, but employees are engaged for the long term; this means you have to have enough work to justify their salaries and keep them engaged.

Your progress through the seven levels is essentially a progression from "I do it" to "We do it" to "They do it." In the beginning you did everything and essentially paid yourself. As you developed your Work Network, you started contracting with others to leverage your time and profits. The moment your investment business began generating reliable

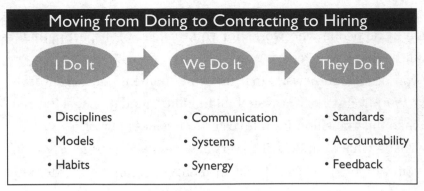

income, those people had the option of bringing in full-time employees to grow it. This is the period when you'll be working with people inside and outside your organization. The 7th Level is where you take on the role of business owner and run your business through the talented leaders you've hired. These leaders are the custodians of your investment business, an asset that still pays you money. While you still will bring vision and values and standards to your business, you'll cease to run it on an everyday basis. That's the gift of the 7th Level business—owning an investment business asset that pays you unearned income while demanding a comparatively small amount of your time.

'TIS BETTER TO GIVE THAN TO RECEIVE: MOVING FROM WEALTH ACCUMULATION TO WEALTH DISTRIBUTION

In late December 2004 *BusinessWeek* published its annual list of the top 50 philanthropists for the year. On one end of the spectrum were Microsoft's Bill and Melinda Gates, who donated an astounding $10 billion to charity—a one-year gift equal to 20 percent of their total net worth. On the other end was Martha Ingram of Ingram Industries, who gave away 30 percent of her net worth, for a total of $116 million in charitable giving. The generosity of those individuals was inspiring and instructive. Clearly, those wealth builders understood that it is, as they say, "better to give than to receive," that money is good for the good it can do. What they also understood is that in order to give a million, you must first receive it.

One of the greatest gifts of wealth building is the ability to share the wealth you've built. Eli Broad of K&B Homes stated that the reason he gave over $1.3 billion to charity in 2004 was, "I've always been interested in making a difference, and I think that in just about all of our giving, the money is making a difference." Fortunately, the gift of great giving is available to all. Many top givers credited their fortunes to what we believe is the most attainable and accessible wealth-building vehicle around: real estate.

My personal wealth-building journey and careful observation of others have helped me understand that there are clear financial stages to a person's life: wealth education, wealth accumulation, wealth protection, and wealth distribution. It's not that complicated if you take a moment to consider it. After all, we have to learn about wealth building in order to do it. Once we've accumulated wealth, it's only natural to want to protect what we have worked so hard to earn. The last stage is the one that is overlooked most often, the time when, having secured our own future, we look to help others. For some people wealth distribution happens in the form of a will. For others it's about sharing their good fortune earlier so that they can see the gifts in action.

Whether you choose to distribute your wealth at the end of your journey or along the way, I encourage you to internalize one important fact: Financial wealth is never truly *owned;* the most one can achieve is to be a good steward for a time and then to pass it on.

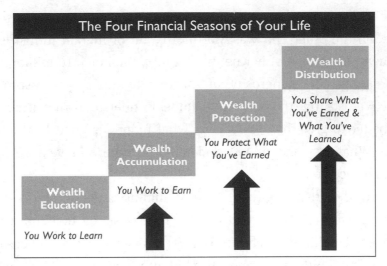

Figure 9

Philanthropy is defined as "the giving and sharing of time, talent, or treasure intended for the common good." It is our hope that as you progress through the four stages of this book—Think a Million, Buy a Million, Own a Million, and Receive a Million—you'll be striving to achieve your personal financial potential as well as your philanthropic potential. Building wealth is a wonderful and rewarding journey, but it's even better when the wealth is shared. As you consider the time when you can truly Receive a Million, I hope you'll choose to receive more than you need and share what you don't.

The journey to Receive a Million ends where you decide to end it. You can reach for $1 million or for more or less. Your personal goals are your own. We encourage you to use Big Models designed for more than you think you'll ever want or need. Never put caps on your financial potential—your potential to buy, own, receive, and even give all the wealth you could imagine.

- You can, if you choose, reach a place in your investment life where you can step out of the day-to-day work of investing and receive $1 million annual pretax income.

- When you can step out of the daily investment business without losing your income, you've reached the *7th Level: The Path to People Leverage*.

  - Your investment business will have three basic components: Acquisition and Disposition, Administration, and Operations.

  - As your business grows, you will hire talent in these areas and, over time, increasingly hand over day-to-day operations to those you recognize have the gift of leadership.

  - The transition toward removing yourself from day-to-day business can be tricky:

    - When you eventually hire a CEO to replace you, you must manage and mentor him or her until you are both confident the job can be done without supervision or safety nets.

    - Accept that your new CEO will bring new strengths to the role and will likely earn the right over time to change and improve your systems.

    - Understand that reaching the 7th Level means using new skills. You will employ business and management skills as you move from "I Do It" to "We Do It" to "They Do It."

  - As you move from wealth accumulation to wealth distribution, strive not only for personal financial potential but also to reach your philanthropic potential. Remember, money is good for the good it can do.

Part Three:

STAYING ON TOP

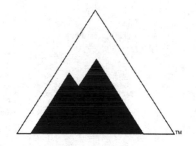

PUTTING IT ALL TOGETHER

The indispensible first step to getting the things you want out of life is this: decide what you want.

Ben Stein

NEVER TAKE YOUR EYE OFF THE BALL

In July 2004, on a summer night made for baseball, Derek Jeter made one of the great catches in baseball history. Playing for the New York Yankees against the rival Boston Red Sox, Jeter saved the day. In the twelfth inning of a tie game, with two men on and two men out, Red Sox outfielder Trot Nixon blooped a high fly ball down the left field foul line. Even with men closer to the ball than he, Jeter took off like a rocket the instant the ball was hit. As he raced over from his shortstop position to make the play, passing at least one other player in the process, his momentum forced him to make a perilous head-first dive into the stands after making the catch. Jeter eventually emerged with the help of fans, his face battered and bruised, holding the ball firmly in his glove and ending the inning. Thanks to Jeter's heroic catch, the Yankees would win the game one inning later. Although baseball through the years has seen some catches just as good, there has never been a better one.

What struck me most about that catch was that Jeter never took his eye off the ball. Not once. And that is what it took because there is only one way to make a play like that: focus. Focus, driven by motivation, supported by knowledge and skill causes one to take action without a thought about not succeeding. Never underestimate the power of purpose and focus. It's how baseball's uncatchable balls are caught, and it's how incredible wealth is attained in the financial world. Whether it's athletic victories or financial wealth, if you want to win, focus on what really matters and never ever take your eye off the ball.

ANYONE CAN DO IT—NOT EVERYONE WILL

My young son and his friends say they want to become financially wealthy someday, and most adults I know say the same thing. It seems everyone wants financial wealth and independence. I believe they can achieve it, but not everyone will. This is a natural law of financial wealth. It is called Pareto's Law.

Earlier I shared Pareto's Principle, or the 80/20 Rule, as the concept of the vital few versus the trivial many. The rule was discovered accidentally during a historical study of the distribution of financial wealth. Pareto was studying wealth! In *The 80/20 Principle* Richard Koch explains that what Pareto uncovered was both astonishing and predictable: Twenty percent of the people will own 80 percent of the income and wealth in any society, in any economy, at any time. Some will become financially wealthy, but most won't. This predictable imbalance takes concrete form in the haves and the have-nots. However, it is actually the tale of the willful and the wishful because whether you're in the 20 percent or the 80 percent is a choice—your choice. Financial wealth and independence may be predictably imbalanced, but they are neither preordained nor predestined. You and you alone get to decide your financial future.

I believe Pareto was right: Not everyone will become financially wealthy. But I also believe that anyone can. The formula is simple: focus driven by purpose. Basically, you have a choice: to focus or not. What you do with this choice will make all the difference in your financial world. Don't spend the majority of your time on minor things: Don't major in the minors. Decide what matters to you, decide how to go get it, and then focus on getting it. Give it passionate intention and serious attention. Don't just give it time and effort: Give it focused time and focused effort.

A Financial Track to Run On

If you want to be a Millionaire Real Estate Investor, you need a map that will get you there. You need a proven financial track to run on that accomplishes four things:

1. Establishes your financial base camp
2. Protects your future
3. Funds your future
4. Helps you stay the course

This simple track not only will set the stage for you to invest but also will provide the investment plan you need.

Stage 1: Establish Your Base Camp

The first stage in building a financial track to run on is to establish your financial base camp. The key to this is to incorporate the Net Worth Model into your life. The first step is to create a personal budget and stick to it. This will allow you to make sure you don't spend all your money and will have some to invest. A personal budget will challenge you to live well—but well below your affordable means until your financial wealth has been accumulated. By following a budget you will begin to understand why you buy expensive things after you become wealthy and not before. In the end you'll come to understand that the first step to becoming a millionaire is to live a controlled-consumption lifestyle.

The second step in establishing your financial base camp is to keep an ongoing net worth worksheet: your wealth-building scorecard. Allocate an hour each week to looking it over and asking one question: "How can I grow my net worth and cash flow?" Each time you purchase something, you will begin to connect the dots between what you do with money and the way it affects your financial wealth. Over time you will come to understand why millionaires say that financial wealth is not the same as earned income and that saving is not the same as investing.

The last step in building your base camp is to avoid debt. Although this is simple to say, it is hard to do. The trick is to make a commitment to avoid financing your personal costs of living. Unfortunately, many people get wrapped up in a "borrow and buy" lifestyle. Millionaires do the exact opposite, adopting the mantra "save up, then buy," especially for major purchases. Don't let your credit card do your saving for you. As a rule, try to pay by cash or cash equivalent. In other words, treat your credit card like cash and pay off the balance each month. Millionaires don't use debt-carrying plastic credit. They have no interest in paying high interest, and neither do you. If you can, buy on the basis of "needs" and avoid a "wants" purchasing lifestyle. When something breaks, always think "repair" first, "used" second, and "new" last. Your goal is to avoid non-asset-based debt at all costs. But in the end, if you must incur debt, try to make sure that the debt term and asset longevity match up.

STAGE 2: PROTECT YOUR FUTURE

The next step to creating your financial track is to protect your future. There are four fundamental ways to do this:

1. Set up an emergency fund
2. Purchase a home

3. Obtain adequate insurance

4. Create an estate plan

The first thing to do to protect your future is to save three to six months of living expenses for an emergency fund. You need a safety net so that no matter what happens you have options. Expect this reserve amount to go up as your net worth goes up.

Next, purchase a home. This not only is forced savings, it also secures the one asset that determines your lifestyle more than any other. As with any other purchase, buy on the basis of needs first and wants second. Buy what you think you can afford, not what a lender will lend you. Buy with your family's plans in mind. Don't "underbuy," necessitating a move too soon, or "overbuy," anticipating more income in the future. It's a tight line to walk, but you must walk it. If you do "underbuy," you probably will end up making this your first rental property. "Overbuy" and it might put you in the poorhouse. Don't become "house rich and income poor." The real key to freedom here lies in putting your payments on a fast path to owning your home free and clear. (Some might disagree with this advice, but as a real estate professional who has seen both sides of this argument, I say do it. Two extra payments a year on a 30-year mortgage pays off your home in 20 years! Do the math.)

Third, protect your future by insuring it in key areas. You will need adequate disability insurance to protect a minimum lifestyle. You will need adequate life insurance to help support your family and pay any estate taxes. You will need the best affordable health insurance for you and your family. You will need adequate replacement value and liability insurance for your home, car, and personal property. If you get your insurance agent, accountant, and estate planning attorney together, you should be able to figure all this out in about an hour.

Finally, create an estate plan. It must include simple but carefully considered entity planning, appropriate trusts and wills, and strategies to minimize or eliminate inheritance taxes and maximize creditor protection. The investment you make early on for the services of an excellent estate planning attorney will in the end make you money. When Sam Walton was a young man just starting out in business and could least afford it, he set up his estate plan. As a result, at the end of his life one of the greatest personal fortunes ever amassed was transferred to his heirs with little to no taxes paid. Millionaires get this, and so should you.

STAGE 3: FUND YOUR FUTURE

This is where the fun (or perhaps we should say the "fund") begins. It's time to put the five real estate models together and start the process of finding your future by first funding it. Let's step back for a second, look at the big picture, and see how all of what we've covered works. Sometimes an aerial view puts things in perspective.

We've covered all the major steps of a Millionaire Real Estate Investor's investment path. When you take them all together, they add up to the six-step investment plan you will follow. It's time to take the instruction and make it strategic.

1. Get Motivated

Visualize your life: what you would be doing and what your life would be like if you didn't have to work for a living. Can you see it? These are your Big Goals. Can you verbalize what you will get from living that life? These are your Big Whys. While holding on to this clear mental picture, write down the monthly dollar amount you would need to fund it. Go a step further and figure out how much capital you will need to have invested to deliver this monthly amount in the form of unearned income. What you will have is your Big Goals, your Big Whys, and your future cash flow and net worth targets. The last two are your

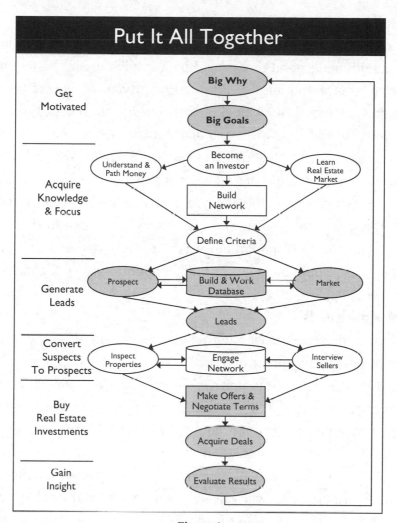

Figure 1

financial wealth-building goals. Make sure you've accounted for family growth, education costs, expected needs, and some unexpected ones. If you have these two numbers, you have the drivers of your investment plan. You're in harmony; your financial targets match your personal goals. These financial numbers are in touch and in sync with your biggest reasons for living big, and that is where the true motivation to build wealth comes from.

2. Acquire Knowledge and Focus

It's time to become an investor. To achieve this you have to do what investors do: understand money and path it, pick the real estate market you want to invest in and learn it, and build your work and leads networks and develop them. School is never out for the successful. Be clear about your "must-focus" areas and master them. Remember, you learn to earn before you niche to get rich. Put together a reading list each year and read those books. And do the same for instructional audio tapes, videos and DVDs. Attend one seminar a year about a topic you need to know better. Hang out with your network members and listen to their experience and advice. Most important, wake up every day and say, "I'm an investor. Today could be the day I find an opportunity and make a deal."

3. Generate Leads

With money, knowledge, and relationships behind you, it's time to generate investment opportunity leads. First, put your Criteria down on paper. If they're not written down, you probably don't have them. Next, memorize this list so that it becomes like a song in your head you can't help remembering. Now go prospect and market for leads that meet your Criteria. Pick a few methods and give them enough time to see if they will work. Since your Criteria, niche, and target geographic market create a unique formula, you will have to work with your lead generation approach for a while to begin to see predictable results. Time-block your calendar for lead generation time and protect that time. Set the goal of generating a lead a day, put those leads into your database, and then work them.

4. Convert Suspects to Prospects

Suspects and prospects are completely different. One won't, and one will. One wastes your time, and one is worth your time. One costs you money, and one makes you money. One isn't worth any effort, and one is worth all the effort. The trick is to be able to figure out quickly which is which. When you can do that, you're doing some of the most critical work investors do. You'll pick your prospects by inspecting the property, interviewing the seller, and getting your network involved. Your goal is to be able to say, "My prospects are looking up." You'll be able to say this when you know about a property that meets your Criteria and is owned by a seller who will meet your Terms.

5. Buy Real Estate Investments

When an investment opportunity shows up, move quickly to control the property. Simply put, make an offer. Since your real estate contracts will have an evaluation option period, you haven't committed to buy yet, but you have committed to try to buy. Begin the negotiation process by making an offer whose Terms make the property match your Criteria. Negotiate with the seller with the win-win goal of meeting his or her selling objectives while meeting your Criteria to invest. If you and the seller can agree, you've acquired a deal!

6. Gain Insight

Once you've acquired an investment property, follow through on your strategy for it: improve and sell or improve and hold. You'll need to evaluate your deal as you go along and ask your network to do the same thing. Some deals will be better than others. That's the way it goes for every investor. Some will be home runs, and some will be bunts, and you want to eliminate or at least limit your strikeouts. Remember that success is the result of good judgment, good judgment is the result of experience, and experience is the result of bad judgment. You'll make mistakes, but as long as you buy it right, all mistakes are survivable. In the end your experiences and the feedback you get from others will give you knowledge and insights that will help you create even better deals in the future. That's what you want: lots of experience and better and better deals.

STAGE 4: STAY THE COURSE

The final stage of building your financial track is to create and sustain energy so that you can stay the course. Don't worry about the economy or the market. Warren Buffett says he doesn't. It's your Criteria that matter, not the conditions that might create their availability. Stick to your plan and invest on the basis of your Criteria. The chart below lays out the specific approach you should take. You will need to devote about 10 hours a week to this wealth-building program. You can do a little each day, or you can do a week's worth each weekend. The choice is yours. Just stay on course.

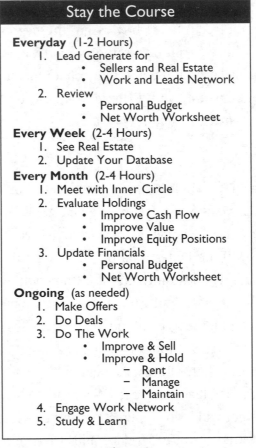

Figure 2

The Millionaire Real Estate Investor

As straightforward as this looks, implementing it can be challenging. Successful investing and wealth building is a process, not an event. It's an endurance race, not a quick sprint, and you will need to create and store energy to run it. Burnout lurks behind every property you must go see and every seller you must interview and negotiate with. You cannot afford to let this happen to you. You must guard against weariness and distractions so that you can continue investing and enjoying it. It's a long haul, and if you don't stay the course, you will be shortchanging your investment plan and yourself. You'll need an energy plan to become and remain a millionaire investor.

The Millionaire Real Estate Investor's Energy Plan

The world is made up of energy. The things we think of as solid are just energy; the things we think of as liquid are just energy; the earth is energy; the sky is energy; we are energy. You are energy too. All these things are energy in different forms, but at the deepest level it's all still energy.

Recognize this simple and undeniable fact: You and I are energy. We receive it and transmit it; we find it and lose it; we store it and leak it; we conserve it and spend it; we breathe it in and we breathe it out; we hold it in and we let it go; we are more of who we are when we have a lot of it and less than we can be when we have only a little. Energy comes to us when we are doing the right things and leaves us when we aren't. When we focus on what matters most for our lives, we are connecting to the right kinds of energy and our lives burn bright and surge ahead. If you want to maximize your life opportunities, you have to slow down enough to refuel with the energy that matters. Because you are matter and you do matter, and to get the most out of your life you have to connect your life to energy that does matter.

In our research on top sales performers we came to understand a simple formula they used to bring energy into their personal and professional lives. As we interviewed our Millionaire Real Estate Investors, we discovered they had a strong force powering their investing. They approached their real estate investment activities with vitality and endurance, and as we got to know them, we got a true sense of their personal energy. As we probed, we realized they were similar to the top performers we had studied in other areas: They had an unspoken energy plan they practiced that renewed them personally and gave them the energy they needed to do the activities that mattered most to them.

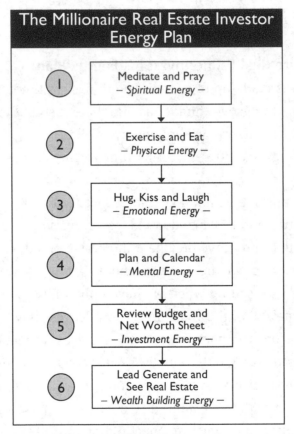

Figure 3

Remember our definition of wealth: it's abundance. An abundant life is a life focused not on just anything but on the things that matter most.

A wealthy life is a life that is filled with abundance in the areas that matter. Millionaires are individuals who have an abundance of financial wealth. But what good is money if you lose everything else to get it? The true "abundant life" millionaire gets this and therefore seeks to find energy not just financially but in the other areas that matter. If you want the best energy possible and the most abundant life possible, try the following simple formula:

Each morning meditate or pray for clarity and guidance; fill your soul with spiritual energy. Then exercise for cardio and muscular strength and eat properly for nutrition; fill your body with physical energy. Hug, kiss, and laugh with your loved ones for connectedness and joy; fill your heart with emotional energy. Plan and calendar your day for focus; fill your mind with mental energy. Review your personal budget and net worth worksheets for financial clarity; fill your finances with investment energy. Finally, lead generate and see real estate for investment opportunities; fill your time with wealth-building energy.

Do all this before noon every day you can. Why so early in the day? Because it is far easier to control your time at the beginning of the day than at the end of it when you may be tired or distracted. It won't be possible to do it every single day, but when you do, energy will flow so powerfully into your life that you will float and fly through the day. The goal in life is not to be a disciplined person but to be a person of selected disciplines. With the energy plan you are selecting the disciplines and energies you want and making time to bring them into your life. If you make sure these things get done, you will be pulled through the rest of the day achieving and accomplishing at levels you never dreamed were possible. Energy will have come into your life and will

> *"Have fun every day. Make every day a wonderful day. When you get as old as I am, they don't make ugly days. They're all pretty."*
>
> Jimmy Napier
> Millionaire Real Estate Investor
> Chipley, FL

be fueling it. You will have become an abundant person, a person of wealth in the areas that matter most.

MONEY DOESN'T CARE

The world doesn't care if you're a millionaire, and certainly money doesn't care. You're the one who cares, and that is as it should be. You should care because it's your life. The key to having money is wanting it and knowing why you want it. The key to being a millionaire is wanting a lot of money and doing what it takes to get it. The key to being happy with a lot of money is understanding what money can and can't do for you.

We all have priorities in life: the people who matter the most and the things we'd most like to do and have. Money, whether we have it or not, isn't intended to define or redefine our priorities. It is intended to help finance them. Money is just money. It will expose and amplify you, but it won't change you. It's simply a medium of exchange that gives you freedom and allows you to buy what you need. The key to happiness is not more money. Happiness is happiness. Our life purpose is to have the best life possible in the time allotted us. It's not the amount, it's the value, and you can't buy that. Money doesn't buy value as it pertains to the best life possible. Money merely reflects what you value and does what it's told. Money sits there until it's called. So put money in its proper place. When you know why you want money and are realistic about what it will do for you, you are in a great place to go call it.

You want it, you know why you want it, and you are ready to go get it, but make no mistake about it: Money has its own rules and disciplines, and it doesn't care who you are. If you break its rules, it'll break you. In other words, when you break money's rules, you're broke. Don't be financially illiterate. Learn the rules and enjoy the rewards. It's your life. Money doesn't care about it one way or another, but you do.

TIME TO GET GOING

This book is about three interconnected things: making money—by investing—in real estate. It's a package deal. We hope you're now Thinking Big, Thinking Like an Investor, and Thinking Real Estate. Anyone can become a millionaire, and if you take the steps we've outlined, you'll be able to change the title of this book to *The Millionaire Real Estate Investor: Anyone Can Do It—and I Did!*

Godspeed and good fortune.
Gary, Dave, and Jay

PROFILES OF REAL-LIFE MILLIONAIRE REAL ESTATE INVESTORS

Although this book has only three names on its cover, it contains the wisdom and expertise of many people from different social, economic, and cultural backgrounds. Fortunately for the authors, the two things those people all have in common are a passion for real estate and a willingness to share their wisdom. Without both, we would not have been able to craft a comprehensive book that speaks so powerfully about building financial wealth. For this we are immensely grateful.

Because each person's story of how he or she became a Millionaire Real Estate Investor was compelling and inspirational and because we had a limited amount of space, it was extremely difficult to select only 21 stories to share. We fretted, we scratched our heads, and we wrangled over who to choose before finally deciding. The amazing individuals featured in the pages that follow were chosen because of the breadth, depth, and diversity of their investment journeys. Separately, the thread of their individual stories may not have been the most colorful or the most fantastic, but as a whole their successes weave a rich tapestry that fully illustrates what it takes to become a Millionaire Real Estate Investor. These people see the endless possibilities of wealth building through real estate. They were our inspiration, and we hope they will inspire you.

PORTRAIT OF A MILLIONAIRE REAL ESTATE INVESTOR

JOE ARLT
Virginia Beach, VA

Years Investing: 8

Number of Deals in 2004: 30

Career Deals: 500 or more

Current Units Owned: 400

Areas of Expertise: Lease options; subject-to acquisitions; and VA foreclosures

Real Estate License: Yes

Do you hate infomercials? Think people never buy that stuff? Or if they do, never do anything with it? Joe Arlt will tell you different. The former certified public accountant with, in his words, a "fancy Ivy League" MBA could be the poster child for late-night infomercials. He changed his life after watching one by real estate investor John Burley. Arlt's interest was piqued enough that he took one of Burley's five-day boot camps in January 1996.

"I made two decisions after the seminar: I wanted to give real estate a try, and I didn't want to continue living in New Jersey," Arlt recalls.

He immediately started investing part-time, driving from New Jersey to Virginia Beach (his soon-to-be new home) to take advantage of the many repossessed houses surrounding the large military base that were financed by the Veteran Affairs Administration. Arlt put his finance and accounting background to work and started buying the properties subject to the existing mortgage or on a wrap. He then resold each property on a wrap. Arlt now owns 250 single-family homes in the area and has an ownership interest in more than 250 other properties across the country.

"I do long-term lease option agreements," he says. "I've created a transaction where the people moving into the house are basically buying it, but I get to treat it like a rental, so taxwise it's viewed as an investment, not a dealer property."

Arlt, who got his real estate license in 1997, serves as the chief operations officer of the business he established with Burley, who serves as the president. When scouting deals, they look for a deal that will give them a 50 percent annual return on their net investment. Their main goal with lease options is to create cash flow.

"If I'm wrapping for cash flow, I want price and terms," Arlt says. "And when I'm dealing with tenants on these lease options, I'm always skeptical and always prepare for the worst."

It took a while to hone their buying and leasing formula, but they found a method that yields a solid return. For example, if they purchase a house for $70,000, they spend about $10,000 for the down payment and closing costs. Arlt and Burley then price the house at $87,900 and market it as a 10-year lease-option agreement with the ability to exercise the option to buy after one year. After the tenant-owner makes a down payment of, say, $4,000, their total net investment is only $6,000. The renters usually pay 10 percent interest because they are not qualified buyers, with part of the rent going toward the total purchase price. On a deal like this Arlt and Burley net about $4,200 a year. This may seem like a trickle, but when you factor in the large volume of deals they conduct, the cash flow becomes a waterfall.

"I'll be doing this business probably until I die or until I can't do it anymore," Arlt says. "Real estate is a great investment because if you buy it right, you can't go wrong."

PORTRAIT OF A MILLIONAIRE REAL ESTATE INVESTOR

DON BECK

Philadelphia, PA

Years Investing: 25

Number of Deals in 2004: 0

Career Deals: 65

Units Owned: 105

Areas of Expertise: 20–40 unit complexes

Real Estate License: Yes

Don Beck had been an elementary school teacher for 12 years when he bought his first home and in the process changed his life.

"It was a duplex," he says. "I lived in one half, rented out the other, and from then on it was just 'get out of my way.'"

It had taken Beck two years to build up the courage to make that first buy in 1979. But over the next five years he bought 80 more units, and by 1984 he had decided to retire from teaching. However, not everyone congratulated him on his decision to pursue financial independence over the security of a nine-to-five job.

"I walked into the principal's office and turned in my resignation," he says. "The principal said, 'I guess the real estate's been going pretty well.' I told him it was. But with that, he picked up the phone and called the school psychiatrist to check me out because I was tenured and my wife was pregnant with our first child."

Beck knew that he wasn't crazy and that becoming a full-time investor would bring more rewards than just money. It gave him time and freedom. After their child was born, Beck carted his newborn daughter around with him while he looked for more investment opportunities and worked as a landlord. Instead of pouring all his energy into other people's children, he had ample time to devote to his own.

"Investing gave me a lot of flexibility to adjust my schedule around my family," he says. "It gave me the chance to be a homeroom dad and attend all my kids' school plays and sporting events and to be there when they came home from school."

While Beck started out buying duplexes, he eventually settled on midsize complexes of 20 to 40 units. He initially developed this strategy when the high prices of single-family homes in his suburban Philadelphia market meant they couldn't generate cash flow. However, he soon learned that apartment complexes had other advantages.

"I've got one roof, one heater, and one on-site manager taking care of everything, instead of 20 single-family homes with 20 roofs and 20 heaters and a full-time maintenance guy running all over the place to take care of them," he says. "Plus, if one tenant moves out, I lose only one-twentieth of my income."

Beck's recipe for success includes one ingredient that many investors overlook: failure. Making a few lousy deals early on, he says, is ultimately how investors learn they can move beyond failure. It helps them break out of a confining comfort zone and learn the skills, the discipline, and the courage to make bigger, bolder deals that *don't* flop.

"But fail fast," he jokes. "There's less zeros at the end."

After two decades of investing and acquiring 100 units, Beck is still disciplined. But rather than using that discipline to pore through real estate books on his lunch hour as he did when he was a teacher with duplex dreams, he now disciplines himself to know when to stop.

"You have to be careful that it doesn't consume you," he says. "I simply don't need another 50 or 100 units."

Even though Beck is happy to manage what he has and leave acquisition to others, he still insists that nothing else even comes close to the benefits of real estate investing. With only a small percentage down or even nothing down, you get 100 percent control of a valuable asset. You get tax advantages. And of course you get someone else paying off the mortgage.

"To this day I still say that if anyone can come up with an investment that can do better than that, please tell me what it is and I'll probably get into it," he says. "But of course, no one can."

PORTRAIT OF A MILLIONAIRE REAL ESTATE INVESTOR

DWAN BENT-TWYFORD
AND SHARON RESTREPO

DelRay Beach, Florida, and Bailey, Colorado

Years Investing: 13

Number of Deals in 2004: 75–100

Career Deals: Over 1,000

Units Owned: Three commercial buildings,
one duplex; two lots; and 12 single family homes.

Areas of Expertise: Short sales and wholesaling;
rehabbing; and subject-to acquisitions.

Real Estate License: No (Dwan) and Yes (Sharon)

Business partners Sharon Restrepo and Dwan Bent-Twyford launched their careers as Millionaire Real Estate Investors from the most unlikely places. Restrepo was a 25-year-old widow and Bent-Twyford was a recently divorced 29-year-old mother when each decided to bet it all on real estate—and they won big.

Restrepo and her husband dreamed of rehabilitating houses before he was killed in a motorcycle accident. Alone and in mourning, Restrepo decided to keep her husband's dream alive and used the settlement money from his death to buy a dilapidated single-family house. Since she knew nothing about houses or investing, she decided that the best way to learn and avoid getting taken advantage of was to do all the renovations herself, from repairing a falling-down roof to cleaning up a mold infestation so bad that it made her sneeze blood. The experience taught her about rehabbing, but more important, it also taught her a valuable lesson: don't fall in love with the house. She spent so much time and energy fixing the house, she forgot that the point was creating not the house of her dreams but the bottom line. With all her fancy tweaks and touches, the house ended up being too expensive to sell. Fortunately, she was able to lease-option the house.

"I probably made a whopping 500 bucks on that house," Restrepo says. "But during the time I bought and sold that one I bought and sold three others, and they were home runs."

Bent-Twyford's first deal was more lucrative than her future partner's. Broke and alone after her divorce, she happened to meet some investors who bought and flipped foreclosures. Bent-Twyford borrowed $3,000 from an aunt to buy a car, got a list of preforeclosures, and with her baby on her hip started knocking on doors. After about a dozen nos she found a seller. Like Restrepo, she fixed it up herself.

"I took all the classes at Home Depot to learn to tile, lay carpet, everything," Bent-Twyford says. "It got to the point where when the guys at the store saw me coming, they'd run because I asked too many questions."

Her house sold in two days, earning Bent-Twyford $22,000.

"I thought I was rich," she says. "I wept because I was so happy."

The two investors met at a small seminar—they were the only women there, and so they started chatting—and soon formed a partnership to do rehabs. But after several years of successful rehabbing and learning exactly how to find a great deal, they branched out into wholesaling.

"It's a lot less work," Restrepo says, "and since you get good deals under contract and then find *other* people to buy them, you don't even have to own the property."

Then they mastered short sales. But no matter what kind of investment they try, both agree that some of their most valuable lessons are those they learned at the outset. Restrepo always comes back to the lesson she learned on that first house.

"Any time you make an emotional decision concerning your business, you will lose money," Restrepo says. "Every time we lost money it was because we compromised a business rule or made an emotional decision."

For example, when they were first rehabbing, they had a system where they always had three houses in the works: One was on the market, one was being worked on, and one was just bought. At one point they were down to two houses, both of which were up for sale, and were feeling desperate to buy. They walked into a house where the numbers seemed to work, trying to ignore the insects flying around them.

"Swarming termites," Restrepo says with a laugh. "We were literally swatting termites away while we were saying to each other, 'Seems pretty good. What do you think?' That was another deal where I think we made about $500."

Bent-Twyford says another lesson they learned in the "salad days" was the need for absolute commitment in order to succeed.

"I think a lot of people who get involved in investing don't always put 100 percent into it because they have a job," she says. "But for me it was do or die because I didn't want to put my daughter in day care. After you wait tables at Denny's, you'll do anything to not do that again."

Restrepo and Bent-Twyford agree that the beauty of real estate is that with just a little courage and pluck, a path begun for simple reasons—to keep a dream alive or to avoid waiting tables—is one that eventually can lead to financial independence.

PORTRAIT OF A MILLIONAIRE REAL ESTATE INVESTOR

DYCHES BODDIFORD
Marietta, GA

Years Investing: 24

Number of Deals in 2004: 40

Career Deals: Hundreds

Units Owned: Owns industrial land, timber land, and commercial properties, as well as "plenty" of residential rentals

Areas of Expertise: Discounted mortgages; distressed property; and development

Real Estate License: No

It's every employee's worst nightmare: the Friday afternoon staff meeting after which no one needs to come back on Monday, the day when your paycheck, your sole source of income and financial stability, vanishes overnight. It's the day your company downsizes, and despite years of stellar performance, you and your coworkers are laid off.

Atlanta investor Dyches Boddiford was called into the president's office for one of those meetings in 1991. But for Boddiford, who already had spent a decade building his real estate portfolio, losing a vice presidency in a computer company was not a nightmare but an opportunity: it was the push he needed to go to work for himself as a full-time real estate investor, a move he had wanted to make for a while.

"I got up Monday morning, had a shower, shaved, did everything like I was going to work," he says, "but instead of getting into my car, I just went down to my little home office and started hitting it full-time."

Because Boddiford had built more than one stream of income, he could keep afloat when his primary income dried up. Not one to let a lesson go by unlearned, Boddiford varies his approach to real estate investment deals and never depends on a single investment strategy to fit every situation. While the former sales executive concentrates on rental properties in middle-class neighborhoods, he is no stranger to lease options, fixing and flipping, owner financing, and developing resorts and manufactured housing lots.

"Having a toolbox of strategies allows me to pick the one that is right for the deal rather than trying to make every opportunity fit into one cookie cutter," he says.

As the Atlanta real estate market goes through its inevitable cycles, that toolbox enables Boddiford to adjust to its whims. In general, he believes that there is no "right" time to buy but firmly believes that different strategies work better at some times than at others. "Time in the market is more important than timing the market," Boddiford says.

For example, while Atlanta recently had a soft rental market, the city still enjoyed solid sales and healthy appreciation. Boddiford looked for the first time into buying properties through conventional mortgages. His reason? The interest rates. Boddiford had bought virtually all his previous properties through cash or owner financing. However, with interest rates at historic lows, he reasoned that the low-rate mortgages would themselves be an investment that he could later sell through owner financing once rates moved back up. But, he says, "no matter what cycle the market is in, you always need to buy the property right on price and/or terms."

Boddiford also applies this flexible approach when evaluating his investment portfolio. Once a year he sells off his weakest-performing properties, which he determines by ranking them according to a variety of criteria: how hard they are to rent, the desirability of their neighborhoods, and how much maintenance they require. Once he determines the 20 or 30 percent that do the least for him, he figures out a way to use a tax-deferred 1031 exchange to leverage his money into a more profitable property.

To develop this kind of dexterity with the tools of real estate, Boddiford advises new investors to invest in their education first. "In the real estate area, you're going to pay for an education one way or another," he says. "You've got two options: you can go to classes and learn from other people and their mistakes, or you can go out in the real world and make your own mistakes. And it's always less expensive and less time-consuming to learn from somebody else."

For his own education, Boddiford took real estate licensing courses at the local community college and, of course, talked to other investors. But just as he warns against skimping on education, he warns just as strongly against getting so caught up in the books and courses that you forget to buy anything. At some point, he says, you have to take the plunge. That's what Boddiford did: after an intensive six-month search, he bought his first three properties on three consecutive days and, true to form, using three kinds of financing. In other words, at least some of your education has to come from your own experiences.

"The worst thing you can do is learn continually without putting some of it into practice," he says. "It's called 'analysis paralysis.' Beginning investors get paralyzed by thinking they have to learn everything about every strategy. But you don't. You just have to learn enough to get started."

But as in Boddiford's case, once you get started, there's no limit to the kinds of deals that can be made. Boddiford's new tactic is manufactured housing and coastal development. But as he says, "there are so many areas I could move into. That's what I love about investing in real estate."

PORTRAIT OF A MILLIONAIRE REAL ESTATE INVESTOR

RENATA CIRCEO
Atlanta, GA

Years Investing: Owned rentals for 16 years; serious investor for 4 years

Number of Deals in 2004: 5

Career Deals: 21

Units Owned: Five single-family homes; two duplexes; six condos; and an 18-unit apartment building

Areas of Expertise: Buy, & Hold; fixer-uppers; and middle and high-end homes.

Real Estate License: Yes

Many beginning investors have to combat their share of naysayers as they launch their real estate investment careers. Usually the biggest critics are people who aren't investors but are quick to say, "Tenants are a pain" or to make ominous predictions that you'll "lose your shirt."

Keeping other people's fears from infecting your drive to invest can be a challenge. An even more challenging situation, though, occurs when the person doubting you is your own father. That's what happened to Renata Circeo when as a young college graduate, she approached her father—a buy-and-hold investor in single-family houses—about a loan for the down payment on her first condo.

"He said, 'I know you want to get into real estate, but I think you're a little young,'" says Circeo, now 15 years older and much richer. "I said, 'I know, Dad. I just wanted to give you first right of refusal.' And I went and found another investor."

That was in 1988. After living in her first property for six years and letting roommates pay down the mortgage, Circeo bought a second house. Six years later she picked up the pace, buying another five.

Circeo's strategy is to keep the number of units she owns to a handful, because she enjoys her work in the entertainment business too much to give it up for full-time investing. With this in mind, she carefully shapes her investment strategy to fit into her nights and weekends.

"I'm a classic overachiever," she says. "And I've learned that things suffer when you spread yourself too thin."

One aspect of this strategy is to focus on higher-end properties in which she can maximize her cash flow and long-term appreciation without having to deal with a huge number of units. A firm believer in the "worst house—best neighborhood" approach, she finds run-down properties that need a little sweat equity and rents them out to stable middle-class tenants, keeping turnover and maintenance low.

Circeo also tailors her financing to fit her strategy of long-term security rather than short-term cash flow. Her technique is to pull equity out of her current holdings to buy more houses. This works especially well with the well-maintained houses in pleasant, safe neighborhoods she already likes to buy. Those houses have enormous potential for appreciation, and a little work can mean huge equity gains. Circeo says one of her best deals was her second house, a five-bedroom, two-and-a-half-bathroom that she paid $151,000 for in 1994.

"It was a beautiful house, huge yard, but not well taken care of," she says. "The inside was absolutely filthy, with holes in the wall, and the refrigerator was getting ready to fall into the basement because the ice maker had been leaking for at least two years."

But what some people would have walked away from, Circeo walked into, and her eye for a diamond in the rough paid off. A year after she bought it, the newly fixed-up house was appraised for $215,000, and by 2003 it was valued at $349,000, equity she could then pull out to buy more.

Another tool Circeo likes to use is interest-only loans, which reduce her monthly payment significantly. Even though she pays them off like 15-year fixed mortgages, this type of loan gives her the option of dropping down to the minimum payment if one of her houses has a maintenance emergency or unexpected vacancy or she needs the cash. (The risk of high-rent single-family houses is that vacancies are much more expensive.)

But even as her net worth grows, Circeo finds that many people still express their doubts about single women investing alone.

"There is still this perception of, 'Oh, don't go out and do it. Wait until you get married and have some security,'" she says.

The solution, she found, was to go to investment clubs and other events where she could build a network of strong professional women who were also going at it alone and succeeding.

"Seek those people out," she says. "Seek out the women who can be your mentors and don't let the doubters bring you down."

PORTRAIT OF A MILLIONAIRE REAL ESTATE INVESTOR

JERRY CLEVENGER
Kansas City, MO

Years Investing: 9

Number of Deals in 2004: 112

Career Deals: 800

Units Owned: 53 single-family homes and 2 commercial buildings

Areas of Expertise: Foreclosures; wholesaling

Real Estate License: No

Everyone knows that money is important. However, just about everyone also knows that many things are more important than money, especially time. Nevertheless, most of us stay on the grind, unable or unwilling to take the kind of leap of faith Jerry Clevenger took in 1997.

Clevenger had a solid career in banking, rising eventually to president of the mortgage division, when he started investing in real estate in the mid-1980s. It was a fluke, actually: He was hired to ghostwrite a chapter about foreclosures and realized he could master the business easily. He started spending his free time doing research at the courthouse and hunting down leads.

Clevenger always thought real estate would be just a part-time money-making hobby until he got full custody of his two children. Suddenly, time became more important than money. Clevenger realized that even though he earned a comfortable six-figure income at his day job, it came with a six-day-a-week schedule that would leave him precious few moments with his kids. He quit his job and started investing full-time, thinking that stepping off the corporate ladder would be a financial sacrifice with emotional rewards.

"The main thing was to have time with my kids," Clevenger says. "I could be home during the day, drive them to school, and be there when they came home from school."

However, he discovered that his leap turned out to not be such a big sacrifice after all. In his first year as a full-time investor he made three times what he had at the bank. More important, being willing to sacrifice his paycheck so that he could focus on his relationships gave him both time and money.

Clevenger's investing success came through mastering foreclosures, mostly of single-family houses or duplexes. However, he doesn't just hit the courthouse steps, and he definitely doesn't go at it like the Lone Ranger, patrolling his territory for the elusive great deal. Instead, he finds his best deals by working with real estate agents who comb the market for him.

"In the beginning I thought I could do everything myself, from finding them to selling or renting them," Clevenger says. "But I went from just doing a few deals to doing a lot more deals and more profitable ones by using agents."

By developing a level of trust with a few agents Clevenger is able to pursue more complicated transactions such as REOs (bank-owned foreclosures) and short sales (buying foreclosed-upon houses for less than what's owed on the mortgage). He also can act fast. He did that in one instance when an agent who had been watching an REO property called him early one morning to say the price had been dropped from $65,000 to $39,000. Clevenger immediately faxed in an offer for $42,000, which was accepted.

"I immediately sold the house for $54,000, and I'd never seen it," he says. "So is that agent worth it? You bet. She gets a well-earned commission on the acquisition, and I walk out making $12,000."

Clevenger says agents are particularly valuable for new investors, who too often buy the wrong property or buy too high because they jump at the word *foreclosure*.

"I've found that if I advertise a house and say 'foreclosure,' I will get three times the calls I will get on any other house," he says. "People just assume it's a good deal, but that's not always true. One month there were over 600 foreclosures in our area. Out of those 600, maybe 50 of them were okay deals. Fifteen were absolutely great deals."

In trying to find the absolutely great deal, Clevenger warns investors to assess not only a property's physical condition and market conditions but also the financial condition.

"Just because it's an old mortgage doesn't mean it's a good deal," he says. "You'll find that people may have signed forbearance agreements or filed for bankruptcy. I can show you lots of those where on paper you think this is a good deal, but then when you get all the facts in, it's not."

Clevenger and his wife now own 53 single-family and two multifamily properties worth more than $4 million. He still has time to spend with his son and daughter, now college age, who benefit not only from the extra time with their dad but also from hands-on, close-up exposure to their lucrative future careers.

"They know how to repair a basement. They know how the mortgage industry works," he says. "My daughter knew when she was a freshman in high school that in college she'd get her MBA, specialize in real estate, and start flipping houses."

PORTRAIT OF A MILLIONAIRE REAL ESTATE INVESTOR

DON DeROSA

Atlanta, GA

Years Investing: 7

Number of Deals in 2004: 30–40

Career Deals: 100–150

Units Owned: Over 35

Areas of Expertise: Subject-to acquisitions; short sales; and fix and flip

Real Estate License: No

"There's a million ways to make a million dollars in real estate investing. Start by picking one." That's what veteran investor Don DeRosa tells his beginning students, and the former Airborne Express manager should know. He became a full-time investor in real estate by focusing on one technique at a time.

"Once I find something I enjoy, I pour everything into it and master it," he says. "Once you master it, it pushes you toward the top."

DeRosa began pouring himself into real estate investing in 1993, inspired in part by the fact that his parents had rented duplexes successfully. The first approach he decided to master was the "subject to."

"The first four properties I bought, I bought for one dollar apiece, subject to the existing financing," he says. "I gave them each one dollar in earnest money and closed the deals over the kitchen table."

But it wasn't until 2001 that DeRosa became a full-time investor. He was pushed into it when, like many investors, he got laid off from a job he didn't like as much as investing anyway.

"The day I lost my job was the happiest day of my life," he says. "I wanted to send my employer a thank-you note."

Once he went full-time, DeRosa gradually branched out from "subject" to deals by learning the ins and outs of short sales. Of course, trial rarely comes without error, and DeRosa made his share of mistakes as he experimented with different approaches. Rehabbing, for example, proved particularly challenging.

"The first rehab I did was a disaster," he says. "I did everything wrong: I paid too much, had no due diligence, and picked the wrong contractor. But I learned a ton. It was a $40,000 mistake, but I probably saved myself a million dollars because I never repeated those mistakes again."

Nevertheless, the fact that doing something new almost inevitably involves some of those beginners' mistakes underscores the value of getting good at one thing rather than dabbling in every idea in the book and never mastering anything.

"Investing is like muscle memory," he says. "It takes less time and energy the more you do it."

These days DeRosa focuses on short-selling second mortgages. He says his tight focus helps him make the key move that separates successful investors from the rest: systematizing and automating as many of the details as possible. For example, when people call with homes to sell, he knows they need instant personal attention. But these days he gets so many calls that he has both a receptionist and a full-time answering service trained to follow scripts that flag the calls with a potential to turn into a good deal and close the door quickly on overleveraged ones that won't work.

As DeRosa spends his days looking for properties, his four assistants do the same thing, armed with spreadsheets on pocket PCs that compute the profit margin on any property. If they find one that fits DeRosa's criteria—for example, he wants to see at least $20,000 net profit and a 200 percent ROI—they are authorized to make an offer.

DeRosa says his focus also helps with one of the hardest parts of the business: getting the phone to ring. After all, building a reputation as an investor in a certain kind of deal means that people in your community know who to call when they come across that type of deal.

"You have to get leads coming in before you can make an offer and find anything to buy," he says.

After 10 years in the business, mastering one approach after another, DeRosa now has depth *and* breadth, along with a business so systematized that he can just about walk away and let it run on autopilot. It's a position, he says, that all investors can reach if they're disciplined about the way they build their knowledge.

"Learn one way to buy," he says. "Get good at it and then learn a second way. Then a third way . . ."

PORTRAIT OF A MILLIONAIRE REAL ESTATE INVESTOR

ELMER DIAZ
Houston, TX

Years Investing: 20

Number of Deals in 2004: 36

Career Deals: Over 200 fix and flip wholesale;
over 200 fix and flip retail; over 600 apartment rentals
owned; and over 200 single-family rentals owned

Units Owned: 56 single family homes; 42 apartments

Areas of Expertise: Wholesale; fix and flip;
fix and rent.

Real Estate License: No (but co-owns three real estate offices)

Few investors can lose it all and bounce back, and fewer still can do it twice. But Houston investor Elmer Diaz did just that, learning several valuable lessons in the process: that making a million isn't as hard as keeping it and that neither means anything if you can't help people along the way.

Diaz bought his first house as a college student—using a student loan to make the $1,500 down payment on an FHA foreclosure—and rented it out to his college buddies. His younger brother managed the property, and Diaz leveraged the equity into two more houses and another duplex. His budding investing career took a turn for the worse, along with the rest of the Houston economy, with the 1980s oil bust. Diaz lost his first property.

"I was sweating bullets when the constable walked in to serve the papers. I thought I was going to jail!" he says. "I told him that I'd never broken the law. He smiled and said, 'There's nothing wrong. You're just one of the 250,000 people who are losing houses in Texas.'"

Because Diaz's other properties weren't as leveraged as that one, he was able to keep them, survive the loss, and thrive. Soon he jumped straight from fixing up single-family houses and renting them into working with large complexes. By 1994, when he was in his early thirties, he was a millionaire, and by 1996 he owned 600 units and 100 houses. But while he was acquiring those units, he was failing to acquire the skills that would help him manage them properly.

"I did everything backward," he says. "I should have had the systems in place before growing to this next level. You have to start by learning the building blocks of the business."

The crash came quickly. In the last few months of 1996 the haphazard way he had built his empire caught up with him. Without effective systems in place to hold contractors and managers accountable, his properties deteriorated and had high vacancy rates. His employees began stealing from him—one contractor stole enough materials to build himself a house. Diaz sustained a $50,000 negative cash flow for six months running, and finally, in December, his business hit bottom.

"I was about $4 million in debt. My personal debt was about half a million," he recalls. "I woke up on December 15 in tears and said, 'God, get me out of this.'"

Diaz never filed for bankruptcy but sold off most of his holdings and spent three years repaying debts. Diaz describes it as a painful, humbling time but one that taught him important spiritual lessons. His financial straits taught him the true value of money and its ultimate purpose: to help people. That epiphany hit him hard during Christmas 1997, when his father-in-law had a car accident and needed $3,000 to buy another car to get to work. Diaz wanted to help but couldn't until a $3,000 settlement check from an old, forgotten-about lawsuit appeared in his mailbox.

"That was a turning point for me. It showed me that when you are on the right path, money will show up," he says. "And the right path is the spiritual path. The spiritual path is helping people."

Diaz learned important business lessons as well. His downfall came because he let his business get too complex and didn't take the time to implement systems to support his real estate empire. Having grown older, wiser, and grayer since his financial collapse, Diaz now urges newbies to start as simply as possible. Rather than landlording, which requires mastering a whole suite of skills, he recommends wholesaling. By finding deals and selling them to more experienced investors, beginners can hone the most basic skill of all while they're building up their reserves.

"You've got to get good at buying houses. You've got to learn how to spot a good deal," he says. "The second thing is that you've got to learn how to evaluate what kind of shape a house is in. A lot of people get good at buying but not at understanding the mechanics of the house. They don't understand that changing that wall is not $500, it's $1,500, and that's what takes some people to the cleaners."

As investors grow their businesses, Diaz recognizes that different people will take different paths. But by the time they're ready to branch out, the wise ones will have mastered the basics. And that, he says, boils down to just one thing: buying right.

"The hardest part of this business is finding the deals," he says. "They're out there. But you have to spend a lot of time looking for those deals."

But as Diaz knows, when an investor is prepared, time spent finding deals is an investment with rewards that aren't just material but spiritual.

PORTRAIT OF A MILLIONAIRE REAL ESTATE INVESTOR

DAVID FAIRWEATHER
Bethesda, MD

Years Investing: 29

Number of Deals in 2004: 10

Career Deals: A "couple hundred."

Units Owned: Over 700

Areas of Expertise: Does a little of everything but considers his strengths to be in assessing property values and adding value

Real Estate License: Yes

The United States is a country where people tend to praise speed and daring more than patience and caution. But David Fairweather believes that while decisive action has its place, a smart investor more often will look like the slow and steady tortoise than the jumpy, impatient hare. His emphasis on safety dates back to the time when, as a young man from a lower-income background, he ended the family tradition of lifelong renting, faced his fears, and bought his own home. That was in 1971, and the home he bought cost $42,000.

"When I bought my first house, I put my life's savings into it," he says. "I wasn't very old, but it was my life savings."

When he sold that house a few years later for $109,000, his *profit* was $67,000. That single event convinced him that no matter what his day job was—he currently earns a comfortable living as a real estate broker—he would build his wealth through real estate investing. But no matter how many properties he buys, and he buys enough that people kid him about "buying them like other people buy shoes," part of him will always remember that cautious young man putting it all on the line to buy his first home. For Fairweather, caution is key, and maintaining the reserves to get you through an eviction, a maintenance emergency, or a market shift gives you a financial cushion to soften the blows. For investors who are just starting out, he recommends keeping at least three to six months' reserves per property.

"Reserves are the most important thing in real estate," he says. "You can't get hurt if you keep a lot of money as reserves."

Fairweather recognizes that at first this may seem like a sacrifice and that it may be tempting to plow ahead with more acquisitions. "Just give it time," he says. "As your number of properties grows, those reserves start building up faster than they're depleted because it's unlikely that something will go wrong with all your properties at once." That means that eventually this cautious approach results in greater flexibility, options, and freedom. For example, having plenty of reserves allows Fairweather to respond to the market in ways that keep him from needing even more reserves, for example, by enabling him to maintain a competitive edge by keeping rents low to minimize vacancies.

"Rents are very market-driven, and you can lose your tenants based on what else they can rent," he explains. "So if you're basing your rents on some formula attached to the value of your house, you'll see your tenants walking out the door."

Fairweather's approach extends into an aspect of the business he says many investors ignore: maintaining the properties. "The government doesn't give you depreciation for nothing," he jokes, and goes on to say that what you spend on roof repairs, HVAC servicing, and lawn maintenance will make all the difference in the long term.

"The trick to gaining wealth through real estate is to own it a very long time and take very good care of it," Fairweather says. "But you don't get anything for it if you let it run into the ground. So maintaining your properties ensures that they'll be around for a long time and so will your tenants."

Keeping tenants happy isn't just good for business. For Fairweather it's simply the right thing to do.

"I'm very grateful to my tenants because they are paying off my building," he says. "I don't know anybody else that's going to do that for me. For the exchange of a decent home, they're willing to pay off the mortgage for me. That's a pretty good trade-off."

In addition, he believes investors need to make a trade-off with themselves, sacrificing short-term toys such as a new car or a vacation to put money back into the business. It's one more way, Fairweather says, that taking a cautious, conservative approach will yield huge returns over the long haul.

"You can make a tremendous amount of money as a real estate investor if you treat it like a business," he says. "It's not a hobby. It's not a casual thing you do. The reward you reap is commensurate with the effort you make."

PORTRAIT OF A MILLIONAIRE REAL ESTATE INVESTOR

TAMARA FULLER
Columbia, MD

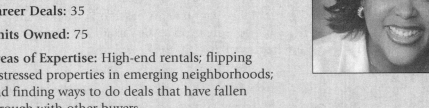

Years Investing: Owned rentals for 6 years;
Investing seriously for $3^1/_2$ years

Number of Deals in 2004: 11

Career Deals: 35

Units Owned: 75

Areas of Expertise: High-end rentals; flipping
distressed properties in emerging neighborhoods;
and finding ways to do deals that have fallen
through with other buyers.

Real Estate License: No ("But my real estate agent loves me!")

Success in real estate investing depends in part on defining your Criteria. Some people look for all-cash deals, some look for the biggest multifamilies they can find, and some specialize in rehabbing diamonds in the rough.

For Tamara Fuller, one of her Criteria is fireplaces.

"It's a quirky thing, but almost every home I buy has a wood-burning fireplace," she says with a laugh. "It gives the home that extra touch of warmth."

Of course, it's not *just* the fireplace that Fuller seeks but everything the fireplace stands for. Fuller rents higher-end homes in pleasant neighborhoods in Howard County, Maryland, a turf she chose after extensive research revealed that it had one of the wealthiest and best-educated populations in the United States. After all, Fuller is a busy management consultant who got into investing as an alternative to putting her money into underperforming stocks, not as a way to spend a lot of time collecting rent or managing contractors.

"I don't have those skills, and I'm not really looking to acquire them," she says. "I like working in a suit, and when I'm not in a suit, I don't want to spend my time chasing tenants or wielding a hammer."

There is a method to Fuller's careful consideration of aesthetics, even though some investors would consider it madness. Fuller is building a brand that she calls Symphony Homes. She chose a niche—nice, comfortable homes for people who can appreciate and take care of them—and maintains that brand no matter what. For example, at one point a downturn in the market meant she had seven vacant homes at once. But rather than dropping her price just to get warm bodies under lease, she worked with realtors, asking them to send her buyers who were looking for a short-term rental as they sought their own homes. Soon she filled all her vacancies—at full price.

"Price contributes to your brand," she says, "and my brand is that I have the best rental homes in Columbia, so they have to be priced accordingly."

As a decidedly non-full-time investor, Fuller emphasizes the need to build a network of professionals to deal with the details. She has a handyman, a property manager, agents who help her find properties, and a regular cleaning staff to return the homes to pristine condition between tenants. But one network she stresses the importance of building early is the financial one.

"Establish relationships with lenders long before you need them," she says. "The time to start courting banks is not when the time bomb is ticking away on a contract that has to close in two weeks."

Before Fuller sought out lenders, she established her financial Criteria. Since she bought her own four-level townhome in the mid-1990s, which she still owns as a rental, Fuller has made it her practice to buy properties that rent for 1 percent of their value and acquires them on 15-year mortgages for faster equity buildup and debt paydown.

"I started buying property in earnest when I was 35," she says. "That means when I'm 50, I'll be basically debt-free and have substantial retirement income."

Besides carefully analyzing the where and how of investing, Fuller has fleshed out her future financial plan. Not yet 40 years old, she is well on her way to attaining her goal of owning 100 units and retiring at age 50. Best of all, she did it in a way that didn't affect her lifestyle negatively.

"The thing you have to remember," she adds, "is that it's not just the money, it's your life."

PORTRAIT OF A MILLIONAIRE REAL ESTATE INVESTOR

RON GARBER
Orange County, CA

Years investing: 20

2004 Deals: 0

Career Deals: 30

Units Owned: 20

Areas of Expertise: Foreclosures, fix and hold

Real Estate License: Yes

Many investors get their start with the help of a mentor, an experienced advisor who may say only a few words, but words with the power to push a novice in a new, life-changing direction. That's what happened to Ron Garber in 1985 when a wise mentor shared with him the "bucket theory" that set Garber on the path to total financial independence.

The theory is this: Everyone has control over three financial "buckets." The first bucket takes care of family obligations; it's the baseline with which you take care of your home, your health, your children's education, and other day-to-day necessities and monthly expenses of life. Once that bucket is full, you can start filling the second bucket: long-term investments. That bucket isn't full until it generates enough income to take care of all the needs of bucket 1 with passive income.

"Then, after you've filled buckets 1 and 2, you've earned the right to play and have toys. That's bucket 3," says Garber. "The problem is that people start backward, and because they start with the play bucket, they aren't able to fill bucket 2 and create substantial wealth by investing."

Garber does things the other way around: His problem was not thinking past bucket 1. While he earned a fine living as a top-performing RE/Max agent, he and his wife were careful and conservative financially, for example, paying down the mortgage on his own home to own it free and clear as quickly as possible. But the bucket theory made Garber realize that he needed to pay more attention to his long-term investments.

Fortunately, financial planning is something Garber takes very seriously. At the end of each year he and his wife take a cruise where they can clear their minds and focus on their futures. On that year's cruise Ron and his wife decided on a course of action. Their life—bucket 1—cost about $5,000 a month. They already had discipline from paying off their own home, and because Garber was already working hands-on in the owned real estate market, he was in the perfect position to master foreclosures. So, they reasoned, five paid-off single-family houses in the $110,000 range would generate about $5,500 in monthly cash flow and allow them to live comfortably off the passive income.

As planned, the couple bought five rental properties and poured as much of Garber's salary as possible into paying them down. Three and a half years later they had done it: five houses, free and clear, netting a little more than $5,000 a month. As usual, at the end of that year they went on their financial planning cruise.

"Well, we've zeroed it out," said Garber. "We've done it. What do you want to do next?"

His wife thought for a moment. "Let's do it again," she said.

"Once we had the model, it was easy to just say, 'Let's do it again,'" he says. "We knew what price range to buy in and how to fix them up." Now that they had a proven model, they only needed to replicate it.

But one thing was different: they now had their rental income in addition to Garber's salary, and so they could move even faster. Two years and five more paid-down properties later the Garbers embarked on their annual cruise with the knowledge that whatever happened, they could count on $10,000 a month in passive income. Once again, Garber asked his wife what she wanted to do next.

She didn't have to think about it. "Let's do it again," she said.

This time it took only a year and a half to come up with five more paid-off houses. Then, when the California real estate market took off, their rental income skyrocketed along with it. Now Garber owns 20 rental properties free and clear, all three of his buckets are overflowing, and he sees no reason to buy more real estate.

"My focus became taking what I had and really shining it up and adding to it," he said. "For example, I add bedrooms or bathrooms or whatever I need to add to the value of the existing portfolio."

But that doesn't mean he's done investing. Having learned the power of systems, models, and mentors, he sold his brokerage firm to his own protégé, and applied the model he developed in real estate to buying small businesses. Like houses, many businesses are undervalued, and many have values that can be increased dramatically through small, targeted fixes to carefully researched weaknesses. Best of all, though, is the feeling that comes from knowing you've found a model that works.

"When I was a broker, I didn't trust that there was a duplicable model for my success no matter how successful I was or how many awards I won," he says. "That was a terrible feeling. So now I tell everyone that it's the models and systems that make the difference—the difference between success with a bad ride and success with a great ride."

PORTRAIT OF A MILLIONAIRE REAL ESTATE INVESTOR

BILL GOACHER
Asheville, NC

Years Investing: 32

Number of Deals in 2004: Only one fix & flip because he's "still working a $1 million office rehab from previous year"

Career Deals: 175–200

Units Owned: 108

Areas of Expertise: Adaptive rehab of old commercial buildings (converts to art studios, work spaces, warehouses and live-work units); has also rehabbed single-family homes

Real Estate License: No

As in the old saying about beauty, disaster is also in the eye of the beholder. At least that's what Bill Goacher believes. He likes to tell a story about some rehabbers in Asheville, North Carolina, who had jacked up an old house on a steep hill to fix its foundation. That was simple enough until the house started to shift a little, and then a little more. And then the whole house rolled off its foundation and down the hill, ending up as a big pile of rubble.

Disaster? Sure. But as Goacher points out, the investors still ended up with a nice clear lot in a very desirable neighborhood.

"They sold the lot for $30,000 and ended up making $5,000," he says. "They had anticipated making $35,000 or $40,000, but they still made five grand! So I'd say that in real estate the real disasters are few and far between."

The former industrial engineer started investing in real estate more than 30 years ago to avoid the potential disaster of becoming an "odd lotter." After five years of investing in the stock market and getting poor returns, Goacher attended a stock-buying seminar in hopes of turning his investments around.

"The guy teaching the seminar told us that an odd lotter is somebody who buys fewer than 100 shares," Goacher recalls. "A savvy investor watches what the odd lotters are doing, the small guys, and he does just the opposite because the odd lotters are always wrong. So I said, 'Hey! I'm one of those. I'm always wrong!' I only had a $6,000 nest egg at that time, so I started looking to buy real estate."

Where Goacher fell short as a wizard of Wall Street, he more than made up for it as a guru of Main Street, snatching up more than $5 million worth of properties during his career. Even with that volume of deals Goacher's only "disaster" was a multifamily property where he only broke even for nine years.

Of course, most of his deals were not even close to that "disaster." The key, Goacher says, is learning to see what others might miss, and that means knowing your market. The best way to do this, Goacher tells new investors, is to look at 50 or 100 houses before making an offer on a single one. That way, when the right property comes along, you can write an offer immediately. However, he likes to put it a bit more colorfully.

"You can't steal in slow motion," he says.

Part of finding the deal, Goacher says, is *making* the deal by ignoring the asking price and instead offering only what the house is worth based on capitalized rent.

It also means thinking creatively and seeing a deal where someone else might see an eyesore. One of Goacher's biggest successes was an old brick building in a mostly abandoned industrial section of Asheville. At that time, the mid-1980s, no one saw value in large, vacant urban property, and lenders laughed at him when he applied for a loan.

"I can tell you, nobody's going to lend you money for that building," one banker said to him. "That area is full of vandals. And the building is terrible! It's got no windows."

"Yes, it does," Goacher shot back. "I've counted them; there's 82 windows in it. There's just not very much glass."

In the end, Goacher's eye for a deal proved the skeptical banker wrong. He owner-financed the $130,000 mortgage on the 26,000-square-foot building and rented out its 14 units to entrepreneurs and artists. His bold purchase marked the beginning of the neighborhood's revitalization. Soon the rest of the old warehouses and factories were snatched up, and when Goacher finally sold that first building in 2002, it fetched a tidy $535,000.

Like just about anyone who does anything for 30 years, Goacher has evolved over time. Now he pursues industrial and commercial projects rather than residential. But he still says residential is the way to start, with a combination of rehabs and long-term holds to both create income and build wealth.

"You might do a dance that would be 'Flip, flip, keep. Flip, flip, flip, keep. Then flip, keep, keep. Then flip, flip, keep, keep,'" Goacher says. "And eventually you get to the point where you build up your portfolio to where you have some of those that will build wealth, which are the buy, fix up, and keeps."

Goacher has reached—and exceeded—that point. But whether it's residential, industrial, or commercial properties, he's ready to keep dancing.

PORTRAIT OF A MILLIONAIRE REAL ESTATE INVESTOR

ROB HARRINGTON, JR.

Framingham, MA

Years Investing: Over 25

Number of Deals in 2004: 6 commercial buildings

Career Deals: Over 200

Units Owned: Hundreds

Areas of Expertise: Takes problem properties and converts use; improves properties through efficient property management (increases the NOI); and commercial real estate

Real Estate License: Yes

Everyone's heard the old saying that the three most important things in real estate are "location, location, location." Rob Harrington echoes this saying when he explains the top reasons why he invests.

"I love real estate. I love real estate. I love real estate," he says.

The Massachusetts-based investor found his true love early. He was just 19 years old when he used savings, including money earned delivering papers, to buy his first property. It was a single-family house he converted into apartments and rented to fellow college students. Although the property generated cash flow, it also emptied his savings account, and so Harrington teamed up with other investors to buy more. By the time he graduated he owned 11 properties, all purchased in the high-interest-rate environment of the early 1980s. Contrary to many investors' thinking, Harrington believes it's best to buy when rates are high because that's when prices most accurately reflect the true value of a property.

"When rates are high, the property can't hold as much debt and therefore doesn't hold a lot of value," he says. "But when interest rates increase, the property can hold more debt and therefore is more valuable."

That kind of big-picture thinking saved Harrington from the tragedy that thinned the ranks of real estate investors in the 1980s: the Tax Act of 1986. As apartment complexes became the favored tax shelter of the wealthy, Harrington realized that prices were being driven upward artificially by people who didn't care about a property's ability to generate cash flow.

"People were falsely creating value in the depreciation," he says. "People were making investment decisions based on tax advantages."

As prices rose and people seemed to be buying high on the assumption that they could always sell higher, Harrington realized it was time to act. He sold all 35 of his units at the peak of the market and then bought more when the market crashed after the tax laws took away the value of depreciation.

But while big-picture thinking has been an important part of his strategy, Harrington says careful attention to details—maintenance, vacancies, taxes—is what makes him successful today. Every month he evaluates all his properties on the basis of one line item—for example, taxes in February, electric bills in March, heating bills in April—and figures out ways to reduce his costs in that area of expenses. In other words, he works line item by line item, not building by building, to shave costs.

"The key in real estate is to watch your nickels and dimes," Harrington says. "If you watch your nickels and dimes, the dollars will follow."

These days Harrington has his formula down: he does his numbers based on a 15-year mortgage and looks for properties he can improve just a little to charge more rent. He encourages new investors to find their own niche but says the key to becoming as much of a raving real estate fan as he is is to get off on the right foot.

"Make sure the first property you buy is a winner," he says. "Make sure you look at everything. Ask yourself if you can reduce expenses to increase the net operating income or what you can do to make someone want to live in your building rather than someone else's. If you make it on the first deal, you'll make it on the next ones."

PORTRAIT OF A MILLIONAIRE REAL ESTATE INVESTOR

CARLOS HERBON

Ogden, UT

Years Investing: 15

Number of Deals in 2004: One 156-unit mixed use building

Career Deals: 50

Units Owned: 261

Areas of Expertise: Buy & Hold

Real Estate License: Yes

In 1970 Carlos Herbon and his wife came to the United States from Argentina with only $120 in their pockets. The couple stepped off the plane in Los Angeles and bought two hot dogs for five dollars. "We said, 'Wow, our money isn't going to last long,'" Herbon recalls.

Fortunately, Carlos and his wife didn't let their lack of funds and the cost of living in the United States discourage them from seeking a better way of life. While they've pursued many ways of making a living in the United States, from construction to owning a jewelry import business, the way they've made it, and made it big, is through owning and renting properties. They've made the improbable journey from having $120 to being Millionaire Real Estate Investors. The Herbons, like thousands of other immigrants before them, were able to achieve the American dream of financial independence. They did this through being inventive, overcoming setbacks, and doing whatever it took. The Herbons and their three sons truly have the mindset of Millionaire Real Estate Investors.

"You can do anything you want to do as long as you have the big desire to do it," Herbon says. "It has to be an obsession. But you have to have a plan first, then have the obsession to execute it. And you have to dream big."

Like many other investors, Herbon first became interested in real estate investing through the back door: he and his wife bought a duplex because they had difficulty finding a place to rent with three young boys. They bought it for $15,000 in the 1970s and rented out the other unit. Instantly Herbon saw the value of being a landlord: using other people's money to pay the mortgage. However, it was his next property that created his real estate obsession: leverage. He bought the triplex next door for $1,000 down against a $5,000 mortgage.

"When we left Argentina, you had to pay cash for properties. There were no loans," Herbon recalls. "But here it's easy. You can control a lot of money by leveraging into properties."

The monthly payments on the triplex were only $50, but the rental market was much hotter than that, and so Herbon was able to rent it to college students for a total of $900 a month. From that moment on he and his wife were sold, and they've been in the buy-and-hold mode ever since. "We never sell any properties," Herbon says. "There's no reason to sell. If you need money, you go to the properties and take out equity, and the renters pay for that."

Their strategy has paid off. Herbon, his wife, and their three sons now own more than $3 million in property, which brings in about $30,000 a month in rent. Each family member plays a role in the business, which is operated out of their house. Herbon is a real estate agent, his wife is a loan officer, and their sons manage and maintain the properties. They've been so successful at real estate investing that they've turned to helping other people launch their own careers while continuing to acquire at least one property each month.

During the last three years Herbon has worked with a dozen investors. He finds deals for them, shows them why it's a good deal, and then coaches them through the entire acquisition and rental process. He also provides them with the checklists they need to find good renters, keep vacancies down, and manage the properties. For Herbon, working with investors not only generates a commission and builds his clientele but also gives him an opportunity to help others realize their dreams.

"I tell people that a failure is just an experience," Herbon says. "Anything that goes wrong is just another thing that you know for the future."

PORTRAIT OF A MILLIONAIRE REAL ESTATE INVESTOR

VENA JONES-COX
Cincinnati, OH

Years Investing: 15

Number of Deals in 2004: 35–50

Career Deals: Over 500

Units Owned: 35–50

Areas of Expertise: Wholesaling; no-money-down acquisitions; and lease options

Real Estate License: Yes

You'd think that growing up the daughter of one of Cincinnati's best-known real estate investors would infect anyone with the investing bug. Not Vena Jones-Cox. Instead, helping her father manage 13 apartment buildings convinced her *not* to go into real estate.

"I was pressed into service all the time to answer phones, clean stoves, and paint," she says. "I decided that I was absolutely not going to get into real estate."

Instead, she studied sociology at college and got a job at Procter & Gamble. However, a mere six weeks of the day-to-day grind drove her right back to real estate, especially after a seminar on wholesaling taught her that investing in real estate does not have to mean following in her father's footsteps and being a landlord. Jones-Cox decided to brave a new investing trail and focus on wholesaling. She sold most of her deals to a single client with whom she had a strong, long-standing relationship: her father.

She chose wholesaling because she didn't want to deal with tenants and didn't think rehabbing was worth the risk.

"Rehabbing is an extraordinarily risky venture," she says, explaining that it's easy for costs to run over or contractors to rip you off. "I've seen people put money up for materials and then never see the contractor again. I've seen contractors cover things up instead of fixing them, like not doing the drywall or wiring and saying they did."

However, she soon recognized that wholesaling, while a lucrative job, was just that— a job, not a wealth-building strategy. She finally settled on lease options as her long-term approach.

"You get all the same benefits you get with a rental, such as cash flow and depreciation, but the big upside is that your tenant buyers take on responsibility for repairs and maintenance," she says. "Your tenants help you maintain the property and increase its value by improving it."

The strategy, she says, also helps her maximize the number of properties she can buy.

"You're leveraging the tenant-owners' money," Jones-Cox says. "If your goal is to acquire lots of properties and you're holding all of them without pulling out the money, you have to earn the additional money to buy more properties. But with lease options you pull out the equity every two to five years and then use that money to purchase more property."

One thing Jones-Cox admits is that even those who have been steeped in real estate for decades can get into a bad deal. She looks back with humor but little fondness on a four-bedroom 1966 home in the suburbs. It seemed like a good deal: she bought it subject to, with $1,800 down and $1,200 to repave the driveway. But just three months after the first tenants moved in, the basement flooded with water. Later it flooded with sewage. Horrified, the first tenants moved out and were replaced by new tenants, who ended up getting evicted. When Jones-Cox tried to sell the property to some contractors, they discovered maintenance problems, from black mold to a cracked heating exchange, that caused them to back out. The house stood vacant and unsold for quite a while.

"I wrote a poem about that house," she jokes. "It won the 'worst deal of the year' from our Real Estate Investors' Association."

After 15 years in the business Jones-Cox is now working on a new approach: allowing herself to let go of the details. For example, she just farmed out her short sales to a woman who gets 30 percent of each deal.

"We're in the advanced investor stage where we're less interested in squeezing every dime out of the deal and more interested in doing lots of deals and making them as easy as possible," she says.

Systems are key, she says, from screening potential buyers in lease options, to marketing wholesale deals, to managing rehabs. Nevertheless, she recognizes that developing systems doesn't make it any easier for some people to relinquish control of a lovingly built business. That's something else she knows from personal experience: Her father, now 76, still works 10 hours a day. But that's just another difference of opinion between a successful father and a daughter with different approaches to running their investments.

"I believe that the more you're able to say, 'This isn't something I need to be doing, and therefore I can give it up,' the more opportunities there are for growth," she says.

PORTRAIT OF A MILLIONAIRE REAL ESTATE INVESTOR

CATHY MANCHESTER
Gray, ME

Years Investing: 5

Number of Deals in 2004: 6

Career Deals: 20

Units Owned: 22 units and 2 raw land

Areas of Expertise: Fix and flip; residential rental; and seasonal rentals

Real Estate License: Yes

Every investor tells the story about his or her favorite deal. The crown jewel in Cathy Manchester's portfolio is the four-bedroom, two-bathroom oceanfront house with the boarded up windows. The house had gone under contract almost as soon as it hit the market, but the owners didn't want to let anyone do inspections, and so it just sat.

Manchester didn't care. She knew from the location and the size that it was a pearl waiting to be snatched up. She immediately bought it for $499,000 and put $20,000 into rehabs. After the renovations were completed, Manchester began renting out her beach house for $4,000 a week during the summer. But what made the deal even sweeter was that the house was appraised for $750,000, which created a wonderful opportunity to leverage the equity.

"The best part is, I not only have a house that brings in substantial rent during the season, I've got access to a $250,000 equity line," Manchester says. "I use this equity line like cash to buy other properties and flip them."

Manchester swears by equity lines. First, they're fast: no loan approvals, no appraisals, no paperwork. On top of that she saves thousands of dollars in closing costs and fees. Of course, Manchester knows this strategy isn't appropriate for *every* deal.

"If I'm going to hold a property a long time, I'll get a mortgage. If I'm looking to flip it for quick cash, I won't," she says. "There's no sense taking out a mortgage and paying $2,500 in closing costs and doing all that paperwork if you're going to flip it in less than a year."

The equity line is just one of the creative ways Manchester leverages her properties to squeeze every bit of revenue out of them. For example, she bought a six-unit apartment building that was underutilizing its downtown parking lot. Instead of pushing rents to their maximum—many of the tenants were elderly and couldn't easily afford it— she concentrated on renting out the 18 underutilized parking spaces for $300 a year each. Another creative move was helping an investor buy an ugly, dated house that no one wanted even though its oceanfront property was gorgeous. She helped the investor buy the house for $270,000 and gift the structure to the fire department for a total tax write-off. Once the fire department had finished its training (which meant they burned it down), the owners cleared away the debris and sold the empty lot for $360,000.

"I just find properties where the numbers aren't great and figure out ways to make them great," she says.

Manchester says her real estate license helps a lot in this regard. Simply taking away the commission, for example, makes flips with slim profit margins a lot more appealing.

"I just bought a single-family house for $142,000 and will sell it for $165,000. Hopefully, I'll do it with no real estate agent other than myself, and of course I bought it with my equity line," she says. "Now, for an investor it wouldn't work. But with no commission and no closing costs, I'll make about $13,000, and for doing nothing other than shuffling some papers around, that's a very minimal risk with a great reward."

Manchester stresses that it doesn't take a license to get the good deals. As an agent, her first priority is helping her clients find the deal of their dreams.

"As an agent, there's nothing better than helping your investor-clients make money," she says.

Manchester says that investing is not all that hard. Her 18-year-old daughter, for example, bought and sold her first property (raw land) for an $11,000 profit. She put that into a condo, which she plans to update and sell for a profit a couple of years down the road. "So here's a young kid who is doing deals while in college," she says. "So it's pretty easy once you focus on doing it."

These days Manchester's life as a successful real estate agent and investor is worlds apart from the 15 years she spent as chief of police in every way but one: she still gets to help people.

"I was really concerned when I got into real estate that it would all be about the money and not about helping people," she says. "But it wasn't! I was totally blown away with what a difference we can make in people's lives. That's what hooked me."

PORTRAIT OF A MILLIONAIRE REAL ESTATE INVESTOR

BARBARA MATTSON
Rockford, IL

Years Investing: 7

Number of Deals in 2004: 30

Career Deals: Over 150

Units Owned: 100

Areas of Expertise: Judicial sales (foreclosures); assisting other investors; and auctions

Real Estate License: Yes

Many people get into real estate investing to get rich. Barbara Mattson got into it to survive.

Mattson was a home health care nurse when her husband, a construction worker, injured his back on the job and was confined to bed. For nine months Mattson supported the family on her nurse's paycheck, fought to get worker's compensation to pay the medical costs, and juggled bills that grew bigger and heavier each month. She never dropped the ball but did come close.

"I paid Peter by borrowing from Paul like a lot of other people," Mattson says. "I always kept my bills paid, but I was in a rotating nightmare."

She also bought her bored, bedridden husband a set of tapes on investing to listen to. He never paid attention to them, but Mattson did, and that changed both of their lives. When worker's compensation finally paid up, she took the $20,000 settlement and, rather than paying off debt, bought her first investment property.

"I thought, 'If I can build up enough to replace Tom's income, it won't be so bad if he really can never work again,'" she says. "My philosophy became survival."

Mattson didn't just survive but thrived. She soon got her real estate license, initially to stop paying other people commissions, and soon afterward got her broker's license. She now owns three real estate companies in addition to 100 rental properties.

"My life went from total negative to total positive," she says. "It was amazing."

Now Mattson focuses her investing on helping other people achieve their dreams. As someone who knows what it's like to struggle, she takes particular pleasure in helping people in financial distress. For example, she takes over the mortgages of people in foreclosure and lets them stay in their homes in a lease-option deal. This gives them a chance to preserve their credit and often buy their homes back once they've straightened out their lives. She also offers a rent-to-own program for potential buyers with poor credit.

"They have three years to repair their credit using me as their mortgage company," Mattson explains. "Then they turn around and refinance me out, and they're in the home that they wanted."

There is no shortage of ways to help people, Mattson says. For example, she recently struck a win-win deal with an elderly woman whose vacant house was trashed by vandals. The house was completely destroyed: Every window, every pipe, and every light bulb was smashed. The owner didn't have the money, ability, or interest to rehab the house. She approached Mattson, who assumed her $20,000 mortgage debt in a deal called a quick-claim, put $15,000 into rehab, and got the house reappraised for $70,000. Mattson then took out $56,000 of the home's equity, gave the owner $20,000, and kept the rest.

"She didn't want to deal with the house and didn't care about the money," Mattson says. "So everybody won. That's the kind of deals I put together, ones where everybody wins. That's why I love what I do."

Mattson loves it so much that she wants to help as many people as possible experience the way real estate can turn a person's life around. She offers sponsorships for single moms and members of minority groups to earn real estate licenses.

"I'm helping them see that these options are open to them," she says. "I want them to see how great this work is. Not only am I making money for myself, I get to help others learn how to do it. I love my job!"

PORTRAIT OF A MILLIONAIRE REAL ESTATE INVESTOR

Jimmy and Linda McKissack

Denton, TX

Years Investing: 12

Number of Deals in 2004: About 30

Career Deals: 150 or more

Units Owned: 95

Areas of Expertise: Foreclosures; and buy & hold

Real Estate License: Yes

Not having enough savings to invest in real estate is the most common excuse people give for not making those investments. What's less common, though, is to hear people say they had to get into real estate investing so that they could *save* money. But that prompted Jimmy and Linda McKissack to start investing in a "forced savings account." In the early 1990s the couple was making plenty of money as successful real estate agents but spending it all.

"I had a lot of cash, but I had no wealth," says Jimmy, a former nightclub owner. "And the cash would always disappear as soon as we got it, so we'd end up broke again."

Investing in bricks and mortar, they realized, would put their funds in a place they couldn't easily access. As Jimmy puts it, "Real estate is pretty much a forced savings account because your money's tied up in an asset that's appreciating."

They started buying three-bedroom, two-bathroom brick homes in middle-class neighborhoods in and around Dallas, and for the first time in their lives they began to have not only cash but wealth. By 2003 they had a net worth of $10 million, the bulk of it directly tied to their real estate holdings: 48 single-family properties, a fourplex, a duplex, a small complex, commercial space, and a residential development.

However, their "newfound" success didn't erase the memories of their financial ups and downs during the 1980s. For one thing, Jimmy had a successful restaurant that went belly-up when he tried to expand.

"We made a lot of money in Denton and decided to go down to Dallas and build a real big place down there," he recalls. "We took all our money and all the money we could borrow and did that deal and lost our rear ends down there."

They also had lived through the 1980s in Texas, a time when other investors were so highly leveraged that they ended up owing more money on their properties than the properties were worth. Their memories of losing it all and watching the same thing happen to others shaped their conservative investment approach.

"We watched people lose everything because they were too leveraged," Linda says. "We wanted an approach that would not overleverage us."

When they started out, they developed a formula that emphasized long-term security. They'd put 20 percent cash down on each deal. Each property had to be at least 10 percent below market value, and it had to generate cash flow at a minimum of $200 a month after taxes, insurance, principal and interest, and property management fees on a 15-year mortgage. Although their approach has evolved over time—these days, for example, they do some 100 percent financing deals—every deal is still at least 80 percent loan-to-value.

While the McKissacks recognize that their approach isn't for everyone, especially not those who don't have access to much cash, Linda says it's what fits their lifestyle, comfort zone, and long-term goals.

"Not everyone might like it, but I'd recommend it to my children because it would help their business survive the ups and downs," Linda says. "And that way they'd get to keep whatever they built."

Of course, like anyone who's built a business, Jimmy and Linda have had snags along the way. They like to laugh about the property one of their partners bought on the courthouse steps based on a drive-by inspection, not realizing that the whole back side of the house was missing. Not only that, the previous owner took everything in the house when he left: the sink, water heater, doors, windows—*everything*.

But despite the inevitable drawbacks both Jimmy and Linda believe their biggest mistake was that they didn't start investing sooner. Jimmy thinks that if they had started a property management company sooner, they would have saved a lot of headaches. For Linda the mistake was that they didn't buy more and buy bigger.

"I wish we had learned more about how to exchange smaller properties for eightplexes and learned more about apartment units," she says. "If you're going to do this, you might as well do it big."

But what matters the most, she says, is that they did it.

"That's the message I give people who are always waiting for the right time to do something," she says. "Do it now."

PORTRAIT OF A MILLIONAIRE REAL ESTATE INVESTOR

BILL O'KANE
Chicago, IL

Years Investing: 28

Number of Deals in 2004: 5

Career Deals: 50–55

Units Owned: 2,800 residential units and over 200,000 square feet of commercial space

Areas of Expertise: Rehabbing and repositioning; management; and investing in highly appreciating locations

Real Estate License: Yes

An investor's mindset is something that's built up over a lifetime. Many investors can look back on some moment in their childhood or some life-changing experience that shaped their outlook. For Bill O'Kane serving as an altar boy in his church taught him the lesson he believes all investors must learn: preparation can defeat fear.

"The priest made sure you knew the routine and knew what you had to do," he says. "So even though I was up there in front of a thousand people, I wasn't nervous at all."

Investing isn't that different, O'Kane says. It's doing your research, learning your market, and knowing exactly what to do when an opportunity comes your way that can conquer the new-investor jitters and ultimately lead to success. These days O'Kane is prepared for whatever the market throws his way. Since he borrowed half of the $7,000 down payment and bought his first three-flat in Chicago in 1978, he's accumulated scores of multifamily units and one large office building. For O'Kane, finding a good deal is a matter of negotiation and figuring out where everyone's willing to sacrifice.

"I've always enjoyed the art of the deal," he says. "One of my rules is that I always find out the other person's priorities and compare them to my priorities. If there's not a conflict there, you should be able to make a deal."

His ability to find a win-win solution is illustrated by the first "trophy building" he bought in 1986. It was a 31-unit apartment building with six storefronts, worth about $1.2 million. However, the seller was demanding no less than $1.4 million, a price O'Kane wasn't willing to pay.

"The negotiation was breaking down," O'Kane recalls. "But then they offered to loan me the $400,000. That allowed me to get a $1 million loan from a lender, and they actually gave me a check for $400,000 at closing."

That building, which O'Kane bought for nothing down, is worth around $8 million today.

O'Kane says another way preparation is key is in finding deals in the first place. O'Kane knows his market inside and out—"Almost down to the per-foot level," he says—and also knows where to go for financing. In fact, doing research to find investor-friendly lenders actually helps him find investor-friendly properties.

"When you find the lenders who want to work with investors, they will be a valuable resource on what's going on in the marketplace," O'Kane says.

O'Kane is a firm believer in the old saying about location. What he wants in a property more than anything else is that it be in the next hot area.

"There's an old line: 'Buy on the fringe and wait,'" he says. "I think properties appreciate the most when you buy them in a neighborhood that's going to 'pop' in a few years."

O'Kane stresses that it takes knowledge of the marketplace to know what the "new hot market" will be: a brand-new subdivision on the outskirts of town or a transitioning urban neighborhood. But no matter where it is and what is going on in the marketplace, O'Kane is adamant that there's only one good time to buy: now.

"It's kind of like a football game," he explains. "You take what the other team's defense is giving you. If they're shutting down a long pass, you go for a short pass. If they're letting you run, then run."

PORTRAIT OF A MILLIONAIRE REAL ESTATE INVESTOR

WENDY PATTON
Detroit, MI

Years Investing: 19

Number of Deals in 2004: 30

Career Deals: Over 650

Units Owned: 39 (She's "trying to get down to 30 from the 175 owned in 2002")

Areas of Expertise: Lease options; subject-to acquisitions; and rehabbing

Real Estate License: Yes

When people talk about "creative finance," they're usually not talking about the way Wendy Patton got started in real estate. Patton used credit cards, and lots of them, to launch her investing career. As a recent college graduate burdened with student loans and earning an entry-level salary, Patton took advantage of the cash advances her numerous credit cards offered. She took cash advance after cash advance to put down payments on her ever-growing portfolio of rental properties.

"I still have my cards, and they stretch 50 feet long," she says. "Literally. I have them taped together to show people. That's what I thought 'zero down' meant."

While Patton's version of creative financing was definitely on the short list of what not to do, it did allow a 21-year-old woman with little knowledge and few resources to get started in the business. Of course, Patton's knowledge and resources quickly expanded as she threw herself into as many courses as she could find—she estimates she's spent $50,000 on courses—and networked with the local investing group. In fact, they're the ones who persuaded her to make the leap and buy her first property.

It was 1985, and Patton had just graduated from college with a negative $20,000 net worth when she moved from Colorado to Detroit to take a job with Electronic Data Systems. There was a housing shortage in Detroit, and so the company put her and many of her coworkers in a hotel for six months. But almost as soon as she got to town, she sought out the investors' group, which gave her the credit card idea. After a short stay in the hotel Patton bought a house and got two coworkers to move in with her. Each one paid $250, which more than covered Patton's $438 monthly payment. From there she just kept going.

"I bought three more rentals within four months," she says. "I really didn't know what I was doing, but I just did it. Everyone else was hanging out at bars on Saturday night, and I was painting my rentals."

These days Patton doesn't recommend running up six-digit credit card bills to buy property.

"I never went bankrupt, but there were many months when I was terrified I couldn't make the payments," she says. "It was a very, very, very dangerous way to do it."

However, she *does* recommend the other half of the strategy that got her where she is today: buying and selling houses on lease options. After all, most lenders would have considered her totally unqualified when she started out and was buying hundreds of thousands of dollars of property each year on a $25,000 salary. By lease-optioning from an owner, she could skip the credit check and income verification, plus her payments would be lower than they would have been if she had been taking out a new mortgage. Then, when she had control of the property, she could turn around and lease-option it to a tenant, pocketing the difference.

"It's control without ownership," she says. "You're able to control these properties by using their equity, but without having to own or maintain them because your tenant is acting as the homeowner. When they improve the property, the equity increases, but you get to leverage that, not them."

In almost 20 years of investing Patton also tried rehabbing, land development, and commercial property but never found anything she liked as much as lease options, and now she's considered an expert by her peers. By 2003, the year after she finally paid off the last of her credit card bills, she had done more than 600 lease-option deals, primarily single-family houses. Now she's at the point where she's gotten so good at structuring deals that the next step is to do *fewer* deals, only the most profitable ones. However, one thing she won't scale back on is her desire to learn.

"I go to as many courses and seminars as I can," she says, "even now that I don't need it as much. I'm happy to spend $1,000 on a person's course if it's going to teach me one tidbit, one idea that will make me $100,000."

PORTRAIT OF A MILLIONAIRE REAL ESTATE INVESTOR

DON AND RYAN ZELEZNAK
Phoenix, AZ

Years Investing: 30 (7 years for Ryan)

Number of Deals in 2004: 6 office/condo buildings;
4 single-family homes; 3 condos; also building 12
office/condo buildings with over 1,400 units
(they'll keep and rent 5–10% and sell the rest)

Career Deals: Thousands

Units Owned: 100,000 square feet of office space;
20 residential rentals; 70 acres of commercial land;
12 office/condo projects; 4 commercial projects; 2,500
lot golf community; and currently building over 1,400 residential homes.

Areas of Expertise: Real estate syndication (over 5,000 units in 70s and 80s);
fix and flips (over 1,200); as well as foreclosures; wraps; lease options;
and developing opportunity for clients.

Real Estate License: Yes

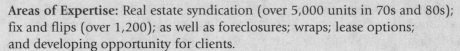

If you're good at what you do, eventually the business comes to you. That is how Don Zeleznak built not one but several businesses, finding and making real estate deals not in one but in two states, using different strategies.

In 1974 Zeleznak was a financial manager in Minnesota when he and his wife moved from their condo into a house big enough for them and their new baby, Ryan (now an investing whiz in his own right). But instead of selling the condo, they rented it out. A couple of years later, when they moved again, they did the same thing. Those simple decisions planted the seeds of a massive investment syndication business: Zeleznak found people who wanted to sell their properties and brought investors to the table. He crafted the deals, which eventually involved hundreds of units.

"We started small, and the deals got bigger and bigger," he says. "Over the course of that six-year period I probably had 300 investors, and we had syndicated about a hundred million dollars of residential deals."

Zeleznak quickly became a multimillionaire, and his phone never stopped ringing: everyone seemed to know that he was the go-to guy if you wanted to buy or sell. He also started a management company that eventually handled 5,000 units. But by the early1980s Zeleznak was ready for a change. First, most of his syndication deals involved people who used their investments as tax shelters, and he knew that the proposed tax laws would change everything. Second, the long Minnesota winters were starting to become a drag. In 1984 he sold it all and moved to Arizona.

"For the first year and a half all I did was play tennis and relax," he says. "I was unwinding from a very busy six to eight years."

But Zeleznak wasn't satisfied simply relaxing, and so soon he threw himself and his son into a new business, one he continues to this day: wrapping loans to nonqualified buyers and putting together wrap deals for other investors. It's a win-win situation, he explains. Investors make a profit, and people whose poor credit would shut them out from traditional financing finally can buy homes of their own. While the deals involve some risk for the investors and buyers, Zeleznak says most have very happy endings.

"Out of the 1,100 deals we've done, we've taken back about 47 or 48 properties on foreclosure," he says. "So we have around a $4^1/_2$ percent default rate, which is pretty good considering the types of credit issues these people are challenged with."

One of the big advantages of wraps, he says, is that they aren't as labor-intensive. Besides working with Ryan to continue their mortgage wrap deals, Zeleznak has been focusing lately on developing and financing large-scale commercial deals, which are also less management-intensive.

"Remember, I was involved in rentals in a very big way in the Midwest and know the headaches that go along with that," he says. "But how do you think people treat the property if they plan to own it?"

Zeleznak attributes his success with wraps, like his earlier successes, to an investor's mindset that allows him to see opportunity within calculated risks. It's not a mindset he believes everyone has, though, and he tells a story about his grandmother to illustrate that.

"She gave me $10,000 to invest because that money was earning only 5 percent at the bank," he says. "I put her into a conservative mutual fund; she couldn't sleep at night because she had read all these articles about the downturn of the stock market."

When he transferred her money into a bond fund, she started sending him articles about how the government was falling apart.

"That's when I said, 'Grandma, it's time to put the money back in the bank,'" he says.

But for Zeleznak, who has the mindset, the skills, and the knowledge to recognize and act on a good deal, there's *no* good time to put money in the bank. Whether it's a rental, a rehab, or a wrap, Zeleznak and his son consider the possibilities and act.

APPENDIX A
The Millionaire Real Estate Investor's Personal Budget Worksheet

On the following pages are blank copies of the Millionaire Real Estate Investor's Personal Budget Worksheet and the subworksheets you'll need to complete it. Electronic copies of these forms are available at www.KellerINK.com. Good luck and keep budgeting for Net Worth.

Sample Personal Budget Worksheet

Monthly Income

(1)	Earned Income	$
(2)	Unearned Income	$
	Gross Monthly Income	$
(1)	Tithe ___ %	$
(2)	Save ___ %	$
(3)	Invest ___ %	$
(4)	Tax ___ %	$
	Net Spendable Income	$

Expenses

		Current	Required	Discretionary
(5)	Housing ___ %	$	$	$
(6)	Food ___ %	$	$	$
(7)	Automobile ___ %	$	$	$
(8)	Insurance ___ %	$	$	$
(9)	Entertainment ___ %	$	$	$
(10)	Clothing ___ %	$	$	$
(11)	Medical ___ %	$	$	$
(12)	Debt Service ___ %	$	$	$
(13)	School/Child Care ___ %	$	$	$
(14)	Travel/Vacation ___ %	$	$	$
(15)	Misc. ___ %	$	$	$
	Total Current Expenses	$		
	Total Required Expenses		$	
	Total Discretionary Expenses			$

Budget Analysis

Net Spendable Income	$
Less Required Expenses	$
Total Surplus/Deficit	$

A Personal Budget Income Breakout Worksheet

INCOME
- (1) Earned
  - Salary $_____
  - Other $_____
  - Total Earned $_____

- (2) Unearned
  - Interest $_____
  - Dividends $_____
  - Rental Income $_____
  - Assets Sold $_____
  - Notes $_____
  - Other $_____
  - Total Unearned $_____

GROSS MONTHLY INCOME $_____
- (1) Tithing
  - Charitable Giving $_____
  - Church Donations $_____
  - Other $_____
  - Total Tithe   – $_____

- (2) Savings
  - Cash Reserve $_____
  - Other $_____
  - Total Savings   – $_____

- (3) Investments
  - Pre Tax $_____
  - IRAs $_____
  - Business (Private) $_____
  - Stocks/Bonds $_____
  - Real Estate $_____
  - Annuities $_____
  - Collectables $_____
  - Other $_____
  - Total Investments   – $_____

- (4) Tax
  - Income $_____
  - Other $_____
  - Total Tax   – $_____

NET SPENDABLE INCOME $_____

EXPENSES

(5) Housing

Mortgage	$_____
Insurance	$_____
Taxes	$_____
Electricity	$_____
Gas	$_____
Water	$_____
Sanitation	$_____
Lawn Care	$_____
Cleaning	$_____
Telephone	$_____
Cable	$_____
Internet	$_____
Maintenance	$_____
Other	$_____

Total Housing $_____

(6) Food

Groceries	$_____
Other	$_____

Total Food $_____

(7) Automobile

Payments	$_____
Gas	$_____
Insurance	$_____
Maintenance/Repair	$_____
Other	$_____

Total Automobile $_____

(8) Insurance

Life	$_____
Medical	$_____
Disability	$_____
Other	$_____

Total Insurance $_____

SUBTOTAL EXPENSES (5-8) $_____

EXPENSES

     (9) Entertainment

          Entertainment $_____

          Magazines/Paper $_____

          Other $_____

     Total Entertainment $_____

     (10) Clothing

          Clothing $_____

          Other $_____

     Total Clothing $_____

     (11) Medical

          Co-Pay $_____

          Prescriptions $_____

          Other $_____

     Total Medical $_____

     (12) Debt Service

          Credit Cards $_____

          Loans/Notes $_____

          Other $_____

     Total Debt Service $_____

     (13) School/Child Care

          School $_____

          Child Care $_____

          Other $_____

     Total School/Child Care $_____

     (14) Travel/Vacation

          Travel $_____

          Vacation $_____

          Other $_____

     Total Travel/Vacation $_____

     (15) Miscellaneous

          Gifts $_____

          Other $_____

     Total Miscellaneous $_____

SUBTOTAL EXPENSES (5-8) $_____

SUBTOTAL EXPENSES (9-15) $_____

TOTAL EXPENSES $_____

APPENDIX B
The Millionaire Real Estate Investor's Personal Balance Sheet

Below is a blank copy of the Millionaire Real Estate Investor's Personal Balance Sheet. An electronic copy will be made available at www.KellerINK.com. This is the tool you'll use to track your assets and liabilities—your growing Net Worth.

Sample Personal Balance Sheet	January 1, Last Year	January 1, This Year	Annual % Increase	Current Total	YTD% Increase
ASSETS					
Retirement Accounts	$	$	%	$	%
Equity Investments					
Businesses Private	$	$	%	$	%
Businesses Public					
Stocks	$	$	%	$	%
Bonds	$	$	%	$	%
Annuities	$	$	%	$	%
Total Equity Investments	$	$	%	$	%
Cash/Savings	$	$	%	$	%
Insurance	$	$	%	$	%
Collectibles	$	$	%	$	%
Personal Property	$	$	%	$	%
Real Estate Personal	$	$	%	$	%
Real Estate Investments	$	$	%	$	%
Notes Receivable	$	$	%	$	%
Other Assets	$	$	%	$	%
TOTAL ASSETS	$	$	%	$	%
LIABILITIES					
Car Loans	$	$	%	$	%
Credit Card Debt	$	$	%	$	%
Mortgage Debt	$	$	%	$	%
School Loans	$	$	%	$	%
Other Debt	$	$	%	$	%
TOTAL LIABILITIES	$	$	%	$	%
NET WORTH	$	$	%	$	%
ANNUAL CASH FLOW (EARNED)	$	$	%	$	%
ANNUAL CASH FLOW (UNEARNED)	$	$	%	$	%

APPENDIX C
The Millionaire Real Estate Investor's Criteria Worksheet

Below is a blank copy of the Millionaire Real Estate Investor's Criteria Worksheet. An electronic copy will be made available for download at www.KellerINK.com. This is the tool you'll use to define your investment Criteria. You have to know what you're looking for to know when you've found it.

The Millionaire Real Estate Investor's Criteria Worksheet (1 of 2)

1) **LOCATION**
   - ❑ Country
   - ❑ State/Province
     - ❑ Taxes
     - ❑ Rentals Laws
     - ❑ Weather
   - ❑ County/Parrish
   - ❑ City/Town
     - ❑ Taxes
     - ❑ Services
   - ❑ Neighborhood
     - ❑ School District
     - ❑ Crime
     - ❑ Transportation
     - ❑ Shopping/Recreation
   - ❑ Street
     - ❑ Traffic
     - ❑ Size
   - ❑ Lot
     - ❑ Zoning
     - ❑ Adjoining Lots
     - ❑ Lot Size
     - ❑ Trees
     - ❑ Privacy
     - ❑ Landscaping
     - ❑ Orientation/View

2) **TYPE**
   - ❑ Single Family
     - ❑ Home
     - ❑ Condo
     - ❑ Town Home
     - ❑ Mobile Home
     - ❑ Zero Lot/Garden
   - ❑ Small Multi Family
     - ❑ Duplex
     - ❑ Fourplex
   - ❑ Large Multifamily/Commercial
   - ❑ Land/Lot
   - ❑ New/Preconstruction
   - ❑ Resale
   - ❑ Urban
   - ❑ Suburban
   - ❑ Exurban
   - ❑ Rural
   - ❑ Resort/Vacation
   - ❑ Farm/Ranch

3) **ECONOMICS**
   - ❑ Price Range
     - ❑ From $_____
     - ❑ To $_____
   - ❑ Discount   ___%
   - ❑ Cash Flow $_____ / Mo
   - ❑ Appreciation ___% /Yr

4) CONDITION
   - ❑ Needs No Repair
   - ❑ Needs Minor Cosmetic
   - ❑ Needs Major Cosmetic
   - ❑ Needs Structural
   - ❑ Needs Demolition

5) CONSTRUCTION
   - ❑ Roof
   - ❑ Walls (Exterior)
   - ❑ Foundation
   - ❑ Plumbing
   - ❑ Water/Waste
   - ❑ Wiring
   - ❑ Insulation
   - ❑ Heating/AC

6) FEATURES
   - ❑ Age/Year Built ____
   - ❑ Beds ____
   - ❑ Baths ____
   - ❑ Living ____
   - ❑ Dining ____
   - ❑ Stories ____
   - ❑ Square Feet ____
   - ❑ Ceilings ____ ft.
   - ❑ Parking/Garage
   - ❑ Kitchen
   - ❑ Closets/Storage
   - ❑ Appliances (Gas/Electric)
   - ❑ Floor Plan (Open, In-law)
   - ❑ Patio/Deck
   - ❑ Basement
   - ❑ Attic
   - ❑ Lighting
   - ❑ Walls (Interior)
   - ❑ Laundry Room

7) AMENITIES
   - ❑ Office
   - ❑ Play/Exercise Room
   - ❑ Security System
   - ❑ Furniture/Furnishings
   - ❑ Sprinkler System
   - ❑ Workshop/Studio
   - ❑ In-Law Suite
   - ❑ Fireplace(s)
   - ❑ Pool
   - ❑ Hot Tub
   - ❑ Ceiling Fans
   - ❑ Window Treatments
   - ❑ Satellite Dish
   - ❑ Internet (Broadband)
   - ❑ Sidewalk
   - ❑ Energy Efficient Features
   - ❑ Other:
     - ❑ _____
     - ❑ _____
     - ❑ _____
     - ❑ _____
     - ❑ _____
     - ❑ _____

APPENDIX D
The Millionaire Real Estate Investor's Cost of Repair Worksheet

Below is a blank copy of the Millionaire Real Estate Investor's Cost of Repair Worksheet. As with the other forms and worksheets, an electronic copy is available for download at www.KellerINK.com. This is the tool you'll use to calculate the repair costs on any Buy & Hold or Buy & Sell you might consider.

While it may not appear to be the case, this spreadsheet is far from comprehensive. That was not our intent. The level of detail is meant to get you to think about the fine points involved in your repairs. You may have used the back of an envelope to estimate repair costs when you were formulating the initial offer; however, between contract and close you'll want to do your due diligence in detail while you still have a chance to renegotiate the terms or pull out.

While it's true that every house has a surprise (sometimes a big one), many beginning investors run into trouble through the accumulation of lots of small bills. For example, rewiring an electrical outlet for $20 may seem like too small cost to account for in the grand scheme of a $10,000 rehab project, but if your property has 25 outlets, you now have a $500 bill. That little bill adds up to 5 percent of your total costs. One 5 percent oversight won't kill your profits, but three or four might.

The organization of this worksheet is also meant to be instructive. Instead of categorizing repairs by room (kitchen, bedroom, bathroom, etc.) or type (carpentry, painting, masonry, etc.), we've opted for categories that in some ways describe the relative risk of the repairs. There is a natural escalation of risk for the investor from Cosmetic Minor to Cosmetic Major and on to the highest level of risk, Structural. The more repairs you have in these increasingly unpredictable categories, the larger your contingency factor should be. There is much less guesswork involved in Fixtures/Appliances and Landscaping, the two categories that round out the repair worksheet. Remember to do your due diligence in detail. The deal, after all, is in the details.

Cost of Repair Worksheet

	Cost of Repair Summary			
1	Cosmetic Minor	+ $	0.00	
2	Cosmetic Major	+ $	0.00	
3	Structural	+ $	0.00	
4	Fixtures/Appliances	+ $	0.00	
5	Landscaping	+ $	0.00	
	Contingency Factor	+ $	0.00	10 %
Total Cost of Repair		= $	-	

1	Cosmetic Minor Sub-Worksheet		
Cleanup			
	Interior Cleaning	+ $	
	Exterior Powerwash	+ $	
Electrical			
	Install GFCIs	+ $	
	Lights	+ $	
	Outlets	+ $	
	Fuse box	+ $	
Roof			
	Shingle Repair	+ $	
	Attic Vents	+ $	
	Rain Caps	+ $	
	Gutters/Downspouts	+ $	
Chimney/Hearth			
	Cleaning	+ $	
	Repair	+ $	
Kitchen			
	New Countertops	+ $	
	New Backsplash	+ $	
Flooring			
	Carpet	+ $	
	Tile	+ $	
	Vinyl	+ $	
	Laminate	+ $	
Plumbing			
	Fixture instillation	+ $	
	Replace bibs	+ $	
	Update Gas Valves/Hoses	+ $	
Carpentry			
	Shelving	+ $	
	Rehang/Adjust Doors	+ $	
	Trim/Molding	+ $	
	Misc Mill Work/Repair	+ $	

About the Authors

Gary Keller is a self-made millionaire and cofounder of Keller Williams Realty, the largest real estate franchise system in the world. With more than 30 years of industry and investing experience, he's been involved in thousands of transactions. He is also the author of the bestselling *The Millionaire Real Estate Agent* and *The Wall Street Journal* #1 bestseller *The ONE Thing*.

Gary is married to Mary Pfluger and they have one child, John Christian. He enjoys playing guitar, reading, movies, sports, and spending as much time as possible with his family and friends.

Dave Jenks served as dean of Keller Williams University and vice president of research and development at Keller Williams Realty. Dave has been in the real estate industry since 1981, has taught for the Dale Carnegie Institute, and owned his own training company, the Leadership Connection, Inc. He is the father of three and grandfather of nine. He loves travel, reading, and golf.

Jay Papasan is vice president of learning and executive editor at Keller Williams Realty, as well as coauthor of the #1 *WSJ* bestseller *The ONE Thing*. A graduate of the New York University graduate writing program, his freelance work has appeared in *Texas Monthly* and *Memphis Magazine*. Jay lives in Austin with his wife, Wendy, their children, Gus and Veronica, and their dog, Taco. Currently, he and Wendy co-own a successful real estate investment business and sales team, the Papasan Properties Group.

House Numbers	+ $	
Mail Box	+ $	
FIXTURES SUBTOTAL	= + $	
APPLIANCES		
Dishwasher	+ $	
Oven	+ $	
Range	+ $	
Hood	+ $	
Microwave	+ $	
Water Heater	+ $	
HVAC	+ $	
Refrigerator	+ $	
Trash Compactor	+ $	
Disposal	+ $	
Alarm System	+ $	
Garage door opener	+ $	
Sump Pump	+ $	
Radiators	+ $	
Other	+ $	
Other	+ $	
Misc.		
Labor	+ $	
Contractor Fees	+ $	
APPLIANCES SUBTOTAL	= $	
Total Fixtures/Appliaces	= $	

5	Landscaping Sub-Worksheet	
Lawn		
Resod	+ $	
Reseed	+ $	
Mowing/Trimming	+ $	
Trim Hedge/Shrubs	+ $	
Trim Trees	+ $	
Watering	+ $	
Plants/Beds		
New Beds	+ $	
Flowers	+ $	
Shrubs/Hedges	+ $	
Trees	+ $	
Retaining Walls		
Timber	+ $	
Paint	+ $	
Stain	+ $	
Replace/Install	+ $	
Misc		
Labor	+ $	
Contractor Fees	+ $	
Pavers/Stepping Stones	+ $	
Sprinkler System	+ $	
Decorative Urns/Statues	+ $	
Fertilizer	+ $	
Mulch/Gravel	+ $	
Top Soil	+ $	
Storage Shed	+ $	
Trash Container Rental	+ $	
Debris/Garbage Removal	+ $	
Total Lanscaping	= $	-

Handicap Access

Ramp	+ $	
Railing	+ $	
Debris/Garbage Removal	+ $	

Exterior Walls

Driveway Patching/Repair	+ $	
Trim/Siding Repair	+ $	
Skirt Replacement	+ $	
Patch/Repair Masonry	+ $	
Paint	+ $	
Screens	+ $	
Replace Window Panes	+ $	
Shutters	+ $	
Weather Striping/Caulking	+ $	

Interior Walls

Patch Dry Wall/Plaster	+ $	
Paint	+ $	
Rehang/Adjust Doors	+ $	
Trim	+ $	
Crown Molding	+ $	

Misc

Labor	+ $	
Contractor Fees	+ $	
Trash Container Rental	+ $	
Debris/Garbage Removal	+ $	
Total Cosmetic Minor	= $	

2	Cosmetic Major Sub-Worksheet

Electrical

Rewiring Throughout	+ $	
	+ $	

Plumbing

Install New Pipes/Lines	+ $	
Line Repair/Replacement	+ $	

Pool/Spa

Demo/Fill	+ $	
Pump/Filtration	+ $	
Addition	+ $	

Carpentry

Custom Built-ins	+ $	
Decorative Woodwork	+ $	

Flooring

Hardwood	+ $	
Tile	+ $	

Exterior Walls

Siding Replacement	+ $	
Skirt Replacement	+ $	
Masonry	+ $	
New Driveway	+ $	
New Deck	+ $	
New Porch/Stoop	+ $	
New Patio	+ $	

Interior Walls

Framing	+ $	
New Door	+ $	
New Window	+ $	
Replace Dry Wall	+ $	

Misc

Labor	+ $	_____
Contractor Fees	+ $	_____
Garage Door	+ $	_____
Trash Container Rental	+ $	_____
Debris/Garbage Removal	+ $	_____
Total Cosmetic Major	= $	_____

3	**Structural Sub-Worksheet**

Foundation Repair

Slab	+ $	_____
Pier & beam	+ $	_____
Replace HVAC Ducts/Vents	+ $	_____

Roof

Shingles/Surface	+ $	_____
Decking	+ $	_____
Trusses /Trim	+ $	_____
Septic Repair/Replacement	+ $	_____
Walls Interior New/Demolish	+ $	_____
Walls Exterior New/Demolish	+ $	_____
Gas Line Repair/Replacement	+ $	_____

Misc

Labor	+ $	_____
Contractor Fees	+ $	_____
Trash Container Rental	+ $	_____
Debris/Garbage Removal	+ $	_____
Total Structural	= $	_____

4	**Fixtures/Appliances Sub-Worksheet**

FIXTURES

Lighting

Ceiling Lights	+ $	_____
Wall Lights	+ $	_____
Ceiling Fans	+ $	_____
Exterior Lights	+ $	_____

Bathroom

Medicine Cabinet	+ $	_____
Countertops	+ $	_____
Vanity	+ $	_____
Cabinets	+ $	_____
Shower	+ $	_____
Bathtub	+ $	_____
Mirrors	+ $	_____
Toilet	+ $	_____

Kitchen

Cabinets	+ $	_____
Island	+ $	_____

Misc Fixtures

Labor	+ $	_____
Contractor Fees	+ $	_____
Parts/Tools	+ $	_____
Door Knobs/Hinges	+ $	_____
Cabinet Pulls/Hinges	+ $	_____
Window Coverings	+ $	_____
Screens	+ $	_____
Gas Alarm	+ $	_____
Smoke Alarm	+ $	_____
Keys/Locks/Lock Boxes	+ $	_____

Next you'll use the code shown above to add a map centered on the user's current location to the Oak Top House app.

To use the Google Maps API to display a map centered on the user's current location:

1. Return to **script.js** in your editor, and then in the `createDirections()` function, comment out the two `console.log` statements.

2. Before the closing `}`, enter the following statements:

```
1   var currPosLat = position.coords.latitude;
2   var currPosLng = position.coords.longitude;
3   var mapOptions = {
4       center: new google.maps.LatLng(currPosLat, currPosLng),
5       zoom: 12
6   };
7   var map = new google.maps.Map(document.getElementById("map"),↵
8       mapOptions);
```

3. Scroll down to the `fail()` function, comment out the `console.log()` statement, and then enter the following statement to display feedback for browsers that don't provide location information:

```
document.getElementById("map").innerHTML =↵
    "Unable to access your current location.";
```

4. Save your changes to **script.js**, and then switch to **oaktop.htm** in your editor.

5. At the bottom of the body section, just before the existing `script` element that references the script.js file, add the following `script` element:

```
<script src="https://maps.googleapis.com/maps/api/js?v=3.exp↵
    &sensor=true"></script>
```

Before you can use the `Map()` and `LatLng()` constructors, your app has to load the Google Maps JavaScript library using the URL in this `script` element. The `sensor` argument in the URL lets Google know that your script uses the API with positioning hardware via the `geolocation` object.

6. Save your changes to **oaktop.htm**, and then in your browser, refresh or reload **oaktop.htm**.

7. Click **Directions**, and then click the **Allow once**, **Share Location**, or similar button to authorize your browser to share your location information with your app. After a

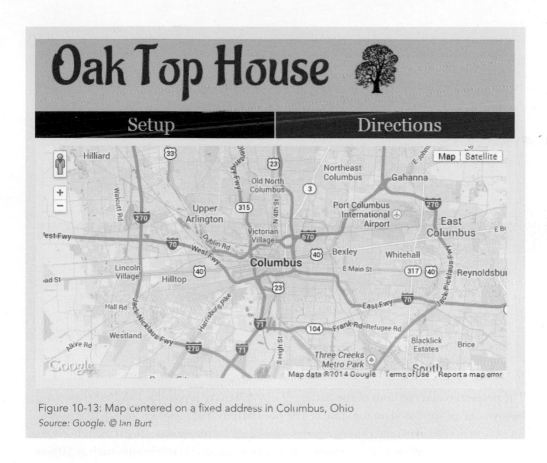

Figure 10-13: Map centered on a fixed address in Columbus, Ohio
Source: Google. © Ian Burt

New APIs are constantly under development to take advantage of the evolving capabilities of mobile devices. The following sections describe a few APIs that enable web apps to work with hardware available in mobile devices.

Using the Battery Status API

The **Battery Status API** adds a `battery` property to the `Navigator` object, which provides access to properties and methods related to the device battery. Table 10-10 describes the `battery` properties and Table 10-11 describes its events.

PROPERTY	DESCRIPTION
charging	Boolean with a value of `true` if the device is charging
chargingTime	Time until battery is fully charged (in seconds)
dischargingTime	Time until system will be shut down due to low battery (in seconds)
level	Current level of charge, on a scale from 0 to 1

Table 10-10: Properties of the `battery` object

EVENT	DESCRIPTION
chargingchange	The value of the `charging` property changes
chargingtimechange	The value of the `chargingTime` property changes
dischargingtimechange	The value of the `dischargingTime` property changes
levelchange	The value of the `level` property changes

Table 10-11: Events of the `battery` object

The properties and methods of the Battery Status API make it possible to adjust the behavior of an app based on the state of a device's battery. For instance, an app that uses a lot of system resources, and thus consumes significant battery power, might include code to restrict its activity when a device's battery level reaches a certain minimum, such as 10% or 15%. This API could also enable the automatic saving of form field values to a cookie when a device's battery reaches a critically low threshold, to avoid a user losing form entries.

At the time this book was written, only Firefox supported the Battery Status API.

Using the Device Orientation API

The **Device Orientation API** provides access to data from specialized hardware in many mobile devices for detecting changes in position and speed. A device's **gyroscope** detects its orientation in space, and its **accelerometer** detects changes in speed. The Device Orientation API lets your apps react to changes in the data provided by this hardware through the `deviceorientation` and `devicemotion` events.

The `deviceorientation` event reports a set of coordinates with the property names `alpha`, `beta`, and `gamma`. Each property corresponds to one of the three dimensions, analogous to the x, y, and z axes used in geometry. By comparing changes in orientation mathematically, your code can respond to user actions including tilting a device. You could use the `deviceorientation` event to create, for instance, a game that simulates a marble on a flat board, with the user tilting the device back and forth and side to side to get the marble into a hole in the center of the board without falling off one of the edges. Based on changes in the orientation of the device, your app would run code changing the direction of the marble's movement.

The `devicemotion` event reports values for acceleration and rotation. You could use this event in an app that provides directions, for instance, to determine if a user is moving or standing still.

Using the WebRTC API

The WebRTC API—short for web real-time communication—enables apps to receive data from a device's camera and microphone, as well as to send and receive audio, video, and other types of data in real time. The WebRTC API combines components of several other APIs to enable the video, audio, and communication aspects of real-time communication. As this API evolves, it should eventually enable text and video chat using only HTML and JavaScript, rather than requiring either native apps or back-end servers.

Short Quiz 2

1. What is the parent object of the `geolocation` property?

2. Why is it useful to add a second timeout to supplement the timeout in the `getCurrentPosition()` method?

3. Why do you need to use an additional API, such as the Google Maps API, to display a map based on geolocation information?

Enhancing Mobile Web Apps

When you create an app with mobile users in mind, it's important to account for some of the limitations of handheld devices. In this section, you'll explore a few development practices that can make your apps work better and more reliably for mobile users.

Testing Tools

Mobile devices run different browsers than desktop computers. Even though Chrome, Firefox, Safari, and Internet Explorer all make mobile versions available for different mobile operating systems, the mobile versions are distinct from the desktop versions, and may have different capabilities, limitations, and even bugs. For all of these reasons, it's important to test your apps on the mobile platforms that you expect your users to be running.

A professional web development department or studio often maintains a large collection of mobile devices for testing mobile apps on various operating systems and with different screen sizes and resolutions. However, because most developers don't have the resources to maintain a collection of mobile devices, other options exist. A number of services are available online that enable developers to interact with virtual versions of many mobile devices. You can locate some of these services by searching on "mobile device testing service."

In addition, the makers of mobile operating systems and browsers all provide free programs that simulate interactions with their devices or software. Table 10-12 lists the names of such software for iOS, Android, and Windows Phone.

COMPANY	OPERATING SYSTEM	SIMULATION SOFTWARE
Apple	iOS	Xcode
Google	Android	Android SDK
Microsoft	Windows Phone	Windows Phone SDK

Table 10-12: Software used to simulate mobile devices

> ## Best Practices | *Choosing Mobile Devices for Testing*
>
> Although exhaustive testing on a wide variety of mobile devices is often only possible for large organizations, it's still important for small-scale developers to test on some mobile hardware. Relying only on tools that run on a desktop computer is never a good idea. To decide which devices are important to test on, research the operating systems and versions used by your target audience. Although many developers test primarily on their own smartphones, it's important to recognize that both Apple iOS and Google Android account for significant shares of mobile device usage. Therefore, at a minimum, you should test on one device running a recent version of each of these operating systems. As a student or a developer early in your career, you may find that borrowing devices from friends is sufficient to cover your testing needs.

Minimizing Download Size

The amount of data that a user needs to download to use a web app is more of an issue on a mobile device than on a desktop computer, for two reasons. First, although mobile devices can connect to the Internet via a home network with a fast connection, many mobile users access the web when connected to the mobile networks of their wireless providers (such as AT&T or Verizon in the United States). While mobile speeds are increasing on a regular basis, most are still significantly slower than the fastest home broadband connections. Therefore, to ensure that users can view and use your web app on a mobile network soon after they request it, your app should require users to download as little data as possible.

The other reason it's important to limit the amount of data that mobile users must download is that many mobile broadband plans include data caps that limit the amount of data a user can download each month. Many users purchase monthly plans that provide a set amount of data transfer every month for activities like viewing web pages and checking email, and these users want to avoid being charged extra by their providers or having their access cut off if they hit the limit. Your app can support its users in this goal by downloading only the minimum amount of data necessary for the current task.

Web developers have come up with a number of strategies for minimizing download size, including loading scripts responsively and minifying files.

Loading Scripts Responsively

For small web apps, it's common to include all JavaScript code in a single .js file and to reference that file at the bottom of the body section, where it is downloaded when the page first loads. However, as your web apps become more complex, they will include code that isn't needed unless a user chooses a specific option. In this case, you can reduce the amount of code that needs to be downloaded when the app is first loaded by dividing up the JavaScript code into multiple files, and downloading each file only when it's needed.

In the Oak Top House app, when the page first loads, only the code related to room setup is necessary. The code that loads and displays the map isn't needed unless a user clicks the Directions button. Because script.js contains only a few functions related to displaying the map, there's no need to break the file up. However, the Google Maps API file is currently downloaded automatically when the page loads, but isn't needed unless a user clicks the Directions button. You'll change the code so this file only loads if needed. Figure 10-14 illustrates the changes you'll make.

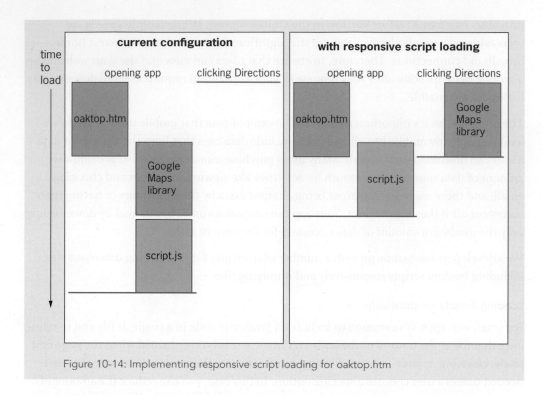

Figure 10-14: Implementing responsive script loading for oaktop.htm

The left side of Figure 10-14 illustrates how the initial view of the web app currently loads. The browser starts by loading oaktop.htm, followed by the Google Maps library, and then the script.js file. Clicking the Directions button starts no additional downloading, as all the necessary code has already been downloaded. The right side of Figure 10-14 illustrates how responsive script loading could reduce the amount of data loaded when a user first opens the app. In this scenario, only script.js would be loaded when the page first loads, reducing the amount of data to download initially and letting users interact with the app more quickly. When users click the Directions button, the app would then download the Google Maps library, which still consists of less data than loading the initial page of the app in the configuration on the left.

Next, you'll add code to load the Google Maps library only when a user clicks the Directions button.

To implement responsive script loading:

  1. Return to **oaktop.htm** in your editor, scroll down to the bottom of the document, and then delete the `script` element that references the URL *maps.googleapis.com*.

2. Save your changes to **oaktop.htm**, and then switch to **script.js** in your editor.

3. In the `loadDirections()` function, comment out the line `geoTest();`.

4. Just before the closing `}`, add the following `if` statement:

```
1      // to minimize data use, download map only if needed and↵
2        not already downloaded
3    if (typeof google !== 'object') {
4      var script = document.createElement("script");
5      script.src = "https://maps.googleapis.com/maps/api/js?↵
6        v=3.exp&sensor=true&callback=geoTest";
7      document.body.appendChild(script);
8    }
```

The condition in line 3 uses the `typeof` operator to check the data type of the `google` object. If the Google Maps library has not been loaded, then the data type is `undefined`; otherwise, the data type is `object`. The remaining statements are executed only if the data type is not `object`—that is, if the library has not yet been loaded. This avoids an unnecessary request for the library if a user clicks Directions, then clicks Setup, and then clicks Directions a second time. Lines 4–7 of the code create a new `script` element, assign the Google Maps library URL as the `src` attribute, and append the new node to the document body. The `script` element `src` value in lines 5–6 includes the `callback` argument, which specifies `geoTest()` as the function to call after the library has loaded.

Programming Concepts | *Asynchronous Callbacks*

The callback argument in the Google Maps library URL is an example of an asynchronous callback. A synchronous callback is a callback that is executed immediately. By contrast, an asynchronous callback waits for something else to happen before running. In this code, the asynchronous callback to the `geoTest()` function isn't executed until the library itself finishes loading from the specified URL. This ensures that the browser loads the Google Maps API objects before executing the `geoTest()` code, which references them.

Your updated `loadDirections()` function should match the following:

```
1   function loadDirections() {
2       document.querySelector("nav ul li:first-of-type").↵
3           className = "";
4       document.querySelector("nav ul li:last-of-type").↵
5           className = "current";
6       document.getElementById("setup").style.display = "none";
7       document.getElementById("location").style.display =↵
8           "block";
9   //   geoTest();
10      // to minimize data use, download map only if needed and↵
11          not already downloaded
12      if (typeof google !== 'object') {
13          var script = document.createElement("script");
14          script.src = "https://maps.googleapis.com/maps/api/js?↵
15              v=3.exp&sensor=true&callback=geoTest";
16          document.body.appendChild(script);
17      }
18  }
```

5. Save your changes to **script.js**, and then refresh or reload **oaktop.htm** in your browser. In a larger web app, you might notice that the page loads more quickly. However, because your app uses a relatively small amount of code, the difference is imperceptible.

6. Click **Directions**, and then if necessary click the **Allow once**, **Share Location**, or similar button. The map loads just as it did previously.

Minifying Files

In a large web app, it's important for developers to remove every unneeded character to reduce the download size as much as possible. One commonly used method is **minifying** files, which removes comments, indents, and line breaks, and tweaks code in other ways to make it smaller.

Note | *Reversing the minifying process by inserting indents and line breaks is known as prettifying.*

As long as you follow the rules and best practices of writing JavaScript, indents and line breaks are part of your code only to make it easier for you and other developers to make sense of it. JavaScript processors, however, do not use these characters, or comments, when parsing your code. When preparing to publish an app, many developers minify their JavaScript code to reduce the file size as much as possible. Although the savings is just a handful of characters in a small app, file size reductions for larger sites can be hundreds of kilobytes. You make the minified version of your code available as part of the published app, but you should keep the nonminified version for use when you make any changes or enhancements to your app, as the minified version is next to impossible for humans to work with.

Next you'll examine a minified file and use an online minifying service to minify your script.js file.

To minify the script.js file:

1. In your editor, open **modernizr.custom.64298.js** from the Chapter folder in the Chapter10 folder included with your data files. This file contains the Modernizr library code that the Oak Top app uses to ensure feature compatibility across different browsers. As Figure 10-15 shows, all the indents and line breaks have been removed from the code, though it does contain one comment.

Figure 10-15: Minified code for the Modernizr library

Source: Aptana Studio 3

2. Close **modernizr.custom.64298.js**, return to **script.js** in your editor, and then save a copy with the name **script.min.js** to the same directory. Including ".min" in the filename is a common way to indicate that a file contains minimized code. Also, because minification removes comments, it's important to keep the original version of a minified file for making future edits. Including .min in the minified filename makes it easy to keep two versions of the file—one minified and one not—and tell them apart by the filename.

3. Select all the contents of the file, and then copy them to the Clipboard.

4. In your browser, open **jscompress.com**. This is a free online JavaScript minifier. Figure 10-16 shows the web page.

Figure 10-16: jscompress.com

Source: jscompress.com.

Note | If jscompress.com *is not available, perform a web search on "free online javascript minifier" to identify another minifier app to use instead.*

5. Click in the **Javascript Code Input** box, paste the contents of the Clipboard, and then click the **COMPRESS JAVASCRIPT** button. As Figure 10-17 shows, the app removes comments, indents, and line breaks and displays the result.

Online Javascript Compression Tool

Copy & Paste Javascript Code	Upload Javascript Files	Output

Compressed Javascript Output

```
"use strict";function setUpPage(){var e=document.querySelectorAll("#room
div");zIndexCounter=e.length+1;for(var t=0;t<e.length;
t++){e[t].style.msTouchAction="none";if(e[t].addEventListener)
{e[t].addEventListener("mousedown",startDrag,false);
e[t].addEventListener("touchstart",startDrag,false);
e[t].addEventListener("mspointerdown",startDrag,false);
e[t].addEventListener("pointerdown",startDrag,false)}else if(e[t].attachEvent)
{e[t].attachEvent("onmousedown",startDrag)}}document.querySelector("nav ul
li:first-
of-type").addEventListener("click",loadSetup,false);document.querySelector("nav ul
li:last-of-type").addEventListener("click",loadDirections,false)}function
startDrag(e){this.style.zIndex=zIndexCounter;zIndexCounter++;
if(e.type!=="mousedown"){e.preventDefault();
this.addEventListener("touchmove",moveDrag,false);
this.addEventListener("mspointermove",moveDrag,false);
this.addEventListener("pointermove",moveDrag,false);
this.addEventListener("touchend",removeTouchListener,false);
```

Figure 10-17: Minified code

Source: jscompress.com.

6. Select the contents of the Compressed Javascript Output box, copy it to the Clipboard, return to **script.min.js** in your editor, delete the existing contents of the file, and then paste the minified code from the Clipboard.

7. Save your changes to **script.min.js**, switch to **oaktop.htm** in your editor, and then edit the `script` element at the bottom of the body section to reference the filename for the minified code, as follows:

```
<script src="script.min.js"></script>
```

8. Save your changes to **oaktop.htm**, refresh or reload **oaktop.htm** in your browser, drag one of the furniture boxes, and then click **Directions**. Even though your JavaScript code is now minified, the app continues to work as it previously did.

Short Quiz 3

1. Why is it useful to test mobile web apps on services that run on a desktop computer?

2. Why is it important to minimize the download size of your mobile web app?

3. What does it mean to minify a file?

Summary

> Touch events focus on responding to a user's finger touches on a touchscreen.

> To ensure that the operating system interface does not respond to events generated when users interact with your app, you use the `preventDefault()` method.

> Pointer events are different than touch events; they aim to handle input from a mouse, finger, or stylus with each event.

> The Geolocation API provides access to a user's latitude and longitude coordinates.

> A number of desktop tools exist for testing mobile web apps virtually.

> It's important to minimize the download size of a mobile web app to reduce download time over slower mobile connections as well as to use as little of a user's data allowance as possible. Two techniques for achieving this are loading scripts responsively and minifying files.

Key Terms

accelerometer—Hardware in a mobile device that detects changes in speed.
API key—A string of characters that you incorporate into any request your code makes using a proprietary API such as the Google Maps API to verify that your use is licensed.
asynchronous callback—A callback that waits for something else to happen before running.
Battery Status API—An API that provides access to properties and methods related to the device battery.
callback—An argument that contains or references executable code.
data transparency—The process of making it clear to users what information your app wants to collect from them and how you intend to use it.
Device Orientation API—An API that provides access to data from specialized hardware in many mobile devices for detecting changes in position and speed.
geocoding— Converting a physical address to a pair of latitude and longitude coordinates.
Geolocation API—An API that provides access to a user's latitude and longitude coordinates.
gesture—A touch interaction for a browser or device activity such as scrolling the page or viewing device notification.
gyroscope—Hardware in a mobile device that detects its orientation in space.
mouse events—Events based on the actions of a mouse or a touchpad.
minifying—A method of reducing the size of a JavaScript file that removes comments, indents, and line breaks, and tweaks code in other ways to make it smaller.

multitouch—A type of touchscreen device that allows for multiple touches on the screen at the same time.

pointer events—A set of events that aims to handle input from a mouse, finger, or stylus with each event.

stylus—A pointing device that looks like a pencil and allows for precise input on a touchscreen.

synchronous callback—A callback that is executed immediately.

touch cascade—The process through which a browser on a touchscreen device responds to a touch by checking for an event handler for multiple events, including some mouse events.

touch events—A set of events for responding to finger touches on a touchscreen.

WebRTC API—An API that enables apps to receive data from a device's camera and microphone, as well as to send and receive audio, video, and other types of data in real time.

Review Questions

1. Which type of events focus on responding to finger touches on a touchscreen?
   a. Mouse events
   b. Touch events
   c. Pointer events
   d. Drag events

2. Which type of events aim to handle input from a mouse, finger, or stylus with each event?
   a. Mouse events
   b. Touch events
   c. Pointer events
   d. Drag events

3. Mobile devices use touch to perform browser and device interactions, known as _____, for activities such as scrolling the page.
   a. touches
   b. points
   c. clicks
   d. gestures

4. _____ devices allow for multiple touches on the screen at the same time.
   a. Pointer
   b. Desktop
   c. Touchpad
   d. Multitouch

5. In the touch events model, which of the following is an array containing the coordinates of all touches on the current element?
   a. `touches`
   b. `targetTouches`
   c. `changedTouches`
   d. `touchesXY`

6. You can access methods of the Geolocation API using the `geolocation` property of the _____ object.
   a. `Window`
   b. `Screen`
   c. `Navigator`
   d. `Document`

7. The *success* and *fail* arguments of the `getCurrentPosition()` method, which are executable code, are examples of _____.
   a. callbacks
   b. properties
   c. API keys
   d. minifiers

8. Which option property do you add to a `getCurrentPosition()` request to specify a length of time to wait before cancelling the request?
   a. `enableHighAccuracy`
   b. `timeout`
   c. `maximumAge`
   d. `coords`

9. Converting a physical address to a pair of latitude and longitude coordinates is known as _____.
   a. minifying
   b. geolocation
   c. a callback
   d. geocoding

10. If your browser does not ask whether you want to share your location information while testing an app that uses geolocation, you may need to _____.
    a. implement touch events
    b. implement pointer events
    c. clear your saved geolocation preferences
    d. minify your files

11. Which API provides access to properties and methods related to the device battery?
    a. Geolocation API
    b. Battery Status API
    c. Device Orientation API
    d. WebRTC API

12. Which API provides access to data from a device's gyroscope and accelerometer?
    a. Geolocation API
    b. Battery Status API
    c. Device Orientation API
    d. WebRTC API

13. Which API enables apps to receive data from a device's camera and microphone, as well as to send and receive audio, video, and other types of data in real time?
    a. Geolocation API
    b. Battery Status API
    c. Device Orientation API
    d. WebRTC API

14. A(n) _____ waits for something else to happen before running.
    a. minifier
    b. prettifier
    c. asynchronous callback
    d. synchronous callback

15. _____ removes comments, indents, and line breaks, and tweaks code in other ways to make it smaller.
    a. Minifying files
    b. Responsively loading scripts
    c. Implementing the Geolocation API
    d. Implementing touch events

16. What is a touch cascade?

17. Why is it useful to add a timeout to a `getCurrentLocation()` request using the `setTimeout()` method of the `Window` object?

18. Explain the roles of the Geolocation API and the Google Maps API in displaying a map showing a user's current position in your app.

19. What is a gyroscope? What is an accelerometer? Explain how data from these devices can be useful in a web app.

20. Explain how to load a script responsively.

Hands-On Projects

Hands-On Project 10-1

In this project, you'll add support for touch events to a puzzle app in which users drag tiles to form a picture.

1. In your text editor, open the **script.js** file from the HandsOnProject10-1 folder in the Chapter10 folder, add your name and today's date where indicated in the comment section, and then save the file.

2. In the `setUpPage()` function, below the statement that sets an event listener for the `mousedown` event, enter the following statement:

```
puzzlePieces[i].addEventListener("touchstart", startDrag, ↵
    false);
```

3. Within the `startDrag()` function, after the statement `event.preventDefault()`, add an `if` statement that checks if `event.type` is not equal to `mousedown`, and if so executes the following two statements:

```
this.addEventListener("touchmove", moveDrag, false);
this.addEventListener("touchend", removeTouchListener, false);
```

4. Below the code you entered in the previous step, enclose the code creating event listeners for the `mousemove` and `mouseup` events in an `else` statement. Your `if/else` statement should match the following:

```
1  if (event.type !== "mousedown") {
2      this.addEventListener("touchmove", moveDrag, false);
3      this.addEventListener("touchend", removeTouchListener, ↵
4          false);
5  } else {
6      this.addEventListener("mousemove", moveDrag, false);
7      this.addEventListener("mouseup", removeDragListener, ↵
8          false);
9  }
```

5. Within the `getCoords()` function, below the statement `var coords = []`, add an `if` statement that checks both `event.targetTouches` and `event.targetTouches` `.length` for truthy values, and if they are present, executes the following statements:

```
var thisTouch = event.targetTouches[0];
coords[0] = thisTouch.clientX;
coords[1] = thisTouch.clientY;
```

6. Below the code you entered in the previous step, enclose the statements assigning values to `coords[0]` and `coords[1]` in an `else` statement. Your `if/else` statement should match the following:

```
1   if (event.targetTouches && event.targetTouches.length) {
2       var thisTouch = event.targetTouches[0];
3       coords[0] = thisTouch.clientX;
4       coords[1] = thisTouch.clientY;
5   } else {
6       coords[0] = event.clientX;
7       coords[1] = event.clientY;
8   }
```

7. Below the `removeDragListener()` function, add the following `removeTouchListener()` function:

```
1   // remove touch event listeners when dragging ends
2   function removeTouchListener() {
3       this.removeEventListener("touchmove", moveDrag, false);
4       this.removeEventListener("touchend", removeTouchListener, ↵
5           false);
6   }
```

8. Save your changes to **script.js**, open **index.htm** in a desktop browser, and then drag one of the tiles at the bottom to the grid to verify that mouse events still work. Figure 10-18 shows the app in a desktop browser.

Figure 10-18: index.htm in a desktop browser

© Jason Bucy

9. Open **index.htm** in a mobile browser that uses touch events, such as Safari Mobile or Chrome Mobile, and then drag one of the tiles at the bottom to the grid to verify that touch events now work. Figure 10-19 shows the app in a handheld browser. Note that if you're using a touch device running Windows 8, the page will scroll at the same time that the tiles move. If you complete Hands-on Project 10-2, you'll enhance the app to make it work better on these devices.

Drag the tiles to form the picture

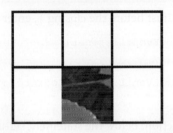

Figure 10-19: index.htm in a handheld browser

Hands-On Project 10-2

In this project, you'll enhance the app from Hands-on Project 10-2 to support pointer events.

1. In the file manager for your operating system, copy the completed contents of the HandsOnProject10-1 folder to the HandsOnProject10-2 folder.

2. In your text editor, open the **script.js** file from the HandsOnProject10-2 folder, change "Hands-on Project 10-1" to **Hands-on Project 10-2** in the comment section, and then save your changes.

3. In the **script.js** file, in the `setUpPage()` function, within the `for` statement, just before the `if` statement, add the following statements to disable interface gestures for IE versions 10 and higher:

    ```
    // disable IE10+ interface gestures
    puzzlePieces[i].style.msTouchAction = "none";
    puzzlePieces[i].style.touchAction = "none";
    ```

4. Within the `if` statement, just before the closing `}`, enter the following statements:

    ```
    1   puzzlePieces[i].addEventListener("mspointerdown", startDrag, ↵
    2       false);
    3   puzzlePieces[i].addEventListener("pointerdown", startDrag, ↵
    4       false);
    ```

5. In the `startDrag()` function, below the statement setting an event listener for the `touchmove` event, add the following statements:

    ```
    this.addEventListener("mspointermove", moveDrag, false);
    this.addEventListener("pointermove", moveDrag, false);
    ```

6. In the `startDrag()` function, below the statement setting an event listener for the `touchend` event, add the following statements:

    ```
    1   this.addEventListener("mspointerup", removeTouchListener, ↵
    2       false);
    3   this.addEventListener("pointerup", removeTouchListener, ↵
    4       false);
    ```

7. In the `removeTouchListener()` function, below the statement removing an event listener for the `touchmove` event, add the following statements:

    ```
    this.removeEventListener("mspointermove", moveDrag, false);
    this.removeEventListener("pointermove", moveDrag, false);
    ```

8. In the `removeTouchListener()` function, below the statement removing an event listener for the `touchend` event, add the following statements:

```
1   this.removeEventListener("mspointerup", removeTouchListener, ↵
2       false);
3   this.removeEventListener("pointerup", removeTouchListener, ↵
4       false);
```

9. Open **index.htm** in a browser that uses pointer events, such as Internet Explorer version 10 or later on a touchscreen device, and then drag one of the tiles at the bottom to the grid to verify that pointer events now work.

Hands-On Project 10-3

In this project, you'll add functionality to an app to get the user's current position and display it on a map.

1. In your text editor, open the **index.htm** file from the HandsOnProject10-3 folder, add your name and today's date where indicated in the comment section, and then save the file. Repeat for **script.js**.

2. In the **script.js** file, enter code to create a function with the name `createMap()`. Add a parameter named `position` to the function declaration. Within the function:
   a. Declare variables named `Lat` and `Lng`.
   b. Set the value of `Lat` to the `latitude` value of the `coords` property of the `position` argument, and set `Lng` to the corresponding `longitude` value.
   c. Declare a variable named `mapOptions`, and set its value to an object containing the following properties:

   ```
   center: new google.maps.LatLng(Lat, Lng),
   zoom: 10
   ```

   d. Declare a variable named `map`, and set its value to the following:

   ```
   new google.maps.Map(document.getElementById("map"), ↵
       mapOptions)
   ```

3. Below the `createMap()` function, declare a new function named `fail()`. The function should contain a single statement that sets the `innerHTML` value of the element with the `id` value `map` to the string **Unable to access your current location**.

4. Below the `use strict` statement, declare a new function named `geoTest()`. It should contain an `if/else` statement that checks the value of the `navigator.geolocation` property. If the value is truthy, the function should call the `getCurrentPosition()` method, running the `createMap()` function on success

or the `fail()` function on failure. If the `navigator.geolocation` value is falsy, the function should call the `fail()` function.

5. Below the use strict statement, define a global variable named `waitForUser`. Within the `geoTest()` function, set the value of `waitForUser` to a timeout that waits 10 seconds and then calls the `fail()` function. Within the `createMap()` function, add a statement that clears the `waitForUser` timeout.

6. Save your changes to the **script.js** file, return to the **index.htm** file in your editor, and then just above the existing script element at the bottom of the body section, add the following script element for the Google Maps API:

    ```
    <script src="https://maps.googleapis.com/maps/api/js?↵
        v=3.exp&sensor=true&callback=geoTest"></script>
    ```

7. Save your changes to the **index.htm** file, open the **index.htm** file in your browser, allow your app to access your current position, and verify that a map is displayed showing your current location, as shown in Figure 10-20. (*Note*: Your location will not necessarily match the one shown in Figure 10-20.) Repeat the test, denying permission to access your location, and verify that the failure message you specified is displayed instead. Note that the app includes buttons with the names of three cities, which you'll use to enhance the app in a later project.

Figure 10-20: Map displaying current location
Source: Google.

Hands-On Project 10-4

In this project, you'll enhance the app you worked on in Hands-on Project 10-3 with timeouts. You'll also geocode the three cities listed at the top of the screen.

1. In the file manager for your operating system, copy the completed contents of the HandsOnProject10-3 folder to the HandsOnProject10-4 folder.

2. In your text editor, open the **index.htm** file from the HandsOnProject10-4 folder, change "Hands-on Project 10-3" to "Hands-on Project 10-4" in the comment section, in the `title` element, and in the `h1` element, and then save your changes.

3. Open the **script.js** file, and then in the comment section, change "Hands-on Project 10-3" to **Hands-on Project 10-4**.

4. In the **script.js** file, within the `geoTest()` function, add a 10-second timeout to the `getCurrentPosition()` call.

5. Below the `use strict` statement, declare a global variable named `waitForUser`.

6. At the start of the `geoTest()` function, use the `waitForUser` variable to set a 10-second timeout using the `setTimeout()` method. The timeout should call the `fail()` function.

7. In the `createMap()` function, just after the declaration of the `Lat` and `Lng` variables, add a statement that clears the `waitForUser` timeout.

8. Save your changes to script.js, and then in your browser open *maps.google.com* or another geocoding service.

9. Geocode a point in downtown Beijing, China, and then save the coordinates in the **script.js** file in a comment in the `createMap()` function. Repeat for a point in downtown Paris, France, and a point in downtown Rio de Janeiro, Brazil.

10. Save your changes to the **script.js** file.

Hands-On Project 10-5

In this project, you'll further enhance the app you've worked on in Hands-on Projects 10-3 and 10-4. You'll incorporate code that displays a map of each city listed at the top of the screen when you click its button.

1. In the file manager for your operating system, copy the completed contents of the HandsOnProject10-4 folder to the HandsOnProject10-5 folder.

2. In your text editor, open the **index.htm** file from the HandsOnProject10-5 folder, change "Hands-on Project 10-4" to "Hands-on Project 10-5" in the comment section, in the `title` element, and in the `h1` element, and then save your changes.

3. Open the **script.js** file, and then in the comment section, change "Hands-on Project 10-4" to **Hands-on Project 10-5**.

4. In the **script.js** file, in the `createMap()` function, below the `clearTimeout()` statement, enclose the two statements assigning values to the `Lat` and `Lng` variables within an `if` statement that checks the `coords` property of the `position` parameter for a truthy value. After the closing `}` for the `if` statement, add an `else` clause that does the following:
   a. Declares a `city` variable and sets its value to `this.innerHTML`.
   b. Checks if the value of `city` is "Beijing" and if so, sets the values of `Lat` and `Lng` to the geocoding results for Beijing that you stored in a comment.
   c. Repeats Step b for "Paris" and "Rio de Janeiro".
   d. Sets the `innerHTML` value of the element with the `id` value `caption` to the value of the `city` variable.

5. At the top of the document, just below the global variable declaration, add a new function named `setUpPage()`. Within the function, add code to do the following:
   a. Declare a variable named `buttons` that references all the `div` elements within the element with the `id` value `cities`.
   b. For each element referenced by the `buttons` variable, add an event listener that responds to the `click` event and calls the `createMap()` function.

6. At the bottom of the document, add an event listener that calls the `setUpPage()` function when the app finishes loading in a browser.

7. Save your changes to the **script.js** file, open the **index.htm** file in your browser, and then allow your browser to access your location if necessary. Verify that a map showing your current location is still displayed. Then click each of the three buttons at the top of the app, and verify that each one displays a map showing that city and changes the caption text above the map to the name of the city displayed, as shown in Figure 10-21.

Figure 10-21: Caption displaying name of city
Source: Google.

Case Projects

Individual Case Project

In your individual web site, enhance your existing page about browser security to show users their current location on a map. Note that you must specify a height and width using CSS for the element in which you display the map; these dimensions can be any size you choose. Also enhance the page to display the user's latitude, longitude, and altitude, with a label for each value.

Group Case Project

Divide into two or three subgroups, with each group taking responsibility for downloading, installing, and becoming familiar with the testing tool for a touchscreen or mobile operating system: Google Android, Apple iOS, and, optionally, Microsoft Windows Phone. Note that the testing tools for Apple iOS can be installed only on an Apple Mac computer, so ensure that the subgroup responsible for this OS includes at least one member with the necessary hardware.

In your group, download your group's tool using the appropriate URL:

> **Android**: *https://developer.android.com/sdk/index.html*
> **iOS**: *https://developer.apple.com/xcode/downloads/*

> **Windows Phone**: *http://www.visualstudio.com/en-us/downloads#d-express-windows-8* (Visual Studio Express for Windows Phone)

Read the documentation at the same URL or included with the tool to learn how to open and test a web app using the tool. Open your Group Case Project web app in your subgroup's tool, and then test the following aspects of your app:

> Appearance on at least three virtual devices with different screen sizes

> Functionality of your navigation interface

> Functionality of your form

Note the results of each test, even if the result is that the app performs the same as on a desktop computer.

Share your results with the other subgroups, and then as a group create a report describing the following:

> Areas where your app functioned as you expected in each OS

> Areas where your app functioned unexpectedly in each OS

> Aspects of the app that you would have liked to test in each tool, but may have been unable to

> At least two advantages and two disadvantages of each tool

C H A P T E R

UPDATING WEB PAGES WITH AJAX

When you complete this chapter, you will be able to:

> Describe the steps involved in using Ajax to update data

> Create an HTTP request and interpret an HTTP response

> Request and receive server data using the `XMLHttpRequest` object

> Process data received from a web service and add it to the DOM

> Update app data using JSON-P

DHTML makes web pages dynamic by combining JavaScript, HTML, CSS, and the Document Object Model (DOM). DHTML does a great job of making web pages more dynamic and will continue to be a vital technique in web page development. The fact that DHTML runs entirely within a user's web browser was once considered an advantage because it made server data and other external resources unnecessary. However, as the Internet matured and broadband access became commonplace, developers began demanding a way to make their web pages interact more dynamically with a web server. For example, consider a browser's request for a web page. In response, the web server returns the requested page. If the user wants to refresh the web page, the web server returns the entire page again—not just the changed portions of the page. For web page data that must always be up to date, such as stock prices, continuously reloading the entire page can be too slow, even at broadband speeds. Additionally, many mobile users have limits on the amount of data they can use. One solution is to use Ajax, which you'll learn about in this chapter.

Introduction to Ajax

Ajax is a technique that allows web pages displayed on a client computer to quickly interact and exchange data with a web server without reloading the entire page. Ajax relies on a client-side programming language, such as JavaScript, and a data interchange format, such as JSON or XML. When the technique was first used, it was practical only with JavaScript and XML, and was originally given the name AJAX, which stood for Asynchronous JavaScript and XML. Today, the technique is used more commonly with JSON than with XML as a data format, and can also be used with other programming languages besides JavaScript. For these reasons, the term "Ajax," rather than the acronym "AJAX," is used to describe the general technique.

It's important to note that the first developers to use Ajax did not invent anything new. Rather, they improved web page interactivity by combining languages and technologies with the key component of Ajax, the XMLHttpRequest object, which is available in modern web browsers. The **XMLHttpRequest object**—commonly referred to as the **XHR object**—uses HTTP to exchange data between a client computer and a web server. Unlike standard HTTP requests, which usually replace the entire page in a web browser, the XMLHttpRequest object can be used to request and receive data without reloading a web page. By combining the XMLHttpRequest object with DHTML techniques, you can update and modify individual portions of your web page with data received from a web server.

Google was one of the first commercial websites to implement an Ajax application—its Google Suggest search functionality. As you type a search item in the Google website, Google Suggest lists additional search suggestions based on the text you type. For example, if you type "solar", search suggestions like those shown in Figure 11-1 appear.

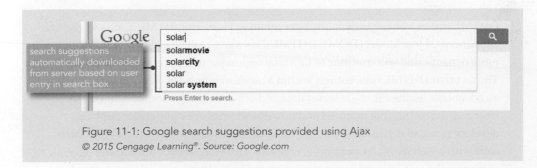

Figure 11-1: Google search suggestions provided using Ajax
© 2015 Cengage Learning®. Source: Google.com

The important thing to understand is that as you type each letter, JavaScript code uses the XMLHttpRequest object to send the string in the text box to the Google server, which attempts to match the typed characters with a list of suggestions. The Google server then returns the suggestions to the client computer (without reloading the web page), and JavaScript code populates the suggestion list with the response text.

Figures 11-2 and 11-3 illustrate the difference between a standard HTTP request, which returns an entire web document, and an HTTP request with the XMLHttpRequest object, which returns data without reloading the current page.

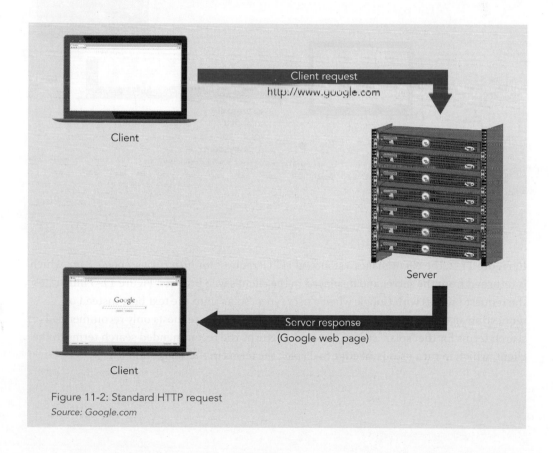

Figure 11-2: Standard HTTP request
Source: Google.com

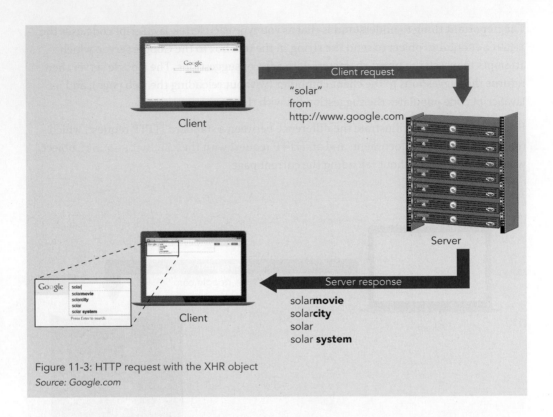

Figure 11-3: HTTP request with the XHR object

Source: Google.com

In Figure 11-2, the client makes a standard HTTP request for *http://www.google.com*, which is returned from the server and displayed in the client's web browser. Figure 11-3 illustrates the request process with Google when a user types "solar" into the text box. Instead of requesting an entire web page, the XMLHttpRequest object requests only recommended search terms for the "solar" string. The server returns the recommended search terms to the client, which in turn uses JavaScript to display the terms in the suggestion list.

In this chapter, you'll enhance a web app for Whole Spectrum Energy Solutions, based in Tucson, Arizona. The company sells and installs products that generate energy from sources like wind and solar power. To make potential customers aware of the amount of solar energy at their disposal, the company wants the web app to display the amount of solar power available in the next week at a location specified by the user. To accomplish this, you need to use Ajax to access weather forecast information. Figure 11-4 shows the final version of the app in a desktop browser, and Figure 11-5 shows the app in a mobile browser.

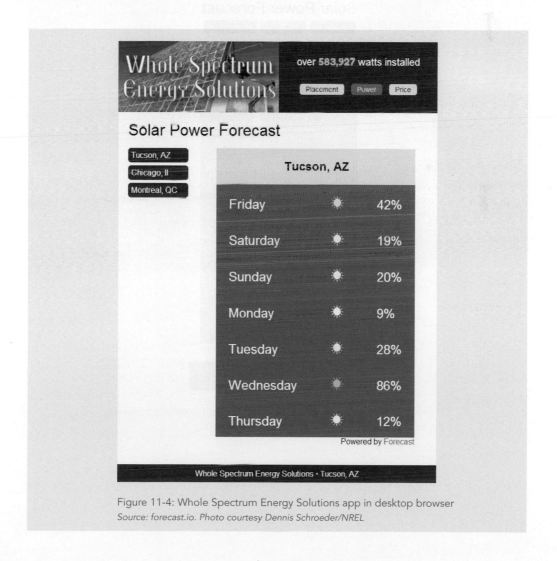

Figure 11-4: Whole Spectrum Energy Solutions app in desktop browser
Source: forecast.io. Photo courtesy Dennis Schroeder/NREL

Figure 11-5: Whole Spectrum Energy Solutions app in mobile browser

Source: forecast.io. Photo courtesy Dennis Schroeder/NREL

Notice that the app includes buttons for three specific locations: Tucson, AZ; Chicago, IL; and Montreal, QC. The app design calls for eventually integrating geolocation to automatically show forecast data for the user's current location. For testing purposes while you're setting up Ajax, however, the app will default to showing the forecast for Tucson, AZ, when it loads; you can then click buttons to load data for the other two cities.

Understanding the Limitations of Ajax

Recall from Chapter 9 that the same-origin policy restricts how JavaScript code in one tab (or window or frame) accesses a web page in another tab on a client computer. For tabs to view and modify the elements and properties of documents displayed in other tabs, they must use the same protocol (such as HTTP) and exist on the same web server. Historically, an Ajax app that used JavaScript could not use the XMLHttpRequest object to directly access content on another domain's server; the data requested with the XMLHttpRequest object had to be located on the web server where the JavaScript program is running. In other words, you could not directly bypass your own web server and grab data off someone else's web server.

In recent years, though, web servers and browsers have implemented changes to the way they handle HTTP requests that relax this restriction. In fact, current versions of all modern browsers can directly access data on third-party servers as long as the servers themselves support third-party requests. However, many web servers do not support third-party requests. In addition, Internet Explorer 8 and 9, as well as Android browser version 2.3 and earlier, do not support requests for third-party data even if the target server allows such requests.

The same-origin policy applies only to JavaScript and not to other programs running on a web server. This means that you can use a server-side script as a proxy to access data from another domain. In computer terms, a **proxy** is a server that acts for or performs requests for other clients and servers. The server-side proxy script can return the data to the client computer as it is requested with the XMLHttpRequest object. Using a proxy remains a common technique for working around the same-origin policy to access third-party content. Because you want to ensure that the Whole Spectrum Energy Solutions app works for users of IE8 and 9, as well as Android browser 2.3, you'll implement an XMLHttpRequest object in your app that uses a proxy.

Accessing Content on a Separate Domain

The purpose of the same-origin policy is to prevent malicious scripts from modifying the content of other windows, tabs, and frames, and to prevent the theft of private browser information and information displayed on secure web pages. However, the ability of one web server to access web pages and data on another web server is the foundation of the World Wide Web. Although you should never attempt to pass off content from another website as your own, there are legitimate reasons why you would use a server-side script to access data from another domain. One common use is to display data provided by a web service, which is a data source made available on one domain for use on other domains across the web. Web services do not contain graphical user interfaces or even command-line interfaces. Instead, they simply provide services and data in response to requests that use the methods and properties of their APIs; it is up to the client accessing a web service to provide an implementation for a program that calls the web service.

Programming Concepts | *Widgets*

Some organizations that offer web services want their content to be available as widely as possible across the web. Rather than relying on programmers to implement an API to access and display their content, these organizations offer prepackaged code known as widgets that enable even users with a minimal understanding of HTML and CSS to add content from the service to a web document. Social networks such as Twitter enable users to share content by generating widget code that they can paste into another web document. Widgets often contain code that uses Ajax to fetch and update content from the service, without requiring users to write the code themselves.

One example of a web service is a service that provides real-time prices of commodities such as crude oil, natural gas, gold, or silver. You could incorporate calls to this service in your own app, which could periodically call methods of the web service that return the most recent trading prices for the commodities. When you incorporate data from a web service into an app that runs in a browser, you need to know only which method of the web service to call for each type of commodity, such as a `getSilverPrice()` method that returns the current price of silver. There are many potential uses of the data from any given web service; it is up to you to store or display the data in your web app. In the case of Ajax, you might pass the data to a JavaScript program running on a client.

For the Whole Spectrum Energy Solutions app, you'll request and use data from forecast.io, a web service that provides real-time weather data, including a forecast, for a specified location. A forecast.io request has the following format:

```
https://api.forecast.io/forecast/apikey/latitude,longitude
```

The *apikey* term represents an API key, which is a unique identifier assigned by the service to each person or organization that wants to access the service. Unlike Google Maps, which allows a limited number of requests per day without an API key, all forecast.io requests must include an API key.

The *latitude* and *longitude* terms represent latitude and longitude values provided as positive or negative floating-point numbers.

The data returned by forecast.io is a string representation of a JSON object. Recall that JSON (JavaScript Object Notation) represents data using the same syntax used to represent the contents of JavaScript objects. You can use the JSON.parse() method to convert the returned string to a JavaScript object, and then you can simply reference the property values within the object and add them as content using the DHTML methods you've used in previous chapters.

Your web app will rely on a server-side script as a proxy to retrieve weather information from forecast.io. This script is written in PHP, which is a programming language specifically designed to run on web servers. Your PHP proxy script executes when it is passed latitude and longitude values with the XMLHttpRequest object. After the PHP script retrieves the weather information for the specified coordinates, it returns the data to the JavaScript code that called it.

The Whole Spectrum Energy Solutions app will rely on the following PHP code to retrieve data from the forecast.io service. This code downloads a JSON file from forecast.io that contains the weather data, and assigns the file to the variable name $WeatherSource. Then the script forwards the string to the client with a readfile statement, which is similar to JavaScript's document.write() statement. The focus of this book is JavaScript programming, not PHP programming, so you will not analyze the following code any further. However, PHP shares many similarities with JavaScript, so you may be able to figure out some statements in the following code on your own.

```
1   <?php
2   $WeatherSource = "https://api.forecast.io/forecast/apikey/"↵
3       . $_GET["lat"] . "," . $_GET["lng"];
4   header("Content-Type: application/json");
5   header("Cache-Control: no-cache");
6   readfile($WeatherSource);
7   ?>
```

Given the JavaScript skills you have learned in this book, and with a little additional study, you can easily learn PHP or any other server-side language. For now, keep in mind that any PHP scripts you see in this chapter are server-side scripting programs; they serve as a counterpoint to the JavaScript programs you've created in this book, which are client-side scripting programs. In fact, client-side and server-side scripting languages share much of the same syntax and functionality.

Skills at Work | *Web Developer Job Titles and Roles*

Web developers who work for large organizations often have a specific focus in both their job skills and responsibilities. The arena of web development can be divided up in several different ways, but one of the most common is between developers who focus on client-side code and those who work on the server. A web developer who works primarily with HTML, CSS, and client-side JavaScript is known as a front-end developer. A developer who works mainly with server-side languages and libraries such as PHP, SQL, and node.js, on the other hand, is known as a back-end developer. Some web developers have skills and responsibilities for both client-side and server-side code; these developers are known as full-stack developers. Even if your goal is a job as a front-end developer, it's important that you build at least basic familiarity and skill with some widely used server-side languages, because both front-end and back-end developers must understand in general how each other's code works and how the code from each side works together.

Running Ajax from a Web Server

Throughout this book, you have opened web pages directly from your local computer or network with your web browser. However, in this chapter, you will instead open files from a web server. Opening a local file in a web browser requires the use of the `file:///` protocol. Because Ajax relies on the `XMLHttpRequest` object to retrieve data, you must open your Ajax files from a web server with the HTTP (`http://`) or HTTPS (`https://`) protocol. You can turn a computer into a web server by installing web server software on it. Popular web server software in use today includes Apache HTTP Server (typically referred to as Apache), Nginx (pronounced "engine-ex"), and Microsoft Internet Information Services (IIS).

Next, you'll move your data files onto your web server and you'll examine the HTML and JavaScript files for the Whole Spectrum Energy Solutions app.

To move and examine the data files:

1. If necessary, follow the instructions in Appendix A, "Building a Web Development Environment," to install and configure a web server and PHP.

2. In the file manager for your operating system, navigate to the location where you store your data files, click the **Chapter11** folder to select it, and then press **Ctrl** + **C** (Win) or **command** + **C** (Mac) to copy the folder.

3. While still in your file manager, navigate to the location where your web server is installed, click the name of the folder that contains publicly accessible files, and then press **Ctrl** + **V** (Win) or **command** + **V** (Mac) to paste a copy of the Chapter11 folder.

Note | *In Apache, the default folder for HTML content is called* htdocs. *In Nginx, the folder name is* html. *For IIS, the default folder is* wwwroot.

4. In your text editor, open the **solar.htm** and **script.js** files from the Chapter folder in the copy of the Chapter11 folder that you just created on your web server.

Note | *If you're using a Mac and get the error message "Access Forbidden" in your browser when trying to open a file from your web server, switch to Finder, open the Applications folder, open the Utilties folder, and then double-click the Terminal application to open it. In Terminal, type*

```
chmod -R 777 /Applications/XAMPP/htdocs
```

and then press return. Close Terminal and then repeat Step 4.

Caution | *For the rest of this chapter, it's important that you work with the copy of the Chapter11 folder on your web server and not the original copy stored in the location of your data files. No changes you make in the original data files will be reflected in the browser when you open files through your server.*

5. In the comment section of each file, enter your name and today's date in the appropriate places, and then save your changes.

6. In the **solar.htm** file, examine the body section. Notice that the file includes a mostly empty table. You'll write JavaScript to place some of the data returned by forecast.io in the empty table cells.

7. In the **script.js** file, examine the contents. The file declares two global variables, creates a function named `getWeather()`, and creates event listeners. The event listeners call the `getWeather()` function when a user clicks one of the three location buttons, as well as when the page loads. The `getWeather()` function checks if a button was clicked, and if so, uses the button text as the value of the `selectedCity` variable. It then sets values for the `latitude` and `longitude` local variables based on the `selectedCity` value. You'll complete this function to submit an Ajax request to forecast.io using the `latitude` and `longitude` values to get weather forecast data for the relevant city.

Short Quiz 1

1. Name two data formats that can be used with Ajax.

2. What does the `XMLHttpRequest` object do?

3. Explain the relationship between a proxy and JavaScript's same-origin policy when creating an Ajax request.

Working with HTTP

Using Ajax to update data involves the following four steps:

1. Instantiate an `XMLHttpRequest` object for the web browser where the script will run.

2. Use the `XMLHttpRequest` object to send a request to the server.

3. Receive the response from the server containing the requested data.

4. Process the data returned from the server, and incorporate the data into the app.

Figure 11-6 illustrates the general steps involved in using Ajax to update data.

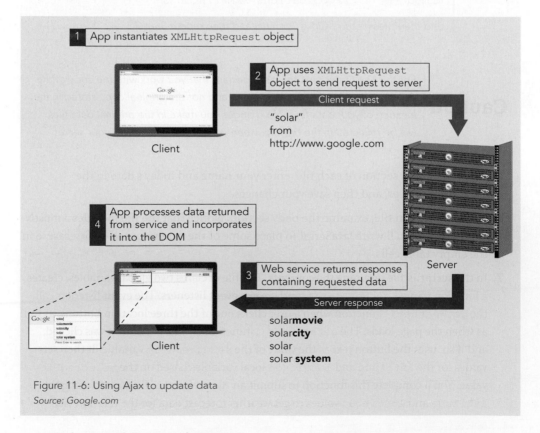

Figure 11-6: Using Ajax to update data

Source: Google.com

Figure 11-7 illustrates the use of Ajax with a proxy server.

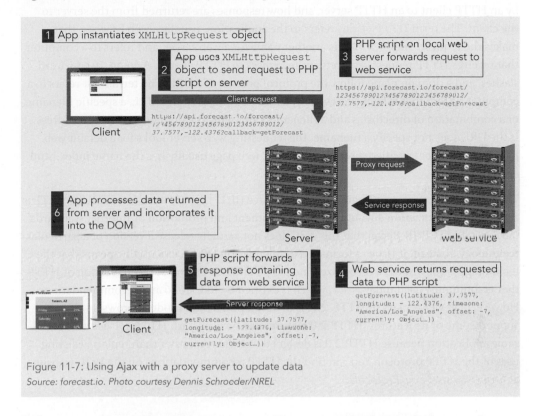

Figure 11-7: Using Ajax with a proxy server to update data
Source: forecast.io. Photo courtesy Dennis Schroeder/NREL

Before you start using the XMLHttpRequest object, you need to know a little more about HTTP to understand how Ajax exchanges data between client computers and web servers.

When discussing HTTP, it's helpful to start by reviewing basic terminology. As you know, when a user attempts to access a web page, either by entering its URL in a browser's Address box or clicking a link, the user's browser asks a web server for the web page. This process is known as a request. The web server's reply (which might consist of the requested web page or a message about it) is known as the response. Every web page is identified by a unique address called the Uniform Resource Locator, or URL. A URL consists of two basic parts: a protocol (usually HTTP) and either the domain name for a web server or a web server's Internet Protocol address.

> **Note** An Internet Protocol address, or IP address, is another way to uniquely identify computers or devices connected to the Internet. An IP address consists of four groups of numbers separated by periods, such as 74.125.224.72. Each Internet domain name is associated with one or more unique IP addresses.

Hypertext Transfer Protocol (HTTP) is a set of rules that defines how requests are made by an HTTP client to an HTTP server, and how responses are returned from the server to the client. The term HTTP client refers to the application, usually a web browser, that makes the request. HTTP server is another name for a web server, and refers to a computer that receives HTTP requests and returns responses to HTTP clients. A colon, two forward slashes, and a domain name follow the protocol portion of a URL. The term host refers to a computer system that is being accessed by a remote computer. In a URL, a specific filename, or a combination of directories and a filename, can follow the domain name or IP address. If the URL does not specify a filename, the requesting web server looks for a default web page in the root or specified directory. A default web page usually has the name index.html or default.html.

The W3C and the Internet Engineering Task Force (IETF) jointly develop HTTP. The IETF is a volunteer organization devoted to the development and promotion of Internet standards, most notably TCP/IP. Recall that the W3C does not actually release a version of a particular technology. Instead, it issues a formal recommendation, which essentially means that the technology is (or will be) a recognized industry standard. The most recent version of HTTP that is commonly used today is 1.1, which is defined by RFC 2616 and recommendations. However, a newer version of HTTP, 2.0, is in development and modern browsers already support some of its features. HTTP 2.0 features can be used with HTTP 1.1 features in the same application because HTTP 2.0 is designed to enhance, rather than replace, existing uses of the HTTP protocol. You can find the HTTP recommendations on the W3C website at *http://www.w3.org/Protocols*.

> **Note**
>
> Although HTTP is probably the most widely used protocol on the Internet, it is not the only one. HTTP is a component of Transmission Control Protocol/Internet Protocol (TCP/IP), a large collection of communication protocols used on the Internet. Other common protocols include Hypertext Transfer Protocol Secure (HTTPS), which provides secure Internet connections that are used in web-based financial transactions and other types of communication that require security and privacy; and Internet Message Access Protocol (IMAP), which is used for storing and accessing email messages.

Understanding HTTP Messages

Most people who use the web don't realize what is going on behind the scenes when it comes to requesting a web page and receiving a response from a web server. HTTP client requests and server responses are both known as HTTP messages. When you submit a request for a web page, the HTTP client opens a connection to the server and submits a request message.

The web server then returns a response message that is appropriate to the type of request. The request and response messages are in the following format:

```
Start line (request method or status returned)
Header lines (zero or more)
Blank line
Message body (optional)
```

The specific contents of each line depend on whether it is part of a request or response message. The first line either identifies the method (such as GET or POST) for requests or the status returned for a response. Following the first line, each message can include zero or more lines containing headers, which define information about the request or response message and the contents of the message body. The RFC 2616 recommendation defines 47 HTTP 1.1 headers, which are categorized as generic headers, which can be used in request or response messages, or headers that are specific to a request, a response, or the message body. The format for using a header is

```
header: value
```

For example, the following lines define two generic headers that can be used in either request or response messages, Connection and Date:

```
Connection: close
Date: Wed, 27 June 2018 18:32:07 GMT
```

The Connection header specifies that the HTTP connection should close after the web client receives a response from the web server. The Date header identifies the origination date and time of the message in Greenwich Mean Time.

One generic header that requires special mention for Ajax applications is the Cache-Control header, which specifies how a web browser should cache any server content it receives. Caching refers to the temporary storage of data for faster access. Most web browsers try to reduce the amount of data that needs to be retrieved from a server by caching retrieved data on a local computer. If caching is enabled in a web browser, the browser will attempt to locate any necessary data in its cache before making a request from a web server. While this technique improves web browser performance, it goes against the reason for using Ajax, which is to dynamically update portions of a web page with the most recent data from a server. For this reason, you should always include the Cache-Control header when creating an Ajax connection, and you should assign it a value of no-cache, as follows:

```
Cache-Control: no-cache
```

A blank line always follows the last header line. Optionally, a message body can follow the blank line in the messages. In most cases, the message body contains form data for POST requests or some type of document (such as a web page or XML page) or other type of content (such as an image file) that is returned with a server response. However, message bodies are not required for either request or response messages. For example, with a GET request, no message body is necessary because any form data that is part of the request is appended to the URL. Response messages are also not required to include a message body. This may seem strange—if a server doesn't return a web page, then what is returned? What's the point in sending a request to a web server if it doesn't return anything? Although GET and POST requests are by far the two most common types of HTTP requests, five other methods can be used with an HTTP request: HEAD, DELETE, OPTIONS, PUT, and TRACE. Most of these methods are rarely used. However, the HEAD method is usually used for returning information about a document, but not the document itself. For example, you may use the HEAD method to determine the last modification date of a web page before requesting it from the web server.

The browser tools that are part of all modern browsers include network tools that enable you to examine the HTTP headers associated with a web document and its related files, such as CSS and JavaScript files. Next you'll open the solar.htm file in a browser and you'll examine the method and other information associated with each of the document's HTTP requests.

To use browser tools to examine the HTTP requests for the solar.htm document:

1. Open a browser, then, in the Address box type
   http://localhost/Chapter11/Chapter/solar.htm, and then press **Enter**. The browser opens the Whole Spectrum Energy Solutions app from your local web server. The document displays everything except the solar forecast information, which you'll add later in the chapter.

2. Open the developer tools for your browser, and then click the **Network** button. The Network tools show details about each network request or response related to the current document. The Network tools capture data only when they're open, so the list of requests is currently empty.

3. If you're using Internet Explorer, press **F5** to enable network traffic capturing.

4. Refresh or reload the document. As Figure 11-8 shows, each browser displays a list of HTTP requests. Notice that each request lists the method, which is GET for all requests related to solar.htm.

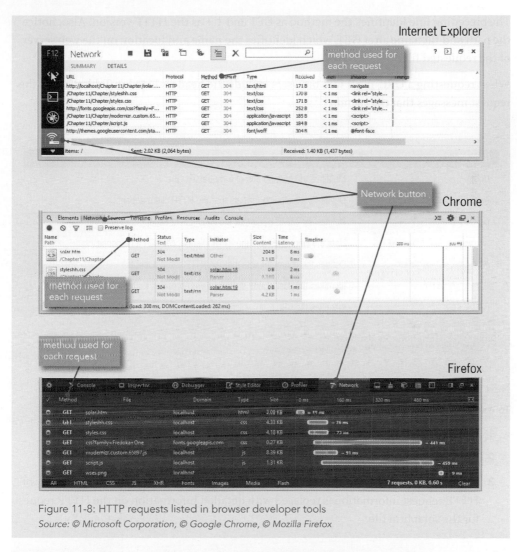

Figure 11-8: HTTP requests listed in browser developer tools

Source: © Microsoft Corporation, © Google Chrome, © Mozilla Firefox

Later in this chapter, you will learn more about managing the response messages returned from a server. First, however, you will learn about sending a request message.

Sending HTTP Requests

Without a scripting language such as JavaScript, most web browsers are usually limited to using the GET and POST methods with an HTTP request. The GET method is used for standard web page requests, but it can have a query string or form data appended to the URL. For example, in the request for solar.htm from your local web server, the browser creates a request message that begins with the following start line:

```
GET /Chapter11/Chapter/solar.htm HTTP/1.1
```

The preceding line identifies the method as GET and 1.1 as the HTTP version. Also, notice the path and filename after GET, which identifies the name and location on the web server of the requested file.

When requesting a URL, most web browsers include the headers listed in Table 11-1 in the request messages that they send.

HEADER	DESCRIPTION
Host	Identifies the host portion of a requested URL
Accept-Encoding	Defines the encoding formats that the HTTP client accepts
Accept	Defines the MIME types that the HTTP client accepts
Accept-Language	Lists the languages that the HTTP client accepts in a response
Accept-Charset	Defines the character sets that the HTTP client accepts
User-Agent	Identifies the user agent, such as a web browser, that submitted the request
Referer	Identifies the URL from which the request was made (that is, the referring URL)

Table 11-1: Common request headers

Next you'll examine the request headers for the solar.htm page in your browser.

To examine the request headers in your developer tools:

1. Return to the solar.htm file in your browser.

2. In the developer tools, locate the first entry in the Network list, for solar.htm.

3. Click (Chrome or Firefox) or double-click (IE) **solar.htm** in the list. The summary of HTTP request information is replaced with detailed information on the HTTP request for the solar.htm file.

Note | In IE, the filename may be listed with its full path, as http://localhost/Chapter11/Chapter/solar.htm. *If it is, you should double-click this string.*

4. If necessary, scroll down the right side of the developer tools pane to view the request headers, as shown in Figure 11-9. Note that in Firefox, the request headers are displayed below the response headers.

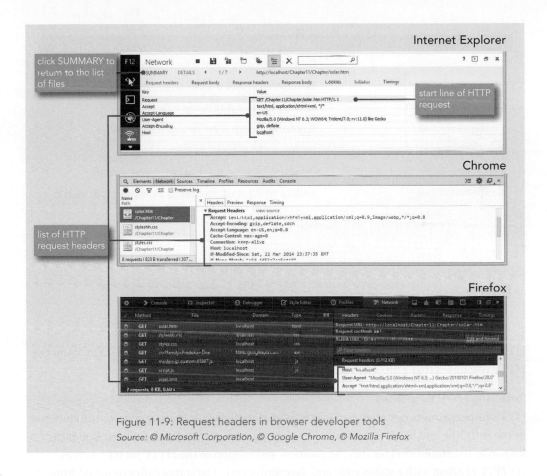

Figure 11-9: Request headers in browser developer tools

Source: © Microsoft Corporation, © Google Chrome, © Mozilla Firefox

5. Examine the headers displayed. Note that different browsers may display different numbers of headers.

6. Repeat Steps 3 and 4 to examine the request headers for styles.css and script.js.

> **Note** | *If you're using IE, click SUMMARY to return to the list of files.*

A POST request is similar to a GET request, except that any submitted data is included in the message body immediately following the blank line after the last header. To provide more information about the message body, requests made with the POST method usually include some of the headers listed in Table 11-2.

HEADER	DESCRIPTION
Content-Encoding	Defines the encoding format of the message body
Content-Language	Identifies the language of the message body
Content-Length	Identifies the size of the message body
Content-Location	Specifies the location of the message body contents
Content-Type	Identifies the MIME type of the message body
Expires	Defines the expiration date of the message body contents
Last-Modified	Identifies the last modification date of the message body contents

Table 11-2: Common message body headers

Note | *The message body headers listed in Table 11-2 are used for response messages as well as request messages.*

HTTP requests are only the first part of an HTTP connection. Next, you will learn about the HTTP responses that a browser receives from a web server.

Receiving HTTP Responses

HTTP response messages take the same format as request messages, except for the contents of the start line and headers. Instead of containing a request method, the start line (also known as the status line) returns the protocol and version of the HTTP server (such as HTTP/1.1) along with a status code and descriptive text. The status codes returned from an HTTP server consist of three digits. The codes that begin with 1 (101, 102, etc.) are purely informational, indicating that the request was received and how the server plans to proceed. Codes that begin with 2 indicate a successful request. The following list summarizes the types of messages provided by the three-digit codes that begin with 1 through 5. Table 11-3 lists the most common response codes.

> 1*xx*: (informational)—Request was received

> 2*xx*: (success)—Request was successful

> 3*xx*: (redirection)—Request cannot be completed without further action

> 4*xx*: (client error)—Request cannot be fulfilled due to a client error

> 5*xx*: (server error)—Request cannot be fulfilled due to a server error

CODE	TEXT	DESCRIPTION
200	OK	The request was successful.
301	Moved Permanently	The requested URL has been permanently moved.
302	Moved Temporarily	The requested URL has been temporarily moved.
304	Not Modified	The client already has the current version of the requested content.
404	Not Found	The requested URL was not found.
500	Internal Server Error	The request could not be completed due to an internal server error.

Table 11-3: Common response codes

For successful requests with HTTP 1.1, the start line in the response message consists of the following status line:

```
HTTP/1.1 200 OK
```

Zero or more response headers follow the status line. Table 11-4 lists the most common response headers.

HEADER	DESCRIPTION
Vary	Determines whether the server can respond to subsequent requests with the same response
Server	Returns information about the server software that processed the request
Location	Redirects clients to a different URI

Table 11-4: Common response headers

Note | Because responses return documents (such as an HTML document) or other types of files (such as image files), response messages usually include one or more of the message body headers listed in Table 11-4.

The response returned from a server can be much more involved than the original request that generated it. The initial request from an HTTP client for a web page often results in the server issuing multiple additional requests for resources required by the requested URL, such as style sheets, images, and so on.

Next, you'll use browser developer tools to examine the response headers for the solar.htm file.

To examine response headers using developer tools:

1. Return to solar.htm in your browser, and then ensure that the developer tools pane is open and displaying the network tools.

2. Open the response headers using the instructions for your browser:

    ◆ **Internet Explorer**—Click **SUMMARY** to return to the URL list, double-click **http://localhost/Chapter11/Chapter/solar.htm** in the list, and then click **Response headers**.

    ◆ **Chrome**—In the list of resources, click **solar.htm**, and then on the right side of the developer tools pane scroll down to view the response headers.

    ◆ **Firefox**—In the list of resources, click **solar.htm**. Note that the response headers are displayed above the request headers.

    Figure 11-10 shows the response headers in each browser.

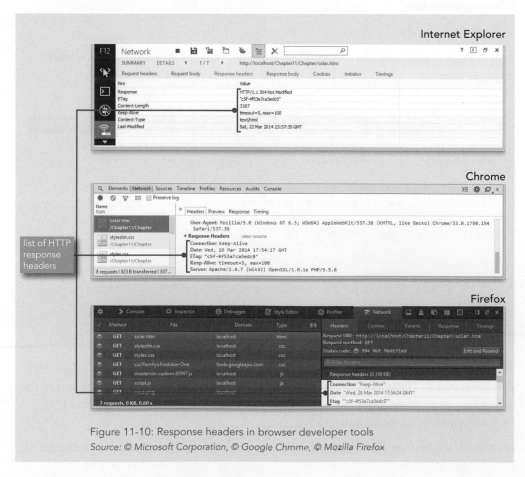

Figure 11-10: Response headers in browser developer tools
Source: © Microsoft Corporation, © Google Chrome, © Mozilla Firefox

3. Examine the headers displayed.

4. Repeat Steps 2 and 3 to examine the response headers for styles.css and script.js.

Now that you understand the basics of HTTP requests and responses, you're ready to begin assembling the components necessary to add an Ajax request to the Whole Spectrum Energy Solutions app. You'll start by examining the contents of the solar.php file, which you'll use as a proxy for your cross-domain request. You'll then request your own API key from the forecast.io web service, and you'll finalize the solar.php file by incorporating your API key into the URL for the HTTP request.

> **Caution**
>
> The forecast.io service gives a unique API key to each account holder. You are responsible if your API key is used for requests that violate the guidelines of the service. For this reason, you should never share your API key with another person

To obtain an API key for forecast.io and incorporate it into the solar.php file:

1. In your editor, open **solar.php** from the Chapter folder on your local server.

> **Caution**
>
> Be sure to open solar.php from the copy of the Chapter11 folder on your web server and not from the original copy stored in the location of your data files.

The file contains the following PHP statements:

```
1    <?php
2    $WeatherSource = "https://api.forecast.io/forecast/apikey/" .↵
3       $_GET["lat"] . "," . $_GET["lng"];
4    header("Content-Type: application/json");
5    header("Cache-Control: no-cache");
6    readfile($WeatherSource);
7    ?>
```

Lines 1 and 7 contain the opening and closing `php` tags. These tags mark all the code between them as PHP code. Lines 2 and 3 are a single statement that creates a string variable named `$WeatherSource`. The first part of the string is a URL for accessing data from the forecast.io service. In line 3, `$_GET["lat"]` references the value of the `lat` parameter passed as part of the query string, and `$_GET["lng"]` references the value of the `lng` parameter. The periods serve to concatenate the parts of the statement into a single string; they serve the same role in PHP as the plus sign (+) in JavaScript. Lines 4 and 5 use the PHP `header()` function to create two response headers. PHP uses the `header()` function to define a header that will be returned with a response. Line 4 creates the `Content-Type` header and assigns it a value of "application/json". Line 5 creates the `Cache-Control` header and assigns it a value of "no-cache". Line 6 then uses the PHP `readfile()` function to return the forecast data as the body of the HTTP response.

To complete the solar.php file, you need to replace the placeholder "apikey" in line 2 with an actual API key.

2. In your browser, open the URL **developer.forecast.io**.

3. At the top of the page, click **Register**.

4. In the form that opens, enter your email address and a password, and then click the **Create an account** button.

5. On the page that opens, scroll to the bottom of the page, click in the **API Key** box to select its contents, and then press **Ctrl + C** (Win) or **command + C** (Mac) to copy your API key to the Clipboard.

6. Return to **solar.php** in your editor, select the text **apikey** in the second line of code, press **Backspace** (Win) or **delete** (Mac) to delete it, and then press **Ctrl + V** (Win) or **command + V** (Mac) to paste your API key in its place. Your completed code for **solar.php** should match the following, except that the string at the start of line 3 should match the API key you received from forecast.io:

```
1   <?php
2   $WeatherSource = "https://api.forecast.io/forecast/↵
3       12345678901234567890123456789012/" . $_GET["lat"] .↵
4       "," . $_GET["lng"];
5   header("Content-Type: application/json");
6   header("Cache-Control: no-cache");
7   readfile($WeatherSource);
8   ?>
```

7. Save your changes to **solar.php**, and then close **solar.php** in your editor.

You have completed the configuration of the PHP file for your proxy server. In the next section, you'll create and configure an XMLHttpRequest object to request data from the proxy to be displayed in your app.

Short Quiz 2

1. How many lines does an HTTP message have, and what is the content of each line?

2. What is the function of the Cache-Control header, and what value should you generally specify for this header when requesting data with Ajax?

3. Explain the meaning of the HTTP status codes 304 and 404.

Requesting Server Data

The XMLHttpRequest object is the key to incorporating Ajax functionality in JavaScript code because it allows you to use JavaScript and HTTP to exchange data between a web browser and a web server. More specifically, you use the methods and properties of an instantiated XMLHttpRequest object with JavaScript to build and send request messages, and to receive and process response messages. The XMLHttpRequest object contains the methods listed in Table 11-5 and the properties listed in Table 11-6.

METHOD	DESCRIPTION
abort()	Cancels the current HTTP request
getAllResponseHeaders()	Returns a text string containing all of the headers that were returned with a response in *header: value* format, separated by line breaks
getResponseHeader(*header_name*)	Returns a text string containing the value assigned to the specified header
open(*method, URL*[, *async, user, password*])	Specifies the method and URL for an HTTP request; assigning a value of true to the *async* argument performs the request asynchronously, while a value of false performs the request synchronously; the default is true
send([*content*])	Submits an HTTP request using the information assigned with the open() method; the optional *content* argument contains the message body
setRequestHeader(*header_name, value*)	Creates an HTTP header using the *header_name* and *value* arguments

Table 11-5: XMLHttpRequest object methods

PROPERTY	DESCRIPTION
onreadystatechange	Specifies the name of the event handler function that executes whenever the readyState property value changes
readyState	Contains one of the following values, which represent the state of the HTTP request: 0 (uninitialized), 1 (open), 2 (sent), 3 (receiving), or 4 (loaded)
responseText	Contains the HTTP response as a text string, such as a JSON string
responseXML	Contains the HTTP response as an XML document
status	Contains the HTTP status code (such as 200 for "OK" or 404 for "Not Found") that was returned with the response
statusText	Contains the HTTP status text (such as "OK" or "Not Found") that was returned with the response

Table 11-6: XMLHttpRequest object properties

> **Note**
>
> *A newer standard, known as XMLHttpRequest2, adds additional properties and methods to the XMLHttpRequest object. However, Tables 11-5 and 11-6 focus on the properties and methods of the original standard because they are the most widely used.*

Instantiating an XMLHttpRequest Object

The first step for using Ajax to exchange data between an HTTP client and a web server is to instantiate an XMLHttpRequest object. Unlike some other built-in JavaScript objects like arrays, there is no object literal form for creating an XMLHttpRequest object. Instead, you instantiate an XMLHttpRequest object with the XMLHttpRequest constructor, as follows:

```
var httpRequest = new XMLHttpRequest();
```

The XMLHttpRequest object was originally created by browser manufacturers specifically to allow a document to request XML data. Although its name has not changed, its capabilities have gone far beyond what its name suggests. Today, the XMLHttpRequest object is standardized by the W3C and the WHATWG, which is another web standards organization.

> **Note**
>
> *To instantiate an XMLHttpRequest object in Internet Explorer 6 or older, you must use different syntax than that used for modern browsers. The apps created in this book are intended to support IE 8 and higher, so older IE syntax is not covered in this book.*

Most JavaScript programmers use a `try/catch` statement to instantiate an `XMLHttpRequest` object. For example, the following code declares a variable named `httpRequest` and then attempts to use the `XMLHttpRequest` constructor in the `try` statement to declare an `XMLHttpRequest` object. If the web browser running the code does not contain an `XMLHttpRequest` constructor, then it is not a modern browser. If this is the case, the `try` statement throws an exception.

```
1   var httpRequest;
2   try {
3       httpRequest = new XMLHttpRequest();
4   }
5   catch (requestError) {
6       document.getElementById("main").innerHTML = "Your browser↵
7           does not support this content";
8       return false;
9   }
```

Note that the `try` statement does not throw a custom error, but instead relies on the JavaScript processor to throw its own error. The catch statement then specifies a custom message to be displayed. This avoids requiring conditional logic for a simple `try/catch` situation.

Opening and closing HTTP connections represent a significant bottleneck in loading a web page, increasing the amount of time it takes for a document to load. To improve performance between client requests and server responses, HTTP/1.1 automatically keeps the client-server connection open until the client or server explicitly closes it by assigning a value of `close` to the `Connection` header. This means that you can make your Ajax programs faster by reusing an instantiated `XMLHttpRequest` object instead of re-creating it each time you send a server request. The following code demonstrates how to create a global variable named `curRequest`, which is assigned an instantiated `XMLHttpRequest` object in a function named `getRequestObject()`. This function is only called once, when the web page first loads. After the `getRequestObject()` function creates the appropriate `XMLHttpRequest` object, the last statement in the function returns the `curRequest` variable to a calling statement. Notice the `if` statement in line 14 that follows the `getRequestObject()` function. If the `curRequest` variable has a falsy value, then it has not been instantiated with the `XMLHttpRequest` object and the `getRequestObject()` function is called. The `return` statement in the `getRequestObject()` function returns the `httpRequest` variable, which represents the `XMLHttpRequest` object. The statement that called the `getRequestObject()` function then assigns the `XMLHttpRequest` object to the `curRequest` variable. However, if the `curRequest` variable does *not* have a falsy value, the web page has already been loaded, so the `getRequestObject()` function is bypassed because the `XMLHttpRequest` object already exists.

```
1    var curRequest = false;
2    var httpRequest;
3    function getRequestObject() {
4        try {
5            httpRequest = new XMLHttpRequest();
6        }
7        catch (requestError) {
8            document.getElementById("main").innerHTML = "Your↵
9                browser does not support this content";
10           return false;
11       }
12       return httpRequest;
13   }
14   if (!curRequest) {
15       curRequest = getRequestObject();
16   }
```

Next, you'll add code to the Whole Spectrum Energy Solutions app that instantiates an `XMLHttpRequest` object.

To add code to the Whole Spectrum Energy Solutions app that instantiates an `XMLHttpRequest` object:

1. Return to the **script.js** document in your text editor.

2. Near the top of the document, add the following statement to the global variables section:

```
var httpRequest = false;
```

This statement instantiates a variable named `httpRequest` and sets its value to `false`. You'll use this variable to track whether an existing HTTP request is open, which will enable you to reuse an existing request rather than slowing down page loading by opening up more than one.

3. Below the global variable declarations, add the following code to create a function named `getRequestObject()`:

```
function getRequestObject() {

}
```

4. Within the `getRequestObject()` function, add the following statement:

```
try {
    httpRequest = new XMLHttpRequest();
}
```

This statement uses the `XMLHttpRequest()` constructor within a `try` statement to instantiate an `XMLHttpRequest` object and assign it as the value of the `httpRequest` variable.

5. Before the closing } for the `getRequestObject()` function, add the following statements:

```
1    catch (requestError) {
2        document.querySelector("p.error").innerHTML =↵
3            "Forecast not supported by your browser.";
4        document.querySelector("p.error").style.display = "block",
5        return false;
6    }
7    return httpRequest;
```

If the preceding `try` statement generates an error, this code catches the error, displays a message for users, and returns `false`. If no error is thrown, the statement in line 7 returns the `httpRequest` object to the statement that called the `getRequestObject()` function.

Opening and Sending a Request

After you instantiate an `XMLHttpRequest` object, you use the `open()` method with the instantiated object to specify the request method (such as GET or POST) and URL. The following statement is the `open()` method used by a web app that displays stock prices:

```
stockRequest.open("get","StockCheck.php?" + "checkQuote=" +↵
    tickerSymbol);
```

The statement specifies the GET method and a URL named StockCheck.php, which is a PHP proxy script that retrieves the stock information from a web service. The requested stock is appended to the URL as a query string in the format `checkQuote=tickerSymbol`. The value assigned to the *tickerSymbol* variable is passed to the function containing the `XMLHttpRequest` code.

In addition to the arguments specifying the method and the URL, the `open()` method also accepts three optional arguments. The third argument, *async*, can be assigned a value of `true` or `false` to determine whether the request is handled synchronously or asynchronously. If you omit the *async* argument, it defaults to a value of `true`, which performs the request asynchronously. The fourth and fifth arguments—a username and password—are necessary only if the web server requires authentication. The following statement demonstrates how to handle the request synchronously and pass form field values containing a username and password to the `open()` method:

```
var user = document.getElementById("username").value;
var pw = document.getElementById("password").value;
stockRequest.open("get", "StockCheck.php?" + "checkQuote=" +↵
    tickerSymbol, false, user, pw);
```

Best Practices | *Never Include a Password Value in Your JavaScript Code*

As you've seen, the developer tools included with all modern browsers enable you to view the HTML, CSS, and JavaScript code for any page you open. This means that anyone accessing a web app that you publish online can view all of this code as well. To avoid the public release of private information such as a password or API key, you should never include these as part of public JavaScript code. (Note that it's fine to send a password that a user enters in a form with JavaScript.) In addition to facilitating cross-domain access, using a proxy server for Ajax enables you to protect any sensitive data that you might need to include in your code, such as an API key, because code such as PHP that is run on the server and not on the client is not visible to users.

In the last section, you learned how to reuse an instantiated `XMLHttpRequest` object instead of re-creating it each time you send a server request. When you reuse an existing `XMLHttpRequest` object, it may already be in the process of sending a request to the server. To improve performance, you should call the `abort()` method of the `XMLHttpRequest` object to cancel any existing HTTP requests before beginning a new one. Append the `abort()` method to an instantiated `XMLHttpRequest` object and call the method before calling the `open()` method, as follows:

```
1  var user = document.getElementById("username").value;
2  var pw = document.getElementById("password").value;
3  stockRequest.abort();
4  stockRequest.open("get", "StockCheck.php?" + "checkQuote=" +↵
5      tickerSymbol, false, user, pw);
```

After you have defined the basic request criteria with the `open()` method, you use the `send()` method with the instantiated `XMLHttpRequest` object to submit the request to the server. The `send()` method accepts a single argument containing the message body. If GET is specified with the `open()` method, you must pass a value of `null` to the `send()` method, as follows:

```
stockRequest.send(null);
```

Recall that when a web browser submits an HTTP request, it usually includes various response and message body headers. When running basic GET requests with the `XMLHttpRequest` object, you do not usually need to specify additional HTTP headers. For example, the following statements are all you need to open and send a request with the stock quote web page:

```
1   stockRequest.abort();
2   stockRequest.open("get", "StockCheck.php?" + "checkQuote=" +↵
3       tickerSymbol, false, user, pw);
4   stockRequest.send(null);
```

POST requests are a little more involved. With form data, a web browser automatically handles the task of creating name-value pairs from form element `name` attributes and field values. When submitting form data as the message body with the `XMLHttpRequest` object, you must manually build the name-value pairs that will be submitted to the server. The first statement in the following code creates a variable named `requestBody` that is assigned the value `"checkQuote="`; the URI-encoded value is assigned to the `tickerSymbol` variable. The last statement then passes the `requestBody` variable as an argument to the `send()` method.

```
var requestBody = "checkQuote=" +↵
    encodeURIComponent(tickerSymbol);
stockRequest.send(requestBody);
```

With POST requests, you must submit at least the `Content-Type` header before executing the `send()` method to identify the MIME type of the message body. You should also submit the `Content-Length` header to specify the size of the message body, and submit the `Connection` header to specify that the connection with the server should be closed after the response is received. Use the `setRequestHeader()` method to specify HTTP headers and values to submit with the HTTP request. You pass two arguments to the method: the name of the header and its value. For example, the following code uses the `setRequestHeader()` method to define the `Content-Type`, `Content-Length`, and `Connection` headers before submitting the request for the stock quote web page:

```
1   stockRequest.abort();
2   stockRequest.open("post","StockCheck.php");
3   var requestBody = "checkQuote=" +↵
```

```
 4      encodeURIComponent(tickerSymbol);
 5   stockRequest.setRequestHeader("Content-Type",↵
 6      "application/x-www-form-urlencoded");
 7   stockRequest.setRequestHeader("Content-Length",↵
 8      requestBody.length);
 9   stockRequest.setRequestHeader("Connection", "close");
10   stockRequest.send(requestBody);
```

Next, you will add a function that instantiates, opens, and submits an XMLHttpRequest object.

To add a function that instantiates, opens, and submits an XMLHttpRequest object:

1. Return to the **script.js** document in your text editor.

2. Within the getWeather() function, just before the closing }, enter the following code:

```
if (!httpRequest) {
   httpRequest = getRequestObject();
}
```

This if statement checks if the httpRequest variable already has a truthy value, indicating that an existing HTTP request is available for use. If not, the statement on the second line calls the getRequestObject() function to instantiate an XMLHttpRequest object.

3. Below the code you entered in Step 2 and before the closing }, enter the following statements:

```
1   httpRequest.abort();
2   httpRequest.open("get","solar.php?" + "lat=" + latitude +↵
3      "&lng=" + longitude, true);
4   httpRequest.send(null);
```

The statement in line 1 cancels any existing HTTP requests before beginning a new one. The statement in lines 2–3 opens a new HTTP request, specifying GET as the method. The second argument concatenates the filename solar.php with the string lat=; the value of the latitude variable determined earlier in the function; the string &lng=; and the value of the longitude variable. For the default city of Tucson, AZ, the resulting URL would be solar.php?lat=37.7577&lng=-122.4376. The statement in line 4 specifies a request body value of null.

4. Save your changes to **script.js**, and then return to **solar.htm** in your browser.

5. Verify that the network tools are open in the developer tools pane, and then refresh or reload solar.htm.

6. In the file list, click **solar.php?lat=37.7577&lng=−122.4376**. This is the request created by the `XMLHttpRequest` object stored in the `httpRequest` variable for the default location of Tucson, AZ.

7. On the right side of the pane, examine the request and response headers.
   Figure 11-11 shows the response headers in Chrome. The response headers include the headers and values you specified in the solar.php file for `Cache-Control` and `Content-Type`. Even though you have received a response, notice that the document displays no additional content. After you receive data from a web service, you need to add additional JavaScript code to parse the results and place them in your layout. You'll do this in the next section.

Figure 11-11: Response headers for default HTTP request in solar.htm

Source: forecast.io. Photo courtesy Dennis Schroeder/NREL

8. Switch to your browser console, type **httpRequest.responseText**, and then press **Enter**. The `httpRequest` variable references the results of your HTTP request. The value of the `responseText` property of an `XMLHttpRequest` object is any non-XML data returned. As Figure 11-12 shows, your request returned a long string of labels and values, starting with latitude, longitude, and time zone. You'll explore how to access and incorporate this data into your app in the next section.

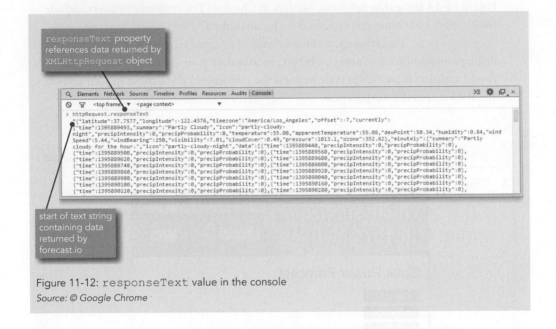

Figure 11-12: `responseText` value in the console
Source: © Google Chrome

Short Quiz 3

1. What is the purpose of keeping an HTTP connection open and reusing it, rather than closing it?

2. What method should you call before beginning a new HTTP request using an existing `XMLHttpRequest` object, and why?

3. What `XMLIttpRequest` property references the non-XML results of an HTTP request?

Receiving Server Data

After you submit a request with the `XMLHttpRequest` object, the message body in the server response is assigned to the object's `responseXML` or `responseText` properties. These properties contain the HTTP response as an XML document and as a text string, respectively. Note that the message body is only assigned to the `responseXML` property if the server response includes the `Content-Type` header assigned a MIME type value of `text/xml`.

Processing XML Data in a Response

You can process the contents of the `responseXML` property by assigning property values to document nodes. For example, the following statements demonstrate how to manipulate the value assigned to the `responseXML` property for the stock quote web page.

```
1   var stockValues = stockRequest.responseXML;
2   document.getElementById("ticker").innerHTML = stockValues.
3       getElementsByTagName("ticker")[0].childNodes[0].nodeValue;
4   document.getElementById("openingPrice").innerHTML =
5       stockValues.getElementsByTagName("open")[0].childNodes[0].
6       nodeValue;
7   document.getElementById("lastTrade").innerHTML = stockValues.
8       getElementsByTagName("lastTrade")[0].childNodes[0].nodeValue;
9   document.getElementById("lastTradeDT").innerHTML =
10      stockValues.getElementsByTagName("lastTradeDate")[0].
11      childNodes[0].nodeValue + " " + stockValues.
12      getElementsByTagName("lastTradeTime")[0].
13      childNodes[0].nodeValue;
14  document.getElementById("change").innerHTML = stockValues.
15      getElementsByTagName("change")[0].childNodes[0].nodeValue;
16  document.getElementById("range").innerHTML = stockValues.
17      getElementsByTagName("rangeLow")[0].childNodes[0].
18      nodeValue + " - " + stockValues.getElementsByTagName
19      ("rangeHigh")[0].childNodes[0].nodeValue;
20  var volume = parseInt(stockValues.getElementsByTagName
21      ("volume")[0].childNodes[0].nodeValue);
22  document.getElementById("volume").innerHTML =
23      volume.toLocaleString();
```

The first statement assigns the value of the returned `responseXML` property to a variable named `stockValues`. The remaining statements then use the `innerHTML` property and node properties to assign the values of the XML document stored in the `stockValues` variable to the appropriate elements.

Processing Text Data in a Response

The value of the `responseText` property can be any text string. In practice, this content is almost always a JSON string. For example, the `responseText` value shown in Figure 11-11 for the `httpRequest` object, which you viewed in the previous set of steps, is a JSON string.

To work with the contents of a JSON string, you first use the `parse()` method of the JavaScript `JSON` object to convert the string to an object. You can then access the property values of the new object and add them to the appropriate DOM elements.

For instance, if the `stockRequest` object returned JSON instead of XML, you could use the following statement to parse the `responseText` value and store the result as an object with the name `stockValues`:

```
var stockValues = JSON.parse(stockRequest.responseText);
```

You could then simply assign some of the object's property values as the `innerHTML` values of DOM elements, as follows:

```
1    document.getElementById("ticker").innerHTML =↵
2        stockValues.ticker;
3    document.getElementById("openingPrice").innerHTML =↵
4        stockValues.open;
5    document.getElementById("lastTrade").innerHTML =↵
6        stockValues.lastTrade;
7    document.getElementById("lastTradeDT").innerHTML =↵
8        stockValues.lastTradeDate;
9    document.getElementById("change").innerHTML =↵
10        stockValues.change;
11   document.getElementById("range").innerHTML =↵
12        stockValues.rangeLow + " - " + stockValues.rangeHigh;
13   var volume = parseInt(stockValues.volume);
14   document.getElementById("volume").innerHTML =↵
15        volume.toLocaleString();
```

The specific procedures for accessing the values of the `responseText` and `responseXML` properties with JavaScript also depend on whether you submitted a synchronous or asynchronous request.

Sending and Receiving Synchronous Requests and Responses

The value of the `open()` method's third argument determines whether the HTTP request is performed synchronously or asynchronously. A **synchronous request** stops processing the JavaScript code until a response is returned from the server. To create a synchronous request, you should check the value of the XMLHttpRequest object's status property, which contains the HTTP status code (such as 200 for "OK" or 404 for "Not Found") returned with the response, to ensure that the response was received successfully.

The following statements demonstrate how to use the returned status code and response string:

```
1    stockRequest.abort();
2    stockRequest.open("get", "StockCheck.php?" + "checkQuote=" +↵
3       tickerSymbol, false);
4    if (stockRequest.status === 200) {
5       stockRequest.send(null);
6       var stockValues = JSON.parse(stockRequest.responseText);
7       document.getElementById("ticker").innerHTML =↵
8          stockValues.ticker;
9    ...
10   }
11   else {
12      document.write("<p>HTTP response error " +↵
13         stockRequest.status + ": " + stockRequest.statusText +↵
14         "</p>");
15   }
```

The second statement passes a value of false as the third argument of the open() method to create a synchronous request. The if statement then determines whether the value assigned to the status property is 200. If so, the response was successful and the statements within the if statement execute. The statements within the if statement are the same ones you saw previously for manipulating the value assigned to the responseText property for the stock quote web page. If any other status code is returned, the else statement prints a message with the status code and text.

Although synchronous responses are easier to handle than asynchronous responses, one major drawback is that a script will not continue processing until a synchronous response is received. Therefore, if the server doesn't respond for some reason (perhaps because it is running slowly due to high traffic or maintenance requirements), your web page will appear to be unresponsive. Users can stop the script by clicking the browser's Stop button. However, a synchronous request with the send() method does not contain any mechanism for specifying the length of time allowed for receiving a response. To ensure that your script continues running if a server problem occurs, you should use asynchronous requests with the `send()` method.

Sending and Receiving Asynchronous Requests and Responses

An **asynchronous request** allows JavaScript to continue processing while it waits for a server response. To create an asynchronous request, you pass a value of `true` as the third argument of the `open()` method, or you omit the argument altogether. To receive a response for an asynchronous request, you must use the `XMLHttpRequest` object's `readyState` property and `readystatechange` event. The `readyState` property contains one of the following values, which represents the state of the HTTP request: 0 (uninitialized), 1 (open), 2 (sent), 3 (receiving), or 4 (loaded). The `readystatechange` event fires whenever the value assigned to the `readyState` property changes. You assign this event the name of a function that will execute whenever the `readyState` property changes. For example, the `open()` method in lines 2–3 of the following code defines an asynchronous request because it includes a value of `true` as the method's third argument.

```
1    stockRequest.abort();
2    stockRequest.open("get","StockCheck.php?" + "checkQuote=" +↵
3        tickerSymbol, true);
4    stockRequest.send(null);
5    stockRequest.onreadystatechange = fillStockInfo;
```

Line 5 in the above code assigns a function named `fillStockInfo()` as the event handler function for the `readystatechange` event. Note that this code specifies the event handler using the event property value rather than by creating an event listener. In this situation, using this syntax can be easier because you're setting other properties of this object and you generally don't need to specify more than one event handler for this event.

The value of the `readyState` property is updated automatically according to the current statement of the HTTP request. However, you cannot process the response until the `readyState` property is assigned a value of 4, meaning that the response is finished loading. For this reason, you include an `if` statement in the event handler function that checks the value assigned to the `readyState` property. As shown in the following example for the `fillStockInfo()` function, once the `readyState` property is assigned a value of 4 and the `status` property is assigned a value of 200, the `if` statement processes the response:

```
1    function fillStockInfo() {
2        if (stockRequest.readyState === 4 && stockRequest.status↵
3            === 200) {
```

```
4          var stockValues = stockRequest.responseText;
5          document.getElementById("ticker").innerHTML =↵
6              stockValues.ticker;
7       ...
8    }
9  }
```

Your code for the Whole Spectrum Energy Solutions app already includes the `true` parameter in the `open()` method, meaning that the `XMLHttpRequest` object sends and receives asynchronous requests and responses. Next you'll create the `fillWeather()` function, which will process the forecast data received from the `XMLHttpRequest` object. You'll include conditional code to check for appropriate `readyState` and `status` values before processing the data, and you'll add a statement to the `getWeather()` function that fires the `fillWeather()` function when the value of the `readyState` property changes.

To create the `fillWeather()` function to process the forecast data:

1. Return to the **script.js** document in your text editor, and then below the `getWeather()` function, enter the following code to create the `fillWeather()` function:

```
function fillWeather() {

}
```

2. Within the `fillWeather()` function, enter the following `if` statement to process the request result only for appropriate `readyState` and `status` property values:

```
if(httpRequest.readyState === 4 && httpRequest.status === 200) {
}
```

3. Within the `if` statement you entered in the previous step, enter the following statement to parse the `responseText` value and assign the resulting JSON object to the `weatherReport` variable:

```
weatherReport = JSON.parse(httpRequest.responseText);
```

4. Scroll up to the `getWeather()` function, and then just before the closing `}`, enter the following statement to configure the `fillWeather()` function as the event handler for the `readystatechange` event of the `httpRequest` object:

```
httpRequest.onreadystatechange = fillWeather;
```

5. Save your changes to **script.js**, and then in your browser, refresh or reload **solar.htm** from your local web server.

6. In your browser console, type **weatherReport**, press **Enter**, and then complete the following instruction for your browser:

- **Internet Explorer**—Click the **triangle** to the left of "[object Object]."
- **Chrome**—Click the **triangle** to the left of "Object."
- **Firefox**—Click [**object Object**].

The contents of the JSON object assigned to the variable name `weatherReport` are shown in the browser console. Figure 11-13 shows the object contents in Chrome.

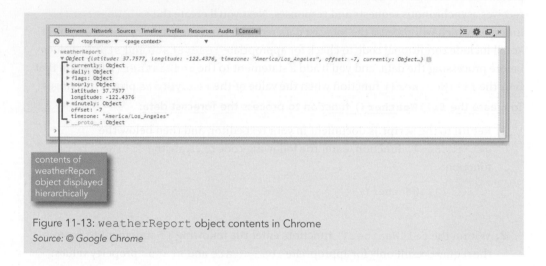

contents of weatherReport object displayed hierarchically

Figure 11-13: `weatherReport` object contents in Chrome
Source: © Google Chrome

The object value displayed for the `weatherReport` variable confirms that `fillWeather()` was called as the event handler when the `readyState` value changed, that the request resulted in successful values for the `readyState` and `status` properties, and that the `JSON.parse()` method successfully converted the string received to an object.

The final step in implementing an Ajax request is to add data provided by the web service to DOM elements in your app and to perform any other final tasks based on the data. The forecast data provided by forecast.io includes daily forecasts for the current day and the seven days that follow. The design for the Whole Spectrum Energy Solutions app incorporates two properties from each daily forecast: `date` and `cloudCover`. The `date` property is a UTC date value. You can use a `Date` object method to extract a value for the day of the week from this property. The `cloudCover` value is a decimal number between 0 and 1 that indicates the amount of cloud cover forecast for that day. The owners of Whole Spectrum Energy Solutions suggested subtracting this value from 1 to give an approximation of the measure of full sun for the day. You'll then do two things with this value. First, you'll use methods of the Math object to convert it to a percentage, which you'll display on the page. Then you'll assign a color to the sun icon in the middle cell of each row based on the percentage value calculated for the amount of sun. This enables the app to provide a visual representation of the solar intensity expected each day, ranging from pale yellow (little sun) to dark orange (full sun). Next you'll add code to incorporate this data into the app.

To add the forecast data to the app:

1. Within the `if` statement and below the statement you entered in the previous step, enter the following statements to place and style selected forecast data:

```
1    var days = ["Sunday","Monday","Tuesday","Wednesday",↵
2       "Thursday","Friday","Saturday"];
3    var dateValue = new Date(weatherReport.daily.data[0].time);
4    var dayOfWeek = dateValue.getDay();
5    var rows = document.querySelectorAll("section.week table↵
6       tbody tr");
7    document.querySelector("section.week table caption").↵
8       innerHTML = selectedCity;
9    for (var i = 0; i < rows.length ; i++) {
10      var firstCell = rows[i].getElementsByTagName("td")[0];
11      var secondCell = rows[i].getElementsByTagName("td")[1];
12      var thirdCell = rows[i].getElementsByTagName("td")[2];
13      firstCell.innerHTML = days[dayOfWeek];
14      if (dayOfWeek + 1 === 7) {
15         dayOfWeek = 0;
16      } else {
17         dayOfWeek++;
18      }
19      var sun = Math.round((1 - weatherReport.daily.data[i].↵
20         cloudCover) * 100,0);
21      if (sun > 90) {secondCell.style.color = "rgb(255,171,0)";}
22      else if (sun > 80 && sun <= 90) {secondCell.style.color =↵
23         "rgb(255,179,25)";}
24      else if (sun > 70 && sun <= 80) {secondCell.style.color =↵
25         "rgb(255,188,51)";}
26      else if (sun > 60 && sun <= 70) {secondCell.style.color =↵
27         "rgb(255,196,77)";}
```

```
28      else if (sun > 50 && sun <= 60) {secondCell.style.color =↵
29          "rgb(255,205,102)";}
30      else if (sun > 40 && sun <= 50) {secondCell.style.color =↵
31          "rgb(255,213,128)";}
32      else if (sun > 30 && sun <= 40) {secondCell.style.color =↵
33          "rgb(255,221,153)";}
34      else if (sun > 20 && sun <= 30) {secondCell.style.color =↵
35          "rgb(255,230,179)";}
36      else if (sun > 10 && sun <= 20) {secondCell.style.color =↵
37          "rgb(255,238,204)";}
38      else if (sun <= 10) {secondCell.style.color =↵
39          "rgb(255,247,230)";}
40      secondCell.style.fontSize = "2.5em";
41      thirdCell.innerHTML = sun + "%";
42  }
43  document.querySelector("section.week table caption").↵
44      style.display = "block";
45  document.querySelector("section.week table").style.display =↵
46      "inline-block";
```

Line 3 fetches the `time` property for the first `data` array in the object, which references the forecast for the current day. Line 4 then uses this date to identify the current day of the week. Line 9 starts a `for` loop that assigns the data for each day to a different row in the table. After adding the day of the week to the table, lines 19–20 look up the `cloudCover` value from the forecast and perform calculations on it. The `cloudCover` value is a number between 0 and 1. Lines 19–20 subtract the `cloudCover` value from 1, multiply the result by 100 to create a percentage, and then round the result to 0 decimal places to avoid any issues with floating-point math. Lines 21–39 then assign a color to the sun icon in the middle cell of each row based on the value calculated for the amount of sun.

2. Save your changes to **script.js**, and then in your browser, open **https://developer.forecast.io/terms_of_use.txt**. This document describes the terms under which you may use the forecast.io service in your own apps. Note that the second paragraph says, "Any public or user-facing application or service made using the Forecast API must prominently display the message "Powered by Forecast" wherever data from the Forecast API is displayed. This message must, if possible, open a link to *http://forecast.io/* when clicked or touched."

3. Close the terms of use document, return to **solar.htm** in your browser, scroll down to the end of the code for the table, and then just after the closing </table> tag, add the following element:

```
<p class="credit">Powered by <a href="http://forecast.io">↵
   Forecast</a></p>
```

This text and link credit forecast.io using the method requested in the terms of use for the service.

4. Save your changes to **solar.htm**, return to **script.js** in your editor, and then near the end of the fillWeather() function, just after the second document .querySelector statement you entered in Step 1, add a statement to make the credit line visible, as follows:

```
1        document.querySelector("section.week table caption").↵
2            style.display = "block";
3        document.querySelector("section.week table").style,↵
4            display = "inline-block";
5        document.querySelector("section.week p.credit").style.↵
6            display = "block";
7        }
8    }
```

The style sheet for the app sets the visibility for p.credit to none when the app loads. The statement you added makes the credit line visible whenever data is subsequently displayed.

5. Save your changes to **script.js**, and then in your browser, refresh or reload **solar.htm** from your local web server. The forecast data is now processed and displayed. Your browser should match the app shown in Figure 11-4.

Refreshing Server Data Automatically

When an app displays data that changes regularly, it can be useful to automatically refresh the data. For instance, during market hours, the price of a stock can change every second or every few seconds. To keep such data up to date, you can use JavaScript's setTimeout() or setInterval() methods, specifying the function that sends a request to the server. If the stock app used a getStockQuote() function to initiate an HTTP request, you could simply add a `clearTimeout()` statement followed by a `setTimeout()` statement to the end of the function, as follows:

```
1    function getStockQuote(newTicker) {
2        if (!stockRequest) {
3            stockRequest = getRequestObject();
4        }
5        if (newTicker) {
6            tickerSymbol = newTicker;
7        }
8        stockRequest.abort();
9        stockRequest.open("get","StockCheck.php?" +↵
10           "checkQuote=" + tickerSymbol, true);
11       stockRequest.send(null);
12       stockRequest.onreadystatechange = fillStockInfo;
13       clearTimeout(updateQuote);
14       var updateQuote = setTimeout('getStockQuote()', 10000);
15   }
```

Short Quiz 4

1. What is the first step in working with the contents of a JSON string returned as the value of the `responseText` property?

2. What is the difference between a synchronous and an asynchronous request?

3. To ensure that your script continues running if a server problem occurs, should you use a synchronous or asynchronous request? Why?

Creating Cross-Domain Requests Without a Proxy Server

The Ajax method you've implemented in this chapter uses PHP code on a web server as a proxy to access and return content from a different domain. This is a widely used strategy for working around JavaScript's same-origin policy. However, developers use other methods in this situation as well. This section describes two of those methods: JSON-P and CORS. JSON with padding, or JSON-P, requests JSON content using a `script` element rather than an `XMLHttpRequest` object. With Cross-Origin Resource Sharing, or CORS, the server for a web service sends a special HTTP response header that indicates that the response data may be used on other domains. Table 11-7 lists some advantages and disadvantages for each of these three strategies.

STRATEGY	ADVANTAGES	DISADVANTAGES
XHR with proxy	Enables use of XHR object for any request.	Requires web server configuration.
	Can be used with XML, JSON, or other text data.	Requires knowledge of PHP.
	Supported by almost all browsers in use.	
JSON-P	Allows direct request without a proxy.	Response data must be JSON.
	Supported by almost all browsers in use.	Any password or API key is exposed to the end user.
CORS	Allows direct request without a proxy.	Not yet widely supported by web services.
	Can be used with XML, JSON, or other text data.	Not supported by IE8 or IE9.
	Purpose-built, not a workaround.	
	Supported by current versions of all modern browsers.	

Table 11-7: Comparison of XHR proxy, JSON-P, and CORS

Updating Content with JSON-P

When developers began looking for ways to work around the same-origin policy for Ajax requests without using proxies, they looked to one of the few HTML elements that's not subject to the policy: the `script` element. A web document can load a script from another domain, and it's left up to the developer to ensure that any script loaded in an app is from a trusted source. You already took advantage of this aspect of the `script` element in Chapter 10 to load the Google Maps library in your app using a `script` element. Developers recognized they could use a `script` element to call a program running on a web server, which could return the requested content in JSON format. Because the data is being returned within a `script` element, the object is treated as the parameter for a function call, and the called function processes the JSON object passed to it, parsing the data and adding it to the web page just like a function that processes the content of an `XMLHttpRequest` object. Figure 11-14 illustrates the process of using JSON-P to update data.

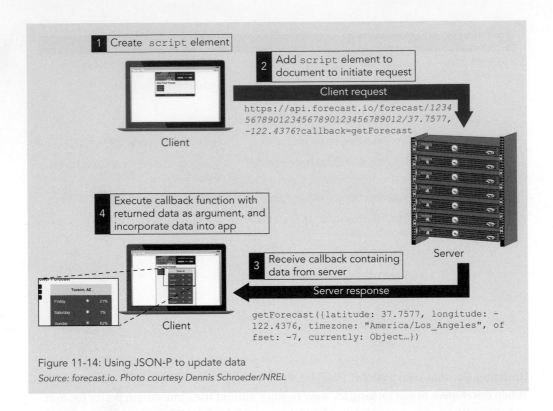

Figure 11-14: Using JSON-P to update data
Source: forecast.io. Photo courtesy Dennis Schroeder/NREL

All the information needed to create a JSON-P request is packaged into the URL specified for the `src` attribute of the `script` element. Although each web service specifies exactly how to craft a JSON-P URL for its service, it generally consists of two parts: the request information and a callback query string. The request information includes the URL of the service along with any parameters that you would pass for any type of data request to that service, such as an API key and a stock symbol or latitude and longitude values. In fact, the first part of the `src` value is often the same as the URL used for a proxy. The second part of the `src` value, the callback query string, appends a keyword and the name of a function in your app that should be called to process the data returned from the web service. The keyword is often "callback."

For instance, the following is the form of the URL used in the Whole Spectrum Energy Solutions PHP proxy to request forecast data from forecast.io:

```
https://api.forecast.io/forecast/apikey/latitude,longitude
```

The forecast.io service supports JSON-P using a query string with the "callback" keyword. This means you could create a JSON-P request to forecast.io using the following URL form:

```
https://api.forecast.io/forecast/apikey/latitude, ↵
    longitude?callback=getForecast
```

This modified version of the URL adds a question mark, which starts a query string. Then it adds the parameter name `callback` with the value `getForecast`, which is the name of the function that will handle the returned data. The forecast.io service would still use the first part of the URL to generate the requested data, just as it did with your XHR request using a proxy. The service would then return a JavaScript statement like the following, which calls the `getForecast()` function you specified, with the JSON string resulting from your query as an argument:

```
getForecast({latitude: 37.7577, longitude: -122.4376, ↵
    timezone: "America/Los Angeles", offset: -7, ↵
    currently: Object...})
```

The final step in implementing JSON-P would then be to modify the `getForecast()` function to accept the data as a parameter, and to remove both the `if` statement that checks the `readyState` and `status` properties, and the `JSON.parse()` statement, which is no longer necessary.

The forecast.io API supports JSON-P requests, and the owners of Whole Spectrum Energy Solutions would like to see a version of the app using JSON-P instead of XHR with a proxy. Next, you'll create a copy of the script.js file and modify it to request and display the same data using JSON-P.

To create a version of your app that uses JSON-P:

1. Return to script.js in your editor, and then save a copy of the file with the name **scriptJSONP.js** in the Chapter11/Chapter folder on your local server.

2. Within the `getWeather()` function, delete the following lines of code:

```
1    if (!httpRequest) {
2        httpRequest = getRequestObject();
3    }
4    httpRequest.abort();
5    httpRequest.open("get","solar.php?" + "lat=" + latitude + ↵
6        "&lng=" + longitude, true);
7    httpRequest.send();
8    httpRequest.onreadystatechange = fillWeather;
```

> **Note** | *The preceding code is crossed out to indicate that you should delete it from your code, and not enter it as new code.*

3. Switch to **solar.php** in your editor, then, in line 2, select your API key, and then press **Ctrl + C** (Win) or **command + C** (Mac) to copy it to the Clipboard.

4. Return to **scriptJSONP.js** in your editor and then, within the `getWeather()` function, just before the closing }, type **var url = "https://api.forecast.io/forecast/**

5. Press **Ctrl + V** (Win) or **command + V** (Mac) to paste your API key after the quote you typed in the previous step, and then immediately after the API key type the following:

```
/" + latitude + "," + longitude + "?callback=getForecast";
```

Your completed `var` statement should match the following, with your API key in place of the *apikey* text:

```
var url = "https://api.forecast.io/forecast/apikey/" +
    latitude + "," + longitude + "?callback=getForecast";
```

6. Below the code you just entered, and just before the closing }, enter the following statements:

```
1   var script = document.createElement("script");
2   script.id = "jsonp";
3   script.src = url;
4   document.body.appendChild(script);
```

These statements create a new `script` element as a document fragment, assign it an `id` value of `jsonp` and a `src` value equal to the `url` variable you constructed above, and then add the `script` element to the document.

7. Below the `getWeather()` function, add the following `getForecast()` function:

```
1   function getForecast(forecast) {
2       try {
3           fillWeather(forecast);
4       }
5       finally {
6           var script = document.getElementById("jsonp");
7           script.parentNode.removeChild(script);
8       }
9   }
```

The `getForecast()` function serves as the callback function for your JSON-P request. It accepts a single parameter, `forecast`, which is the data returned from the forecast.io service. The `try/finally` construct allows you to call the `fillWeather()` function with the forecast data, and then only after that succeeds, remove the script you added in the `getWeather()` function. This keeps your code clean and avoids adding multiple duplicate `script` elements to your code as a result of repeated requests.

8. In the `fillWeather()` function, add the parameter name `weatherReport` between the parentheses in the function declaration, delete the `if` statement at the start of the function as well as its closing bracket near the end of the function, and then delete the statement at the start of the function that assigns a value to the `weatherReport` variable. The following code shows the updated start and end of the function:

```
1    function fillWeather(weatherReport) {
2        if(httpRequest.readyState == 4 && httpRequest.status ==↵
3            200) {
4            weatherReport = JSON.parse(httpRequest.responseText);
5            var days = ["Sunday","Monday","Tuesday","Wednesday",↵
6                "Thursday","Friday","Saturday"];
7        ...
8            thirdCell.innerHTML = sun + "%";
9        }
10           document.querySelector("section.week table caption").↵
11               style.display = "block";
12           document.querySelector("section.week table").style.↵
13               display = "inline-block";
14           document.querySelector("section.week p.credit").style↵
15               .display = "block";
16       }
17   }
```

9. Save your changes to scriptJSONP.js, switch to solar.htm in your editor, and then in the `script` element at the end of the body section, change the `src` value to **scriptJSONP.js**, as follows:

```
<script src="scriptJSONP.js"></script>
```

10. Save your changes to solar.htm, and then in your browser, refresh or reload solar.htm. The forecast data is displayed just as it was earlier using the XHR proxy request.

11. In your browser tools, switch to the view that shows the HTML code for the current page (IE: **DOM Explorer**; Chrome: **Elements**; Firefox: **Inspector**), scroll to the bottom of the document code, and then watch the code as you refresh or reload the document. Notice that a second `script` element is added at the end of the body section, and then quickly removed. This is the `script` element being added to make the JSON-P call, and then being cleaned up after the data is received.

It's important to recognize that incorporating content from another domain using JSON-P opens a potential security hole in your website. If the site from which you're requesting data is compromised by malicious code, the content you receive from that site is a potential route to attack your site as well. For this reason, it's important to use JSON-P only with a web service that you trust.

In addition, a JSON-P request that requires authentication such as a password or API key exposes these sensitive credentials to end users. For this reason, you should generally use JSON-P that requires authentication only with trusted users, such as in an app that is used only by your organization's employees.

Updating Content with CORS

While JSON-P is a reasonable solution for many cross-domain requests, developers continued working on a method for enabling cross-domain requests within an `XMLHttpRequest` object. The result was the Cross-Origin Resource Sharing (CORS) specification, which is one part of a new specification known as XMLHttpRequest2, which enables additional properties, methods, and events for an `XMLHttpRequest` object.

While JSON-P leverages a gap in the same-origin policy within a user's browser and relies on sites using the technique for non-malicious purposes, CORS instead enables a content provider that wants to share its content to configure its server to convey that permission in its HTTP response to an `XMLHttpRequest`. At its simplest, this involves configuring the web server for the service to return the `Access-Control-Allow-Origin` HTTP response header with a value that includes the requesting domain. This header lets the user's browser know that the cross-domain request is authorized, permitting an exception to the same-origin policy.

Microsoft has enabled CORS through a new object, `XDomainRequest`, instead of adding it to the existing `XMLHttpRequest` object. This means that for support across all modern browsers, code to access a web service using CORS must first check whether the user's browser defines an `XDomainRequest` object.

Short Quiz 5

1. What is JSON-P? What is CORS?

2. List at least one advantage and one disadvantage of using XHR with a proxy, JSON-P, and CORS.

3. Describe the potential security implications of using JSON-P.

Summary

⟩ Ajax is a technique that allows web pages displayed on a client computer to quickly interact and exchange data with a web server without reloading the entire page.

⟩ The XMLHttpRequest object uses HTTP to exchange data between a client computer and a web server.

⟩ Using a proxy is a common technique for working around JavaScript's same-origin policy to access third-party content with Ajax.

⟩ When a user attempts to access a web page, the user's browser sends a web server an HTTP request. The web server replies with an HTTP response.

⟩ Hypertext Transfer Protocol (HTTP) is a set of rules that defines how requests are made by an HTTP client to an HTTP server, and how responses are returned from an HTTP server to an HTTP client. The term "HTTP client" refers to the application, usually a web browser, which makes the request. "HTTP server" is another name for a web server and refers to a computer that receives HTTP requests and returns responses to HTTP clients.

⟩ When a user attempts to access a web page, the user's browser sends a web server an HTTP request. The web server replies with an HTTP response.

⟩ You use the methods and properties of an instantiated XMLHttpRequest object with JavaScript to build and send request messages, and to receive and process response messages.

⟩ The first step for using Ajax to exchange data between an HTTP client and a web server is to instantiate an XMLHttpRequest object.

⟩ After you instantiate an XMLHttpRequest object, you use the open() method with the instantiated XMLHttpRequest object to specify the request method (such as GET or POST) and URL.

⟩ To improve performance, you should call the abort() method of the XMLHttpRequest object to cancel any existing HTTP requests before beginning a new one.

⟩ After you have defined the basic request criteria with the open() method, you use the send() method with the instantiated XMLHttpRequest object to submit the request to the server.

> After you submit a request with the `XMLHttpRequest` object, the message body in the server response is assigned to the `XMLHttpRequest` object's `responseXML` or `responseText` properties.

> A synchronous request stops the processing of the JavaScript code until a response is returned from the server; an asynchronous request allows JavaScript to continue processing while it waits for a server response.

> To ensure that your script continues running if a server problem occurs, you should use asynchronous requests with the `send()` method, rather than synchronous requests.

> The `readystatechange` event fires whenever the value assigned to the `readyState` property changes. To process the results of an Ajax request, you assign this event the name of a function that will execute whenever the `readyState` property changes.

> JSON with padding, or JSON-P, requests JSON content using a `script` element rather than an `XMLHttpRequest` object.

> With Cross-Origin Resource Sharing, or CORS, the server for a web service sends a special HTTP response header that indicates that the response data may be used on other domains.

Key Terms

Ajax—A technique that allows web pages displayed on a client computer to quickly interact and exchange data with a web server without reloading the entire page.

asynchronous request—An HTTP request that allows JavaScript to continue processing while it waits for a server response.

back-end developer—A developer who works mainly with server-side languages and libraries such as PHP, SQL, and node.js.

caching—The temporary storage of data for faster access.

Cross-Origin Resource Sharing— A technique for requesting data from a server on a different domain in which the server for a web service sends a special HTTP response header that indicates that the response data may be used on other domains.

CORS—*See* Cross-Origin Resource Sharing.

front-end developer—A web developer who works primarily with HTML, CSS, and client-side JavaScript.

full-stack developer—A web developer who has skills and responsibilities for both client-side and server-side code.

headers— Lines in an HTTP message that define information about the request or response message and the contents of the message body.

host—A computer system that is being accessed by a remote computer.

HTTP client—The application, usually a web browser, that makes a request.

HTTP messages—HTTP client requests and server responses.

HTTP server—A computer that receives HTTP requests and returns responses to HTTP clients.

JSON with padding—A technique for requesting data from a server on a different domain that requests JSON content using a `script` element rather than an `XMLHttpRequest` object.

JSON-P—*See* JSON with padding.

PHP—A programming language specifically designed to run on web servers.

proxy—A server that acts for or performs requests for other clients and servers.

request—The process by which a user's browser asks a web server for the web page.

response—The reply from a web server to a request, which might consist of the requested web page or a message about it.

synchronous request—An HTTP request that stops processing JavaScript code until a response is returned from the server.

web service—A data source made available on one domain for use on other domains across the web.

widget—Prepackaged code made available by a web service that enables even users with a minimal understanding of HTML and CSS to add content from the service to a web document.

XHR object—*See* `XMLHttpRequest` object.

XMLHttpRequest object—A JavaScript object that uses HTTP to exchange data between a client computer and a web server.

Review Questions

1. Which object uses HTTP to exchange data between a client computer and a web server?

   a. `JSON`

   b. `Math`

   c. `XMLHttpRequest`

   d. `Ajax`

2. A server that acts for or performs requests for other clients and servers is a(n) _____.

   a. proxy

   b. Ajax

   c. request

   d. response

3. A data source made available on one domain for use on other domains across the web is a(n) _____.
   a. server
   b. web service
   c. HTTP server
   d. HTTP client

4. Which of the following is the first step in using Ajax to update data?
   a. Receive the response from the server, containing the requested data.
   b. Process the data returned from the server and incorporate the data into the app.
   c. Use the `XMLHttpRequest` object to send a request to the server.
   d. Instantiate an `XMLHttpRequest` object for the web browser where the script will run.

5. When a user's browser asks a web server for a web page, the process is known as a(n) _____.
   a. header
   b. request
   c. response
   d. host

6. A web server's reply when a user's browser asks for a web page is known as a(n) _____.
   a. header
   b. request
   c. response
   d. host

7. The temporary storage of data for faster access is known as _____.
   a. parsing
   b. caching
   c. a request
   d. a response

8. An HTTP response code indicating a successful request begins with which digit?
   a. 1
   b. 2
   c. 3
   d. 4

9. Which property of an `XMLHttpRequest` object contains a JSON string returned from a web service?
   a. `value`
   b. `innerHTML`
   c. `responseXML`
   d. `responseText`

10. Which type of request stops processing JavaScript code until a response is returned from the server?
    a. Synchronous
    b. Asynchronous
    c. JSON
    d. XML

11. Which type of request allows JavaScript to continue processing while it waits for a server response?
    a. Synchronous
    b. Asynchronous
    c. JSON
    d. XML

12. When using an asynchronous request, you cannot process the response until the `readyState` property is assigned a value of _____.
    a. 1
    b. 2
    c. 3
    d. 4

13. Which method of updating content involves the server for a web service explicitly indicating that data may be used on other domains?
    a. Ajax
    b. Ajax with a proxy
    c. JSON-P
    d. CORS

14. Which of the following does a JSON-P request use?
    a. An `XMLHttpRequest` object
    b. A `script` element
    c. A proxy
    d. A `meta` element

15. Which response header is used by CORS?
    a. `Vary`
    b. `Server`
    c. `Access-Control-Allow-Origin`
    d. `Location`

16. Explain how a proxy is used for an Ajax request.

17. What is the difference between a standard HTTP request and a request that uses the `XMLHttpRequest` object?

18. Why do you need to run an app using Ajax from a web server to test it rather than opening it as a local file?

19. Why do you not normally send a `Connection` header with a value of `close`?

20. Explain why incorporating content from another domain using JSON-P opens a potential security hole in your website.

Hands-On Projects

> **Caution** Ensure that all the files for your projects are located in the public directory of your web server, rather than in the original location of your data files.

Hands-On Project 11-1

In this project, you'll use the API for the Bing search engine to return search results to a web app using Ajax.

1. In your text editor, open the **search.htm** and **script.js** files from the HandsOnProject11-1 folder in the copy of the Chapter11 folder that you created on your web server. In the comment section of each file, enter your name and today's date in the appropriate places, and then save your changes. Note that the search.htm file contains a form displaying an input box and a submit button.

2. In the **script.js** file, after the "use strict" statement, declare a global variable named `httpRequest` with a value of `false`. Below the variable declaration, create a function named `getRequestObject()` that contains the following `try/catch/return` statements:

```
1   try {
2       httpRequest = new XMLHttpRequest();
3   }
```

```
4    catch (requestError) {
5        return false;
6    }
7    return httpRequest;
```

3. Below the `getRequestObject()` function, add the following `getResults()` function:

```
1    function getResults(evt) {
2        if (evt.preventDefault) {
3            evt.preventDefault();
4        } else {
5            evt.returnValue = false;
6        }
7        var entry = document.getElementsByTagName("input")[0].value;
8        if (!httpRequest) {
9            httpRequest = getRequestObject();
10        }
11        httpRequest.abort();
12        httpRequest.open("get","search.php?q=" + entry, true);
13        httpRequest.send();
14        httpRequest.onreadystatechange = displaySuggestions;
15    }
```

4. Below the `getResults()` function, add the following `displaySuggestions()` function:

```
1    function displaySuggestions() {
2        if(httpRequest.readyState === 4 &&↵
3            httpRequest.status === 200) {
4            searchResults = JSON.parse(httpRequest.responseText);
5            var items = searchResults.d.results;
6            var articleEl = document.getElementsByTagName↵
7                ("article")[0];
8            for (var i = 0; i < items.length; i++) {
9                var newDiv = document.createElement("div");
10                var head = document.createDocumentFragment();
11                var newP1 = document.createElement("p");
```

```
12          var newP2 = document.createElement("p");
13          var newP3 = document.createElement("p");
14          var newA = document.createElement("a");
15          head.appendChild(newP1);
16          newA.innerHTML = items[i].Title;
17          newA.setAttribute("href", items[i].Url);
18          newP1.appendChild(newA);
19          newP1.className = "head";
20          newP2.innerHTML = items[i].Url;
21          newP2.className = "url";
22          newP3.innerHTML = items[i].Description;
23          newDiv.appendChild(head);
24          newDiv.appendChild(newP2);
25          newDiv.appendChild(newP3);
26          articleEl.appendChild(newDiv);
27      }
28  }
29 }
```

5. Below the `displaySuggestions()` function, add the following code to create an event listener:

```
1  var form = document.getElementsByTagName("form")[0];
2  if (form.addEventListener) {
3      form.addEventListener("submit", getResults, false);
4  } else if (form.attachEvent) {
5      form.attachEvent("onsubmit", getResults);
6  }
```

6. Save your changes to **script.js**, and then in your browser navigate to **datamarket.azure.com** and follow the instructions to log in or sign up for a Microsoft account. Search for the Bing Search API, and then sign up for the free subscription level. Then in your account settings, locate your account key, select it, and copy it to the Clipboard.

7. In your editor, open **search.php**, and then near the top of the file, delete the text `accountkey` and paste your account key from the Clipboard in its place.

8. Save your changes to **search.php**, and then in your editor return to **search.htm**. Just before the closing `</form>` tag, enter the following p element containing credit information:

```
<p class="credit">Powered by <a href="http://bing.com">↵
  Bing</a></p>
```

9. Save your changes to **search.htm**, and then in your browser open the URL *http://localhost/Chapter11/HandsOnProject11-1/search.htm*. In the search box, enter the name of your school, and then click **Search**. After a short delay, the search results are displayed on the same page, as shown in Figure 11-15. Note that you may have to wait up to 20 seconds for results to be displayed.

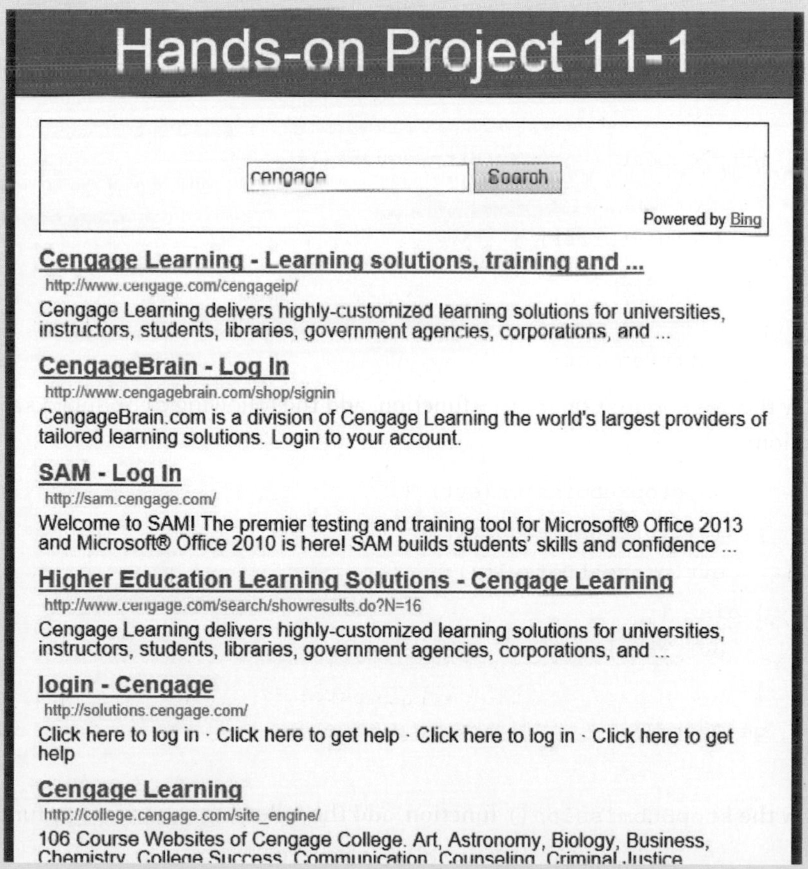

Figure 11-15: Search results

Hands-On Project 11-2

In this project, you'll use a PHP script to fetch market information for a stock based on a stock symbol that a user specifies.

1. In your text editor, open the **stocks.htm** and **script.js** files from the HandsOnProject11-2 folder in the copy of the Chapter11 folder that you created on your web server. In the comment section of each file, enter your name and today's date in the appropriate places, and then save your changes. Note that the **stocks.htm** file contains a form displaying an input box and a submit button, as well as `table` and `figure` elements for displaying results.

2. In the **script.js** file, after the "use strict" statement, declare a global variable named `httpRequest` with a value of `false`. Declare a second global variable named `entry` with a value of `^IXIC`.

3. Below the variable declarations, create a function named `getRequestObject()` that contains the following `try/catch/return` statements:

```
1  try {
2      httpRequest = new XMLHttpRequest();
3  }
4  catch (requestError) {
5      return false;
6  }
7  return httpRequest;
```

4. Below the `getRequestObject()` function, add the following `stopSubmission()` function:

```
1  function stopSubmission(evt) {
2      if (evt.preventDefault) {
3          evt.preventDefault();
4      } else {
5          evt.returnValue = false;
6      }
7      getQuote();
8  }
```

5. Below the `stopSubmission()` function, add the following `getQuote()` function:

```
1  function getQuote() {
2      if (document.getElementsByTagName("input")[0].value) {
```

```
3        entry = document.getElementsByTagName("input")[0].value;
4    }
5    if (!httpRequest) {
6        httpRequest = getRequestObject();
7    }
8    httpRequest.abort();
9    httpRequest.open("get","StockCheck.php?t=" + entry, true);
10   httpRequest.send();
11   httpRequest.onreadystatechange = displayData;
12   }
```

6. Below the getQuote() function, add the following displayData() function:

```
1    function displayData() {
2    if(httpRequest.readyState === 4 && httpRequest.status ===
3        200) {
4        var stockResults = httpRequest.responseText;
5        var stockItems = stockResults.split(/,|\"/);
6        for(var i = stockItems.length - 1; i >= 0; i--) {
7            if(stockItems[i] === "") {
8                stockItems.splice(i, 1);
9            }
10       }
11       var articleEl = document.getElementsByTagName↵
12           ("article")[0];
13       document.getElementById("ticker").innerHTML =↵
14           stockItems[0];
15       document.getElementById("openingPrice").innerHTML =↵
16           stockItems[6];
17       document.getElementById("lastTrade").innerHTML =↵
18           stockItems[1];
19       document.getElementById("lastTradeDT").innerHTML =↵
20           stockItems[2] + ", " + stockItems[3];
21       document.getElementById("change").innerHTML =↵
22           stockItems[4];
23       document.getElementById("range").innerHTML =↵
```

```
24          (stockItems[8] * 1).toFixed(2) + " &ndash; " +↵
25          (stockItems[7] * 1).toFixed(2);
26      document.getElementById("volume").innerHTML =↵
27          (stockItems[9] * 1).toLocaleString();
28      var chartSrc = "http://ichart.yahoo.com/t?s=" + entry;
29      document.getElementById("chart").src = chartSrc;
30      document.getElementById("chart").style.display =↵
31          "inline";
32    }
33  }
```

7. Below the `displayData()` function, add the following `formatTable()` function:

```
1   function formatTable() {
2     var rows = document.getElementsByTagName("tr");
3     for (var i = 0; i < rows.length; i = i + 2) {
4         rows[i].style.background = "#9FE098";
5     }
6   }
```

8. Below the `formatTable()` function, add the following code to create event listeners:

```
1   var form = document.getElementsByTagName("form")[0];
2   if (form.addEventListener) {
3     form.addEventListener("submit", stopSubmission, false);
4     window.addEventListener("load", formatTable, false);
5     window.addEventListener("load", getQuote, false);
6   } else if (form.attachEvent) {
7     form.attachEvent("onsubmit", stopSubmission);
8     window.attachEvent("onload", formatTable);
9     window.attachEvent("onload", getQuote);
10  }
```

9. Save your changes to script.js, and then in your browser open the URL
    http://localhost/Chapter11/HandsOnProject11-2/stocks.htm. The current information
    for the default stock symbol, which is the NASDAQ composite, is displayed, as shown
    in Figure 11-16.

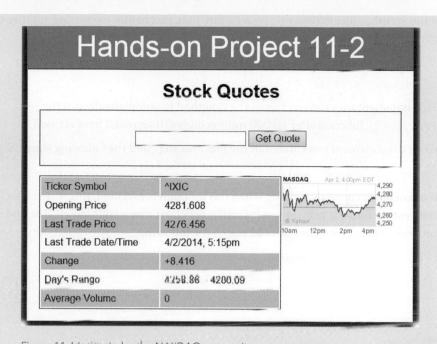

Figure 11-18: Quote for the NASDAQ composite

10. In the search box, type **YHOO**, and then click **Get Quote**. After a short delay, trading information for Yahoo! is displayed.

Hands-On Project 11-3

In this project, you'll enhance the stock quote app you created in Hands-on Project 11-2 to refresh the data automatically every 10 seconds.

1. In the file manager for your operating system, copy the completed contents of the HandsOnProject11-2 folder in the public folder on your web server to the HandsOnProject11-3 folder.

2. In your text editor, open the **stocks.htm** and **script.js** files from the HandsOnProject11-3 folder. In **stocks.htm**, change "Hands-on Project 11-2" to **Hands-on Project 11-3** in the comment section, in the `title` element, and in the `h1` element, and then save your changes. In script.js, change "Hands-on Project 11-2" to **Hands-on Project 11-3** in the comment section, and then save your changes.

3. In the **script.js** file, in the `getQuote()` function, just before the closing }, enter the following statement:

```
var updateQuote = setTimeout('getQuote()', 10000);↵
    // refresh every 10 seconds
```

This statement uses the `setTimeout()` method to automatically run the `getQuote()` function after 10,000 milliseconds (10 seconds) have elapsed.

4. Above the statement you entered in the previous step, add the following statement:

```
clearTimeout(updateQuote);
```

If a timeout is currently running when this function is executed, this statement clears the existing timeout before the next statement starts a new countdown. The end of your `getQuote()` function should match the following:

```
1        httpRequest.onreadystatechange = displayData;
2        clearTimeout(updateQuote);
3        var updateQuote = setTimeout('getQuote()', 10000);↵
4            // refresh every 10 seconds
5    }
```

5. Save your changes to stocks.htm, and then in your browser open the URL *http://localhost/Chapter11/HandsOnProject11-3/stocks.htm*. The current information for the default stock symbol, which is the NASDAQ composite, is displayed.

6. Watch the values displayed in the table for 10 seconds. If you are viewing the page during trading hours for U.S. stock markets (generally 9:30 am–4:30 pm Eastern time), one or more of the values should change after 10 seconds have elapsed.

7. Close the page or tab displaying stocks.htm to ensure that your browser does not continue to generate requests for data.

Hands-On Project 11-4

In the United States, each zip code is part of a single city and state. This means that in general, it's redundant to ask a user to enter both a zip code and city and state information. In this project, you'll enhance an address form using an Ajax request to autocomplete city and state fields based on a zip code entered by a user. You'll do this using the zippopotam.us service. Because this service enables CORS for all domains, you'll create your Ajax request without a PHP proxy.

1. In your text editor, open the **address.htm** and **script.js** files from the HandsOnProject11-4 folder in the copy of the Chapter11 folder that you created on your web server. In the comment section of each file, enter your name and today's date

in the appropriate places, and then save your changes. Note that the **address.htm** file contains a form containing three labeled input boxes.

2. In the script.js file, after the "use strict" statement, declare a global variable named `httpRequest` with a value of `false`.

3. Below the variable declarations, add the following code to create an event listener:

```
1   var zip = document.getElementById("zip");
2   if (zip.addEventListener) {
3       zip.addEventListener("keyup", checkInput, false);
4   } else if (zip.attachEvent) {
5       zip.attachEvent("onkeyup", checkInput);
6   }
```

This code uses the `keyup` event, which fires when a user releases a key on the keyboard.

4. Above the code you entered in the previous step, create a function named `getRequestObject()` that contains the following `try/catch` statements:

```
1   try {
2       httpRequest = new XMLHttpRequest();
3   }
4   catch (requestError) {
5       // display city & state fields and labels for manual input
6       document.getElementById("csset").style.visibility = "visible";
7       // remove event listeners so additional input is ignored
8       var zip = document.getElementById("zip").value;
9       if (zip.addEventListener) {
10          zip.removeEventListener("keyup", checkInput, false);
11      } else if (zip.attachEvent) {
12          zip.detachEvent("onkeyup", checkInput);
13      }
14      return false;
15  }
16  return httpRequest;
```

By default, the `csset` fieldset, containing the city and state fields and labels, is hidden. If the browser doesn't support Ajax, the `catch` statement makes the city and state fields and labels visible so users can complete them manually.

5. Below the `getRequestObject()` function, add the following `checkInput()` function:

```
1    function checkInput() {
2        var zip = document.getElementById("zip").value;
3        if (zip.length === 5) {
4            getLocation();
5        } else {
6            document.getElementById("city").value = "";
7            document.getElementById("state").value = "";
8        }
9    }
```

This function checks if users have entered five digits in the zip box, which is the minimum length for a U.S. zip code. If so, the function calls the `getLocation()` function, which you'll create in the next step to send the Ajax request. Otherwise, the app assumes that the user has deleted the existing entry and clears the values in the city and state fields.

6. Below the `checkInput()` function, add the following `getLocation()` function:

```
1    function getLocation() {
2        var zip = document.getElementById("zip").value;
3        if (!httpRequest) {
4            httpRequest = getRequestObject();
5        }
6        httpRequest.abort();
7        httpRequest.open("get","http://api.zippopotam.us/us/" +↵
8            zip, true);
9        httpRequest.send();
10        httpRequest.onreadystatechange = displayData;
11    }
```

Notice that the `open()` method specifies the URL for the zippopotam.us service itself, rather than the name of a local PHP file. This is because zippopotam.us supports CORS, and thus accepts and returns requests from any domain. The zippopotam.us URL includes `/us/` at the end, indicating a U.S. lookup for the zip code specified by the `zip` variable.

7. Below the `getLocation()` function, add the following `displayData()` function:

```
1    function displayData() {
2        if(httpRequest.readyState === 4 && httpRequest.status ===↵
3            200) {
```

```
4          var resultData = JSON.parse(httpRequest.responseText);
5          var city = document.getElementById("city");
6          var state = document.getElementById("state");
7          city.value = resultData.places[0]["place name"];
8          state.value = resultData.places[0]↵
9              ["state abbreviation"];
10         document.getElementById("zip").blur();
11         document.getElementById("csset").style.visibility =↵
12             "visible";
13     }
14  }
```

The JSON object returned by the hippopotam.us service contains a `places` object with a nested array named `0`. Each element of the array is an object property. Because the property names you need to reference, `place name` and `state abbreviation`, contain spaces, you must use bracket notation rather than dot notation to reference them. The function assigns values returned by the service to the city and state fields and then makes the fields visible in the browser.

8. Save your changes to script.js, and then in your browser open the URL *http://localhost/Chapter11/HandsOnProject11-4/address.htm*. Click in the **Postal Code** box, and then type **06902**. After you release the last key, your request is processed and the city "Stamford" and state "CT" are displayed in the relevant fields, as shown in Figure 11-17.

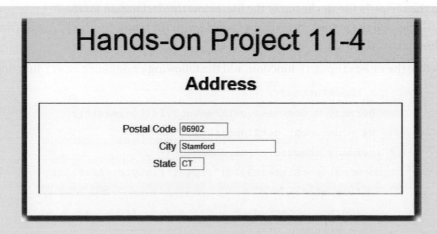

Figure 11-17: City and state fields completed based on Postal Code value

Hands-On Project 11-5

In this project, you'll enhance your address form from Hands-on Project 11-4 to support German postal codes as well as United States zip codes. You'll add Country option buttons to the form, and you'll change the JavaScript code for your Ajax request to pass the country value to the zippopotam.us service.

1. In the file manager for your operating system, copy the completed contents of the HandsOnProject11-4 folder in the public folder on your web server to the HandsOnProject11-5 folder.

2. In your text editor, open the **address.htm** and **script.js** files from the HandsOnProject11-5 folder. In **address.htm**, change "Hands-on Project 11-4" to **Hands-on Project 11-5** in the comment section, in the `title` element, and in the `h1` element, and then save your changes. In **script.js**, change "Hands-on Project 11-4" to **Hands-on Project 11-5** in the comment section, and then save your changes.

3. In the **address.htm** file, just below the opening `<form>` tag, add the following code to create a new fieldset containing country option buttons:

```
1   <fieldset id="countryset">
2       <label for="germany" id="germanylabel">Germany</label>
3       <input id="germany" type="radio" value="germany"↵
4         name="country" />
5       <label for="us" id="uslabel">United States</label>
6       <input id="us" type="radio" value="us" name="country" />
7   </fieldset>
```

4. In the **script.js** file, at the top of the file, below the declaration for the `httpRequest` variable, add a statement declaring a variable with the name `countrySel`. You'll use this to track the country selected by a user.

5. Before the `checkInput()` function, add the following `checkButtons()` function:

```
1   function checkButtons() {
2       var germany = document.getElementById("germany");
3       var us = document.getElementById("us");
4       if (germany.checked || us.checked) {
5           document.getElementById("zipset").style.visibility =↵
6               "visible";
7           if (germany.checked) {
8               countrySel = "de";
```

```
9              } else {
10                countrySel = "us";
11            }
12        }
13    }
```

This function is called when a user clicks one of the country option buttons. The code identifies the checked button and assigns the `countrySel` variable the corresponding country abbreviation used by zippopotam.us.

6. Below the `displayData()` function, enter the following code to create event listeners for the country option buttons:

```
1    var germany = document.getElementById("germany");
2    var us = document.getElementById("us");
3    if (us.addEventListener) {
4        germany.addEventListener("click", checkButtons, false);
5        us.addEventListener("click", checkButtons, false);
6    } else if (us.attachEvent) {
7        germany.attachEvent("onclick", checkButtons);
8        us.attachEvent("onclick", checkButtons);
9    }
```

7. In the `getLocation()` function, in the statement that begins `httpRequest.open`, replace the second occurrence of the string "us" in the URL with " + countrySel + ". Your updated statement should match the following:

```
httpRequest.open("get", ↵
    "http://api.zippopotam.us/" + countrySel + "/" + zip, true);
```

8. In the `getRequestObject()` function, update the `catch` statement to match the following:

```
1    catch (requestError) {
2        // display city & state fields and labels for manual input
3        document.getElementById("zipset").style.visibility = ↵
4            "visible";
5        document.getElementById("csset").style.visibility = ↵
6            "visible";
7        // remove event listeners so additional input is ignored
8        var germany = document.getElementById("germany");
```

```
 9      var us = document.getElementById("us");
10      var zip = document.getElementById("zip").value;
11      if (zip.addEventListener) {
12          germany.removeEventListener("click", checkButtons,↵
13              false);
14          us.removeEventListener("click", checkButtons, false);
15          zip.removeEventListener("keyup", checkInput, false);
16      } else if (zip.attachEvent) {
17          germany.detachEvent("onclick", checkButtons);
18          us.detachEvent("onclick", checkButtons);
19          zip.detachEvent("onkeyup", checkInput);
20      }
21      return false;
22  }
```

The added code expands the existing functionality so the zip field is displayed along with the city and state fields if the browser doesn't support Ajax, and the event listeners are removed from the country option buttons along with the zip field.

9. Save your changes to **script.js**, and then open **styles.css**. In the comment section, change "Hands-on Project 11-4" to **Hands-on Project 11-5**. Locate the style rule for the #csset selector, and then add #zipset as an additional selector for the rule, as follows:

```
#zipset, #csset {
   visibility: hidden;
}
```

10. Save your changes to **styles.css**, and then in your browser open the URL *http://localhost/Chapter11/HandsOnProject11-5/address.htm*. Click the **Germany** option button. The Postal Code field is displayed.

11. In the Postal Code box, type **80333**. As Figure 11-18 shows, the city and state boxes are displayed, identifying the German postal code you entered as München, BY.

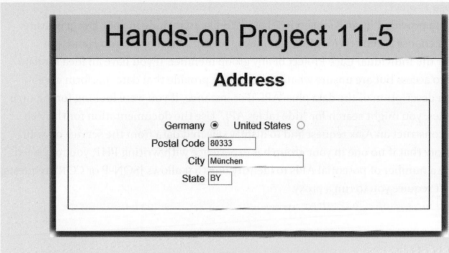

Hands-on Project 11-5

Address

Germany ⦿   United States ○
Postal Code 80333
City München
State BY

Figure 11-18: City and state retrieved for German postal code

12. Press and hold **Shift** as you click the **Refresh** or **Reload** button, click the **United States** option button, enter **06902**, and then verify that Stamford, CT, is displayed.

Case Projects

Individual Case Project

Identify data provided by an Ajax service that you'd like to include in your personal website. You should choose a web service other than those used in the chapter and the Hands-on Projects. If you have an idea for data you'd like to access but are unsure what service might provide that data, perform a web search on a description of the data plus "API." For instance, if you were looking for a source of tide tables, you might search for "tide tables API." Use the documentation for the web service to construct an Ajax request and to display selected data from the service on your website. Note that if you don't have experience with writing PHP, you may need to examine a number of potential APIs to identify one that allows JSON-P or CORS requests, which don't require you to run a proxy.

Group Case Project

Identify data provided by an Ajax service that you'd like to include in your group website. You should choose a web service other than those used in the chapter, the Hands-on Projects, or the Individual Case Project of any group member. If you have an idea for data you'd like to access but are unsure what service might provide that data, perform a web search on a description of the data plus "API." For instance, if you were looking for a source of tide tables, you might search for "tide tables API." Use the documentation for the web service to construct an Ajax request and to display selected data from the service on your website. Note that if no one in your group has experience with writing PHP, you may need to examine a number of potential APIs to identify one that allows JSON-P or CORS requests, which don't require you to run a proxy.

CHAPTER 12

INTRODUCTION TO JQUERY

When you complete this chapter, you will be able to:

> Select elements using jQuery syntax

> Use built-in jQuery functions

In a complex JavaScript project, developers often find themselves reusing code they originally wrote for a different project. The many lines of code that accomplish a specific task can often be generalized to the point that they can be copied and inserted in another project with few if any changes. Individual programmers and organizations have long compiled such useful sets of code into JavaScript libraries, which they can link to new projects to use any code the libraries contain. In addition to such private libraries, a number of free, publicly available libraries are also in common use on the web today. One of the most commonly used is jQuery, which is a library that enables developers to implement many common JavaScript tasks with minimal code. In this chapter, you'll learn what jQuery can do and you'll construct statements using jQuery syntax.

Implementing jQuery

jQuery removes some of the tedious work from coding JavaScript, and also provides a shortcut for some of the complicated parts of writing JavaScript. For starters, jQuery is a cross-browser library, automatically including alternate code where necessary to support different browsers. At the time this book was written, the jQuery Foundation, which maintains the jQuery library, published and supported two versions of jQuery: jQuery 1.x and jQuery 2.x. The first, jQuery 1.x, is backward compatible with Internet Explorer version 6 and later, meaning that it supports IE 6, 7, and 8. By contrast, jQuery 2.x does not support these older versions of IE, but instead supports only IE 9 and later. Because it requires less extra code for these older browsers, the jQuery 2.x library is slightly smaller than jQuery 1.x. This size difference can be significant when developing a complex web app.

In this chapter, you'll work on a web site for Life on Rocks Wildlife Cruises, a company in Monterey, California, that offers boat trips to view marine animals and seabirds. The main page of the site has been designed, and you've been hired to add drop-down menus to the navigation section. The design specifies that when a user moves the mouse pointer over a navigation bar item, the submenu showing its related options should be displayed. When the user moves the mouse pointer off that navigation bar item, the submenu should be hidden. Although you could create these drop-down menus using the JavaScript concepts you've learned in the preceding chapters, jQuery enables you to create this feature using much less code, so you'll use the jQuery library for this task. The owners want their site to work for IE8 users, so you'll use jQuery 1.x. Figure 12-1 shows a working drop-down menu on a desktop browser, and Figure 12-2 shows the system on a handheld browser.

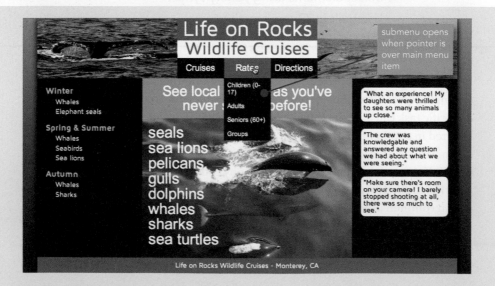

Figure 12-1: Final Life on Rocks site on a desktop browser
© 2015 Cengage Learning®. Source: Jan Roletto/NOAA CBNMS, Steve Lonhart/NOAA MBNMS, Chad King/ NOAA MBNMS

submenu opens when user touches main menu item

Figure 12-2: Final Life on Rocks site on a handheld browser
Source: Steve Lonhart/NOAA MBNMS

Including the Library

The first step in using jQuery is to link the .js file that contains the library to your HTML document. You can download the .js file for any version of the jQuery library for free from *jquery.com*. You can then place the downloaded file in the same location as your HTML document and link to the local file, just as you would for code you write yourself. However, because jQuery is so widely used, you have another option: instead of downloading the file and hosting it on your own server, you can simply specify the location in your HTML document of the jQuery file on a publicly accessible server. Such servers, known as content delivery networks (CDNs), are optimized for quick delivery of files across the globe, and linking to a file on a CDN provides an improved user experience in many situations. jQuery is available through a CDN hosted by *jquery.com*, as well as those maintained by Google, Microsoft, and other companies.

> **Note** | *You can learn more about available jQuery CDNs at jquery.com/download.*

You'll start your work on the Life on Rocks drop-down menus by examining the main web page in your browser and then adding a `script` element that links to a local copy of the jQuery library file.

To examine the Life on Rocks web page and link to the jQuery library:

1. In your text editor, open the **jquery-1.11.1.js** file, located in your Chapter folder for Chapter 12, and then examine the code. This file contains the jQuery library. Note that all the code is written in JavaScript.

2. Open the **jquery-1.11.1.min.js** file from the Chapter folder, and then examine the code. This file contains the minified version of the same code. Because you don't need to make changes to the jQuery library file, you'll link this minified version to your HTML document.

3. In your editor, open the **rocks.htm** file, and then in the comment section, add your name and today's date where indicated.

4. Save your changes, and then scroll through the document and familiarize yourself with its content. The body section contains two `div` elements containing images, followed by a `header` section and a `nav` section. The `nav` section contains an unordered list for the navigation bar elements, and each list item contains a nested unordered list for its submenu. The rest of the page consists of two `aside` elements, an `article` element, and a `footer` element.

5. At the end of the body section, just before the closing `</body>` tag, add the following `script` element to link to the minified jQuery file for version 1.11.1:

```
<script src="jquery-1.11.1.js"></script>
```

6. Save your changes to **rocks.htm**, open **rocks.htm** in a browser, and then move your mouse pointer over the navigation bar. Note that the submenus are hidden and moving the mouse pointer over the navigation bar text has no effect. Your first task will be to write code that displays each submenu when the mouse pointer is over the related navigation bar text.

Starting a jQuery Statement with $

Although all code that makes use of the jQuery library conforms to the rules of JavaScript, jQuery makes use of a few constructions and shortcuts that can give jQuery code the appearance of a different language.

First of all, every jQuery statement begins with $. The $ symbol specifies that any code that follows should be interpreted using the jQuery library.

Programming Concepts *Aliases*

The $ symbol that starts every jQuery statement is an alias, which is an alternative name. By default, the $ alias refers to the `jQuery()` function, which contains all the properties and attributes of the jQuery library. However, the $ alias is a common choice for JavaScript libraries because it is a unique and nonrestricted character. This means that if your app uses more than one library, you may need to replace the default alias for one or more of the libraries with a different alias. jQuery includes a `noConflict()` method that allows jQuery code using the $ alias to coexist with code for another library that also uses $. You can read more about the `noConflict()` method and other parts of the jQuery API at *api.jquery.com*.

Selecting Elements with jQuery

In every jQuery statement, the $ is followed by a reference to the element or elements on which the statement operates, contained in parentheses. To select elements in jQuery, you specify a CSS selector, contained in single or double quotes. For instance, to start a jQuery statement that operates on h1 elements, you use the following syntax:

```
$("h1")
```

Likewise, to select all elements that belong to the odd class, you use the following syntax:

```
$(".odd")
```

Notice that this default jQuery syntax is essentially a concise version of using JavaScript's `querySelectorAll()` method. The following code selects all elements that belong to the odd class, just like the statement above does, but using the JavaScript `querySelectorAll()` method rather than jQuery:

```
document.querySelectorAll(".odd")
```

Instead of using a literal selector, you can also select elements by providing the name of a variable that points to elements in the DOM. You can also use the `this` keyword in an event handler to refer to the element where the event was fired.

In the Life on Rocks navigation bar, the top-level unordered list has the class name `mainmenu`. To select each list item within this list, your jQuery statements must start as follows:

```
$("ul.mainmenu li")
```

Note that this code doesn't end with a semicolon because it's not a complete statement—it's just the selector portion of the statement. Next, you'll learn about methods you can specify to create a complete statement.

Traversing the DOM with jQuery Methods

Once you have selected one or more DOM elements for manipulation, you sometimes need to select one or more other elements based on their relationship to the selected elements. To do so, you move through the DOM from the selection. For instance, you may select a group of headings but want to perform an action on the first `p` element following each heading. jQuery enables you to modify a selection by appending a method to the selection code using dot syntax. For instance, the following code selects all `h2` elements:

```
$("h2")
// returns all h2 elements
```

To modify the selection to the sibling element that follows each `h2` element instead, you use the `next()` method, as follows:

```
$("h2").next()
// returns sibling elements that follow h2 elements
```

Table 12-1 describes several jQuery methods that enable you to traverse the DOM.

METHOD	DESCRIPTION
`children()`	Selects the child elements of each element matched by the main selector
`first()`	Narrows the group of selected elements to the first element
`last()`	Narrows the group of selected elements to the last element
`next()`	Changes the selection to the sibling element immediately following each selected element
`parent()`	Selects the parent element of each element matched by the main selector
`previous()`	Changes the selection to the sibling element immediately preceding each selected element
`siblings()`	Selects the sibling elements of each element matched by the main selector

Table 12-1: jQuery methods for DOM traversal

In the Life or Rocks navigation bar, your drop-down menus will work by showing and hiding the unordered lists that are children of the top-level list items. You can add the `children()` method to your existing selector to change the selected items to the children of the original selection, as follows:

```
$("ul.mainmenu li").children()
```

You can make the code more specific by including a selector within the parentheses for the `children()` method. This narrows the selected items to only those children that match the selector. For instance, to select only the `ul` elements that are children of each list item selected in the previous statement, you could add the `"ul"` selector to the `children()` method, as follows:

```
$("ul.mainmenu li").children("ul")
```

After you have written code to select one or more DOM elements for manipulation, you can then use jQuery methods to manipulate the selection.

Manipulating the DOM with jQuery Methods

Selecting elements in jQuery is generally easier than in plain JavaScript (that is, in JavaScript without jQuery). However, the advantages to jQuery don't stop there. The jQuery API also includes a substantial set of methods for performing actions on the selected elements. Some of the most powerful are the methods that enable you to manipulate DOM elements. Table 12-2 describes several of these methods.

METHOD	DESCRIPTION
addClass()	Adds the specified class name(s) to the selection
clone()	Creates a duplicate of the selection
css()	Retrieves values for one or more CSS properties for the first element in the selection, or sets a specified CSS property to a specified value
height()	Retrieves the calculated height of the first element in the selection, or sets the height of the selected elements
html()	Retrieves the HTML content of the first element in the selection, or sets the HTML content of the selected elements
removeClass()	Removes the specified class name(s) from the selection
val()	Retrieves the value of the first element in the selection, or sets the value of the selected elements
width()	Retrieves the calculated width of the first element in the selection, or sets the width of the selected elements

Table 12-2: jQuery methods for DOM manipulation

Many jQuery methods serve dual functions, allowing you to look up a value or set that value. For instance, if you specify the width() attribute for a selection without a value in the parentheses, the statement returns the existing width value of the selection. However, if you specify the width() attribute with a value in the parentheses, such as width("5em"), the statement sets the width value of the selection to the specified value. The following code illustrates both uses of the jQuery width() method.

```
1   $(".odd").width();
2   /* returns the computed width value for the first element with
3   the class name "odd" */
4   $(".odd").width("5em");
5   /* sets the width of all elements with the class name "odd" to
6   5em */
```

The style sheet for the Life on Rocks site contains a class named show that sets the value of the CSS display property to block. By applying this property to the children of a top-level list item, you make the nested list containing the submenu items visible. The following complete jQuery statement makes all submenus visible by assigning them all the class name show:

```
$("ul.mainmenu li").children("ul").addClass("show");
```

Next, you'll create a JavaScript document, link it to your HTML document, and add a jQuery statement that makes all the submenus visible.

To create a jQuery statement that makes all the submenus visible:

1. In your text editor, create a new JavaScript document containing the following comment, adding your name and today's date where indicated:

```
1   /*  JavaScript 6th Edition
2       Chapter 12
3       Chapter case
4       Life on Rocks Wildlife Cruises
5       Author:
6       Date:
7       Filename: script.js
8   */
```

2. Save the file as **script.js** in the Chapter 12 folder.

3. Below the comment, enter the following jQuery statement:

```
$("ul.mainmenu li").children("ul").addClass("show");
```

This statement selects the `li` elements that are within the `ul` element with the class name `mainmenu`, traverses to the children of the selected elements, and then adds the class name `show` to the child elements.

4. Save your changes to **script.js**, then switch to **rocks.htm** in your editor.

5. At the end of the body section, just before the closing `</body>` tag, enter the following `script` element to link the **script.js** file you just created:

```
<script src="script.js"></script>
```

Caution

Be sure the `script` element that links to the script.js file follows the `script` element that links to the jQuery library file. This order ensures that browsers parse the contents of the jQuery library before attempting to interpret the jQuery statements in script.js. Otherwise, the jQuery syntax in script.js could cause syntax errors if browsers encounter it before parsing the jQuery library.

6. Save your changes to **rocks.htm**, and then refresh or reload **rocks.htm** in your browser. As Figure 12-3 shows, all three submenus are now displayed.

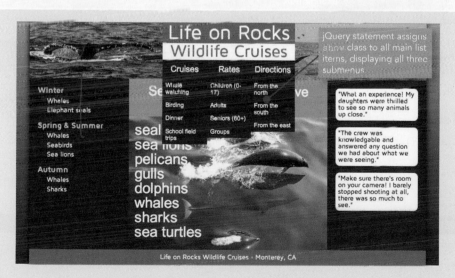

Figure 12-3: Life on Rocks page showing all three submenus
Source: Jan Roletto/NOAA CBNMS, Steve Lonhart/NOAA MBNMS, Chad King/NOAA MBNMS

Now that you understand how to use jQuery methods to modify DOM elements, you'll place your jQuery statement in a named function and specify it as an event handler. This will allow you to link the display of the submenus to user actions.

Specifying an Event Handler

You can group jQuery statements into functions using standard JavaScript syntax. For instance, the following code creates a named function called `display()` that contains the statement you created in the previous steps:

```
function display() {
    $("ul.mainmenu li").children("ul").addClass("show");
}
```

As in plain JavaScript, you can use a named function as an event handler with jQuery by creating an event listener. However, the code to create a backward-compatible event listener in jQuery is much simpler than the corresponding code in plain JavaScript. To create an event listener with jQuery, you create a statement that (1) starts with the jQuery alias ($), (2) specifies a selector for the element(s) associated with the event, and (3) finishes with a method that specifies an event and the action or actions to take in response to the event. Table 12-3 describes the jQuery methods for specifying some common events, and Table 12-4 describes some jQuery properties related to events.

METHOD	DESCRIPTION
`blur()`	Specifies code to execute on `blur` event
`click()`	Specifies code to execute on `click` event
`focus()`	Specifies code to execute on `focus` event
`hover()`	Specifies code to execute when the pointer enters an element, as well as code to execute when the pointer leaves the element
`load()`	Specifies code to execute on `load` event
`submit()`	Specifies code to execute on `submit` event

Table 12-3: jQuery methods for common events

METHOD	DESCRIPTION
`event.currentTarget`	Element currently being targeted by the event
`event.target`	Target element on which the event was fired
`event.type`	Type of event that was fired

Table 12-4: jQuery event properties

Note that each event method has the role indicated when a function name or an anonymous function is specified within the parentheses. If the parentheses are left empty, then each method instead fires the indicated event. For instance, the following code shows two statements that use the `submit()` method. The first specifies the name of a function that handles the submit event when it fires. The second fires the `submit` event on the selected element.

```
1    $("form.order").submit(validateForm);
2    /* specifies validateForm() as event handler when form is
3    submitted */
4    $("form.order").submit();
5    /* fires submit event on form */
```

Next you'll create two functions for the Life on Rocks drop-down menus. The `display()` function will display a submenu, and the `hide()` function will hide a submenu. You'll then add an event handler for the `hover` event, specifying the `display()` function as the code to execute when the pointer enters an element and the `hide()` function as the code to execute when the pointer leaves an element. Your functions will use the `event .currentTarget` property to identify which element's submenu to show or hide.

To create functions and an event listener using jQuery:

1. Return to **script.js** in your editor.

2. Comment out the statement `$("ul.mainmenu li").children("ul") .addClass("show");`

3. Below the commented-out statement, enter the following code to create the `display()` function:

```
function display(event) {

}
```

This function takes a single parameter, `event`, which references the event that fired to call the function.

4. Within the `display()` function, enter the following statement:

```
$(event.currentTarget).children("ul").addClass("show");
```

This statement replaces the selector you previously used (`"ul.mainmenu li"`) with a reference to the `currentTarget` property of the `event` parameter. The value of this property is the `li` element that the mouse pointer is currently over.

5. Below the closing `}` for the `display()` function, enter the following `hide()` function:

```
function hide(event) {
    $(event.currentTarget).children("ul").removeClass("show");
}
```

This function works similarly to the `display()` function, but instead of the `addClass()` method, it uses the `removeClass()` method to remove the `show` class and return the submenu to its default `display` property value of `none`.

6. Below the closing } for the `hide()` function, enter the following statement:

```
$("ul.mainmenu li").hover(display,hide);
```

This statement incorporates the same selector you used in the previous steps to select all top-level list items. It then uses the `hover()` method to specify code to fire in response to the hover event. The method takes two arguments: the first specifies the event handler for when the mouse pointer enters the element, and the second specifies the event handler for when the mouse pointer leaves the element.

7. Save your changes to **script.js**, reload **rocks.htm** in your browser, and then move the mouse pointer over each of the items in the navigation bar. As Figure 12-4 shows, when you move the mouse pointer over a menu item, its submenu is displayed, and when you move the mouse pointer off the menu item, its submenu is once again hidden.

Figure 12-4: Submenu displayed in response to `hover` event
Source: Jan Roletto/NOAA CBNMS, Steve Lonhart/NOAA MBNMS, Chad King/NOAA MBNMS

Short Quiz 1

1. What is the first step in using jQuery in a project?
2. How does every jQuery statement start?
3. How do you select elements in jQuery?

Using jQuery Built-in Effects

In addition to providing a compact syntax for selecting and manipulating elements, jQuery also includes a number of methods that enable you to add visual animations to your apps. Table 12-5 lists several popular jQuery animation methods.

METHOD	DESCRIPTION
animate()	Changes value of one or more CSS properties
fadeIn()	Displays hidden elements by changing their display values to the default and then changing their opacity from 0 to 100
fadeOut()	Hides elements by changing their opacity from 100 to 0 and then changing their display values to none
hide()	Hides elements by changing their display values to none
show()	Displays elements by changing their display values to the default
slideDown()	Displays elements by changing their height from 0 to the full value
slideUp()	Hides elements by changing their height from the full value to 0

Table 12-5: jQuery animation methods

All of these methods can take a value in milliseconds as an argument, allowing you to specify the time frame over which the animation should occur. Certain methods also allow you to specify the keywords `slow` or `fast` to set the speed of the animation.

Although the Life on Rocks submenus now work as the designer intended, you could create the same behavior without using the `show` class simply by using jQuery's `show()` and `hide()` methods. To see how this works, you'll change the `display()` and `hide()` functions to instead use the `show()` and `hide()` methods.

To use the jQuery `show()` and `hide()` methods to display and hide the submenus:

1. Return to **script.js** in your editor.

2. Within the `display()` function, comment out the statement `$ (event .currentTarget) .children ("ul") .addClass ("show");`

3. Within the `display()` function, enter the following statement:

   `$ (event.currentTarget) .children ("ul") .show ();`

   This statement replaces the `addClass ("show")` method with the `show()` method. The `show()` method changes the value of an element's `display` property without requiring you to include a class in your style sheet.

4. Within the `hide()` function, comment out the statement `$ (event.currentTarget) .children ("ul") .removeClass ("show");` and then enter the following statement:

   `$ (event.currentTarget) .children ("ul") .hide ();`

   Similar to the new statement in the `display()` function, this statement replaces the `removeClass ("show")` method with the `hide()` method.

5. Save your changes to **script.js**, refresh or reload **rocks.htm** in your browser, and then move your mouse pointer over the main navigation bar items. Each item's submenu is displayed when the mouse pointer is over it, just as it was in the previous set of steps. The only difference is that your code now uses jQuery's `show()` and `hide()` methods rather than using the `addClass()` and `removeClass()` methods to add and remove a custom class.

Some jQuery animation methods enable you to easily add and experiment with visual effects that might otherwise require writing and debugging many lines of JavaScript. Although the Life on Rocks designer asked only for the submenus to simply be displayed and hidden, you'll finish your work on the site by adding a more gradual animated effect when the menus open. You can show this to the designer to provide a sense of what's possible with jQuery, and you can easily remove it if the designer prefers the menus not to be animated. You'll use the `slideDown()` method for your animation with the `fast` keyword, which will quickly increase the height of a menu as it's displayed, rather than showing it immediately at full height.

To implement the `slideDown()` method to show the submenus:

1. Return to **script.js** in your editor.

2. In the `display()` function, comment out the statement `$(event.currentTarget).children("ul").show();`

3. In the `display()` function, add the following statement:

```
$(event.currentTarget).children("ul").slideDown("fast");
```

This statement is the same as the statement you commented out in the previous step, except that it replaces the `show()` method with the `slideDown()` method and specifies the `fast` keyword for the speed of the `slideDown()` animation. Your completed code should match the following:

```
1   //$("ul.mainmenu li").children("ul").addClass("show");
2   function display(event) {
3   //    $(event.currentTarget).children("ul").addClass("show");
4   //    $(event.currentTarget).children("ul").show();
5       $(event.currentTarget).children("ul").slideDown("fast");
6   }
7   function hide(event) {
8   //    $(event.currentTarget).children("ul").removeClass("show");
9       $(event.currentTarget).children("ul").hide();
10  }
11  $("ul.mainmenu li").hover(display,hide);
```

4. Save your changes to **script.js**, refresh or reload **rocks.htm** in your browser, and then move the mouse pointer over one of the navigation bar items. Instead of the submenu being immediately displayed, it appears to extend down gradually from the related main menu item, similar to closing a blind.

Note | This chapter provided a brief introduction to jQuery syntax, methods, and effects. To learn more about the jQuery library, explore the tutorials online at learn.jquery.com, or search on "jQuery tutorials."

Short Quiz 2

1. What argument do all jQuery animation methods take?
2. What is the difference between using the jQuery `addClass()` method and the `show()` method to display an element with the `display` property value set to `none`?

Summary

> jQuery, one of the most commonly used JavaScript libraries, enables developers to implement many common JavaScript tasks with minimal code.

> To use jQuery, you have to link the .js file containing the library to your HTML document.

> The $ that starts every jQuery statement is an alias, which is an alternative name. The $ alias refers to the jQuery() function, which contains all the properties and attributes of the jQuery library.

> To select elements in jQuery, you specify a CSS selector, contained in quotes.

> jQuery enables you to modify a selection by appending a DOM traversal method to the selection code using dot syntax.

> The jQuery API also includes a substantial set of methods for performing actions on selected elements. Many jQuery methods serve dual functions, allowing you to look up a value or set that value.

> To create an event listener with jQuery, you create a statement that (1) starts with the jQuery alias ($), (2) specifies a selector for the element(s) associated with the event, and (3) finishes with a method that specifies an event and the action or actions to take in response to the event.

> In addition to providing a compact syntax for selecting and manipulating elements, jQuery also includes a number of methods that enable you to add visual animations to your apps.

Key Terms

alias—An alternative name; the $ that starts every jQuery statement is an alias for the jQuery() function.

jQuery—A JavaScript library that enables developers to implement many common JavaScript tasks with minimal code.

plain JavaScript—JavaScript without jQuery.

Review Questions

1. What language is the jQuery library written in?
   a. CSS
   b. JavaScript
   c. HTML
   d. PHP

2. What is a difference between jQuery 1.x and jQuery 2.x?
   a. Only jQuery 1.x is written in JavaScript.
   b. Only jQuery 2.x works with modern browsers.
   c. Only jQuery 1.x supports IE 6, 7, and 8.
   d. jQuery 1.x is smaller than jQuery 2.x.

3. Instead of hosting your own copy of the jQuery library, you can link an HTML document to a copy of the jQuery file _____.
   a. on the W3C website
   b. on a CDN
   c. on the WHATWG website
   d. in the style sheet

4. What is the first step in using jQuery?
   a. Link the .js file that contains the library to your HTML document.
   b. Create a selector.
   c. Enter a method name.
   d. Enter method parameters.

5. Every jQuery statement begins with which character?
   a. #
   b. $
   c. .
   d. {

6. The syntax you use to select elements in a jQuery statement is essentially a concise version of which JavaScript method?
   a. `getElementById()`
   b. `getElementsByClassName()`
   c. `getElementsByTagName()`
   d. `querySelectorAll()`

7. Which of the following selects all p elements in a document?
   a. `$("p")`
   b. `#("p")`
   c. `$.("p")`
   d. `#.("p")`

8. Which jQuery method do you use to add a class name to one or more selected elements?
   a. `clone()`
   b. `addClass()`
   c. `html()`
   d. `removeClass()`

9. What action does a jQuery event method perform if it is called with empty parentheses?
   a. It does nothing.
   b. It creates an event listener on the `window` object.
   c. It removes any matching event listener on the selection.
   d. It fires the indicated event.

10. Which is not part of a jQuery statement to create a backward-compatible event listener?
   a. The jQuery alias
   b. A selector for the element(s) associated with the event
   c. A method that specifies the event
   d. An `if/then` construction

11. Which is the correct syntax to create a function that uses jQuery?
   a. `$(function) name() {}`
   b. `$.function name() {}`
   c. `function name() {}`
   d. `$(name()).function {}`

12. Which of the following is a jQuery animation method?
   a. `focus()`
   b. `addClass()`
   c. `children()`
   d. `show()`

13. All jQuery animation methods can take a value in _____ to specify the length of the animation.
   a. minutes
   b. seconds
   c. microseconds
   d. milliseconds

14. Some jQuery animation methods accept which keywords to set the speed of the animation?
    a. `up` or `down`
    b. `slow` or `fast`
    c. `left` or `right`
    d. `true` or `false`

15. Which is an advantage of using jQuery animation methods rather than coding animations yourself in JavaScript?
    a. Coding the animations yourself might require writing and debugging many lines of JavaScript.
    b. The jQuery animation effects cannot be created with plain JavaScript.
    c. You cannot select certain web page elements without using jQuery.
    d. There is no particular advantage to using one or the other.

16. What is an alias? What is the role of an alias in jQuery?

17. What is the difference between calling a jQuery method with and without parameters?

18. Why should you ensure that the `script` element that links to the jQuery library file comes before any other `script` element for a .js file that includes jQuery code?

19. What are the components of an event listener using jQuery?

20. Why should you avoid including jQuery in a project if you don't need it?

Hands-On Projects

Hands-On Project 12-1

In this project, you'll use jQuery to display the elements containing a recipe's ingredients and instructions when a user clicks the associated headers.

1. In your text editor, open the **index.htm** file from the HandsOnProject12-1 folder in the Chapter12 folder where your data files are stored. In the comment section, enter your name and today's date where indicated, and then save your changes. Note that the file contains an `article` element, which includes an `h2` heading, an `h3` heading followed by an unordered list, and another `h3` heading followed by a `div`.

2. Open **index.htm** in your browser, and then click each of the headings. Notice that only the headings are displayed, and that nothing happens when you click a heading.

3. In your editor, create a new JavaScript file, and save it to the HandsOnProject12-1 folder with the filename **script.js**. Add a comment that includes the book name, chapter number, project number, your name, today's date, and the filename. Save your changes.

4. In the script.js file, add the following code to create a new function named `display` that takes a parameter called `event`:

```
function display(event) {

}
```

5. Within the `display()` function, enter the following jQuery selector to select the `currentTarget` value of the `event` parameter:

```
$(event.currentTarget)
```

   Because this function will be called when a user clicks either of the h3 elements, this selector references the h3 element the user clicked.

6. After the selector you entered in the previous step, type **.next()**. This method traverses the DOM tree to the element that follows the selected element—the ingredients list for the first h3 heading, or the instructions for the second h3 heading.

7. After the method you entered in the previous step, type **.fadeIn("slow");**

   Your completed function should match the following:

```
function display(event) {
    $(event.currentTarget).next().fadeIn("slow");
}
```

8. Below the closing } for the `display()` function, enter the following statement to create event listeners for the h3 elements that call the `display()` function when they are clicked:

```
$("h3").click(display);
```

9. Save your changes to **script.js**, and then in **index.htm**, just before the closing `</body>` tag, add a `script` element that specifies **script.js** as its source.

10. Just before the `script` element you created in the previous step, add a second `script` element that references the **jquery-1.11.1.min.js** file.

11. Save your changes to **index.htm**, open **index.htm** in a browser, and then click the **Ingredients** and **Instructions** headers. The ingredients list is displayed using the jQuery `fadeIn` animation method after you click the Ingredients header, and the instructions are displayed in the same way after you click the Instructions header, as shown in Figure 12-5.

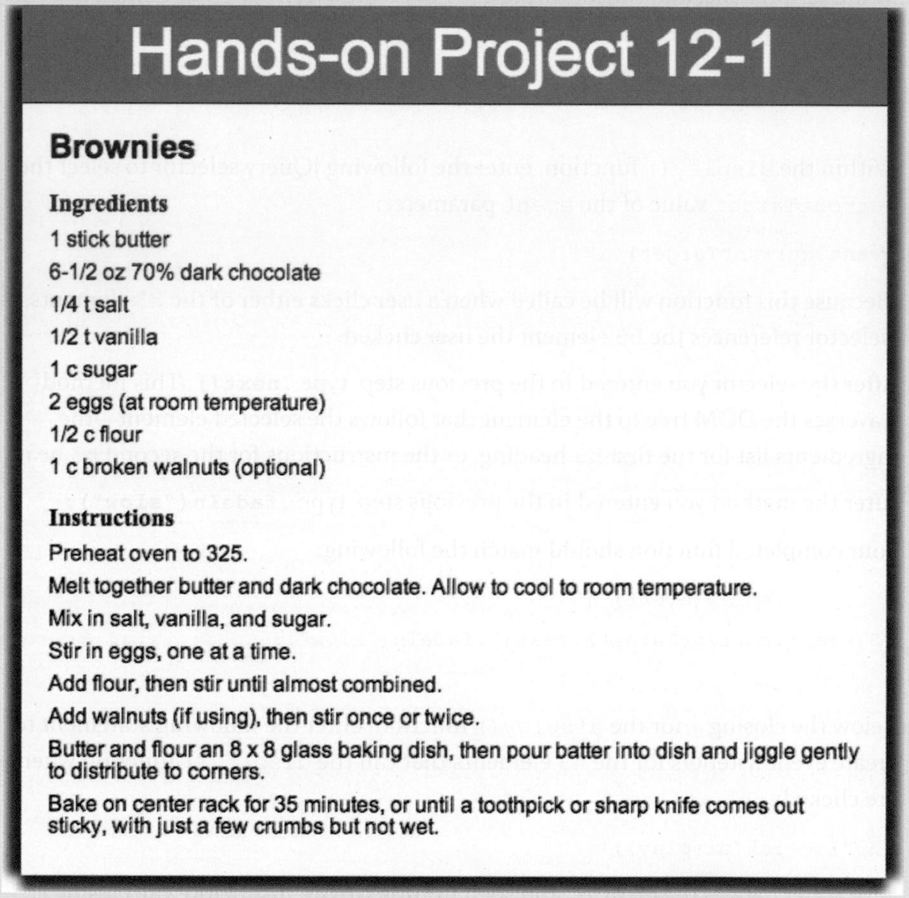

Hands-on Project 12-1

Brownies

Ingredients

1 stick butter
6-1/2 oz 70% dark chocolate
1/4 t salt
1/2 t vanilla
1 c sugar
2 eggs (at room temperature)
1/2 c flour
1 c broken walnuts (optional)

Instructions

Preheat oven to 325.

Melt together butter and dark chocolate. Allow to cool to room temperature.

Mix in salt, vanilla, and sugar.

Stir in eggs, one at a time.

Add flour, then stir until almost combined.

Add walnuts (if using), then stir once or twice.

Butter and flour an 8 x 8 glass baking dish, then pour batter into dish and jiggle gently to distribute to corners.

Bake on center rack for 35 minutes, or until a toothpick or sharp knife comes out sticky, with just a few crumbs but not wet.

Figure 12-5: Recipe document with all content displayed

Hands-On Project 12-2

In this project, you'll code an app that converts a weight in pounds to kilograms using jQuery.

1. In your text editor, open the **index.htm** file from the HandsOnProject12-2 folder in the Chapter12 folder where your data files are stored. In the comment section, enter your name and today's date where indicated, and then save your changes. Note that the file contains a form that accepts a weight in pounds in an `input` field with the `id` value `pValue` and returns a weight in kilograms in a `p` element with the `id` value `kValue`.

2. In your editor, create a new JavaScript file, and save it to the HandsOnProject12-2 folder with the filename **script.js**. Add a comment that includes the book name, chapter number, project number, your name, today's date, and the filename. Save your changes.

3. In the script.js file, add the following code to create a new function named `convert()`:

```
function convert() {

}
```

4. Within the `convert()` function, enter the following two statements to declare local variables:

```
var lb = $("#pValue").val();
var kg = Math.round(lb / 2.2);
```

5. The first statement assigns the variable name `lb` to the value of the element with the id value `pValue`. The second statement uses plain JavaScript to divide the value of `lb` by 2.2, convert it to kilograms, and then round it to zero decimal places.

6. Within the `convert()` function, after the statements you entered in the previous step, enter the following statement to assign the value of the `kg` variable as the content of the element with the id value `kValue`:

```
$("#kValue").html(kg);
```

7. Below the `convert()` function, enter the following statement to add an event listener to the element with the id value `convertButton` that calls the `convert()` function when the element is clicked:

```
$("#convertButton").click(convert);
```

8. Below the statement you entered in the previous step, enter the following statements to clear the `pValue` and `kValue` elements when the document loads:

```
$("#pValue").val("");
$("#kValue").html("");
```

9. Save your changes to **script.js**, and then in **index.htm**, just before the closing `</body>` tag, add a `script` element that specifies **script.js** as its source.

10. Just before the `script` element you created in the previous step, add a second `script` element that references the **jquery-1.11.1.min.js** file.

11. Save your changes to **index.htm**, and then open **index.htm** in a browser. In the Enter weight in pounds box, type **44**, and then click the **Convert to Kg** button. As Figure 12-6 shows, the Weight in kilograms box displays 20.

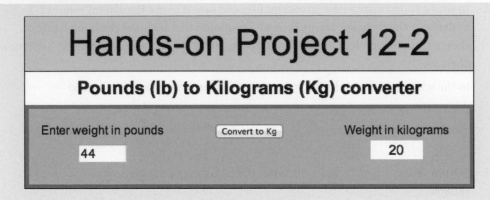

Figure 12-6: Value in pounds converted to kilograms

Hands-On Project 12-3

In this project, you'll recreate an existing form validation script using jQuery.

1. In your text editor, open the **index.htm** and **script.js** files from the HandsOnProject12-3 folder in the Chapter12 folder where your data files are stored. In the comment section of each file, enter your name and today's date where indicated, and then save your changes. Note that the **index.htm** file contains a form that contains four input fields and a Submit button. The **script.js** file contains JavaScript code to validate form input.

2. Open **index.htm** in a browser, and then click the **Submit** button. As Figure 12-7 shows, the background of each field changes to pink, and an error message is displayed at the top of the form.

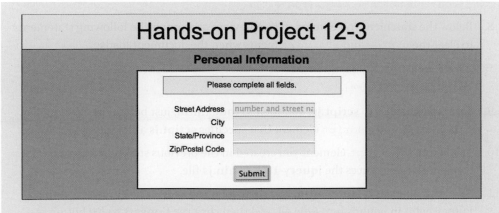

Figure 12-7: Invalid form submission

3. Enter fictitious information in each form field, ensuring that you enter numbers in the final field, and then click the **Submit** button. The submission confirmation page is displayed, confirming that your form entries were valid.

4. Return to the **script.js** file in your editor, and then in the `validateForm()` function, comment out the first five lines of the function, containing the `if/else` statement. After the commented-out section, add the following statement:

```
event.preventDefault();
```

5. Comment out the statement `var errorDiv = document.getElementById("errorText");`

6. Within the `try` statement, comment out the final two lines (`errorDiv.style.display = "none";` and `errorDiv.innerHTML = "";`). Before the closing `}` for the `try` statement, enter the following replacement statements:

```
$("#errorText").hide();
$("#errorText").html("");
```

7. Within the `catch` statement, comment out both existing statements and then enter the following two replacement statements:

```
$("#errorText").show();
$("#errorText").html(msg);
```

8. Within the final `if` statement that checks if the value of the `formValidity` variable is `true`, comment out the existing statement and replace it with the following:

```
$("form").submit();
```

9. Save your changes to **script.js**, refresh or reload **index.htm** in your browser, and then repeat Steps 2 and 3 to test the form and verify that the validation still works with the jQuery code you just added.

Hands-On Project 12-4

In this project, you'll continue your work on the validation code you worked on in the previous project. Next you'll convert the event listener code from plain JavaScript to jQuery.

1. In the file manager for your operating system, copy the completed contents of the HandsOnProject12-3 folder to the HandsOnProject12-4 folder.

2. In your text editor, open the **index.htm** and **results.htm** files from the HandsOnProject12-4 folder. In each file, change "Hands-On Project 12-3" to **Hands-On Project 12-4** in the comment section, in the `title` element, and in the `h1` element. Save your changes to both files and then close results.htm.

3. In your text editor, open the **script.js** file from the HandsOnProject12-4 folder, change "Hands-On Project 12-3" to **Hands-On Project 12-4** in the comment section, and then save your changes.

4. In the **script.js** file, at the bottom of the file, comment out the six lines of code that create event listeners, and then below the commented code, add the following replacement statement:

```
$("#submitBtn").click(validateForm);
```

5. Save your changes to **script.js**, open **index.htm** in your browser from the HandsOnProject12-4 folder, and then repeat Steps 2 and 3 from Hands-On Project 12-3 to verify that the validation function still works as expected.

Hands-On Project 12-5

In this project, you'll continue your work on the validation code you worked on in the previous 2 projects. You'll finish your work by locating and linking to the jQuery library using a CDN rather than a locally stored file.

1. In the file manager for your operating system, copy the completed contents of the HandsOnProject12-4 folder to the HandsOnProject12-5 folder.

2. In your text editor, open the **index.htm** and **results.htm** files from the HandsOnProject12-5 folder. In each file, change "Hands-On Project 12-4" to **Hands-On Project 12-5** in the comment section, in the title element, and in the h1 element. Save your changes to each file, and then close results.htm.

3. In your text editor, open the **script.js** file from the HandsOnProject12-5 folder, change "Hands-On Project 12-4" to **Hands-On Project 12-5** in the comment section, and then save your changes.

4. In your text editor, return to index.htm, scroll to the bottom of the file, and then comment out the script element that links to the local jQuery file.

5. In a browser, open **http://jquery.com/download/**, and read the information about CDNs where the jQuery library is available.

6. Choose a CDN from the list, follow the link to its documentation, and then based on the CDN instructions, replace the link to the jQuery library in your index.htm document with a link to the jQuery version 1.11 library hosted by the CDN. (*Note:* The jQuery 1.11.1 library is not available from a CDN because it is not a major version, but for the purposes of this exercise, version 1.11 is equivalent to the version you've been using.)

7. Save your changes to **script.js**, open **index.htm** in your browser from the HandsOnProject12-5 folder, and then repeat Steps 2 and 3 from Hands-On Project 12-3 to verify that the validation function still works as expected.

Case Projects

Individual Case Project

In your individual website, revise a function to use jQuery selectors and methods. Identify a function that contains at least three selectors that you can replace with jQuery selectors, and that performs at least one DOM traversal or CSS change that you can replace with a jQuery method. Comment out the code you replace rather than deleting it. Be sure to link to the jQuery library in all HTML documents that link to the .js file you've updated. When your revisions are done, test all pages that use the function to ensure they still perform as they did when the function was written in plain JavaScript.

Group Case Project

Examine the documentation of jQuery methods and properties at *api.jquery.com*. As a group, pick a jQuery method that would enhance the appearance or function of one or more pages of your group website. As a group, agree on which sections of your code need to be changed to implement this method. Make the changes as a group, and continue to save and test your changes until the feature works as you expect.

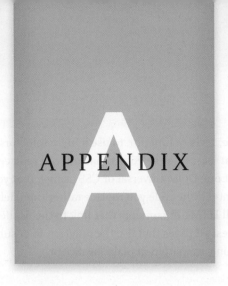

APPENDIX

INSTALLING AND CONFIGURING A TESTING SERVER

For basic web development with HTML, CSS, and JavaScript, you can do most of your testing by opening the files with a web browser installed on your computer. However, some web app functionality can be tested only by moving the code to a web server and opening it in your browser using an HTTP connection. A web server used privately for testing purposes is known as a **testing server**. Applications published on a testing server are available only to the developers working on them, and not to other users of the Internet or a local intranet. When testing is complete and your application is ready to be released, you move your app to a **production server**, which is available to your target audience.

It's common for web developers to install a testing server on the same computer they use to code. Having both the server and client on the same machine enables quick testing of changes while coding or debugging, without needing to be connected to a network or to first transfer files to another machine.

Like any web server, a testing server consists of server software and interpreters. The server software listens for and processes HTTP requests. When necessary, it passes requests along to interpreters of specific languages for parsing and processing, and then forwards the results to the client. Most web servers on the web today are running either Apache, nginx, or Internet Information Services for server software. A commonly used interpreter is the one for PHP.

Installing server software and interpreters is often done using the command line, which is a text-only computer interface in which you type a command for every action you want the computer to execute. Although this is still necessary in some cases for highly customized installations, you can instead install a basic web server using an app that sets up a server with basic functionality using the most common options. This appendix provides instructions for using one such package, known as XAMPP, which is free and available for computers running Windows or Mac OS X. XAMPP installs the Apache web server along with the MySQL database and interpreters for the PHP and Perl languages.

Installing XAMPP for Windows

The following instructions detail installing XAMPP for Windows. These steps are followed by a separate set of instructions for installing XAMPP for Mac OS X.

To install XAMPP for Windows:

1. In your browser, open **apachefriends.org/download.html**. As Figure A-1 shows, the Download page provides links for multiple versions of XAMPP for each operating system.

2. In the XAMPP for Windows section, click the **Download (32 bit)** button for the final version in the list. For instance, on the page shown in Figure A-1, you would click the Download (32 bit) button for version 1.8.3.

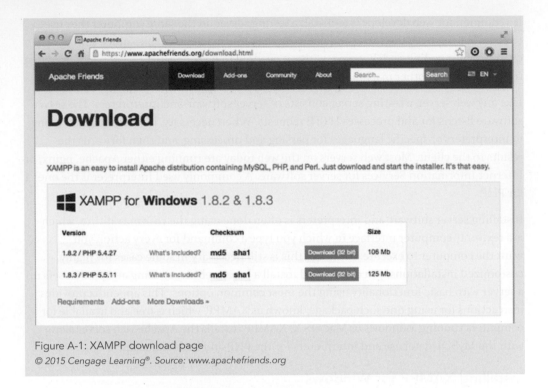

Figure A-1: XAMPP download page
© 2015 Cengage Learning®. Source: www.apachefriends.org

3. When the download is completed, if your browser offers you the option to run the downloaded file, follow the browser instructions to do so. Otherwise, open the folder to which the file was downloaded, locate the downloaded file, and double-click it to start the installer.

4. If Windows asks for confirmation that you wish to install the file, follow the instructions shown to authorize the installation.

5. If a warning is displayed about the interaction of the XAMPP installer with antivirus, click **Yes** to continue with the installation. The installer may also display a window discussing the interaction between XAMPP and Windows User Account Control. Click **OK**. The Setup window is displayed, as shown in Figure A-2.

Figure A-2: Setup window
Source: www.apachefriends.org

6. Click **Next**. The Select Components window is displayed. Ensure that all boxes are checked, as shown in Figure A-3, and then click **Next**.

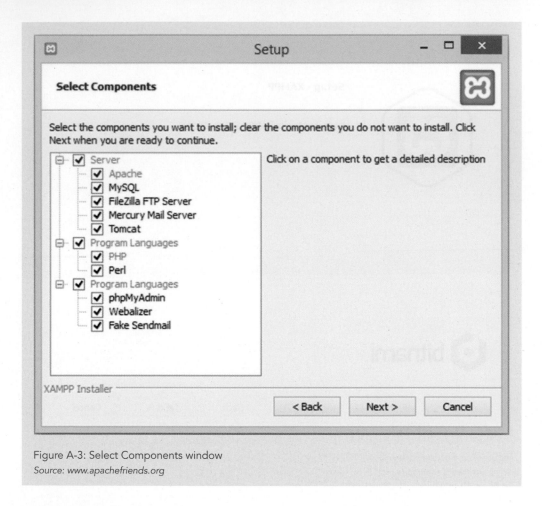

Figure A-3: Select Components window
Source: www.apachefriends.org

7. The Installation folder window is displayed. Ensure that the Select a folder box contains C:\xampp, as shown in Figure A-4. Click **Next**.

Figure A-4: Installation folder window
Source: www.apachefriends.org

> **Note**
>
> *Due to permissions issues, you should not install XAMPP to the Program Files folder. If you change the default directory name, you should choose a name that contains no spaces, to avoid issues with server components.*

8. The Bitnami for XAMPP window is displayed, which offers more information about enhancing an XAMPP installation. Uncheck the **Learn more about Bitnami for XAMPP** box to specify a basic installation, and then click **Next**.

9. The Ready to Install window is displayed. Click **Next**. A progress bar is displayed while the server is installed, as shown in Figure A-5.

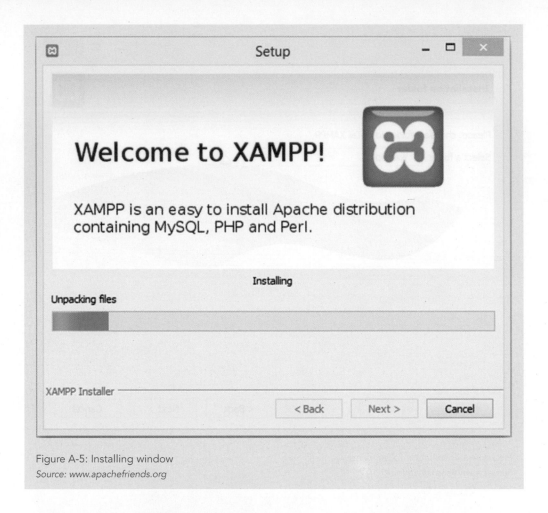

Figure A-5: Installing window
Source: www.apachefriends.org

10. When setup is completed, the Completing the XAMPP Setup Wizard window is
displayed. You need to launch the Control Panel as an administrator, so ensure the
Do you want to start the Control Panel now? box is not checked, and then
click **Finish**. In File Explorer, navigate to **c:/xampp**, right-click the file named
xampp-control with a file type of Application, click **Run as administrator**, and
then in the User Account Control box, click **Yes**. The Control Panel is displayed, as
shown in Figure A-6.

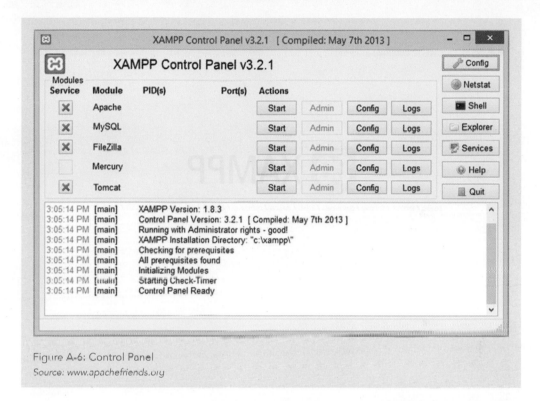

Figure A-6: Control Panel
Source: www.apachefriends.org

11. The Control Panel lists several modules. In the line for the Apache module, click the **Start** button to start the Apache service. If Windows displays a security alert dialog box, click **Allow access** to continue. (*Note:* If you see a Stop button instead of a Start button, the Apache service is already started, so you can skip this step.)

12. To test your XAMPP installation, open your browser then, in the address bar, type **localhost**, and then press **Enter**. Your browser should display the default web document for XAMPP, as shown in Figure A-7. This confirms that your Apache web server is working correctly.

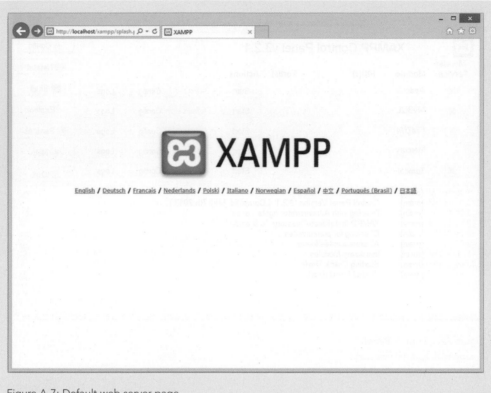

Figure A-7: Default web server page
Source: www.apachefriends.org

To move your own files to the Apache installation so you can open them with an HTTP connection, open **File Explorer**, navigate to the location of your files, copy one or more files or folders to the clipboard, navigate to **c:/xampp/htdocs**, and then paste your copied files or folders. You can then open your files in the browser with the path `localhost/`*`filename`*. For instance, if you copied a file called register.htm to the htdocs folder, you would open this file in a browser by entering `localhost/register.htm`. If you copied a folder called website containing a file called info.htm, you would open this file in a browser by entering `localhost/website/info.htm`.

Installing XAMPP for Mac OS X

The following instructions detail installing XAMPP for Mac OS X.

To install XAMPP in Mac OS X:

1. In your browser, open **apachefriends.org/download.html**, and then scroll down to the XAMPP for Apple section. As Figure A-8 shows, the Download page provides links for multiple versions of XAMPP for each operating system.

2. In the XAMPP for Apple section, click the **Download (64 bit)** button for the final version in the list. For instance, on the page shown in Figure A-8, you would click the Download (64 bit) button for version 1.8.3.

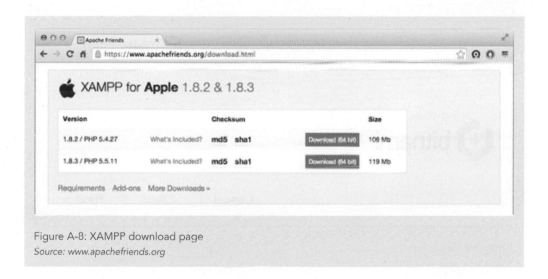

Figure A-8: XAMPP download page
Source: www.apachefriends.org

3. When the download is completed, if your browser offers you the option to run the downloaded file, follow the browser instructions to do so. Otherwise, open the folder to which the file was downloaded, locate the downloaded file, and double-click it to unzip it. In the window that opens, double-click the installer file to run it.

4. If your computer asks for confirmation that you wish to install the file, click **Open**, and then enter your password to confirm installation. The Setup window is displayed, as shown in Figure A-9.

Figure A-9: Setup window
Source: www.apachefriends.org

5. Click **Next**. The Select Components window is displayed. Ensure that all boxes are checked, as shown in Figure A-10, and then click **Next**.

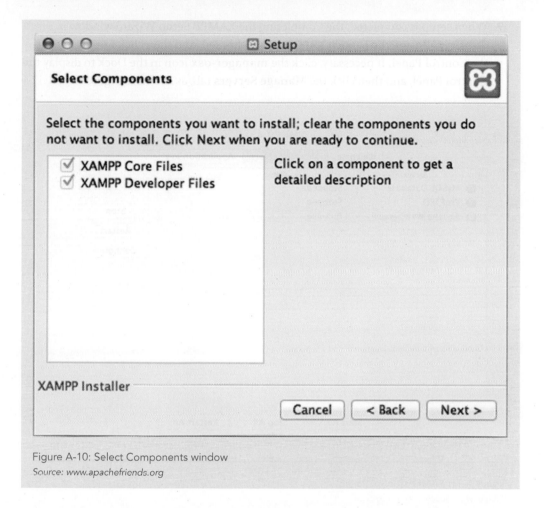

Figure A-10: Select Components window
Source: www.apachefriends.org

6. The Installation Directory window is displayed. On a Mac, XAMPP is always installed to the /Applications/XAMPP directory. Click **Next**.

7. The Bitnami for XAMPP window is displayed, which offers more information about enhancing an XAMPP installation. Uncheck the **Learn more about Bitnami for XAMPP** box to specify a basic installation, and then click **Next**.

8. The Ready to Install window is displayed. Click **Next**. A progress bar is displayed while the server is installed.

9. When setup is completed, the Completing the XAMPP Setup Wizard window is displayed. Ensure the Launch XAMPP box is checked, and then click **Finish** to open the Control Panel. If necessary, click the **manager-osx** icon in the Dock to display the Control Panel, and then click the **Manage Servers** tab, as shown in Figure A-11.

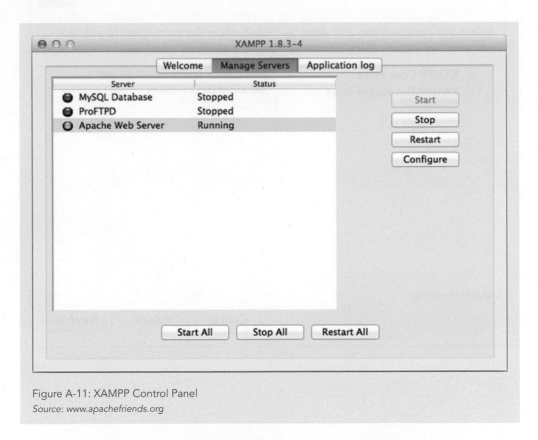

Figure A-11: XAMPP Control Panel
Source: www.apachefriends.org

10. The Control Panel lists several modules. If the status next to Apache Web Server in the list is "Stopped," click **Apache Web Server** in the list, and then click the **Start** button to start the Apache service.

11. To test your XAMPP installation, open your browser then, in the address bar, type **localhost**, and then press **Enter**. Your browser should display the default web document for XAMPP, as shown in Figure A-12. This confirms that your Apache web server is working correctly.

Figure A-12: Default web server page
Source: www.apachefriends.org

To move your own files to the Apache installation so you can open them with an HTTP connection, open **Finder**, navigate to the location of your files, copy one or more files or folders to the clipboard, navigate to **Applications/XAMPP/htdocs**, and then paste your copied files or folders. You can then open your files in the browser with the path localhost/*filename*. For instance, if you copied a file called register.htm to the htdocs folder, you would open this file in a browser by entering localhost/register.htm. If you copied a folder called website containing a file called info.htm, you would open this file in a browser by entering localhost/website/info.htm.

> **Note** | For questions or more information about using XAMPP, you can read existing topics or post your own questions on the XAMPP community forums at community.apachefriends.org. You can do the same at stackoverflow.com.

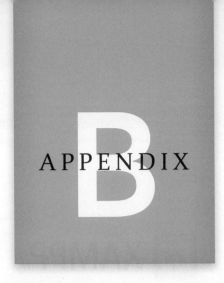

WORKING WITH HTML AND CSS

Writing HTML5

Compared to many other markup languages, HTML5 is not very strict in the elements it requires to be present in a document, or the syntax it requires. However, to ensure that parsers interpret your HTML5 code as you intended, it's advisable to follow some guidelines for the documents you create.

Defining the Document Type

A **DOCTYPE declaration** belongs in the first line of an HTML document and determines the Document Type Definition with which the document complies. A **Document Type Definition**, or **DTD**, defines the elements and attributes that can be used in a document, along with the rules that a document must follow when it includes them. Although many DOCTYPE declarations exist for different versions of HTML and other markup languages, HTML5 uses the following simple DOCTYPE:

```
<!DOCTYPE html>
```

This DOCTYPE declaration should come first in your HTML document, before the opening `<html>` tag that starts the page content.

Specifying the Character Encoding

Every text document, including an HTML5 file, has a **character encoding**, which is the system used to encode the human-readable characters that make up the page in a machine-readable format. Many character encoding systems exist, including ASCII and ISO-8859-1. The standard encoding used across the web today is UTF-8. To specify that your document uses this encoding, you include the following `meta` element in your document's head section:

```
<meta charset="utf-8" />
```

Using Semantic Elements

The `div` element is a useful tool for applying styles to element or groups of elements that don't fit semantically into common HTML tags. However, the added semantic value of more specific tags can enhance the interpretation of your web pages by user agents and crease the value of the information indexed by search engines. To bridge this gap, HTML5 defines a set of elements that serve the same function as the `div` element, but that include semantic value. Table B-1 describes some of these elements.

SEMANTIC ELEMENT	INTENDED USE
article	Standalone piece of work, such as a single entry in a blog
aside	Part of a page that's tangential to the main page content; in a book, this might lend itself to a sidebar or pull quote
footer	Information about a section or document that usually appears at the end, such as attributions and/or footnotes
header	Information about a section or document that usually appears at the beginning, such as a heading, logo, and/or table of contents
hgroup	Group of related elements that include a heading; enables user agents to recognize content such as a tagline as related to a heading
section	Section of content focused on a common theme, such as a chapter of a larger work

Table B-1: HTML5 Semantic Elements

Writing XHTML

XHTML is a version of HTML that's written to conform to the rules of XML. Because XML is a relatively strict language, XHTML documents must include several elements and must conform to a specific syntax.

XHTML Document Type Definitions (DTDs)

When a document conforms to the rules and requirements of XHTML, it is said to be **well formed**. Among other things, a well-formed document must include a DOCTYPE declaration and the `html`, `head`, and `body` elements. As in an HTML5 document, the DOCTYPE declaration belongs in the first line of an XHTML document and determines the Document Type Definition with which the document complies. You can use three types of DTDs with XHTML documents: transitional, strict, and frameset. To understand the differences among the three types of DTDs, you need to understand the concept of deprecated HTML elements. One of the goals of XHTML is to separate the way HTML is structured from the way the parsed web page is displayed in the browser. To accomplish this goal, the W3C decided that several commonly used HTML elements and attributes for display and formatting would not be used in XHTML 1.0. Instead of using HTML elements and attributes for displaying and formatting web pages, the W3C recommends you use the Cascading Style Sheets (CSS) language, which is discussed later in this appendix.

Elements and attributes that are considered obsolete and that will eventually be eliminated are said to be **deprecated**. Table B-2 lists the HTML elements that are deprecated in XHTML 1.0.

ELEMENT	DESCRIPTION
applet	Executes Java applets
basefont	Specifies the base font size
center	Centers text
dir	Defines a directory list
font	Specifies a font name, size, and color
isindex	Creates automatic document indexing forms
menu	Defines a menu list
s or strike	Formats strikethrough text
u	Formats underlined text

Table B-2: HTML elements that are deprecated in XHTML 1.0

The three DTDs are distinguished in part by the degree to which they accept or do not accept deprecated HTML elements. This is explained in more detail in the following sections.

Transitional DTD

The **transitional DTD** allows you to use deprecated style elements in your XHTML documents. The DOCTYPE declaration for the transitional DTD is as follows:

```
<!DOCTYPE html PUBLIC
    "-//W3C//DTD XHTML 1.0 Transitional//EN"
    "http://www.w3.org/TR/xhtml1/DTD/xhtml1-transitional.dtd">
```

Frameset DTD

The **frameset DTD** is identical to the transitional DTD, except that it includes the `frameset` and `frame` elements, which allow you to split the browser window into two or more frames.

The !DOCTYPE declaration for the frameset DTD is as follows:

```
<!DOCTYPE html PUBLIC
    "-//W3C//DTD XHTML 1.0 Frameset//EN"
    "http://www.w3.org/TR/xhtml1/DTD/xhtml1-frameset.dtd">
```

Because frames have been deprecated in favor of layouts using CSS, frameset documents are rarely used. However, you may encounter them if you need to modify an existing web page that was created with frames.

Strict DTD

The **strict DTD** eliminates the elements that were deprecated in the transitional DTD and frameset DTD. The !DOCTYPE declaration for the strict DTD is as follows:

```
<!DOCTYPE html PUBLIC
    "-//W3C//DTD XHTML 1.0 Strict//EN"
    "http://www.w3.org/TR/xhtml1/DTD/xhtml1-strict.dtd">
```

Using the strict DTD ensures that your web pages conform to the most current web page authoring techniques.

Writing Well-Formed XHTML Documents

As you learned earlier, a well-formed document must include a !DOCTYPE declaration and the `html`, `head`, and `body` elements. The following list describes some other important components of a well-formed document:

> All XHTML documents must use `html` as the root element. The `xmlns` attribute is required in the `html` element and must be assigned the `http://www.w3.org/1999/xhtml` URI.

> XHTML is case sensitive.

> All XHTML elements must have a closing tag.

> Attribute values must appear within quotation marks.

> Empty elements must be closed.

> XHTML elements must be properly nested.

Most of the preceding rules are self-explanatory. However, the last rule requires further explanation. **Nesting** refers to how elements are placed inside other elements. For example, in the following code, the a element is nested within the span element, while the span element is nested within an li element.

```
<li><span><a>Contact</a></span></li>
```

HTML parsers can be somewhat forgiving if elements are not closed in the order in which they are opened. For instance, examine the following modified version of the preceding statement:

```
<li><span><a>Contact</span></a></li>
```

In this version, the opening a element is nested within the span element, which, in turn, is nested within the li element. Notice, however, that the closing </a> tag is outside the closing </span> tag. The a is the innermost element. In XHTML, the innermost element in a statement must be closed before another element is closed. In the preceding statement, the span element is closed before the a element. Although the order in which elements are closed generally does not prevent an HTML parser from interpreting the content, the preceding code would prevent an XHTML document from being well formed.

The second-to-last rule in the list ("Empty elements must be closed.") also requires further explanation. One of the most common empty elements in HTML is the img element, which adds an image to the document. You close an empty element in XHTML by adding a space and a slash before the element's closing bracket. For example, the following code shows how to use the img element in an XHTML document.

```
1   <hgroup>
2       <h1>
3           <img src="images/logo.png" alt="" title="" />
4       </h1>
5       <p>Ducks in a Row Organizing Service</p>
6   </hgroup>
```

Working with Cascading Style Sheets (CSS)

Once you have marked up the content of a web document with HTML, you can specify how it should be presented to users by using CSS, a standard set by the W3C for managing the visual design and formatting of HTML documents. A single piece of CSS formatting information, such as text alignment or font size, is referred to as a **style**. Some of the style capabilities of CSS include the ability to change fonts, backgrounds, and colors, and to modify the layout of elements as they appear in a web browser.

CSS information can be added directly to documents or stored in separate documents and shared among multiple web pages. The term "cascading" refers to the ability of web pages to use CSS information from more than one source. When a web page has access to multiple CSS sources, the styles "cascade," or "fall together." Keep in mind that CSS design and formatting techniques are truly independent of the content of a web page. CSS allows you to provide design and formatting specifications for well-formed documents that are compatible with all user agents.

CSS Properties

CSS styles are created with two parts separated by a colon: the **property**, which refers to a specific CSS style, and the value assigned to it, which determines the style's visual characteristics. Together, a CSS property and the value assigned to it are referred to as a **declaration** or **style declaration**. The following code creates a simple style declaration for the color property that changes the color of an element's text to blue:

```
color: blue;
```

CSS Selectors

To apply a style declaration to an HTML document, you need to specify the element or elements to which it applies. You do this using **selectors**. When you associate a selector with one or more style declarations, you create a **style rule**, which has the following general format:

```
1    selector {
2        property: value;
3        property: value;
4        ...
5    }
```

Some of the simplest selectors simply specify an element name, and result in applying associated styles to every occurrence of that element. For instance, the selector p selects all p elements in an HTML document to which it is applied. The following selector applies the foreground color blue to all p elements:

```
p {
    color: blue;
}
```

In addition to selecting all occurrences of an element, you can specify an element id value by preceding its name with the pound symbol (#). Likewise, you can specify a class value by preceding its name with a period (.). Table B-3 describes some basic CSS selectors.

NAME	FORMAT	SELECTS
Element	`element`	All occurrences of the specified element
ID	`#id`	The element with the `id` value `id`
Class	`.class`	All elements with the `class` value `class`
Attribute	`[attribute]`	All elements containing the attribute `attribute`
Attribute value	`[attribute=value]`	All elements containing the attribute `attribute` with a value of `value`

Table B-3: Basic CSS selectors

You can also create style rules using combined selectors to specify multiple types of elements, or to choose elements with specific relationships to other elements. Table B-4 describes common selector combinations.

TYPE	FORMAT	SELECTS
Child	`selector1 > selector2`	Every occurrence of `selector2` that is a child element of `selector1`
Descendant	`selector1 selector2`	Every occurrence of `selector2` that is a descendant (child, grandchild, etc.) of `selector1`
Multiple	`selector1, selector2`	All elements that match `selector1` and all elements that match `selector2`

Table B-4: Common CSS selector combinations

Inline Styles

You can apply styles to a single element in a document using **inline styles**, which uses the `style` attribute to assign inline style information to the element. For instance, the following code assigns the value Verdana to the `font-family` property for a p element:

```
<p style="font-family: Verdana">
    Ducks in a Row Organizing Service
</p>
```

You can include multiple style declarations in an inline style by separating each declaration with a semicolon.

When you change the `style` property of an element using JavaScript, you are adding an inline style.

Internal Style Sheets

You use an **internal style sheet** to create styles within an HTML document that apply to that entire document. You create an internal style sheet within a `style` element placed within the document head, as follows:

```
1   <style>
2     p {
3        color: blue;
4     }
5   </style>
```

Within the `style` element, you create any style instructions for a specific element that are applied to all instances of that element contained in the body of the document.

Inline styles and internal style sheets are rarely written in HTML documents. Instead, web developers generally limit HTML documents to HTML code, and keep CSS code separate in a CSS document.

External Style Sheets

An **external style sheet** is a separate text document containing style declarations that can be used by multiple documents on a website. You create an external style sheet in a text editor, just as you create HTML and JavaScript documents, and you save it with an extension of .css. A style sheet document should not contain HTML elements, only style declarations.

To link the styles in an external style sheet to a web document, you add a `link` element to the head section of the HTML document. You include two attributes in the `link` element: an `href` attribute that is assigned the URL of the style sheet, and the `rel` attribute that is assigned a value of `stylesheet` to specify that the referenced file is a style sheet. For example, to link a document to a style sheet named corpstyles.css, you include the following `link` element in the document head:

```
<link rel="stylesheet" href="corpstyles.css">
```

APPENDIX C

JAVASCRIPT REFERENCE

Comment Types

Line Comments

```
// Line comments are preceded by two slashes.
```

Block Comments

```
/*
This line is part of the block comment.
This line is also part of the block comment.
*/

/* This is another way of creating a block comment. */
```

Reserved Words

abstract	do	if	private	true
boolean	double	implements	protected	try
break	else	import	public	typeof
byte	enum	in	return	var
case	export	instanceof	short	void
catch	extends	int	static	volatile
char	false	interface	super	while
class	final	let	switch	with
const	finally	long	synchronized	yield
continue	float	native	this	
debugger	for	new	throw	
default	function	null	throws	
delete	goto	package	transient	

Commonly Used Events

EVENT	KEYBOARD TRIGGER	MOUSE TRIGGER	TOUCHSCREEN TRIGGER
blur	An element, such as a radio button, becomes inactive		
change	The value of an element, such as a text box, changes		
click	A user presses a key when an element is selected	A user clicks an element once	A user touches an element and then stops touching it
error	An error occurs when a document or image is being loaded		
focus	An element, such as a command button, becomes active		
keydown	A user presses a key		
keyup	A user releases a key		
load	A document or image loads		

Continued on next page...

EVENT	KEYBOARD TRIGGER	MOUSE TRIGGER	TOUCHSCREEN TRIGGER
mouseout		A user moves the mouse pointer off an element	A user stops touching an element
mouseover		A user moves the mouse pointer over an element	A user touches an element
reset	A form's fields are reset to its default values		
select	A user selects text		
submit	A user submits a form		
touchend			A user removes finger or stylus from the screen
touchmove			A finger or stylus already touching the screen moves on the screen
touchstart			A user touches a finger or stylus to the screen
unload	A document unloads		

Primitive Data Types

DATA TYPE	DESCRIPTION
number	A positive or negative number with or without decimal places, or a number written using exponential notation
Boolean	A logical value of true or false
string	Text such as "Hello World"
undefined	An unassigned, undeclared, or nonexistent value
null	An empty value

Escape Sequences

ESCAPE SEQUENCE	CHARACTER
\\	Backslash
\b	Backspace
\r	Carriage return
\"	Double quotation mark
\f	Form feed
\t	Horizontal tab
\n	Newline
\0	Null character
\'	Single quotation mark (apostrophe)
\v	Vertical tab
\x$XX$	Latin-1 character specified by the XX characters, which represent two hexadecimal digits
\u$XXXX$	Unicode character specified by the XXXX characters, which represent four hexadecimal digits

Operators

Operator Types

OPERATOR TYPE	DESCRIPTION
Arithmetic	Perform mathematical calculations
Assignment	Assign values to variables
Comparison	Compare operands and return a Boolean value
Logical	Perform Boolean operations on Boolean operands
String	Perform operations on strings
Special	Various purposes; do not fit within other operator categories

Arithmetic Binary Operators

NAME	OPERATOR	DESCRIPTION
Addition	+	Adds two operands
Subtraction	–	Subtracts one operand from another operand
Multiplication	*	Multiplies one operand by another operand
Division	/	Divides one operand by another operand
Modulus	%	Divides one operand by another operand and returns the remainder

Arithmetic Unary Operators

NAME	OPERATOR	DESCRIPTION
Increment	++	Increases an operand by a value of one
Decrement	––	Decreases an operand by a value of one
Negation	–	Returns the opposite value (negative or positive) of an operand

Assignment Operators

NAME	OPERATOR	DESCRIPTION
Assignment	=	Assigns the value of the right operand to the left operand
Compound addition assignment	+=	Combines the value of the right operand with the value of the left operand (if the operands are strings), or adds the value of the right operand to the value of the left operand (if the operands are numbers), and assigns the new value to the left operand
Compound subtraction assignment	–=	Subtracts the value of the right operand from the value of the left operand, and assigns the new value to the left operand
Compound multiplication assignment	*=	Multiplies the value of the right operand by the value of the left operand, and assigns the new value to the left operand
Compound division assignment	/=	Divides the value of the left operand by the value of the right operand, and assigns the new value to the left operand
Compound modulus assignment	%=	Divides the value of the left operand by the value of the right operand, and assigns the remainder (the modulus) to the left operand

Comparison Operators

NAME	OPERATOR	DESCRIPTION
Equal	==	Returns true if the operands are equal
Strict equal	===	Returns true if the operands are equal and of the same type
Not equal	!=	Returns true if the operands are not equal
Strict not equal	!==	Returns true if the operands are not equal or not of the same type
Greater than	>	Returns true if the left operand is greater than the right operand
Less than	<	Returns true if the left operand is less than the right operand
Greater than or equal	>=	Returns true if the left operand is greater than or equal to the right operand
Less than or equal	<=	Returns true if the left operand is less than or equal to the right operand

Logical Operators

NAME	OPERATOR	DESCRIPTION
And	&&	Returns true if both the left operand and right operand return a value of true; otherwise, it returns a value of false
Or	||	Returns true if either the left operand or right operand returns a value of true; if neither operand returns a value of true, then the expression containing the Or || operator returns a value of false
Not	!	Returns true if an expression is false, and returns false if an expression is true

Special Operators

NAME	OPERATOR	DESCRIPTION
Property access	.	Appends an object, method, or property to another object
Array index	[]	Accesses an element of an array
Function call	()	Calls up functions or changes the order in which individual operations in an expression are evaluated
Comma	,	Allows you to include multiple expressions in the same statement

Continued on next page...

NAME	OPERATOR	DESCRIPTION
Conditional expression	`?:`	Executes one of two expressions based on the results of a conditional expression
Delete	`delete`	Deletes array elements, variables created without the `var` keyword, and properties of custom objects
Property exists	`in`	Returns a value of `true` if a specified property is contained within an object
Object type	`instanceof`	Returns `true` if an object is of a specified object type
New object	`new`	Creates a new instance of a user-defined object type or a predefined JavaScript object type
Data type	`typeof`	Determines the data type of a variable
Void	`void`	Evaluates an expression without returning a result

Values Returned by `typeof` Operator

RETURN VALUE	RETURNED FOR
`number`	Integers and floating-point numbers
`string`	Text strings
`boolean`	True or false
`object`	Objects, arrays, and null variables
`function`	Functions
`undefined`	Undefined variables

Operator Precedence

OPERATORS	DESCRIPTION	ASSOCIATIVITY
`.`	Objects—highest precedence	Left to right
`[]`	Array elements—highest precedence	Left to right
`()`	Functions/evaluation—highest precedence	Left to right
`new`	New object—highest precedence	Right to left

Continued on next page...

OPERATORS	DESCRIPTION	ASSOCIATIVITY
++	Increment	Right to left
--	Decrement	Right to left
-	Unary negation	Right to left
+	Unary positive	Right to left
!	Not	Right to left
typeof	Data type	Right to left
void	Void	Right to left
delete	Delete object	Right to left
* / %	Multiplication/division/modulus	Left to right
+ -	Addition/concatenation and subtraction	Left to right
< <= > >=	Comparison	Left to right
instanceof	Object type	Left to right
in	Object property	Left to right
== != === !==	Equality	Left to right
&&	Logical And	Left to right
||	Logical Or	Left to right
?:	Conditional	Right to left
=	Assignment	Right to left
+= -= *= /= %=	Compound assignment	Right to left
,	Comma—lowest precedence	Left to right

Control Structures and Statements

if Statements

```
if (condition) {
    statements
}
```

if/else Statements

```
if (condition) {
    statements;
}
else {
    statements;
}
```

switch Statements

```
switch (expression) {
    case label:
        statements;
        break;
    case label:
        statements;
        break;
    ...
    default:
        statements;
        break;
}
```

while Statements

```
while (expression) {
    statements;
}
```

do/while Statements

```
do {
    statements;
} while (expression);
```

for Statements

```
for (counter_declaration; condition; counter_operation) {
    statements
}
```

for/in Statements

```
for (variable in object) {
    statements
}
```

break Statements

A `break` statement is a special kind of statement that is used to end the execution of a `switch` statement. To end a `switch` statement once it performs its required task, include a `break` statement at the end of the statements associated with each `case` label.

continue Statements

The `continue` statement halts a looping statement and restarts the loop with a new iteration. You use the `continue` statement when you want to stop the loop for the current iteration, but want the loop to continue with a new iteration.

Built-In Functions

FUNCTION	DESCRIPTION
decodeURI (*string*)	Decodes text strings encoded with `encodeURI()`
decodeURIComponent (*string*)	Decodes text strings encoded with `encodeURIComponent()`
encodeURI (*string*)	Encodes a text string so it becomes a valid URI
encodeURIComponent (*string*)	Encodes a text string so it becomes a valid URI component
eval (*string*)	Evaluates expressions contained within strings
isFinite (*number*)	Determines whether a number is finite
isNaN (*number*)	Determines whether a value is the special value `NaN` (Not a Number)
parseFloat (*string*)	Converts string literals to floating-point numbers
parseInt (*string*)	Converts string literals to integers

Built-In Classes

Array Class

Methods

METHOD	DESCRIPTION
array1.concat(array2 [, array3, ...])	Combines arrays
pop()	Removes the last element from the end of an array
push(value1[, value2, ...])	Adds one or more elements to the end of an array, where value1, value2, etc., are the values to add
reverse()	Reverses the order of the elements in an array
shift()	Removes and returns the first element from the beginning of an array
slice(start, end)	Copies a portion of an array to another array, where start is the array index number at which to begin extracting elements, and end is an integer value that indicates the number of elements to return from the array
sort()	Sorts an array alphabetically
splice(start, elements_to_delete[, value1, value2, ...])	Adds or removes elements within an array, where start indicates the index number within the array where elements should be added or removed; elements_to_delete is an integer value that indicates the number of elements to remove from the array, starting with the element indicated by the start argument; and value1, value2, etc., represent the values to add
unshift(value1[, value2, ...])	Adds one or more elements to the beginning of an array, where value1, value2, etc., are the values to add

Property

PROPERTY	DESCRIPTION
length	The number of elements in an array

Date Class

Methods

METHOD	DESCRIPTION
Date()	Date object constructor
getDate()	Returns the date of a Date object
getDay()	Returns the day of a Date object
getFullYear()	Returns the year of a Date object in four-digit format
getHours()	Returns the hour of a Date object
getMilliseconds()	Returns the milliseconds of a Date object
getMinutes()	Returns the minutes of a Date object
getMonth()	Returns the month of a Date object
getSeconds()	Returns the seconds of a Date object
getTime()	Returns the time of a Date object
getTimezoneOffset()	Returns the time difference between the user's computer and GMT
getUTCDate()	Returns the date of a Date object in universal time
getUTCDay()	Returns the day of a Date object in universal time
getUTCFullYear()	Returns the four-digit year of a Date object in universal time
getUTCHours()	Returns the hours of a Date object in universal time
getUTCMilliseconds()	Returns the milliseconds of a Date object in universal time
getUTCMinutes()	Returns the minutes of a Date object in universal time
getUTCMonth()	Returns the month of a Date object in universal time
getUTCSeconds()	Returns the seconds of a Date object in universal time
getYear()	Returns the year of a Date object
now()	Returns the current time as the number of milliseconds that have elapsed since midnight, January 1, 1970 (ECMAScript 5 and later only)
parse()	Returns a string containing the number of milliseconds since January 1, 1970
setDate()	Sets the date of a Date object
setFullYear()	Sets the four-digit year of a Date object

Continued on next page...

METHOD	DESCRIPTION
setHours()	Sets the hours of a Date object
setMilliseconds()	Sets the milliseconds of a Date object
setMinutes()	Sets the minutes of a Date object
setMonth()	Sets the month of a Date object
setSeconds()	Sets the seconds of a Date object
setTime()	Sets the time of a Date object
setUTCDate()	Sets the date of a Date object in universal time
setUTCDay()	Sets the day of a Date object in universal time
setUTCFullYear()	Sets the 4-digit year of a Date object in universal time
setUTCHours()	Sets the hours of a Date object in universal time
setUTCMilliseconds()	Sets the milliseconds of a Date object in universal time
setUTCMinutes()	Sets the minutes of a Date object in universal time
setUTCMonth()	Sets the month of a Date object in universal time
setUTCSeconds()	Sets the seconds of a Date object in universal time
setYear()	Sets the two-digit year of a Date object
toGMTString()	Converts a Date object to a string in GMT time zone format
toLocaleString()	Converts a Date object to a string, set to the current time zone
toString()	Converts a Date object to a string

JSON Class

Methods

METHOD	DESCRIPTION
parse()	Converts a string value to an object
stringify()	Converts an object to a string value

Math Class

Methods

METHOD	RETURNS
abs(x)	The absolute value of x
acos(x)	The arc cosine of x
asin(x)	The arc sine of x
atan(x)	The arc tangent of x
atan2(x, y)	The angle from the x-axis of the point represented by x, y
ceil(x)	The value of x rounded to the next highest integer
cos(x)	The cosine of x
exp(x)	The exponent of x
floor(x)	The value of x rounded to the next lowest integer
log(x)	The natural logarithm of x
max(x, y)	The larger of x or y
min(x, y)	The smaller of x or y
pow(x, y)	The value of x raised to the y power
random()	A random number
round(x)	The value of x rounded to the nearest integer
sin(x)	The sine of x
sqrt(x)	The square root of x
tan(x)	The tangent of x

Properties

PROPERTY	DESCRIPTION
E	Euler's constant e, which is the base of a natural logarithm; this value is approximately 2.7182818284590452354
LN10	The natural logarithm of 10, which is approximately 2.302585092994046
LN2	The natural logarithm of 2, which is approximately 0.6931471805599453

Continued on next page...

PROPERTY	DESCRIPTION
LOG10E	The base-10 logarithm of *e*, the base of the natural logarithms; this value is approximately 0.4342944819032518
LOG2E	The base-2 logarithm of *e*, the base of the natural logarithms; this value is approximately 1.4426950408889634
PI	A constant representing the ratio of the circumference of a circle to its diameter, which is approximately 3.1415926535897932
SQRT1_2	The square root of 1/2, which is approximately 0.7071067811865476
SQRT2	The square root of 2, which is approximately 1.4142135623730951

Number Class

Methods

METHOD	DESCRIPTION
toExponential(*decimals*)	Converts a number to a string in exponential notation using the number of decimal places specified by *decimals*
toFixed(*decimals*)	Converts a number to a string using the number of decimal places specified by *decimals*
toLocaleString()	Converts a number to a string that is formatted with local numeric formatting style
toPrecision(*decimals*)	Converts a number to a string with the number of decimal places specified by *decimals*, in either exponential notation or in fixed notation
toString(*base*)	Converts a number to a string using the number system specified by *base*
valueOf()	Returns the numeric value of a Number object

Properties

PROPERTY	DESCRIPTION
MAX_VALUE	The largest positive number that can be used in JavaScript
MIN_VALUE	The smallest positive number that can be used in JavaScript
NaN	The value NaN, which stands for "not a number"
NEGATIVE_INFINITY	The value of negative infinity
POSITIVE_INFINITY	The value of positive infinity

RegExp Class

Method

METHOD	DESCRIPTION
test()	Returns a value of true if a string contains text that matches a regular expression or false if it doesn't

Properties

PROPERTY	FLAG	DESCRIPTION
global	g	Determines whether to search for all possible matches within a string
ignoreCase	i	Determines whether to ignore letter case when executing a regular expression
lastIndex		Stores the index of the first character from the last match (no flag)
multiline	m	Determines whether to search across multiple lines of text
source		Contains the regular expression pattern (no flag)

String Class

Methods

METHOD	DESCRIPTION
charAt(index)	Returns the character at the specified position in a text string; returns an empty string if the specified position is greater than the length of the string
charCodeAt(index)	Returns the Unicode character code at the specified position in a text string; returns NaN if the specified position is greater than the length of the string
indexOf(text[, index])	Performs a case-sensitive search and returns the position number in a string of the first character in the text argument; if the index argument is included, then the indexOf() method starts searching at that position within the string; returns −1 if the character or string is not found

Continued on next page...

METHOD	DESCRIPTION
lastIndexOf(*text[, index]*)	Performs a case-sensitive search and returns the position number in a string of the last instance of the first character in the *text* argument; if the *index* argument is included, then the lastIndexOf() method starts searching at that position within the string; returns −1 if the character or string is not found
match(*pattern*)	Performs a case-sensitive search and returns an array containing the results that match the *pattern* argument; returns *null* if the text is not found
search(*pattern*)	Performs a case-sensitive search and returns the position number in a string of the first instance of the first character in the *pattern* argument; returns −1 if the character or string is not found
slice(*starting index [, ending index]*)	Extracts text from a string, starting with the position number in the string of the *starting index* argument and ending with the character immediately before the position number of the *ending index* argument; allows negative argument values
substring(*starting index [, ending index]*)	Extracts text from a string, starting with the position number in the string of the *starting index* argument and ending with the character immediately before the position number of the *ending index* argument; does not allow negative argument values

Property

METHOD	DESCRIPTION
length	The number of characters in a string

Regular Expression Components

Metacharacters

METACHARACTER	DESCRIPTION
.	Matches any single character
\	Identifies the next character as a literal value
^	Matches characters at the beginning of a string

Continued on next page...

METACHARACTER	DESCRIPTION
$	Matches characters at the end of a string
( )	Specifies required characters to include in a pattern match
[ ]	Specifies alternate characters allowed in a pattern match
[^]	Specifies characters to exclude in a pattern match
–	Identifies a possible range of characters to match
|	Specifies alternate sets of characters to include in a pattern match

Quantifiers

QUANTIFIER	DESCRIPTION
?	Specifies that the preceding character is optional
+	Specifies that one or more of the preceding characters must match
*	Specifies that zero or more of the preceding characters can match
{n}	Specifies that the preceding character repeat exactly n times
{n,}	Specifies that the preceding character repeat at least n times
{n1, n2}	Specifies that the preceding character repeat at least $n1$ times but no more than $n2$ times

Character Class Expressions

EXPRESSION	DESCRIPTION
\w	Alphanumeric characters
\W	Any character that is not an alphanumeric character
\d	Numeric characters
\D	Nonnumeric characters
\s	White space characters
\S	All printable characters
\b	Backspace character

Objects of the Browser Object Model

Document Object

Methods

METHOD	DESCRIPTION
getElementById(*ID*)	Returns the element with the id value *ID*
getElementsByClassName(*class1* [*class2* ...])	If one class name, class1, is specified, returns the collection of elements that belong to class1; if two or more space-separated class names are specified, the returned collection consists of those elements that belong to all specified class names
getElementsByName(*name*)	Returns the collection of elements with the name *name*
getElementsByTagName(*tag*)	Returns the collection of elements with the tag (element) name *tag*
querySelectorAll(*selector*)	Returns the collection of elements that match the CSS selector specified by *selector*
write(*text*)	Writes *text* to the document

History Object

Methods

METHOD	DESCRIPTION
back()	Produces the same result as clicking a browser's Back button
forward()	Produces the same result as clicking a browser's Forward button
go()	Opens a specific document in the history list

Property

PROPERTY	DESCRIPTION
length	Contains the specific number of documents that have been opened during the current browser session

Location Object

Methods

METHOD	DESCRIPTION
assign()	Loads a new web page
reload()	Causes the page that currently appears in the web browser to open again
replace()	Replaces the currently loaded URL with a different one

Properties

PROPERTIES	DESCRIPTION
hash	URL's anchor
host	Host and domain name (or IP address) of a network host
hostname	Combination of the URL's host name and port sections
href	Full URL address
pathname	URL's path
port	URL's port
protocol	URL's protocol
search	URL's search or query portion

Navigator Object

Properties

PROPERTIES	DESCRIPTION
appName	Name of the web browser displaying the page
appVersion	Version of the web browser displaying the page
geolocation	API for accessing the user's current location and user permission settings denying or allowing access to that information
onLine	Whether the browser currently has a network connection
platform	Operating system in use on the client computer
userAgent	String stored in the HTTP user-agent request header, which contains information about the browser, the platform name, and compatibility

Screen Object

Properties

PROPERTIES	DESCRIPTION
availHeight	Height of the display screen, not including operating system features such as the Windows taskbar
availWidth	Width of the display screen, not including operating system features such as the Windows taskbar
colorDepth	Display screen's bit depth if a color palette is in use; if a color palette is not in use, returns the value of the pixelDepth property
height	Height of the display screen
pixelDepth	Display screen's color resolution in bits per pixel
width	Width of the display screen

Window Object

Methods

METHOD	DESCRIPTION
alert()	Displays a simple message dialog box with an OK button
blur()	Removes focus from a window or tab
clearInterval()	Cancels an interval that was set with setInterval()
clearTimeout()	Cancels a timeout that was set with setTimeout()
close()	Closes a web browser window or tab
confirm()	Displays a confirmation dialog box with OK and Cancel buttons
focus()	Makes a Window object the active window or tab
moveBy()	Moves the window relative to the current position
moveTo()	Moves the window to an absolute position
open()	Opens a new web browser window or tab
print()	Prints the document displayed in the current window or tab
prompt()	Displays a dialog box prompting a user to enter information
resizeBy()	Resizes a window by a specified amount
resizeTo()	Resizes a window to a specified size
scrollBy()	Scrolls the window or tab by a specified amount

Continued on next page...

METHOD	DESCRIPTION
scrollTo()	Scrolls the window or tab to a specified position
setInterval()	Repeatedly executes a function after a specified number of milliseconds have elapsed
setTimeout()	Executes a function once after a specified number of milliseconds have elapsed

Properties

PROPERTY	DESCRIPTION
closed	Boolean value that indicates whether a window or tab has been closed
document	Reference to the Document object
history	Reference to the History object
innerHeight	Height of the window area that displays content, including the scrollbar if present
innerWidth	Width of the window area that displays content, including the scrollbar if present
location	Reference to the Location object
name	Name of the window or tab
navigator	Reference to the Navigator object
opener	Reference to the window that opened the current window or tab
outerHeight	Height of the entire browser window
outerWidth	Width of the entire browser window
screen	Reference to the Screen object
self	Self-reference to the Window object; identical to the window property
status	Temporary text that is written to the status bar
window	Self-reference to the Window object; identical to the self property

Objects of the Document Object Model

Form Object

Methods

METHOD	DESCRIPTION
reset()	Resets a form without the use of a reset button
submit()	Submits a form without the use of a submit button

Properties

PROPERTY	DESCRIPTION
action	Returns the URL to which form data will be submitted
encoding	Sets and returns a string representing the MIME type of the data being submitted
length	Returns an integer representing the number of elements in the form
method	Sets and returns a string representing one of the two options for submitting form data: "get" or "post"

Events

EVENT	DESCRIPTION
reset	Executes when a form's reset button is clicked
submit	Executes when a form's submit button is clicked

Elements within a Form Object

Methods and Their Associated Form Controls

METHOD	DESCRIPTION	FORM CONTROLS
blur()	Removes focus from a form control	Buttons, check boxes, option buttons, reset buttons, submit buttons, text boxes, text areas, password boxes, file boxes, selection lists
click()	Activates a form control's click event	Buttons, check boxes, option buttons, reset buttons, submit buttons, selection lists
focus()	Changes focus to a form control	Buttons, check boxes, option buttons, reset buttons, submit buttons, text boxes, text areas, password boxes, file boxes, selection lists
select()	Selects the text in a form control	Text boxes, text areas, password boxes, file boxes

Properties and Their Associated Form Controls

PROPERTY	DESCRIPTION	FORM CONTROLS
checked	Sets and returns the checked status of a check box or option button	Check boxes, option buttons
defaultChecked	Determines the control that is checked by default in a check box group or option button group	Check boxes, option buttons

Continued on next page...

PROPERTY	DESCRIPTION	FORM CONTROLS
defaultValue	Specifies the default text that will appear in a form control	Text boxes, text areas, password boxes, file boxes
form	Returns a reference to the form that contains the control	Buttons, check boxes, option buttons, reset buttons, submit buttons, text boxes, text areas, password boxes, file boxes, selection lists, hidden text boxes
length	Returns the number of items within a selection list's options[] array	Selection lists
name	Returns the value assigned to the element's name attribute	Buttons, check boxes, option buttons, reset buttons, submit buttons, text boxes, text areas, password boxes, file boxes, selection lists, hidden text boxes
selectedIndex	Returns an integer that represents the element displayed in a selection list, according to its position	Selection lists
type	Returns the type of form element, such as checkbox, number, password, or submit	Buttons, check boxes, option buttons, reset buttons, submit buttons, text boxes, text areas, password boxes, file boxes, selection lists, hidden text boxes
value	Sets and returns the value of form controls	Buttons, check boxes, option buttons, reset buttons, submit buttons, text boxes, text areas, password boxes, file boxes, hidden text boxes

Events and Their Associated Form Controls

EVENT	DESCRIPTION	FORM CONTROLS
blur	An element, such as an option button, becomes inactive	Buttons, check boxes, option buttons, reset buttons, submit buttons, text boxes, text areas, password boxes, file boxes, selection lists
change	The value of an element, such as a text box, changes	Text boxes, text areas, password boxes, file boxes, selection lists
click	A user clicks an element once	Buttons, check boxes, option buttons, reset buttons, submit buttons
focus	An element, such as a command button, becomes active	Buttons, check boxes, option buttons, reset buttons, submit buttons, text boxes, text areas, password boxes, file boxes, selection lists

INDEX

A

abort() method, 765, 770
aboutNode variable, 324
aboutus variable, 321
abs() method, 483
accelerometer, **716**, 726
Accept-Charset header, 758
Accept-Encoding header, 758
Accept header, 758
Accept-Language header, 758
accept property, 409
accountsPayable()
    function, 259
accountsPayable object, 459
accountsReceivable()
    function, 259
accuracy property, 701
acos() method, 483
acresBox variable, 266
acresComplete variable, 267
action attribute, 624
actual parameters, **79**–80, 134
addCalendarDates() function,
    170–172, 176
addClass() method, 819, 826
addColumnHeaders() function,
    167, 168, 172, 175–177
addEventListener() method,
    81–82, 190–192
addGameInfo() function, 176–177,
    181–184, 186–190, 195–197
adding event listeners, **81**, 134
addition compound assignment
    operator (+=), 100–101,
    113–118, 548
addition operator (+), 39, 100, 103,
    106, 109–110, 128
addition quantifier (+), 562
address property, 496
address sub-object, 495–496
Adobe Dreamweaver, 10
Advanced Research Projects
    Agency. *See* ARPA (Advanced
    Research Projects Agency)
a element, 41–42, 329
agency variable, 539
age variable, 124–125
Ajax, **742**, 792
    accessing content on separate
        domain, 747–750
    cross-domain requests without
        proxy server, 784–790

Hypertext Transfer Protocol
    (HTTP), 752–765
JavaScript, 742
JSON, 742
limitations, 745
moving and examining files,
    750–751
requesting server data, 765–774
running from web server, 750–751
updating data, 752
XML, 742
alert dialog boxes, 228–230
alert() method, **41**–42, 327–328,
    332
alias, **817**, 829
alpha property, 716
altitudeAccuracy property, 701
altitude property, 701
alt property, 409
americanCity argument, 194
amount variable, 220
ampersand (&), 53
anchor, **558**, 598
And operator (&&), 123–125, 418
Android devices, 5
Android mobile web apps, 717
Android SDK, 717
animate() method, 825
anonymous functions, **74**–76, 82,
    134, 506
Apache HTTP Server, 750–751
API. *See* application programming
    interface (API)
API key, **710**, 726, 748, 763–765
appendChild() method,
    312–315, 317, 320, 322
applet element, 856
application programming interface
    (API), **293**, 350
applications
    forcing to close, 166
    testing using cookies, 638–642
appName property, 344
apps, 3
appVersion property, 344
Aptana Studio 3, 10, 214, 272
arguments, **26**, 58, **79**–80, 134
Arguments class, 457
arithmetic operations, 107–108
arithmetic operators, 104, **105**, 134
    binary arithmetic operators,
        106–109

unary arithmetic operators,
    109–112
arithmeticValue variable, 107
ARPA (Advanced Research Projects
    Agency), 2
ARPANET, 2
Array class, 457, **577**–578, 598
Array() constructor, 160
array index operator ([]), 125
array literals, **148**–149, 154, 201
Array object, 160, 458, 537, 583
arrays, **148**, 150, 160, 201, 458
    adding elements, 149–150,
        580–585
    array literals, **148**–149
    combining, 587–588
    converting between strings,
        588–592
    data types, 151
    days of the week or months,
        466–467
    default collection of elements,
        160–162
    displaying contents, 225
    elements, **149**, 158–159, 579–585
    empty, 150, 458, 491
    finding and extracting elements
        and values, 578–579
    identifiers, 148
    index, **149**
    length, 159–160
    manipulating, 577–588
    printing contents, 174
    removing elements, 580–585
    resizing dynamically, 150
    reversing order of elements, 587
    sorting, 586–587
    storing data, 148–162
arrayString variable, 591
article element, 6, 13, 24, 153,
    217, 297, 312–313, 317, 320,
    629, 684, 855
articleEl variable, 313, 322
aside element, 13, 44, 77, 217, 855
asin() method, 483
ASP.NET, 21
assignment operator (=), **35**, 39, 58,
    107, 110, 112–118, 119, 129
assignment operators, 104,
    112–118, 134
assignment statements, 108
assign() method, 343, 344

reference data types, 459
Referer header, 758
referrer property, 296
Regex object, 537
RegExp class, 458
RegExp() constructor, 554, 575–576
RegExp object, 548, **554**–555, 575–576, 599
registerLodging() function, 537, 582–585
registerName() function, 493–494, 496–497, 503–504, 507
regular expressions, **553**–554, 599
  character classes, **567**–574
  HTML code, 577
  methods, 555–556
  multiple characters as single item, 567–574
  patterns, 556–575
  prewritten, 556
  properties, 575–576
  quantifiers, **561**–566
  special escape characters, 570–571
  String class methods, 553
  subexpressions, **566**–567, 570
  substrings, 574–575
  variables, 553
relational operators, **118**–122, 135
reload() method, 343
removeChild() method, 323–326
removeClass() method, 819, 824, 826
removeDragListener() function, 687, 688
removeItem() method, 656
removeSelectDefaults() method, 373
removeTouchListener() function, 690–692, 699
rendering, **7**, 60
  elements, 46
replace argument, 329
replace() method, 343–344, **548**, 553, 576, 599
reprodrights variable, 98, 122
requestBody variable, 771
requests, **3**, 60, **753**, 793
  JSON-P, 786
  opening and sending, 769–774
required attribute, 371, 394–395
required property, 412
reserved words, **33**–34, 60
reset event, 40
resetForm() function, 78, 82–84, 86, 98, 116–117
resizeBy() method, 328
resizeTo() method, 328

responses, **3**, 60, **753**, 793
responseText property, 766, 774, 776–777, 779
responseXML property, 766, 774–775
result variable, 86, 120
return keyword, 86
return statements, **86**, 135
returnValue property, 405
returnValue variable, 86
reverse() method, 577, **587**, 599
rightAdvance() function, 340–341
rightArrow() function, 297, 340–341
riskFactor variable, 124–125
root element, **7**, 60
round() method, 484
Ruby, 21
run-time errors, **214**, 219–220, 280

S

Safari, 1, 4–5, 19, 221
salesPrice variable, 87–88
salesTax variable, 35
salesTotal variable, 36–37, 480
same origin policy, **659**–660, 663, 745, 747
schoolName property, 515
scientificNames[] array, 586–587
scientific notation, **93**–94, 135
Screen object, 291–292, **346**–348, 351
screen property, 327
script element, 23–25, 31, 45–48, 50, 53, 60, 74, 78, 94–95, 272–273, 374, 653, 661, 712, 720–721, 725, 784–786, 788–790, 816, 821
scripting engines, **19**–21, 60, 213
scripting hosts, **20**, 60
scripting languages, **19**, 21–24, 60
scripts, 23–25, 60
  break code, 245–246
  HTML code, 46
  libraries, **50**–52
  printing metric prefixes, 94–96
  processing, 46
  stepping through, 251–253
  variable declarations, 47
scrollBy() method, 328
scrollTo() method, 328
search() method, 543, **544**–548, 553–556, 556, 576, 599
search property, 343, 623, 625–626
secondNum variable, 253
section element, 537, 855

secure attribute, **648**, 663
secure coding, **657**–658, 663
secure property, 636
Secure Sockets Layer (SSL), **647**, 657, 663
security, 657–661
  code injection attack, **658**
  escape characters, **658**
  JavaScript, 21
  privacy of client information, 658–659
  same origin policy, **659**–660
  secure coding, **657**–658
  third-party scripts, **660**–661
  web server security, 657
selectDate() function, 474–478, 482, 488, 494, 500, 507
selectedCity variable, 751
selectedDate element, 495
selectedDate variable, 475
selectedIndex property, 371–374, 378, 392, 414
selected property, 375
select element, 42, 365, 371–381, 391, 395, 414–415
select event, 40
selection lists, 370
  checking for no value, 414–417
  dynamically updating values, 375–381
  removing default values, 371–374
select() method, 388, 410
select object, 371
selectors, **859**–860
s element, 856
self.close() method, 335–337
self property, 327, **328**, 351
semantic elements, 855
send() method, 765, 771, 777
sensor argument, 712
Server header, 761
servers, **16**–18, 60
server-side scripting, **21**–23
sessionStorage property, **655**–656, 663
setCustomValidity() method, 366
setDate() method, 465, 643, 652
setFullYear() method, 465
setHours() method, 465
setInterval() method, 328, **339**, 340–341, 350–351, 489, 783
setItem() method, 656
setMilliseconds() method, 465
setMonth() method, 465
setRequestHeader() method, 765, 771–772
setSeconds() method, 465